Law Society of Ireland

Technology and IP Law

Law Society of Ireland

Technology and IP Law

General Editor

Mark Hyland

Authors

Louise Carey	James Murray
Gerry Carroll	Philip Nolan
Rob Corbet	Andrew Parkes
Maureen Daly	Carol Plunkett
Andy Harbison	René Rosenstock
Mark Hyland	Pearse Ryan
Jeanne Kelly	Colin Sainsbury
Rossa McMahon	Richard Willis
Aoife Murphy	

Published by
Tottel Publishing Ltd
Maxwelton House
41–43 Boltro Road
Haywards Heath
West Sussex
RH16 1BJ

Tottel Publishing Ltd
The Fitzwilliam Business Centre
26 Upper Pembroke Street
Dublin 2

ISBN: 978 184766 094 7
© Law Society of Ireland 2008
First published 2008

All rights reserved. No part of this publication may be reproduced in any material form (including photocopying or storing it in any medium by electronic means and whether or not transiently or incidentally to some other use of this publication) without the written permission of the copyright owner except in accordance with the provisions of the Copyright, Designs and Patents Act 1988 or under the terms of a licence issued by the Copyright Licensing Agency Ltd., Saffron House, 6–10 Kirby Street, London, EC1N 8TS, England. Applications for the copyright owner's written permission to reproduce any part of this publication should be addressed to the publisher.

Warning: The doing of an unauthorised act in relation to a copyright work may result in both a civil claim for damages and criminal prosecution.

This work is intended to be a general guide and cannot be a substitute for professional advice. Neither the authors nor the publisher accept any responsibility for loss occasioned to any person acting or refraining from acting as a result of material contained in this publication.

British Library Cataloguing-in-Publication Data
A catalogue record for this book is available from the British Library

Typeset by Marlex Editorial Services Ltd., Dublin, Ireland
Printed and bound in Great Britain by Athenaeum, Gateshead, Tyne and Wear

ABOUT THE AUTHORS

Louise Carey is a solicitor at Arthur Cox. She has a Bachelors of Civil Law (University College Cork, 1981) and a Diploma in European Law (University College Cork, 1991). She was admitted as a solicitor of the Irish Law Society in 1985 and gained entry to the Register of Trade Mark Agents in 1987. Her areas of practice include a specialism in litigation relating to all the areas of intellectual property, advisory and transactional work relating to intellectual property, and trade mark registration matters. Her knowledge of languages includes English, French and German. She is a member of the Licensing Executives Society (LES) and the Irish Trade Mark and Patents Agents Association.

Gerry Carroll qualified as a solicitor in 1984. He became a partner with WhitneyMoore in 1989 and has been Managing Partner of the firm since 2003. A litigation specialist, he has handled some of the largest and most complex cases to come before the Irish courts. He also has extensive experience of international litigation practice involving European and US courts. Although acting in commercial disputes for clients across a broad range of activity, Gerry has considerable experience of intellectual property, insurance, professional indemnity, professional disciplinary enquiries and aviation matters. In the area of intellectual property he has acted in an advisory capacity and in the conduct of litigation for both plaintiffs and defendants. Gerry has been involved in infringement and revocation patent actions concerning pharmaceutical and veterinary drugs, proceedings alleging infringement of a patent for additives to mud used for drilling for oil and gas, and coronary heart stents.

Rob Corbet is a partner in Arthur Cox. His practice is primarily focused on technological innovation in the areas of IT/IP and he has particular experience in the areas of ebusiness and data protection. Rob has been published and presented internationally on technology law and he has lectured in the Law Society of Ireland for the past eight years. He is the current editor of *Data Protection Ireland*, a member of the editorial board of *Privacy and Data Protection* and he is a member of the Irish Internet Association's Legal Working Group. He has been ranked as a 'leading individual' (Band 1) in IT by Chambers Europe.

Maureen Daly is Partner and Head of Technology & Intellectual Property at Beauchamps Solicitors. She advises on all aspects of IP and IT matters (both contentious and non-contentious) including the protection, defence, enforcement and exploitation of IP rights; the seizure of counterfeit goods; domain name disputes; IP and IT due diligences; website privacy statements and terms & conditions; end-user agreements; software licence agreements; software/website development agreements; support and maintenance agreements; biotechnology collaborations/research agreements as well as joint ventures between academic and commercial organisations; and compliance with consumer protection and data protection legislation.

Maureen has lectured extensively on IP and IT issues. She is also the author of numerous articles as well as being the Irish contributor to a book on Character Merchandising in Europe (published by Kluwer Law International). Maureen has an honours science degree in Biochemistry (University College Dublin). In addition to being a solicitor, she is also an Irish registered Trade Mark Attorney and Community Trade Mark Attorney. Maureen is a committee member of the Irish section of the Licensing Executives Society. She is also an officer of the Technology Committee of the International Bar Association. Maureen has been recommended for her work by independent international commentators and guides such as Who's Who Legal, European Legal 500, Practical Law Company Which Lawyer? and Chambers Europe.

Andrew Harbison leads the IT Forensics and Litigation Support practice at Deloitte, Dublin. He founded and led the IT Forensics practice at Ernst & Young. He has provided support to companies and litigators in over 250 cases. He has written extensively on IT Forensics, Computer Fraud and Incident Management. He has advised many of Ireland's largest financial services firms on information security incident response planning.

Mark Hyland, BCL, Dip. Eur. Law, LL.M., is a qualified solicitor working as a professional support lawyer in the Banking Law Group of Matheson Ormsby Prentice. He has published internationally in the Technology/IP Law domain (principally on copyright in the Digital Age and competition law aspects of communications law). Mark also has a strong interest in the Conflict of Laws and how this field of law will operate in the internet era. He lectures for the Law Society of Ireland on its Technology and IP Law module.

Jeanne Kelly is a partner in Mason Hayes+Curran's commercial department. She holds a BCL (International Legal Studies) degree from UCD and the Université de Haute Normandie, Rouen, France. Jeanne advises clients in relation to a wide range of IP and IT issues in the context of research and development projects, mergers and acquisitions and licensing matters. She advises both suppliers and purchasers of IT systems and outsourcing arrangements. Jeanne has advised on a variety of issues including domain name registration and online contract formation as well as franchise and distribution agreements. She advises both public and private clients on contract and data protection issues.

Jeanne has co-authored the second edition of *Business Law* (Oxford University Press). She has also co-authored a book on data protection law in Ireland (Thomson Round Hall, 2004) and the Irish chapter of *Le traite dessins et des modeles* (Greffe, Litec, 2008). At the Law School of the Law Society of Ireland, Jeanne is a guest lecturer in commercial drafting, software licensing law and data protection law. She serves on the domain names sub-committee of the INTA and is currently the president of the Licensing Executives Society, Irish branch. Jeanne is a regular speaker and attender at IP law conferences in Ireland and abroad.

Rossa McMahon is a solicitor in the IP and Technology group at A&L Goodbody. He specialises in intellectual property, technology, outsourcing and commercial agreements. He has BCL and LLB degrees from University College Cork and was awarded the Matheson Ormsby Prentice Information Technology Law Scholarship in 2003 for his research masters on the emerging field of online dispute resolution. Rossa regularly advises clients on data protection, intellectual property rights, gaming and lotteries, franchising, sale of goods and consumer issues. He has also advised public bodies and private companies on outsourcing arrangements and technology procurement. Rossa is a Registered Trade Mark Agent and has published a number of articles in the Commercial Law Practitioner, Tottel's Communications Law and the journal of the Chartered Institute of Arbitrators.

Aoife Murphy joined WhitneyMoore in 1995 and became a partner in 2005. She practices extensively in commercial litigation, with a particular emphasis on intellectual property. Aoife advises on all aspects of intellectual property issues, patents, trade marks, copyright and design and related intellectual property matters. She has been involved in infringement and revocation patent actions concerning pharmaceuticals, coronary heart stents and EPOS systems. Aoife has advised on the protection of domain name and internet related rights, the protection of confidential information and issues arising out of international commerce and e-commerce generally. She has also advised on data protection issues. She works closely in this area with the in-house advisers of multinational companies, intellectual property practitioners in other jurisdictions and with patent and trade mark agents.

James Murray is General Counsel and Company Secretary of Readymix, the Dublin-based PLC. He qualified as a solicitor in 1994 and subsequently worked as an academic at Cambridge University. On returning to Ireland he practised for eight years in the area of commercial litigation – handling a wide range of commercial disputes which included intellectual property matters. He defended one of the earliest IP cases in the Commercial Court, and subsequently handled a series of significant cases which included judicial review, shareholder rights, breach of contract and banking matters. He is presently responsible for management of all legal affairs at Readymix, including commercial contracts, acquisitions/disposals and litigation functions in addition to the protection of intellectual property rights.

Philip Nolan is a partner in the Commercial Department of Mason Hayes+Curran. He studied at University College Dublin, De Paul University, Chicago and the University of Oxford before joining Mason Hayes+Curran, where he completed his training. Philip specialises in commercial law, communications and energy law, intellectual property law and information technology law. He advises a range of both public and private clients and has developed a focused regulatory advisory practice, which includes public procurement law and data protection law.

Philip is a member of the Editorial Board of the Gazette of the Law Society of Ireland. He has taught information technology law, software licensing law, data protection law and commercial law at the Law Society of Ireland's Law School.

Andrew Parkes is a former partner and consultant with Tomkins, European Patent Attorneys and Community Trade Mark Attorneys. He is a Registered Patent Agent in Ireland (1967) and Great Britain (1965). He is a Fellow of the Chartered Institute of Patent Agents and of the Institute of Trade Mark Attorneys. He received a BA (Natural Science and Law) and MA at Cambridge University (1961, 1965). He gained professional experience in England and in Washington DC (1961–2002). He then returned to Ireland and joined Tomkins in 1968. He was President of the Association of Patent and Trade Mark Agents in Ireland in 1989–91 and was also President (1990–1993) and is now Honorary President of the UNION of European Practitioners in Industrial Property. He was a member of the Standing Advisory Committee at the European Patent Office, SACEPO (1992–2002). He is currently Special Reporter (Trade Marks and Designs) in the Study and Work Commission of FICPI – the International Federation of Intellectual Property Attorneys. He contributed the chapter on Ireland in *Gemeinschaftsmarke und Recht der EU-Mitgliedstaaten* (Verlag C.H.Beck, 2006).

Carol Plunkett qualified as a solicitor in 1979. She joined William Fry as a partner in the Litigation Department in 2004, having been a partner in A&L Goodbody and Landwell solicitors in Dublin.

Carol is a highly respected commercial litigator with extensive expertise in all areas and a particular knowledge of intellectual property disputes. She advises on all intellectual property issues, copyright and design, patents, trademarks, confidential information and information technology. Carol has assisted many of the leading brand owners in the protection of their intellectual property in Ireland and has been involved in many leading Irish intellectual property cases.

In addition, she advises on regulatory disputes, having acted over the years for a number of Regulators in the telecommunications, postal, travel and aviation industries. Carol also advises on a range of general commercial litigation matters, including admiralty, breach of contract, company law issues, product liability and professional negligence.

René Rosenstock qualified as a Solicitor in 2001 and works as in-house solicitor with the Commission for Communications Regulation (ComReg). René practices in the areas of competition law, regulatory law and commercial contracts. Prior to joining ComReg, he worked for Matheson Orsmby Prentice Solicitors. Any views expressed in this chapter are not the views of ComReg.

Pearse Ryan is a Partner in the Technology & Life Sciences Group at Arthur Cox. His practise focuses primarily on the areas of IT and outsourcing. Within these areas, Pearse specialises in IT and outsourcing projects in both the public and private sector, acting for both suppliers and customers. Pearse writes on IT and outsourcing relating matters, generally publishing in the UK Society for Computers and Law (SCL) monthly magazine and website (www.scl.org). Pearse is an active member of the SCL as well as a number of other IT and outsourcing related organisations.

Colin Sainsbury qualified as a solicitor in 1984. He worked as a solicitor with A&L Goodbody before joining Elan Corporation, plc in 1994. From 1996 to 2002 Colin was Vice President and General Counsel of Elan Pharmaceutical Technologies (Elan's drug delivery division). In 2002 Colin was promoted to Senior Vice President and played a leading role in the restructuring of Elan that has involved the sale of assets worth in excess of $1.8 billion. Colin was also centrally involved in managing the legal aspects of the SEC investigation into Elan's accounting policies and the related litigation involving class action suits by some Elan shareholders.

Colin, who joined BCM Hanby Wallace as a partner in the Corporate Department in 2004, has extensive international transactional and other experience in the life sciences and technology sectors. The sector-specific experience that Colin gained at Elan has been a significant added value driver in terms of his representation of Irish and multinational clients, including his ability to manage complex international transactions. As General Counsel of Elan's drug delivery business and as a partner in BCM Hanby Wallace, Colin has been involved both in structuring and negotiating transactions with many leading pharmaceutical companies and biotech companies in Europe, the US and Japan. Colin has also played a significant part in the structuring and negotiation of a large number of transactions pursuant to which his life sciences clients acquire rights to products.

Colin is a member of the Business Law Committee of the Law Society of Ireland. Colin is also actively involved in the work of the American Chamber of Commerce Research and Development Committee (which has interacted with a number of state agencies) and is also a member of the Laws Committee of the Licensing Executives Society

Richard Willis is a partner in the Litigation Group of Arthur Cox and focuses on professional negligence, shareholder, financial regulation and technology disputes. He regularly advises on matters before the Commercial Court division of the High Court or under case management in the High Court. He also has extensive experience in injunction applications as well as large scale discovery processes which typically involve electronic discovery processes and associated court applications.

CONTENTS

About the Authors v
Contents ix
Table of Cases xv
Table of Legislation xxi

Part I: Technology

Chapter 1   eBusiness
Rob Corbet

1.1	Overview	3
1.2	Primary legislation	3
1.3	What is so different about electronic contracts?	3
1.4	The legislation	4
1.5	Conclusion	19

Chapter 2   Legal Issues for Start-up Technology Companies
Rob Corbet

2.1	Introduction	21
2.2	Overview	21
2.3	Incorporating a company	21
2.4	Raising finance	23
2.5	Heads of agreement	24
2.6	Due diligence	25
2.7	Intellectual property	26
2.8	Warranties	27
2.9	Subscription and shareholders agreements	27
2.10	Service agreements	28
2.11	Employee share option schemes	28
2.12	Commercial contracts	28
2.13	Useful sources of information	29

Chapter 3   Domain Names – Registration and Disputes
Jeanne Kelly

3.1	What is a domain name?	31
3.2	How do domain name disputes arise?	32
3.3	How did WIPO become involved in resolving these disputes?	32
3.4	What is the UDRP?	33
3.5	What about .com?	34

3.6	Emerging UDRP case law	34
3.7	The emerging principles	35
3.8	Recent .ie disputes	37

Chapter 4 Privacy and Data Protection

Philip Nolan & Rossa McMahon

4.1	Introduction	41
4.2	Privacy as a constitutional and human right	41
4.3	The Data Protection Acts	42
4.4	The Electronic Communications Regulations 2003	52
4.5	The Data Retention Directive 2006	53
4.6	Privacy and data protection in the workplace	54

Chapter 5 IT Contracts

Philip Nolan & Rossa McMahon

5.1	Introduction	57
5.2	Preliminary issues	57
5.3	Legal principles that underpin software licensing	60
5.4	Other relevant legal principles	64
5.5	Software licence agreements	67

Chapter 6 Communications Law

René Rosenstock

6.1	Introduction and background	71
6.2	Key concepts and terms in electronic communications regulation	72
6.3	The legal framework	75
6.4	Enforcement	87
6.5	Competition law and administrative law	90
6.6	The postal sector	91
6.7	Broadcasting and spectrum	94
6.8	Conclusion	95

Chapter 7 Computer Crime in Ireland

Andy Harbison & Pearse Ryan

7.1	Introduction	97
7.2	Computer-specific fraud	98
7.3	Reaction to discovery of computer fraud	106
7.4	Computer fraud and the law	106
7.5	Computer forensics	109
7.6	Computer evidence	109
7.7	Proper computer evidential practice	111
7.8	Best evidence — in a 'paperless' society	112
7.9	Summary	112

Chapter 8   Electronic Discovery

Andy Harbison & Richard Willis

8.1	Introduction	113
8.2	The process of electronic discovery	114
8.3	Categorisation of electronic data	115
8.4	Identification of relevant data	116
8.5	Presentation of evidence	116
8.6	How much data …	116
8.7	Metadata	117
8.8	Legal issues	118
8.9	Discovery in Ireland	119
8.10	The position in the UK	119
8.11	The position in Australia	120
8.12	The position in New Zealand	121
8.13	The position in the USA	121
8.14	General conclusions	122
8.15	Problems for the litigator	123
8.16	Document management systems	124
8.17	Conclusion	124

Chapter 9   Outsourcing

Pearse Ryan

9.1	Introduction	125
9.2	What is outsourcing?	125
9.3	Types of outsourcing	126
9.4	History of outsourcing	127
9.5	Best-of-breed versus end-to-end outsourcing	128
9.6	Commercial drivers	129
9.7	Outsourcing market	130
9.8	Outsourcing contract – key risk issues	131
9.9	Employment law aspects of IT outsourcing	139

Part II: Intellectual Property

Chapter 10   Patents

Gerry Carroll, Aoife Murphy & Andrew Parkes

10.1	Patent law	145
10.2	International conventions and agreements	146
10.3	Patentability	147
10.4	Ideas and know-how	151
10.5	Applying for a patent	152
10.6	Ownership of the right to a patent (ss 15–16, 79–80 of PA 1992)	154

10.7	Infringement (ss 40–46 of PA 1992)	155
10.8	Action for infringement	158
10.9	Remedies for infringement	158
10.10	Defences and statutory exceptions to infringement	162
10.11	Revocation	166
10.12	Amendment	167
10.13	Remedy for groundless threats	168
10.14	Declaration of non-infringement	169
10.15	The role of a patent agent in patent litigation	169
10.16	Miscellaneous matters	169

Chapter 11   Trade Marks

Maureen Daly & Louise Carey

11.1	Introduction	173
11.2	What is a trade mark?	173
11.3	What type of mark can be registered?	173
11.4	Where should a trade mark be registered?	173
11.5	Who should do the filing of the application?	175
11.6	Registrability	175
11.7	Procedure before the Patents Office	176
11.8	The duration of the registration	177
11.9	Limitation on rights	177
11.10	Effects of registration	177
11.11	What constitutes 'infringing use'?	178
11.12	Defences and exceptions to infringement:	178
11.13	Infringement proceedings	179
11.14	Section 24 – Groundless threats of infringement proceedings	179
11.15	Dealings with registered trade marks	180
11.16	Licensing	181
11.17	Exclusive licences	181
11.18	Non-exclusive licensees	182
11.19	Surrender, revocation and invalidity	182
11.20	Certification marks and collective marks	184
11.21	Famous marks	184
11.22	Offences	184
11.23	Jurisdiction	185
11.24	Community trade mark	185

Chapter 12   Copyright

Mark Hyland

12.1	Introduction and overview	189
12.2	Basic concepts of copyright law	195
12.3	The enforcement of copyright	203
12.4	Civil remedies	205

12.5	Criminal remedies	208
12.6	Copyright and Related Rights (Amendment) Act 2007	210
12.7	Conclusions	211

Chapter 13   The Law of Passing Off

James Murray

13.1	Misrepresentation	214
13.2	Made by a trader in the course of trade	216
13.3	To prospective customers	216
13.4	Business or goodwill	217
13.5	Damage	218
13.6	The evolution of passing off – character merchandising	219

Chapter 14   Designs

Andrew Parkes

14.1	Introduction	223
14.2	Legislation	223
14.3	Protectable designs	224
14.4	Infringement	227
14.5	Defences to infringement	228
14.6	Invalidity	229
14.7	Criminal cases	230
14.8	Authorship and ownership of designs	230
14.9	Registration	231
14.10	Effect of exploitation of artistic works	232
14.11	Overlap with trade marks	232
14.12	Conclusion	233

Chapter 15   Confidential Information

Carol Plunkett

15.1	Introduction	235
15.2	What are the essential requirements?	235
15.3	Why should confidential information be protected?	235
15.4	History	236
15.5	The employment cases	237
15.6	The non-employment cases	238
15.7	Celebrities	241
15.8	Remedies	242

Chapter 16   Protection Of Computer Programs And Databases

Carol Plunkett

16.1	Protection of computer programs	243
16.2	International treaty law	244

16.3	Definition of computer program	244
16.4	Protection	245
16.5	Authorship and ownership	245
16.6	Restricted acts	246
16.7	Exceptions to restricted acts	247
16.8	Databases	248
16.9	Conclusion	251

Chapter 17 Life Sciences

Colin Sainsbury

17.1	Introduction	253
17.2	Patents	253
17.3	Trade marks	258
17.4	EU regulatory law	260
17.5	Generic products	263
17.6	The Bolar exemption	265
17.7	Patent Settlement Agreements	267

Index 269

TABLE OF CASES

A

Abbott Laboratories' SPC Application [2004] RPC 20 .... 17.2.1.4.2

Adidas v Charles O'Neill & Co Ltd [1983] ILRM 112 .... 13.1

Adidas v Varga and Petho (DIE2006-0004) 3.8

Aerotel Ltd v Telco Holdings [2006] EWCA Civ 1371 .... 10.3.1.2

Airtours v Commission [2002] ECR II-2585 .... 6.3.3.6

American Cyanamid v Ethicon [1975] AC 396 .... 10.9

An Post v Irish Permanent [1995] IR140 .... 13.1

Antioch Co v Scrapbook Borders Inc 210 FRD 645 .... 8.14.2

B

B&S Ltd v Irish Autotrader Ltd [1995] IR 142 .... 13.1

B&S Ltd v Varga and Petho (DIE2006-0005) 3.8

Bates & Assoc Ltd v Woolworths (NZ) Ltd (15 Nov 2002)
    HC Auckland, CL15/02 .... 8.12

Blayney v Clogau St David's Goldmines Ltd [2003] FSR 361 .... 12.4.1

Bodil Lindqvist v Kammaraklagaren (C-101/01) 4.3.8.2

Boehringer Ingelheim v Swingward (C-348/04) 17.3.2.1

Bristol Myers Squibb v Paranova (C-427/93) 17.3.2.1

British Horse Racing Board Ltd v William Hill Organisation Ltd
    [2001] EWHC 517 (Patents) (9 Febraury 2001), [2001] EWCA Civ 1268
    (C-263/02) 16.8.5

British Sugar plc v NEI Power Projects Ltd [1998] ITCLR 118 .... 9.8.4

Byers v Illinos State Police 53 Fed R Serv 3d 740 .... 8.13

C

C&A Modes Ltd v C&A Waterford Ltd [1978] SSR 126 .... 13.4

Campbell v MGN Ltd UKHL/2004/22 .... 15.7

Campus Oil v Minister for Energy (No 2) [1983] IR 88 .... 10.9

Catnic v Hill and Smith [1982] RPC 183 .... 10.7

CBS Broadcasting Inc v LA Twilight Zone (D2000-0397) WIPO 3.7.3

Children's Television Workshop Inc v Woolworths (New South Wales) Ltd
    [1981] 1 NSWLR 273 .... 13.6

Clearsprings Management Ltd v Businesslinx Ltd [2006] FSR 3 .... 16.5

Coast Stores v Dunnes Stores (9 Oct 2007, unreported) HC 14.4.3

Coco v AN Clarke [1969] RPC 41 .... 15.6

Computer Associates v Altai [1992] 23 IPR 385) 12.2.3

Contech Building Products Ltd v Walsh [2006] IEHC 45 .... 13.1

Copland v UK [2007] ECHR 253 .... 4.6.1

D

Derby & Co Ltd v Weldon (No 9) [1991] 2 All ER 901 ....8.8–8.11
Designer Guild Ltd v Russell Williams (Textiles) Ltd (t/a Washington DC)
(23 Nov 2000) HL 12.2.2
Deutsche Bank AG v Diego-Arturo Bruckner (D2000-0277) WIPO 3.7.2
Douglas v Hello! [2007] UKHL 21 ....15.7
Dyson Appliances Ltd v Hoover Ltd [2001] RPC 544 ....10.9

E

Educational Testing Service v TO EFL (D2000-0044) WIPO 3.7.2
Electricity Supply Board (ESB) v Lislyn Retail Ltd (DIE 2003-0001) 3.8
EMI Records and Ors v Eircom Ltd [2005] IEHC 233,
[2005] 4 IR 148 ....12.7
Eredu v Armet (OHIM ref: ICD000000024, 27 April 2004) 14.3.5
Ervin Warnink BV v J Townsend & Sons (Hull) Ltd [1979] AC 731 13

F

Faccenda Chicken v Fowler [1986] 1 All ER 617 ....15.5
Falcon Travel Ltd v Falcon Leisure Group [1991] IR 175 ....13.5
Football League Ltd v Littlewood Pools Ltd [1950] CH 637 ....16.8.1
Fujitsu Appn [1997] RPC 608 ....10.3.1.2

G

Gabicci plc v Dunnes Stores (1991, unreported) HC 13.1
General Electric Co (D2000-O394) WIPO 3.7.3
General Tire and Rubber Co v Firestone Tyre and Rubber Co
[1975] 2 All ER 173, [1975] 1 WLR 10.3.2, 12.4.1
Gerber Garment Technology Inc v Lectra Systems Ltd
[1997] RPC 443 ....10.9.1, 12.4.1
Glaverbel SA v British Coal Corporation [1995] FSR 225 ....10.7
Guinness Ireland v Kilkenny Brewing Co Ltd [1999] ILRM 531 ....13.4

H

Hutchinion 3G v Mahon (DIE2005-1) 3.8, 6.3.34

I

Ingersoll-Rand Co v Frank Gully (D2000-0021) WIPO 3.7.2
Intel Corporation v Via Technologies Inc [2003] FSR 33 ....10.10.2
Irish Patent No 1121375, Re [2005] IEHC 441 ....10.12
Irish Patent No 52364, Re [2005] IEHC 114 ....10.11
Irvine (Edmund) & Tidswell Ltd v Talksport Ltd
[2002] 2 All ER 414 ....13.6.1, 15.7

K

Kennedy v Ireland [1988] ILRM 472 .... 4.2.2

Kimberly-Clark v Procter & Gamble [2000] RPC 422 .... 10.12

Kirin-Amgen Inc v Transkaryotic Therapies Inc [2002] EWCA Civ 1096
    [2003] RPC 31 .... 10.3.2

L

Ladbroke (Football) Ltd v William Hill (Football) Ltd
    [1964] 1 WLR 273 .... 12.2.2, 12.2.3

Landor & Hawa International Ltd v Azure Designs Ltd
    [2006] EWCA Civ 1285 .... 14.3.3

Lawrence David Ltd v Ashton [1991] 1 All ER 385 .... 15.5

London Economics (Aus) Pty Ltd v Frontier Economics Pty Ltd
    [1999] FCA 932 .... 8.11

Lubrizol v Esso Petroleum [1998] RPC 727 .... 10.7

M

Mansell v Valley Printing Co [1908] 2 Ch 441 .... 12.2.3

Marca Mode CV v Adidas AG and Adidas (C-425/98)
    [2000] ET MR 723 .... 11.10

Marlton v Tectronix UK Holdings [2003] EWHC 383 (Ch) 8.10

Massachusetts Institute of Technology (MIT) (C-431/04) 17.2.1.4.1

McDonald v Bord na gCon (No 2) [1965] IR 217 .... 4.2.4

McGee v Attorney General [1974] IR 284 .... 4.2.2

McGrath v Trintech Technologies Ltd & Trintech Group Plc
    (29 Oct 2004, unreported) HC 8.9

Meadox Medicals v VPI Ltd (1981, unreported) HC 15.5

Medtronic Inc v Guidant Corporation [2007] IEHC 37 .... 10.16.2

Merck & Co Inc v GD Searle & Co [2001] 2 ILRM 363 .... 10.11

Merck v Integra US 74 USPQ 2d 1901 .... 17.6.2

Meters Ltd v Metropolitan Gas Meters [1911] 28 RPC 157 .... 10.9.1

Miss World Ltd Case [2004] IR 394 .... 13.1

Mondich (Mary-Lynn) (D2000-0004) WIPO 3.7.2

Monsanto v Stauffer Chemical Co [1985] RPC 515 .... 17.6.3

N

National Irish Bank v RTÉ [1998] 2 IR 465 .... 15.6

Navitaire Inc v Easyjet Airline Company and BulletProof Technologies Inc
    [2004] EWHC 1725 (Ch) 5.3.2.1

Niemitz v Germany [1992] 16 EHRR 97 .... 4.2.3

Nilesh Mehta v J Pereira Fernandes SA [2006] EWHC 813 (Ch) 1.4.1.4

Norowzian v Arks Ltd [1999] FSR 79 .... 12.2.2

Norwich Pharmacal Co v Customs & Excise Commissioners
 [1974] AC 133 ....10.16.3

O

O'Neill's Irish International Sports Co Ltd v O'Neill's Footwear
 Dryer Co Ltd (30 April 1997, unreported) HC 13.4
Oblique Financial Services v Promise Production Co Ltd
 [1994] ILRM 75 ....15.6
Orange Communications Ltd v Director of Telecommunications
 [2000] 4 IR 136..6.3.34
Orange Telecommunications Ltd v Director of Telecommunications Regulation
 (No 2) [2000] 4 IR 159 ....6.3.34

P

Pitney Bowes Inc v Francotyp-Postalia GmbH [1991] FSR 72, Ch D 10.10.2
Pope v Curl (1741) 2 Atk 342 ....15.4, 15.7
Prince Albert v Strange (1849) 2 De G & Sm 293, 1 Mac & G 25 ....15.4, 15.7
Prince of Wales v Associated Newspapers Ltd
 [2006] EWCA Civ 1776 ....15.7
Procter & Gamble Co v Reckitt Benckiser (UK) Ltd
 [2006] EWHC Ch 3154 ....14.3.5–14.4.1

R

R Griggs Group Ltd v Dunnes Stores (1996, unreported) HC 13.1
Ranbaxy Laboratories Ltd v Warner Lambert Co [2005] IEHC 178
 [2005] IESC 81, [2006] 1 IR 193 ....10.7, 10.14
Ransburg-Gema AJ v Electrostatic Plant Systems Ltd
 [1991] FSR 508, Ch 10.10.2
Ray (Robin) v Classic FM [1998] FSR 622 ....16.5
RCO Support Services v Unison and Others [2002] EWCA
 Civ 464 (CA) 9.9.5
Retail Systems Technology Ltd v McGuire [2007] IEHC 13
 2 February 2007 ....12.4.1
Roberts (Julia) v Russell Boyd (D2000-0210) WIPO 3.7.1
Roche Products Inc v Bolar Pharmaceutical Co 733 F 2d 858 ....17.6.2
Rowe Entertainment Inc v The William Morris Agency Inc
 205 FRD 421 ....8.14.2

S

Saltman Engineering v Campbell Engineering (1948) 65 RPC 203 ....15.6
Schmidt Case C-392/92 [1994] IRLR 302 ....9.9.5
Schneider (Europe) GmbH v Conor Medsystems Ireland Ltd
 [2007] IEHC 63 ....10.16.2
Seager v Copydex (No 1) [1967] RPC 349 ....15.6

Seager v Copydex (No 2) [1969] RPC 250 .... 15.6
Silhouette International Schmied GmbH and Co KG v Hartlauer
    (C-355/96), [1998] ETMR 539 .... 11.12
Simon Property Group LP v mySimon Inc 194 FRD 639 .... 8.14.2
Smart Telecom Ltd v Commission for Communications Regulation (29 July 2005,
    unreported) HC 6.3.3.4
SmithKline and French Laboratories Ltd v Evans Medical Ltd
    [1989] FSR 561 .... 10.12
SmithKline and French Laboratories Ltd v Global Pharmaceuticals Ltd
    [1986] RPC 394 .... 10.16.3
SmithKline Beecham v Genthon BV [2003] IEHC 623 .... 10.9
Sony Music Entertainment (Aus) Ltd v University of Tasmania
    [2003] FCA 532 .... 8.11
South West Water v ICL (1999) BLR 420 .... 9.8.4
Spring Gardens (House of) v Point Blank 1985 FSR 327 .... 15.5
St Albans City and District Council v International Computers Ltd
    [1995] FSR 686, [1996] All ER 481 .... 5.3.1, 9.8.4
Stena v Irish Ferries [2002] RPC 990, [2003] RPC 668 .... 10.10.10.1
Suzen v Zehnacker Gebaudereinigung GmbH Krankenhaussemice
    (C-13/1995), [1997] ICR 662 .... 9.9.5
Symonds Cider v Showerings (Ireland) Ltd [1997] 1ILRM 482 .... 13.3

T

Talk City (D2000-0009) WIPO 3.7.2
Telstra Corporation Ltd v Nuclear Marshmallows
    (D2000-O003) WIPO 3.7.2
Terrapin v Builders Supply (Hayes) [1960] RPC 128 .... 15.6
Tolley v JS Fry and Sons Ltd [1931] AC 333 .... 15.7

U

University of London Press Ltd v University Tutorial Press Ltd
    [1916] 2 Ch 601 .... 12.2.2

V

Veuve Cliquot Ponsardin v The Polygenix Group Co
    (D2000-0163) WIPO 3.7.2
Victor Chandler International v Customs & Excise
    [2000] 2 All ER 315 .... 8.8
Volvo v Veng (C-23/87) 10.10.2
Von Hannover v Germany [2004] ECHR 294 .... 4.2.3, 15.7

W

Watson, Laidlaw & Co Ltd v Pott, Cassels and Williamson
    [1914] 31 RPC 104 .... 12.4.1

Webb v Rose 98 ER 924 ....15.4
Wimmera Industrial Minerals Pty Ltd v RGC Mineral Sands Ltd
　[1998] FCA 299 ....8.11
Winterson (Jeanette) v Mark Hogarth (D2000-0235) WIPO 3.7.1
Witter Ltd v BP Industries Ltd [1996] All ER 573 ....9.8.4
Woodhouse UK v Architectural Lighting Systems
　[2006] RPC 1 ....14.3.5
Wrenn (Laurence), Integrated Multi-Media Solution Ltd v
　Stephen Landamore [2007] EWHC 1833 (Ch), 23 July 2007 ....16.5

Z

Zubulake v USB Warburg LLC (2003) 217 FRD 309 ....8.3.2, 8.14.2–8.14.3

TABLE OF LEGISLATION

Statutes

Child Trafficking and Pornography Acts 1998–2004
    s 9 (1) 4.6.1

Communications Regulation Act 2002
    Pt 3 .... 6.4.2
    s 6 .... 6.3.1
    s 10 .... 6.3.1, 6.7.2
         (1) 6.6.1
    s 11 .... 6.3.1
    s 12 .... 6.3.1, 6.6.1
         (3) 6.5.2
    s 13 (1) 6.3.1.1, 6.6.1
    s 30 .... 6.6.1
    s 39 .... 6.4.2
    s 44 .... 6.4.1.1–6.4.3
    s 45 .... 6.4.3

Communications Regulation (Amendment) Act 2007 .... 6.3.2, 6.4.4

Companies Acts 1963–2006 .... 7.4.1

Competition Act 2002
    s 5 .... 6.3.3.6, 6.5.1
    s 14 .... 6.5.1

Computer Software Copyright Act 1980 .... 16.1.1

Constitution of Ireland
    Art 40 .... 15.6

Consumer Information Act 1978 .... 1.4.3.3

Consumer Protection Act 2007 .... 1.2, 1.4.2.7, 1.4.5.1, 5.3.1
    Pt II 1.4.5.1
    s 2 (1) 5.3.1
    s 8 .... 1.4.5.1
    s 41 .... 1.4.5.1
    s 43 .... 1.4.5.1
    s 44 .... 1.4.5.1
    s 45 .... 1.4.5.1
    s 48 .... 1.4.5.1
    s 49 .... 1.4.5.1
    s 52 .... 1.4.5.1
    s 55 .... 1.4.5.1
    ss 77–84 .... 1.4.5.1

Continental Shelf Act 1968 .... 10.7

Control of Exports Act 2008 .... 5.4.3

Copyright Act 1963 .... 12.1

Copyright (Amendment) Act 1987 .... 12.1.1

Copyright and Related Rights Act 2000 .... 5.3.2.1, 12.1–12.1.1, 14.9.8, 16–16.2.2
   s 2 .... 12.2.2, 16.8.1
      (1) 16.3–16.4
   s 6 .... 12.1.2
   s 17 .... 12.2.1
      (1) 12.2.1
      (2) 12.2.2, 16.4
      (3) 12.2.2, 16.4, 16.8.1
      (4) 12.2.2
   s 18 (1) 12.2.2
      (2) 12.2.2
   s 21 .... 12.2.2
   ss 21–23 .... 16.5
   s 22 .... 12.2.2
   s 23 (1) 12.2.2
      (2) 12.2.2
   s 24 (1) 5.3.2.1
   ss 24–30 .... 12.2.2
   ss 24–36 .... 12.1.2
   s 37 (1) 12.2.3, 16.6
      (2) 12.2.3, 16.6
      (3) 12.2.3
   ss 37–43 .... 12.2.1
   s 38 .... 12.2.3
   s 39 .... 12.1.4, 12.2.3, 16.6, 16.7.3
      (1) 12.2.3
        (a) 16.6.1
      (2) 12.2.3
   s 40 .... 12.1.4, 12.2.3, 12.2.3, 16.6–16.6.2
      (3) 12.1.4
   s 41 .... 12.2.3, 12.2.3, 16.6–16.6.2
   s 42 .... 12.1.2, 12.2.3, 16.6
   s 43 .... 12.2.3, 16.6
      (2) 16.6.3
   ss 44–48 .... 12.2.1, 12.3.3
   s 45 .... 12.3.3
   s 46 .... 12.3.3
   s 47 .... 12.3.3
   s 48 .... 12.3.3
   s 80 .... 5.3.2.1, 16.6.1
      (2) 16.7.1
   ss 80–82 .... 5.3.2.1, 5.5.3, 12.1.4, 16.2.2
   s 81 .... 5.3.2.1
      (1) 16.7.2
      (2) 16.7.2
   s 82 .... 5.3.2.1, 16.6.1–16.7.3
      (2) 16.7.3
   s 87 .... 12.1.4, 16.6.1–16.7.3
   s 107 .... 12.4.5
   ss 107–119 .... 12.1.3
   s 109 .... 12.4.5
   s 113 .... 12.4.5

Copyright and Related Rights Act 2000 (contd)
    s 114 .... 12.4.5
    s 127 .... 12.3.4
        (4) 12.3.1
    ss 127–134 .... 12.3.1
    s 128 .... 12.4.1
        (2) 12.4.1
        (3) 12.4.1
    s 131 .... 12.4.2
    s 132 .... 12.4.3
        (3) 12.4.3
        (5) 12.4.3
    s 133 .... 12.4.4
    s 135 .... 12.3.1
    s 137 .... 12.3.1, 12.4.5
    s 139 .... 12.3.2
    s 140 .... 5.3.2.1, 12.5.1
        (3) 12.5.1
        (4) 12.5.1
        (7) 12.5.1
        (8) 12.5.1
    ss 140–145 .... 12.3.1, 12.5.1
    s 142 .... 5.3.2.1, 12.5.1
    s 143 .... 5.3.2.1, 12.5.1
    s 145 .... 12.4.2, 12.5.2
        (2) 12.5.2
    s 147 .... 12.3.1, 12.5.3
        (4) 12.5.3
    s 148 .... 12.5.4
    s 174 .... 12.1.2
    ss 182–90 .... 12.2.2
    s 244 .... 12.1.2
    ss 255–264 .... 12.3.1
    ss 303–306 .... 12.3.1
    s 319 .... 12.3.1
    s 320(1) 16.8.4
    ss 320–361 .... 12.1.2
    s 321 .... 16.8.3
    s 324 .... 16.8.4
        (3) 16.8.4
    ss 370–374 .... 12.1.4
    ss 370–376 .... 12.1.3
    s 374 .... 12.1.2
    s 375 .... 12.3.1
    ss 375–376 .... 12.1.4
    s 376 .... 12.3.1
    Pt II 12.1.2
    Pt V 5.3.4, 16.8

Copyright and Related Rights Acts 2000–2007 .... 12.1

Copyright and Related Rights (Amendment) Act 2007 .... 12.1, 12.6
    s 7 .... 12.6

Copyright and Related Rights (Amendment) Act 2007 (contd)
    s 8 .... 12.6
    s 12 .... 12.6
    s 42A 12.6

Criminal Damage Act 1991 .... 7.4.1
    s 2 .... 7.2.5, 7.4.1
        (1) 7.4.1
        (3) 7.4.1
    s 3 .... 7.4.1
    s 4 .... 7.4.1
    s 5 .... 7.2.5, 7.4.1

Criminal Evidence Act 1992
    s 5 (1) 7.8

Criminal Justice (Theft and Fraud Offences) Act 2001 .... 7.4.1
    s 9 .... 7.4.1

Data Protection Act 1988 .... 4.3.1
    s 1   (2) 4.3.3.2
        (3B)(a) 4.3.2.2
    s 2   (1) 4.3.3.3
        (5)(b) 4.3.3.2
        (7) 1.4.3.5, 4.3.4
        (8) 4.3.4
    s 2A 4.3.5
        (1) 4.3.5
    s 2B 4.3.6
    s 2C 4.3.3.1, 4.3.3.1
    s 2D 4.3.3.2
    s 3 .... 4.3.7.1
    s 4 .... 4.3.7.3
    s 5   (1) 4.6.1
    s 6 .... 4.3.7.4
    s 6A 4.3.7.5
    s 10 (2) 4.3.3.3
    s 11 .... 4.3.8.1
        (4) 4.3.8.7
    s 16 (1) 4.3.9
    s 23 (8) 1.4.3.5

Data Protection (Amendment) Act 2003 .... 4.3.1
    s 2   (7) 1.4.3.5
    s 3 .... 4.3.3.1, 4.3.3.2
    s 23 (8) 1.4.3.5

Digital Millennium Copyright Act 2000 .... 12.1.4

Electronic Commerce Act 2000 .... 1.2–1.4.1.1
    Annex 1 .... 1.4.1.6
    s 2 .... 8.8
        (1) 1.4.1.4
    s 9 .... 1.4.1.2, 8.8
    s 10 .... 1.4.1.3
    s 13 .... 1.4.1.5

Electronic Commerce Act 2000 (contd)
s 14	1.4.1.6
s 16	1.4.1.6
s 19	1.4.1.2
s 21	1.4.1.7–1.4.1.8
s 24	1.4.1.9

Enterprise Act 2002 .... 6.5.1

European Communities Act 1972 .... 10.10.8.1
    s 3 (3) 6.4.3

European Convention on Human Rights Act 2003
    s 2 .... 4.2.4

Evidence Act 1995 .... 8.11

Federal Food, Drug and Cosmetic Act (US) 17.6.2

Geneva Act 1999 .... 14.2.3

Industrial Designs Act 2001 .... 14.2, 14.3.4
s 2 (1)	14.3.1–14.3.6
(5)	14.2.4
(7)	14.3.7
s 16	14.3.3
(3)	14.3.3
ss 17–18	14.8.1
s 19	14.8.2
(3)	14.8.3
ss 20–29	14.9.1
s 24	14.9.3
ss 25–26	14.9.2
s 32	14.9.5
s 42 (4)	14.4.2
(5)	14.5.2
s 43	14.9.6
s 45 (3)	14.4.1
s 47	14.6.1–14.6.2
s 48	14.5.1
s 50	14.5.3
ss 51–62	14.4.3
ss 52–54	14.4.3
s 56	14.4.4
s 66	14.7.1
ss 69–70	14.7.1
ss 71–72	14.4.3
s 79	14.2.3
s 89	14.9.8

Industrial and Commercial Property (Protection) Acts 1927–1958
.... 10.1, 14.2, 14.3.2, 14.3.6

Intellectual Property (Miscellaneous Provisions) Act 1998 .... 12.1.1, 12.1.3

Interpretation Act 2005
    s 6 .... 4.6.1

Jurisdiction of Courts and Enforcement of Judgments Act 1998
   s 11 .... 15.6
Local Government Act 2001 .... 12.6
Maritime Jurisdiction Act 1959
   s 5 .... 10.7
Paris Act 1971 .... 12.1.3
Patents Act 1964 .... 10.1, 17.6.3
Patents Act 1975 .... 17.6.3
Patents Act 1977 (UK)
   s 61(1)(c) 12.4.1
Patents Act 1992 .... 10.1
   s 9 (2) 5.3.2.2, 10.3.1, 10.4
         (3) 10.3.1.2
         (4) 10.3.1, 17.2.1.1
   s 10 .... 17.2.1.1
         (1) 17.2.1.1
             (a) 17.2.1.2
             (c) 17.2.1.1
         (2) 10.3.1.1, 17.2.1.1
   s 11 (1) 10.3.2
         (2) 10.3.2
         (3) 10.3.2
         (4) 17.2.1.1
         (5) 17.2.1.1
   s 13 .... 10.3.2
   s 14 .... 10.3.1
   s 15 .... 10.6
   s 16 .... 10.6
         (2) 10.6
   s 18 (1) 10.5.3
         (2) 10.5.2
         (3) 10.5.3
   ss 18–22 .... 10.5.2
   s 19 .... 10.5.2
   s 20 .... 10.5.2, 10.12
   s 21 .... 10.5.2
   ss 25–27 .... 10.5.5
   s 29 .... 10.5.1–10.5.3
   s 30 .... 10.5.3
   s 32 .... 10.12
         (2) 10.12
   s 36 (3) 10.9.1.1
   s 37 .... 10.10.6
   s 38 .... 10.9.3, 10.12
   s 40 .... 10.7.1, 10.10.1
         (1) 10.7.2
         (b) 10.7.2
   ss 40–46 .... 10.7
   s 41 .... 10.7.2

Patents Act 1992 (contd)

s 42	10.10.8.1, 17.2.1.4.5, 17.6.1–17.6.3
(1)	10.10.8
(a)	10.7.2, 10.10.7
(b)	10.7.2
(c)	10.7.2, 10.10.9
(g)	17.6.3
s 43	10.10.2
s 44 (3)	10.7.2
s 45	10.7
s 47	10.9
(1)(a)	10.9.2
(2)	10.9
s 49	10.9.1.1
(1)	10.9.1.1
(2)	10.9.1.1
(3)	10.15
s 50	10.9.3
(2)	10.9.3, 10.15
s 51	10.8, 10.9.1.1
(1)	10.8
(2)	10.8
s 52	10.9.4
(2)	10.9.4
s 53	10.13
s 54	10.14
s 55	10.10.5
(2)	10.10.5
s 57	10.11
(5)	10.11
s 58	10.10.4, 10.11
(c)	10.12
(d)	10.12
s 59	10.11
s 63 (5)	10.5.3
ss 63–67	10.3.3
s 66 (1)	10.3.3
(3)	10.3.3
(4)	10.3.3
s 68 (1)	10.10.10.3
(2)(b)	10.10.10.3
s 70 (1)	17.2.1.3
(3)(f)	17.2.1.3
(ii)	17.2.1.3
ss 70–75	10.16.4, 17.2.1.3
s 79	10.6.1
s 80	10.6.1
s 83 (4)	10.10.10.3
s 85 (3)	10.8
(7)	10.8
s 94	10.16.1
s 95	10.8

Patents Act 1992 (contd)
   s 106(7) 10.16.1
   ss 118–124 .... 10.5.6
   s 119 .... 10.5.6
      (4) 10.5.6, 10.11
      (6) 10.5.6
   s 127 .... 10.5.7
   Sch 1 para 4 .... 17.6.3

Patents (Amendment) Act 2006 .... 10.1, 10.16.4
   s 37 (7) 10.10.6
      (8) 10.10.6
   s 53 (3) 10.13
   s 35A 10.10.6
   s 35B 10.10.6
   s 110A 10.10.6
   s 119A 10.10.6

Patents Acts 1992–2006
   s 9 (1) 10.3.1
      (2) 10.3.1
      (3) 10.3.1
   s 10 (1)(c) 10.3.1
      (2) 10.3.1
   s 11 (2) 10.3.2
      (3) 10.3.2
      (4) 10.3.2
      (5) 10.3.2
   s 12 .... 10.3.2
   s 25 .... 10.5.5
   s 40 .... 10.7
   s 45 (1) 10.7
      (3) 10.7
   s 46 .... 10.7
   s 50 (4) 10.9.3
   s 58 .... 10.11
   s 59 (2) 10.3.1
   s 60 .... 10.11
   s 117 .... 10.7
   Sch 2 .... 10.7

Post Office Act 1908
   s 34 (2) 6.6

Postal and Telecommunications Services Act 1983 .... 6.6
   s 12 (1) (a) 6.6
      (b) 6.6
   s 63 .... 6.6
   s 98 (1) 4.6.1

Sale of Goods and Supply of Services Act 1980 .... 5.3.1, 9.8.4
   s 11 .... 1.4.6
   s 39 .... 5.3.1
   s 46 .... 9.8.4
   Sch 1 .... 9.8.4

Sale of Goods and Supply of Services Acts 1893–1980 .... 1.2
    s 12 .... 1.4.6
Sale of Goods Act 1893 .... 5.3.1
    s 13 .... 1.4.6, 5.3.1
    s 14 .... 1.4.6, 5.3.1
    s 15 .... 1.4.6, 5.3.1
Social Welfare Acts 9.9.2
Statute of Frauds 1677
    s 4 .... 1.4.1.4
Trade Marks Act 1996 .... 11.1–11.4.2, 14.11, 17.3.2
    s 2 .... 14.11
    s 6 .... 11.3, 11.6.1
        (2) 14.11
    s 8 .... 11.6.1, 11.19.3
        (1)(b) 11.19.3
        (c) 11.19.3
        (d) 11.19.3
    s 10 .... 11.6.2
        (4) 11.6.2
    s 13 .... 11.10
    s 14 .... 11.10–11.11, 11.24.3
    s 15 .... 11.12
    s 18 .... 11.13
    s 20 .... 11.17, 11.23
    s 22 .... 11.13
    s 23 .... 11.15, 11.23
    s 24 .... 11.14
    s 25 .... 11.13
    s 26 .... 11.15
    s 27 .... 11.15
    s 28 .... 11.15
    s 29 .... 11.15
    s 32 .... 11.16
    s 33 .... 11.17
    s 34 .... 11.18
    s 35 .... 11.17
    s 36 .... 11.17
    s 40 .... 11.7
    s 47 .... 11.8
    s 48 .... 11.8
    s 50 .... 11.19.1
    s 51 .... 11.19.2, 11.24.7
    s 52 .... 11.19.3
        (6) 11.12
    s 53 .... 11.19.3
    s 54 .... 11.20
    s 55 .... 11.20
    s 61 .... 11.21
    s 76 .... 11.19.3

Trade Marks Act 1996 (contd)
 s 92 .... 11.22
 s 93 .... 11.22
 s 94 .... 11.22
 s 96 .... 11.23
 s 99 .... 11.19.2
 Sch 1 .... 11.20
 Sch 2 .... 11.20

Unfair Contract Terms Act 1977 (UK) 9.8.4

Wireless Telegraphy Acts 1926–1988 .... 6.7.2

Statutory Instruments

Civil Procedure Rules (UK) 1999 .... 8.10
 r 31 .... 8.10
 r 31.4 .... 8.10
 r 31.8 .... 8.10
 r 31.12 .... 8.10

Control of Exports Order 2000 (SI 300/2000) 5.4.3

Control of Exports Order 2005 (SI 884/2005) 5.4.3

Data Protection Act 1988 (Section 16(1)) Regulations 2007 (SI 657/2007) 4.3.9

European Communities (Companies) Regulations 1973 (SI 163/1973)
 reg 9 .... 1.4.4

European Communities (Misleading Advertising) Regulations 1988
 (SI 134/1988) 1.4.3.3

European Communities (Legal Protection of Computer Programs)
 Regulations 1993 (SI 26/1993) 12.1.1–12.1.2, 16.2.2

European Communities (Supplementary Protection Certificate) Council
 Regulations 1993 (SI 125/1993) 10.1, 10.3.4, 17.2.1.4.2

European Communities (Term of Protection of Copyright) Regulations 1995
 (SI 158/1995) 12.1.1

European Communities (Unfair Terms in Consumer Contracts) Regulations 1995
 (SI 27/1995) 1.2, 1.4.5.2, 5.4.1
 Sch 3 .... 1.4.5.2, 5.4.1

European Communities (Counterfeit and Pirated Goods) Regulation 1996
 (SI 49/1996) 11.13

European Communities (Control of Exports of Dual-Use Items) Regulations 2000
 (SI 317/2000) 5.4.3

European Communities (Legal Protection of Biotechnological Inventions)
 Council Regulations 2000 (SI 247/2000) 10.1, 10.3.1.1, 17.2.1.2
 reg 5(1) 17.2.1.2
 reg 6(1) 17.2.1.2

European Communities (Unfair Terms in Consumer Contracts) (Amendment)
 Regulations 2000 (SI 307/2000) 1.4.5.2

European Communities (Protection of Consumers in Respect of Contracts made by
  Means of Distance Communication) Regulations 2001
  (SI 207/2001) 1.2, 1.4.2.1, 5.3.1, 5.4.2, 6.3.6.4
  reg 3 .... 1.4.2.4–1.4.2.6
  reg 4 .... 1.4.2.7
  reg 5 .... 1.4.2.7
  reg 6 .... 1.4.2.7
  reg 9 .... 1.4.2.7
  reg 10 .... 1.4.2.7
  reg 11 .... 1.4.2.7
  reg 17 .... 6.3.6.4
  reg 18 .... 6.3.6.4
  Sch 3 .... 1.4.2.7

European Communities (Supplementary Protection Certificates)
  (Amendment) Regulations 2001 (SI 648/2001) 10.1

European Communities (Control of Exports of Dual-Use Items)
  (Amendment) Regulations 2002 (SI 512/2002) 5.4.3

European Communities (Data Protection and Privacy in
  Telecommunications) Regulations 2002 (SI 192/2002) 4.4, 6.3.7

European Communities (Postal Services) Regulations 2002
  (SI 616/2002) 6.6.2
  reg 4 .... 6.6.2.1
  reg 5 .... 6.6.2.1
  reg 7 .... 6.6.2.2

European Communities (Community Designs) Regulations 2003
  (SI 27/2003) 14.2.2

European Communities (Directive 2000/31/EC) Regulations 2003
  (SI 68/2003) 1.2–1.4.1.1, 1.4.3.1, 12.1.4
  reg 3(1) 1.4.3.3
  reg 7 .... 1.4.3.3
    (1)(d) 1.4.3.5
  reg 8 .... 1.4.3.5
  reg 9 .... 1.4.3.5
  reg 11 .... 1.4.3.5
  reg 13 .... 1.4.3.6
  reg 14 .... 1.4.3.6
  Sch 1 .... 1.4.3.3

European Communities (Electronic Communications Networks
  and Services) (Authorisation) Regulations 2003 (SI 306/2003) 6.3.4

European Communities (Electronic Communications Networks and Services)
  (Access) Regulations 2003 (SI 305/2003) 6.3.5
  reg 1 .... 6.3.5.1
  regs 9–14 .... 6.3.5.2
  reg 17 .... 6.4.1.1
  reg 18 .... 6.4.1.1
    (5) 6.4.1.1
    (7) 6.4.1.1
    (10) 6.4.1.2
    (12) 6.4.1.2

European Communities (Electronic Communications Networks and Services)
(Data Protection and Privacy) Regulations 2003 (SI 535/2003) 4.4, 6.3.7, 7.2.1
   reg 13 .... 1.4.3.5
      (1)(b) 4.4

European Communities (Electronic Communications Networks and
Services) (Framework) Regulations 2003 (SI 307/2003) 6.3.3, 6.3.3.6
   reg 19 .... 6.3.3.3, 6.5.2
   reg 26 .... 6.3.3.6
   reg 31 .... 6.3.3.7

European Communities (Electronic Communications Networks and Services)
(Universal Service and Users' Rights) Regulations 2003 (SI 308/2003) 6.3.6
   reg 11(1) 6.3.6.2
   reg 14 .... 6.3.6.3
   reg 26 .... 6.3.6.5

European Communities (Copyright and Related Rights) Regulations 2004
(SI 16/2004) 12.1.2
   reg 3 .... 12.1.4

European Communities (Distance Marketing of Consumer Financial
Services) Regulations 2004 (SI 853/2004) 1.4.2.4

European Communities (Artists Resale Right) Regulations (SI 312/2006) 12.1.2
   reg 7 .... 12.1.2
   reg 10 .... 12.1.2

European Communities (Enforcement of Community Judgments on
Trade Marks and Designs) Regulations 2006 (SI 646/2006) 14.2.2

European Communities (Enforcement of Intellectual Property Rights)
Regulations 2006 (SI 360/2006) 10.1, 11.13, 11.24.5, 12.1.2, 14.2.2, 17.3.3
   reg 3 .... 10.16.3
   reg 4 .... 10.9.2
   reg 5 .... 10.9.6

European Communities (Limitation of Effect of Patent) Regulations 2006
(SI 50/2006) 10.1, 10.10.8.1, 17.6.3

European Communities (Patent Agents) Regulations 2006 (SI 141/2006) 10.1

European Communities (Companies) (Amendment) Regulations 2007
(SI 49/2007) 1.2, 1.4.4

European Communities (Electronic Communications Networks and Services)
(Framework) (Amendment) Regulations 2007 (SI 271/2007) 6.3.3.5

Federal Court Rules (Aust)
   reg 1 r 4 .... 8.11

Federal Rules of Civil Procedure (US)
   r 34 .... 8.13

High Court Rules (NZ)
   r 3 .... 8.12

Industrial Designs Regulations 2002 (SI 280/2002) 14.2

Medicinal Products (Control of Placing on the Market) Council Regulations 2007
(SI 540/2007) 17.4.2

Patents Rules 1992 (SI 172/1992) 10.1
    r 27 .... 10.3.1
    r 38 .... 10.10.6
    r 83 .... 10.5.6
    r 93(2) 10.5.3

Patents (Amendment) Rules 2006 (SI 2006/142) 10.1

Patents (Amendment) Act 2006 (Certain Provisions) (Commencement)
    Order 2007 (SI 2007/761) 10.1

Patents, Trade Marks and Designs (Fees) Rules 2001 (SI 482/2001) 10.1

Rules of the Superior Courts 1986 (SI 15/1986)
    Ord 84 .... 6.3.3.4, 6.6.2.6

Rules of the Superior Courts (No 2) (Discovery) 1999 (SI 233/1999) 8.8

Trade Marks (Madrid Protocol) Regulations 2001 (SI 346/2001) 11.4.3

Transfer Regulations (European Communities (Protection of Employees
    on Transfer of Undertakings) Regulations 2003 (SI 131/2003) 9.9–9.9.2

Transfer of Undertakings (Protection of Employment) Regulations 1981 (UK)
    (SI 1794/1981) 9.9.5

European Legislation

Commission Regulation 240/96 .... 10.4

Community Trade Marks Regulation
    Art 4 .... 14.11

Council Common Position 2003/486/CFSP
    Art 2 .... 5.4.3

Council Directive 89/104/EC 11.1, 17.3.2
    Art 28 .... 17.3.2
    Art 30 .... 17.3.2

Council Directive 91/250/EC 16.2.1–16.4
    Art 1(2) 16.4
    Art 6 .... 16.7.2

Council Directive 91/250/EEC 12.1.1–12.1.2

Council Directive 92/100/EEC 12.1.2, 12.6

Council Directive 93/13/EC 1.4.5.2

Council Directive 93/83/EEC 12.1.2

Council Directive 93/98/EEC 12.1.1, 12.1.2

Council Directive 95/46/EC 4.3.1, 7.2.2

Council Directive 96/9/EC 5.3.4, 12.1.2, 16.8–16.8.4
    Art 7 .... 16.8.5

Council Directive 97/66/EC 4.4

Council Directive 97/67/EC 6.6.1

Council Directive 97/7/EC 1.4.2.1

Council Directive 98/44/EC	17.2.1.2
Recital 42	17.2.1.2
Council Directive 98/71/EC	14.2
Art 1 (a)	14.3.1
(b)	14.3.2
(c)	14.3.2
Art 6(1)	14.3.6
(2)	14.3.7
Art 7	14.3.3
(3)	14.3.3
Art 9	14.4.1
Art 10	14.9.6
Art 11	14.6.1–14.6.2
Art 12	14.4.2
Art 13	14.5.1
Art 16	14.9.7
Art 17	14.9.8
Art 18	14.5.2
Recital 13	14.3.5
Recital 14	14.3.3
Council Directive 1999/93/EC	1.4.1.1
Council Directive 2000/31/EC	1.4.1.1, 1.4.3.1, 12.1.4
Art 12	12.1.4
Art 13	12.1.4
Art 14	12.1.4
Council Directive 2001/29/EC	12.1.2, 12.7
Art 5	12.1.2
Art 6 (1)	12.1.2
Art 7	12.1.2
Council Directive 2001/83/EC	17.4.1
Council Directive 2001/84/EC	12.1.2
Council Directive 2001/23/EEC	9.9
Council Directive 2002/19/EC	6.3.5
Council Directive 2002/20/EC	6.3.4
Annex	6.3.4
Council Directive 2002/21/EC	6.3.3
Art 3 (1)	6.3.3.2
Art 4	6.3.3.4, 6.3.5.3
Art 8	6.3.1
Council Directive 2002/22/EC	6.3.6–6.3.6.2
Council Directive 2002/39/EC	6.6.2
Council Directive 2002/58/EC	4.4, 6.3.7
Council Directive 2002/65/EC	1.4.2.4
Council Directive 2003/58/EC	1.4.4
Council Directive 2004/27/EC	17.4.1
Art 6 (1)	17.5.3

Council Directive 2004/27/EC (contd)
   Art 8 (3)(i) 17.5.1
   Art 10 .... 17.4.2.1
      (1) 17.4.2.2–17.5.2
      (2)(b) 17.5.2
      (4) 17.5.4
      (5) 17.4.2.3
      (6) 17.6.1–17.6.3

Council Directive 2004/48/EC 12.1.2, 12.7, 17.3.3
Council Directive 2005/29/EC 1.4.5.1, 5.3.1
Council Directive 2006/116/EC 12.1.2
Council Directive 2006/24/EC 4.5
Council Directive 2008/6/EC 6.6.3, 6.8
Council Regulation 1768/92/EC 10.1, 10.3.4, 17.2.1.4
Council Regulation 3381/94/EC 5.4.3
Council Regulation 40/94/EC 11.1–11.4.2
   Art 9 .... 11.24.3
   Art 93 .... 11.24.4

Council Regulation 1610/96/EC 10.1, 10.3.4
Council Regulation 1334/2000/EC 5.4.3
Council Regulation 141/2000/EC 17.4.2.4
Council Regulation 44/2001/EC 1.2, 1.4.7
   Art 15 .... 1.4.7
   Art 23 .... 1.4.7

Council Regulation 6/2002/EC 14.2
   Art 3 .... 14.11
      (2) 14.3.4
         (a) 14.3.1
         (b) 14.3.2
         (c) 14.3.2
   Art 7 (1) 14.3.6
      (2) 14.3.7
   Art 8 .... 14.3.3
      (3) 14.3.3
   Art 10 .... 14.4.1
   Art 11 .... 14.2.2, 14.9.6
      (2) 14.3.6
   Art 12 .... 14.9.6
   Art 14 .... 14.8.2
   Art 18 .... 14.8.3
   Art 19 .... 14.4.2
      (2) 14.2.2
   Art 20 .... 14.5.1
   Art 22 .... 14.5.3
   Art 24 .... 14.6.2
   Art 25 .... 14.6.1
   Arts 35–48 .... 14.9.1

Council Regulation 6/2002/EC (contd)
 Art 36 .... 14.9.3
    (6) 14.4.1
 Art 37 .... 14.9.4
 Art 38 .... 14.9.2
 Arts 41–43 .... 14.9.2
 Art 50 .... 14.9.5
 Arts 80–92 .... 14.4.3
 Arts 84–87 .... 14.6.2
 Art 89 .... 14.4.3
 Art 96(1) 14.9.7
    (2) 14.9.8
 Art 110 .... 14.5.2
 Recital 10 .... 14.3.3
 Recital 14 .... 14.3.5

Council Regulation 1383/03/EC 10.16.5

Council Regulation 726/2004/EC 17.4.1–17.4.2.2
 Art 14(11) 17.4.2.1

Council Regulation 1891/2006/EC 14.2.3

Council Regulation 1901/2006/EC 17.4.2.5

Council Regulation 1902/2006/EC 17.4.2.5

Council Regulation 816/2006/EC 10.1, 10.16.4, 17.2.1.3

International Treaties and Conventions

Berne Convention for the Protection of Literary and Artistic Works 12.1.3
 Art 2 .... 16.2

Charter of Fundamental Rights of the European Union
 Art 7 .... 4.2.1
 Art 8 .... 4.2.1

Community Patent Convention 1975–1989 .... 10.2.4

EC Treaty 10.10.2
 Art 2 .... 6.1
 Arts 28–30 .... 10.10.2
 Art 36 .... 10.10.2
 Art 81 .... 6.5.1
    (1) 10.10.2
 Art 82 .... 6.3.3.6, 6.5.1–6.6, 10.10.2, 10.10.2, 17.2.1.4.4
 Art 86 .... 6.1
 Art 95 .... 6.1

European Convention on Human Rights
 Art 8 .... 4.2.1–4.2.3, 4.6.1

European Patent Convention 1973–2000 .... 10.2.3, 10.5.6, 10.12, 10.16.1, 17.2.1.1
 Art 52 .... 10.3.1.2
    (2) 5.3.2.2
    (3) 10.3.1.2
    (4) 17.2.1.1
 Art 53 (a) 17.2.1.2

European Patent Convention 1973–2000 (contd)
- Art 54 .... 10.3.1.2
  - (5) 17.2.1.1
- Art 56 .... 10.3.1.2
- Art 69 .... 10.7
  - Protocol 10.7
- Art 105a 10.12
- Art 112(b) 10.3.1.2
- Art 138(3) 10.12

International Convention for the Protection of Industrial Property 10.2.1

International Convention on Civil and Political Rights 1966
- Art 17 .... 4.2.1

Marrakesh Agreement Establishing the World Trade Organization
(the WTO Agreement) 10.2.5

Paris Convention
- Art 4 .... 10.5.5

Patent Co-operation Treaty 10.2.2, 10.5.7, 10.16.1

Trade-Related Aspects of Intellectual Property Rights (TRIPs)
- Agreement 1994 .... 10.2.5, 10.16.4, 12.1.1, 12.3.1
- Art 10(1) 16.2
- Arts 27–34 .... 10.2.5
- Art 27.1 .... 17.2.1.3
- Art 27.2 .... 17.2.1.2
- Art 31 .... 17.2.1.3
- Art 61 .... 12.1.2

Treaty of Rome
- Art 81 .... 12.1.2
- Art 82 .... 12.1.2

Universal Declaration of Human Rights 1948
- Art 12 .... 4.2.1

World Intellectual Property Organization Copyright Treaty 12.1.3, 16.2
- Art 4 .... 16.2

World Intellectual Property Organization Phonograms and Performers Treaty 12.1.3

Part I: Technology

CHAPTER 1

EBUSINESS

Rob Corbet

1.1 Overview

The purpose of this chapter is to assist those advising clients who are doing business online. In particular, the chapter will focus on how to properly conclude contracts over the internet, by email or through other electronic means.

Since 2000, there have been several pieces of legislation which directly impinge upon 'etailers' who offer goods or services for sale to consumers, while those who offer 'business to business' services remotely have also been affected. However, there is an important point to bear in mind throughout this chapter: ebusiness is simply business conducted remotely. Accordingly, all of the usual laws relating to business (contract, sales of goods and services, consumer protection, international laws etc) will apply equally in an online and offline environment. While this chapter will focus on the laws which are specific to electronic transactions, one could not properly advise on ebusiness without first gaining an understanding of the broader ambit of commercial law.

1.2 Primary legislation

The main legislation on which this chapter focuses is the following:

- Electronic Commerce Act 2000;
- European Communities (Protection of Consumers in Respect of Contracts made by means of Distance Communication) Regulations 2001;
- European Communities (Directive 2000/31/EC) Regulations 2003;
- European Communities (Companies) (Amendment) Regulations 2007;
- The Consumer Protection Act 2007;
- European Communities (Unfair Terms in Consumer Contracts) Regulations 1995;
- Sale of Goods and Supply of Services Acts 1893–1980; and
- Council Regulation No 44/2001 on Jurisdiction and the Recognition and Enforcement of Judgments in Civil and Commercial Matters.

Where you are advising a client in a particularly regulated area, such as, for example, financial services or betting, specific legislation will apply which is beyond the scope of this chapter.

1.3 What is so different about electronic contracts?

One of the perceived barriers to ecommerce when it first emerged in the 1990s was that consumers and businesses did not feel that the law would adequately protect them where they bought or sold something online as against when the same sale was made over the counter. Legal scholars tended to focus on the following issues when discussing the legal aspects of an electronic contract:

- the fact that the purchaser and the seller were not present at the same time;

- the fact that purchasers would be resident in foreign jurisdictions where consumer protection, contract and other laws might be quite different to those in the seller's home jurisdiction;
- a perceived lack of security and higher propensity for fraud;
- the expense in pursuing an errant seller who may have little in the way of assets and could be located in a foreign jurisdiction;
- the fact that websites could appear and disappear with alarming rapidity and ease;
- privacy concerns; and
- whether or not a court would admit an electronic contract into evidence in the event of a dispute.

As we will see, the law has started to address many of these issues, particularly in the case of consumers.

1.4 The legislation

1.4.1 Electronic Commerce Act 2000

1.4.1.1 *Background to the ECA*

The Electronic Commerce Act 2000 (ECA) implements the European Union's Electronic Signatures Directive (1999/93/EC) and some of the provisions of the Electronic Commerce Directive (2000/31/EC). The remaining provisions of the Electronic Commerce Directive were implemented in the EC (Directive 2000/31/EC) Regulations 2003 which are considered further below.

1.4.1.2 *Main objectives of the ECA*

Section 9 of the ECA provides an informative overview of the main purpose of the ECA and states that:

> 'Information ... shall not be denied legal effect, validity or enforceability solely on the grounds that it is wholly or partly in electronic form ...'

In the context of contracting online, s 19 of the ECA provides those wishing to conclude electronic contracts with additional clarity and states as follows:

> '19(1) An electronic contract shall not be denied legal effect, validity or enforceability solely on the grounds that it is wholly or partly in electronic form, or has been concluded wholly or partly by way of an electronic communication.
>
> 19(2) In the formation of a contract, an offer, acceptance of an offer or any related communication (including any subsequent amendment, cancellation or revocation of the offer or acceptance of the offer) may, unless otherwise agreed by the parties, be communicated by means of an electronic communication.'

While this is not to say that it was not possible to have a valid contract concluded over the internet or by an exchange of emails prior to the enactment of the ECA, the above provisions did help to remove all ambiguity on the matter.

1.4.1.3 *Excluded areas*

Importantly, however, the ECA does not apply to the law relating to the transfer of land or to the execution of documents such as wills, trusts or enduring powers of attorney, which will still have to be evidenced in traditional paper forms of writing (s 10). Importantly from the point of view of conveyancing solicitors, a contract for the sale of land can be in electronic form while the conveyance itself must be in a traditional form of writing.

1.4.1.4 *Signing an electronic contract*

The traditional procedure for executing a written contract in the offline world is for each of the parties to fix their signatures on the document to indicate that they agree to the terms contained therein (of course, a signature is not necessarily always required for there to be a valid contract – contract terms can be agreed orally or can be ascertained from the circumstances and conduct of the parties.) Where no paper contract existed, this presented a potential difficulty in the context of electronic contracts. The ECA therefore sought to address the discrepancy between paper and electronic signatures.

The ECA makes an important distinction between 'electronic signatures' and 'advanced electronic signatures'.

Under s 2(1) of the ECA, an 'electronic signature' means:

> 'data in electronic form attached to, incorporated in or logically associated with other electronic data and which serves as a method of authenticating the purported originator, and includes an advanced electronic signature.'

This definition would encompass, for example, a scanned version of a handwritten signature or, possibly, a typed name at the foot of an email.

An interesting issue arises in relation to email addresses. For example, an email sent from John.Smith@JohnSmithSolicitors.ie will have sufficient information to constitute an electronic signature regardless of whether John Smith types his name at the foot of the email. The recipient of an email from John Smith can see that the contents of the email are purported to come from John Smith and John Smith's email address is a method of authenticating him. Therefore, the ingredients of an 'electronic signature' as set out above appear to be present.

However, the UK courts have taken a different view. This specific issue of whether or not an email address can constitute an electronic signature arose in the recent UK decision, *Nilesh Mehta v J Pereira Fernandes SA* [2006] EWHC 813 (Ch), (7 April 2006). In this case, the defendant stated in an email that he would give a personal guarantee in the amount of £25,000. The English High Court had to decide whether, for the purposes of s 4 of the Statute of Frauds 1677, the presence of an automatically inserted email address at the top of the email constituted a signature by, or on behalf of, the defendant.

In this case, the email was not 'signed', but the header of the email showed that it came from the defendant's email address, which was the same email address that had appeared on other emails sent by him to the plaintiff's solicitors, which he had signed. The wording of the email in question was such that it contained an offer and contemplated that formal documents would be entered into in relation to the personal guarantee. Notwithstanding that the terms of the guarantee had been subsequently agreed orally by the defendant and the plaintiff's solicitors, the defendant argued that he was not bound to honour the terms of the guarantee on the basis that it had not been 'signed' for the purposes of s 4 of the Statute of Frauds.

The English High Court held that the contents of the email constituted a sufficient note or memorandum for the purpose of s 4 of the Statute of Frauds, as it contained an offer in writing made by the guarantor which contained the essential terms of what was offered, and the offer had been accepted unconditionally by the plaintiff's solicitors (albeit orally). However, the court held that the email did not bear a signature, within the meaning of s 4 of the Statute of Frauds, of either the guarantor or his authorised agent, as the automatic insertion of an email address was not intended as a signature. The inclusion of the email address, in the absence of contrary intention, was incidental, in that the signature or name just happened to appear somewhere rather than being inserted into the document in order to give, and with the intention of giving, authenticity to it.

As an aside, the judge stated that if a party, or a party's agent, sending an email types his, or his principal's, name that would be a sufficient signature, subject to other legal requirements and providing always that the name was inserted into the document in order to give, and with the intention of giving, authenticity to it.

The issue of electronic signatures has yet to come before the Irish courts. However, in the case of a typical purchase concluded on a website, the purchaser will normally be required to type in his or her name and contact details before submitting the order and likewise, the submission of this data would be expected to constitute an electronic signature of the online order.

In contrast, an 'advanced electronic signature' is defined in s 2(1) as an electronic signature which is:

(1) uniquely linked to the signatory;
(2) capable of identifying the signatory;
(3) created using means that are capable of being maintained by the signatory under his, her or its sole control; and
(4) linked to the data to which it relates in such a manner that any subsequent change of the data is detectable.

Encrypted 'digital' signatures using Public Key Infrastructure (PKI) will often meet the requirements of an 'advanced electronic signature'. Without getting into the more complex aspects of cryptography, the use of PKI technology allows the sender of the information to encrypt the contents of the electronic communication so that (i) the recipient can be sure that the email has come from the sender who appears to have sent it, and (ii) the data has not been changed prior to it being received. So, in the earlier example, if John Smith encrypts his email using an advanced electronic signature (engaging typical PKI technology), the email can only be opened and read by the intended recipient. The recipient can be sure that it has been signed by John since only John has the means of encrypting the message with his advanced electronic signature.

The need for advanced electronic signatures stems from the inherent confidentiality and integrity risks that are associated with an open communications network such as the world wide web.

1.4.1.5 *Validity of electronic signatures*

Section 13 of the Act provides that if by law or otherwise the signature of a person or public body is required (whether the requirement is in the form of an obligation or consequences flow from there being no signature) or permitted, then, subject to meeting the requirements of s 13(2), either an electronic signature or an advanced electronic signature may be used. The purpose of s 13 is to provide functional equivalence between hand-written and electronic signatures.

So, going back to one of the earlier examples, where the customer fills out an online order form on a website and enters his or her name, contact details, credit card details etc, in submitting this data online and by clicking a 'Place Order' or similar icon on the screen, this order will be deemed to have been signed by the purchaser using an 'electronic signature' and the electronic signature will be given the same legal validity as if the purchaser had submitted and signed the order in paper form.

1.4.1.6 *Special cases – advanced electronic signatures*

The ECA carves out specific areas where a simple electronic signature will not enjoy functional equivalence to the paper counterpart. For example, where a signature is required to be witnessed (s 14), the signature to be witnessed must be an advanced electronic signature. In addition, the document must contain an indication that the signature is required to be witnessed and the witness must also sign using an advanced electronic signature which meets the requirements of Annex 1 of the ECA (ie the advanced electronic signature both meets the definition in the Act and in addition is based on a 'qualified certificate').

Qualified certificates must contain:

(a) an indication that the certificate is issued as a qualified certificate;
(b) the identification of the certification-service-provider and the State in which it is established;
(c) the name of the signatory or a pseudonym, which shall be identified as such;
(d) provision for a specific attribute of the signatory to be included if relevant, depending on the purpose for which the certificate is intended;
(e) signature-verification data which correspond to signature-creation data under the control of the signatory (in the PKI environment this equates to the use of public keys and related private keys);
(f) an indication of the beginning and end of the period of validity of the certificate;
(g) the identity code of the certificate;
(h) the advanced electronic signature of the certification-service-provider issuing it;
(i) limitations on the scope of use of the certificate, if applicable; and
(j) limits on the value of transactions for which the certificate can be used, if applicable.

The requirement to use an advanced electronic signature based on a qualified certificate also applies where a document is required to be executed under seal (s 16).

So in the case of witnessed signatures and documents executed under seal, these cannot be executed electronically unless an advanced electronic signature is deployed. These situations are not that unusual. For example, a company's Articles of Association may have specific provisions about the use of the company seal in executing certain types of documents. Similarly, some contracts may be executed as deeds under seal. Unless the company's Articles specifically permit the use of advanced electronic signatures in these cases, it would not be advisable to execute such documents electronically and the traditional pen, paper and seal should be applied to the contract.

In other instances, the parties may choose to engage advanced electronic signatures for the added security and integrity which comes with their use. For example, the Revenue Online Service, www.ros.ie uses advanced electronic signatures on its website to ensure both the identity of those who are filing their tax returns online and the integrity of the data which is submitted online. In so doing, the Revenue can be certain that online filings are even more secure than the paper based equivalent.

1.4.1.7 *When is an email/internet communication deemed to have been sent and received?*

Section 21 deals with the time and place of dispatch and receipt of electronic communications. Under the so-called 'Postal rule' acceptance is deemed to occur at the time the written acceptance is posted by the offeree and not the time at which it is received or read by the offeror. Prior to the implementation of the ECA, it was not clear whether the rule applied to electronic communications. Section 21 provides that where an electronic communication enters an information system, or the first information system, outside the control of the originator, then, unless otherwise agreed between the originator and the addressee, it is taken to have been sent when it enters such information system (or first information system). So, in the case of an email, an emailed acceptance of an offer would be deemed to be sent once it passes outside the sender's email system.

Where the recipient has designated an information system for the purpose of receiving electronic communications (for example, a website or an email address), then, unless otherwise agreed or the law otherwise provides, the electronic communication is taken to have been received when it enters that information system. Where the addressee of an electronic communication has not designated an information system the electronic communication is taken to have been received when it 'comes to the attention of the addressee'.

The phrase 'comes to the attention of the addressee' would encompass circumstances where a recipient does not actually open the communication (whether or not he knows that it contains an acceptance of his contract offer). So if a party sent his acceptance of a contract by text message, the recipient will not be entitled to rely upon his failure to open the message to claim that the acceptance was not received by him. Provided the sender of the acceptance has successfully transmitted the text message to the correct number, the failure of the recipient to open the text message does not prevent the communication from being deemed received by him. This is subject to the consent requirement which is dealt with in **1.4.19** below.

1.4.1.8 *Where is an email/internet communication deemed to have been sent from/to?*

The places of dispatch and receipt of an electronic communication are deemed to be the places of business of the parties or, if there is no such place of business, the place where they ordinarily reside (s 21). This can have particular importance in contracts where no jurisdiction and/or governing law clauses are included.

1.4.1.9 *Key requirement – consent*

As we can see from the above, the ECA attempts to remove some of the legal ambiguities previously associated with electronic contracts. Importantly however, the ECA does not compel people to migrate to email or internet in order to validly communicate. The ECA is only there to assist those who wish to communicate and transact by electronic means. It is not designed to over-ride traditional forms of communication if a person does not wish to communicate by email, internet, mobile commerce etc. In light of this, it is a requirement of the ECA that the parties to the communication must consent to the information being provided in electronic form.

Where information is required or permitted to be given to a public body and the public body consents to the giving of the information in electronic form, but requires that the information be given in accordance with particular information technology and procedural requirements, or that a particular action be taken by way of verifying the receipt of the information, these requirements must be met. However, public bodies cannot use this as a means of blocking the introduction of electronic services. Therefore, where a public body introduces technological or procedural requirements it must ensure that those requirements have been made public and are objective, transparent, proportionate and non-discriminatory. An example would be a government body such as a local authority which permits the payment of refuse charges online. Obviously, the local authority will only be able to process payments that are validly submitted on its website. In requiring users of the website to fill out a payment form online, the local authority is laying down its rules regarding how online payments can be made. As these rules are objective, transparent, proportionate and non-discriminatory, they will not offend against the public body provisions in the ECA. Those who do not have internet access will continue to be able to pay their charges by offline means.

Where the recipient of an electronic communication is a private individual, company or other non-public body, that person must consent to receiving the information in electronic form. The ECA is not intended to force people to transact electronically (s 24).

In typical internet contracts, the consent issue does not create a problem as the purchaser will have chosen to volunteer his or her order online and will have accepted the supplier's terms. However, consent may not necessarily have been achieved in the case of a negotiated contract where several drafts have been exchanged by the parties using email. Before such a contract could be finally executed electronically, it would be important to ensure that the parties agree to executing the document by email. This could be achieved by including an appropriate execution clause within the agreement itself.

1.4.2 EC (Protection of Consumers in Respect of Contracts made by means of Distance Communication) Regulations 2001

1.4.2.1 *Background*

The European Communities (Protection of Consumers in Respect of Contracts made by means of Distance Communication) Regulations 2001 (the Distance Contracts Regulations) came into effect on 15 May 2001. The Distance Contracts Regulations significantly impact all ebusinesses or other businesses which provide goods or services to consumers other than in a face-to-face environment.

The Distance Contracts Regulations implement European Directive 97/7/EC which aims to harmonise the laws in respect of distance contracts for consumers throughout the Member States of the European Union, substantially increasing protection for consumers.

1.4.2.2 *Only applies to 'consumers'*

The Distance Contracts Regulations apply to any businesses supplying goods or services to 'consumers' ie persons acting for purposes which are outside their trade, business or profession under 'distance contracts' (see **1.4.2.5**). All businesses covered by the Regulations must ensure that their terms and conditions of sale and their contractual procedures comply with the Distance Contracts Regulations or run the risk of being guilty of one of the many offences contained in the Regulations. In addition, a failure to adhere to the Distance Contracts Regulations may result in the supplier's online contract being unenforceable.

1.4.2.3 *What businesses are affected?*

The Distance Contracts Regulations apply to all businesses that sell goods or services to consumers on the internet, on interactive digital television, by mail order, by telephone or by fax and includes advertising on television or radio, in newspapers or magazines.

1.4.2.4 *Exclusion of financial services*

Financial services are not covered by the Distance Contracts Regulations (Regulation 3) but they are covered by a separate Directive on Distance Marketing of Consumer Financial Services (Directive 2002/65/EC). This latter Directive was transposed by the European Communities (Distance Marketing of Consumer Financial Services) Regulations 2004 (SI 853/2004). Financial services are broadly defined to mean any service of a kind normally provided in the ordinary course of carrying on a banking business, an insurance business or a business of providing credit, personal pensions, an investment service or a payment service. While many of the principles set out in the Distance Contracts Regulations re-appear in the Distance Marketing of Consumer Financial Services Regulations, readers are encouraged to consult the Financial Services Regulations carefully if advising in relation to the remote provision of any kind of banking, insurance, investment, pension or payment services.

1.4.2.5 *Other excluded areas*

The Distance Contracts Regulations also do not apply to:

- vending machines and pay-phones;
- contracts for the construction and sale of property; or
- auctions (which presumably covers internet auctions).

1.4.2.6 *What types of transactions are covered?*

The Distance Contracts Regulations apply to 'distance contracts', which are defined in reg 3 as:

'A contract between a supplier and a consumer which

(a) relates to goods or services,

(b) is made under an organised distance sales or service-provision scheme run by the supplier, and,

(c) is made by the supplier making exclusive use of one or more 'means of distance communication' (see definition below) up to and including the moment at which the contract is made.'

The distance contract must be made pursuant to an *organised distant selling scheme.* The Regulations do not apply therefore if a business does not usually sell to consumers in response to letters, phone calls, faxes or emails. However, even once off transactions may fall under the Regulations if the supplier has an organised means of responding to telephone, email or internet orders.

Another important aspect of the 'distance contract' definition is that *exclusive* use of a method of distance communication must be made. So if a method of face to face communication is used at any stage prior to or at the moment of contract conclusion, the Regulations do not apply.

'Means of distance communication' is defined as 'any method which, without the simultaneous physical presence of the supplier and the consumer, may be used for making a contract between those parties' and Schedule 1 of the Regulations includes the following non-exhaustive examples:
- electronic mail,
- television (teleshopping),
- unaddressed printed matter,
- addressed printed matter,
- standard letter,
- press advertising with order form,
- catalogue,
- telephone (with or without human intervention),
- telephone without human intervention (automatic calling machine, audiotext),
- radio,
- videophone (telephone with screen),
- videotex (microcomputer and television screen) with keyboard or touch screen,
- fax.

1.4.2.7 *How do the Regulations affect online contracts?*

Prior information

A contract will not be enforceable against the consumer if detailed information about the contract including the commercial purpose of the contract is not made clear in an appropriate manner to the consumer in good time prior to the making of the contract (reg 4). Online suppliers must have due regard to principles of good faith in commercial transactions, and to any principles governing the protection of those who are unable to give their consent, such as minors. This would imply that online businesses are obliged to comply with sales guidelines issued from time to time by, for example, the National Consumer Agency or the Advertising Standards Authority of Ireland.

The minimum prior information which must be provided is contained in Schedule 3 of the Regulations and comprises:

- the identity of the supplier and, in the case of contracts requiring payment in advance, the supplier's address;
- the main characteristics of the goods or services;
- the price of the goods or services including all taxes;
- delivery costs, where appropriate;
- the arrangements for payment, delivery or performance;
- the existence of a right of cancellation (the right of cancellation may not apply in certain circumstances, see Paragraph (3) below);
- the cost of using the means of distance communication, where it is calculated other than at the basic rate;
- the period for which the offer or the price remains valid; and
- where appropriate, the minimum duration of the contract in the case of contracts for the supply of goods or services to be performed permanently or recurrently.

The impact of these prior information requirements will in each case depend on the nature of the goods or services being provided by the supplier and so appropriate website notices and terms and conditions should be adopted accordingly.

Confirming the contract terms

A distance contract is unenforceable against a consumer unless the consumer has received confirmation in writing or in another accessible durable medium, such as fax or email, of the prior information outlined above, unless it has already been provided in such manner to the consumer prior to making the contract, eg in a catalogue or advertisement previously provided to the consumer (reg 5).

The 'confirmation information' must also include information on the right of cancellation, the geographical address of the place of business of the supplier to which the consumer may address any complaints, existing after-sales services and guarantees and conditions for cancelling the contract if it is of unspecified duration or longer than one year. One way of achieving this would be to email these details to consumers on receipt of the order for goods and services. Alternatively, the confirmation could be provided by way of a 'splash' page which appears once an order is submitted on a website although it is important that any splash page can be saved or printed by the consumer so that it is accessible to the consumer in the future if required. The purpose of this provision is to provide consumers with a clear record of the primary terms of their contract while allowing them access to appropriate contact information in the event of non-delivery or poor performance of the contract by the supplier.

The confirmation information must be provided during the course of the contract and, at the latest, at the time of delivery of goods where goods not for delivery to third parties are concerned.

The confirmation information requirements do not apply to once-off services (not goods) which are invoiced by a means of distance communication, unless the supplier has failed to provide its geographical address to which the consumer may address complaints (regs 5(3) and 5(4)).

Cooling off periods: the consumer's right to cancel the contract

The consumer has a period of seven working days in which to cancel a distance contract without giving a reason and the only cost payable by the consumer is the direct cost of returning the goods (reg 6). The Regulations do not specify that the cancellation must be in writing nor that the consumer actually return the goods. Therefore, unless these matters are covered in the supplier's contractual terms one can foresee circumstances where a consumer could simply notify the supplier that he or she is exercising the cooling-off right, leaving the onus on the supplier to attempt to recover the goods (at its own cost) after the refund has been granted.

The 'cooling off' period begins as soon as the goods have been received or, in the case of services, from the day the distance contract is concluded. For both goods and services the confirmation information must have been provided before the cooling off period begins to run.

If the confirmation requirements have not been complied with, the cooling off period is extended by up to three months. For example, where the supplier fails to provide the necessary written confirmation required by reg 5 the cooling off period will last seven working days plus the additional three months. Obviously, in commercial terms, the consequences of a three month cooling-off period would be severe.

The consumer's right of cancellation in distance contracts, (unless agreed between the supplier and the consumer), does not apply for the following contracts:

- for services if performance has begun with the consumer's agreement before the cooling off period ends;
- for goods and services the price of which is subject to fluctuations in the financial market e.g. online share trading;
- for customised or perishable goods;
- for supply of audio or video recordings or computer software which was unsealed;
- for the supply of newspapers, periodicals and magazines, (note that the exception does not extend to books); or
- for gaming and lottery services.

The effect of the cooling off period on any supplier will therefore depend on the nature of the goods or services being provided online.

If the consumer exercises the right to cancel the contract during the cooling off period, the supplier must refund any sums paid by the consumer, less the direct cost of returning the goods, as soon as possible after the exercise of the right of cancellation and in any event not later than 30 days. This extends consumer protection to a right of reimbursement beyond circumstances of defective goods/services. The consumer can demand his/her money back even if the goods are in perfectly good condition. This is not necessarily the case in over the counter transactions where consumers are not ordinarily entitled to a refund where the goods are not faulty.

If payment for the goods and services was made under a related credit agreement the cancellation notice has the effect of also cancelling the credit agreement. So if, for example, a website offers customers credit terms on the purchase of goods, the customer's choice to cancel the order automatically cancels the associated credit agreement.

The Regulations exempt contracts for the regular supply of foodstuffs, beverages or other goods intended for everyday consumption from the information and cooling-off provisions for obvious reasons. Similarly, contracts for transport, accommodation, catering or leisure services provided on specific dates are not subject to the cooling-off and prior information requirements. The right of refund does not apply to outdoor leisure events, which by their nature cannot be rescheduled, if so agreed between the supplier and the consumer prior to making the distance contract.

Time limits and substitute goods/services

The supplier must execute the order within a maximum of 30 days (reg 9). If the goods or services in question are out of stock, the supplier must inform the consumer and provide a refund as soon as possible (not later than 30 days). A supplier is entitled to reserve the right to offer goods or services of equivalent quality and price provided the supplier has done so prior to the making of the contract and provided the customer retains the cooling-off right in respect of the substituted goods or services.

Fraudulent credit and debit cards

Regulation 10 provides the consumer with a legal right to demand the immediate cancellation, re-credit or return of any payment, where fraudulent use has been made of his/her credit card, charge card, debit card or store card. The Regulations do not address the issue of whether fraud must be merely alleged or actually proved. However, one of the main commercial risks attaching to online merchants is that transactions can be subject to 'charge-backs' by credit card companies where cardholders dispute a transaction and the merchant has no physical signature evidencing the transaction. As a result of the international rules regarding credit card payments, inevitably it is the merchant and not the banks who suffer charge-backs in these circumstances. There are proposals to amend the Visa rules where merchants adopt the next generation of payment processing technology which the reader should watch for if advising in this area.

Inertia selling

Inertia selling, that is, a demand for payment for an unsolicited service, is prohibited by reg 11.

Consequences of non-compliance

A person who fails to comply with the Regulations is guilty of an offence subject to a fine on summary conviction of up to €3,000. Personal liability may attach to the officers of a company if they have consented or contributed to the breach.

The Director of Consumer Affairs or a consumer organisation may apply to the High Court for an order to effect compliance. Actual loss or damage or recklessness or negligence need not be proved. This power transferred to the National Consumer Agency under the Consumer Protection Act 2007.

The National Consumer Agency has the right to require information and to inspect and retain records and data in the context of investigating compliance with the Distance Contracts Regulations, and may apply to the District Court for warrants if necessary.

The rights conferred on consumers under the Regulations may not be waived and any terms and conditions which attempt to override the Regulations will be void. Similarly, if the contract has a close connection with the territory of a Member State of the EEA, any condition applying the law of a State other than a Member State of the EEA is void (Regulation 19). This means that overseas websites which have a 'close connection' (undefined) with Ireland cannot apply the jurisdiction of a non-EEA country to their online terms and conditions.

1.4.3 European Communities (Directive 2000/31/EC) Regulations 2003

1.4.3.1 *Background*

On 24 February 2003, Ireland implemented the EU Electronic Commerce Directive. The European Communities (Directive 2000/31/EC) Regulations 2003 (E-Commerce

Regulations) introduced important new legal provisions which directly affect all those offering goods or services online, including Internet Service Providers (ISPs) and those involved in direct email marketing activities.

1.4.3.2 *Application*

The E-Commerce Regulations apply to almost all organisations which offer commercial services to customers over the internet or in response to email requests. Unlike the Distance Contracts Regulations, the E-Commerce Regulations are not solely addressed at consumer goods and services and therefore are relevant to all those contracting online whether in a business-to-business or business-to-consumer environment.

1.4.3.3 *More transparency requirements*

In addition to the prior information rights that apply to online consumer contracts, which were addressed under the Distance Contracts Regulations (see above), reg 7 of the E-Commerce Regulations adds an additional responsibility on those offering any 'relevant service'. A relevant service is any service normally provided for remuneration, at a distance, by electronic means and at the individual request of a recipient of the service (reg 3(1)). Certain types of service are excluded in Schedule 1 to the Regulations.

Under reg 7, the following information must be provided by a relevant service provider in a manner which is easily, directly and permanently accessible to the recipients of the service:

1. the name of the service provider;
2. the geographic address at which the service provider is established;
3. the details of the service provider, including his or her electronic mail address, which allows him or her to be contacted rapidly and communicated with in a direct and effective manner;
4. details of how natural persons can register their choice regarding unsolicited commercial communications;
5. where the service provider is registered in a trade or similar public register, the trade or other such register in which the service provider is entered and his or her registration number, or equivalent means of identification in that register,
6. where the activity is subject to an authorisation scheme, the particulars of the relevant supervisory authority,
7. where the service provider is a member of a regulated profession –
    (i) any professional body or similar institution with which the service provider is registered,
    (ii) the professional title of the provider and the Member State where it has been granted, and
    (iii) a reference to the applicable professional rules in the Member State of establishment and the means to access them,
8. where the service provider undertakes an activity that is subject to value-added tax, the company's VAT registration number;
9. in addition to the requirements of the Consumer Information Act 1978, any orders for the time being in force under that Act, the European Communities (Misleading Advertising) Regulations 1988 and of any other enactment, where the relevant service refers to prices, those prices are to be indicated clearly and unambiguously and, in particular, must indicate whether they are inclusive of tax and delivery costs.

The above effectively amounts to a new statutory 'online letterhead' which is designed to provide visitors to a website with transparency as to who they are dealing with.

1.4.3.4 *Country of origin principle*

One of the main principles of the new Regulations is the so-called 'country of origin' principle. This provides that once an online organisation is established in Ireland (in the sense of having a fixed commercial establishment within the State), provided that organisation complies with Irish laws, it should not have to unduly concern itself with meeting the laws of the other member states in the EEA into which it offers its services. However, this provides only limited benefit to consumer-focused websites, as, under the Brussels Regulation (see below), Irish websites can still be subjected to litigation by consumers in other EEA countries where the websites are directed at those countries.

1.4.3.5 *Implications for direct mailings*

A significant additional requirement in the E-Commerce Regulations is that the online entity must also provide a clear choice to customers as to whether or not they wish to receive direct mail. This information must be provided in a manner which is easily, directly and permanently accessible to customers or potential customers and must, at a minimum, be included on the website and at every point where data is captured on a website, such as on log-in pages or online registration forms (reg 7(1)(d)). This new obligation is in addition to the existing data protection laws regarding fair obtaining and fair use of personal data.

In addition, whenever a service provider sends an email or other communication, the commercial nature and identity of the sender of the communication must be clearly identifiable (reg 8). The email must also contain details of how the recipient (where it is an individual as opposed to a company) can register his or her choice regarding further direct mailings.

The terms of any promotional offers, games or competitions must also be clearly and unambiguously presented to the recipient.

The above requirements apply to all email and internet commercial communications. Further requirements exist where the communications are unsolicited such as in the case of junk email ('spam'). Under reg 9, not only must spam be clearly and unambiguously identifiable as such upon receipt, but this must be achieved 'by stating that it is an unsolicited commercial communication.' These conditions are in addition to those in ss 2(7) and 23(8) the Data Protection Acts 1988 and 2003 and in reg 13 of the European Communities (Electronic Communications Networks and Services) (Data Protection and Privacy) Regulations 2003.

Regulated professions who provide online services are the subject of additional provisions in reg 11.

1.4.3.6 *Requirements for online contracts*

While the above provisions are relevant to all those involved in online marketing, for those engaged in concluding online sales or other distance contracts, the E-Commerce Regulations introduce new formal requirements.

Regulation 13 requires that the online service provider must supply the following information prior to an order being placed:

(i) the steps to be followed to conclude the contract;
(ii) whether or not the supplier will file the relevant contract and whether or not it will be accessible;
(iii) the means for identifying and correcting input errors prior to placing the order; and
(iv) the languages in which the contract may be concluded.

If the supplier adheres to any codes of conduct, these must be specified and made available electronically. The supplier's terms and conditions must be made available in a way that allows the recipient to store and reproduce them, for example by confirmation email or in a confirmation page which is capable of being saved by the customer.

The supplier is required to acknowledge receipt of the order without undue delay and by electronic means (reg 14). This could be achieved by a 'splash' page or by a return email to the customer.

1.4.4 EC (Companies) (Amendment) Regulations 2007 (SI 49/2007)

Since 1 April 2007, Irish registered limited liability companies must display basic information regarding company particulars on the company websites and certain company electronic communications, in addition to such information being displayed on certain hard copy company documentation. These requirements apply to all companies who operate a website or send emails regardless of whether or not they are actually selling online.

This requirements arise from amendments to reg 9 of the European Communities (Companies) Regulations 1973 (SI 163/1973) which are contained in the European Communities (Companies) (Amendment) Regulations 2007 (SI 49/2007). While Irish companies have always been required to disclose general company information in their paper-based business letters, the object of this new legislation is to extend those requirements to electronic forms of communication. Specifically, the Irish Regulations and the underlying Directive (2003/58/EC) extend the statutory letterhead requirements to 'letters and order forms' which are defined to mean those in paper form 'or in any other medium', which includes electronic form.

Irish-registered limited liability companies are obliged to display on their websites, company letters and order forms for goods and services (such as emails and faxes, whether or not in paper form), the following information:

- the name of the company and the company's legal form;
- the place of registration of the company, the number with which it is registered and the address of its registered office;
- in the case of a company exempt from the obligation to use the word 'limited' or 'teoranta' as part of its name, the fact that it is a limited company;
- in the case of a company which is being wound up, the fact that it is being wound up; and
- if there is reference to the share capital of the company on any letters or order forms, the reference shall be to the paid-up share capital.

The above is in addition to the existing laws which require every Irish registered limited liability company (unless otherwise exempt) to include in its business letters minimum information about every director and shadow director of the company.

The Regulations do not apply to Irish registered unlimited liability companies or branches of foreign-registered bodies corporate. However, unlimited and branch companies continue to have other statutory disclosure requirements under various company laws.

Failure to comply with the Regulations is a summary offence. Further guidance on the publication requirements for companies and branches can be obtained from the ODCE Information Notice 1/2007/2, available at www.odce.ie.

1.4.5 Consumer Law

In addition to the specific 'electronic' legislation referred to above, the existing array of consumer protection law will, to a large degree, also apply to ebusinesses who are selling to Irish consumers. While a detailed consideration of Irish consumer protection law is beyond the scope of this chapter, readers should remain aware of the growing amount of consumer protection law which may serve to override any contractual terms and conditions of the seller. A brief review of some of the more relevant legislation is considered below.

1.4.5.1 *Consumer Protection Act 2007*

(i) The Consumer Protection Act 2007 provides for the establishment of the National Consumer Agency and provides for the implementation of the Unfair Commercial Practices Directive. Most of the provisions of the Act have been commenced with effect from 1 May 2007. However, at the time of writing, ss 48 and 49, which deal with the prohibition on surcharges in relation to certain methods of payment, such as by credit card, have not been commenced. If and when they are commenced, they will have implications for any websites raising surcharges for card payments.

(ii) The main features of the Consumer Protection Act are the establishment of the National Consumer Agency and the implementation of the Unfair Commercial Practices Directive (Directive 2005/29/EC) in Ireland. This Directive was introduced to strengthen consumer confidence in the Internal Market with the introduction of common standards of consumer protection across the EU. The Consumer Protection Act is relevant to online and offline businesses who sell to consumers.

(iii) Part II of the Consumer Protection Act deals with the establishment of the National Consumer Agency (NCA). The NCA is responsible for investigating and encouraging compliance with Irish consumer law. The NCA takes over the existing functions of the Director of Consumer Affairs. Section 8 of the Act sets out the functions of the National Consumer Agency as follows:

   (a) to promote and protect the interests and the welfare of consumers;
   (b) to enforce the relevant statutory provisions;
   (c) to encourage compliance with the relevant statutory provisions;
   (d) to investigate suspected offences under any of the relevant statutory provisions; and
   (e) to refer cases to the Director of Public Prosecutions where relevant.

(iv) Part III of the Act prohibits unfair, misleading and aggressive commercial practices. A commercial practice is considered to be *unfair* if it is contrary to the general principle of good faith in the traders field of activity and/or the standard of skill that a trader could reasonably be expected to exercise toward the consumers (s 41). A commercial practice is *misleading* if it includes the provision of false information in relation to certain matters or it would be likely to cause the average consumer to be deceived or misled in relation to certain matters (s 43). A commercial practice involving marketing or advertising is misleading if it would be likely to cause the average consumer to confuse a competitor's product with the trader's product, or competitor's trade name, trademark or some other distinguishing feature or mark with that of the trader (s 44). A commercial practice is also misleading if the trader omits or conceals material information that the average consumer would need to make an informed decision (s 45). In addition, a commercial practice is misleading if the trader provides material information in a manner that is unclear, unintelligible, ambiguous or untimely, or fails to identify the commercial intent of the practice.

(v) Section 52 of the Act contains a general prohibition on *aggressive* commercial practices, which are defined as practices involving harassment, coercion or undue influence that impair consumer's freedom of choice and affect their purchasing decisions. Eight aggressive commercial practices are prohibited even without proof that they affect a consumer's decision to enter into a transaction, for example persistent cold calling, exhorting children to buy something being advertised, or stonewalling a customer's claim on an insurance policy (s 55).

(vi) The Act is enforced by both civil and criminal remedies (ss 77–84).

1.4.5.2 *EC (Unfair Terms in Consumer Contracts) Regulations 1995*

(i) The EC (Unfair Terms in Consumer Contracts) Regulations 1995 as amended by the EC (Unfair Terms in Consumer Contracts) (Amendment) Regulations 2000 (Unfair Contracts Regulations) implement Council Directive 93/13/EEC on unfair terms in consumer contracts which aims to harmonise the laws in EU Member States with regard to unduly harsh contract terms in consumer contracts. For the purposes of the Unfair Contracts Regulations, a contractual term is regarded as being unfair if, contrary to the requirements of good faith, it causes a significant imbalance in the parties' rights and obligations under the contract to the detriment of the consumer, taking into account the nature of the goods or services for which the contract was concluded, and all the surrounding circumstances. If a term in a contract is found to be unfair, it shall not be binding on the consumer. The contract shall however continue to bind the parties, if it is capable of continuing in existence without the unfair terms.

(ii) In making an assessment of good faith under the Unfair Contracts Regulations, particular regard shall be had to:
- the strength of the bargaining positions of the parties;
- whether the consumer had an inducement to agree to the term;
- whether the goods or services were sold or supplied to the special order of the consumer; and
- the extent to which the seller or supplier has dealt fairly and equitably with the consumer whose legitimate interests he has to take into account.

(iii) Schedule 3 of the Regulations includes a list of examples of certain types of clauses which are presumed to be unfair and would therefore not be upheld by a court.

(iv) While the Unfair Contracts Regulations are not specific to internet sales, in drafting any online Terms and Conditions for any Irish retailer, the Unfair Contracts Regulations should be borne in mind.

1.4.6 Sale of Goods and Supply of Services Acts 1893–1980

Section 12 of the Sale of Goods and Supply of Services Acts 1893–1980 (the SOGAs) provides an implied condition that the seller has the right to sell the goods and an implied warranty that the goods are free from any charge or encumbrance and that the buyer will enjoy quiet possession of the goods. Under section 55(3) of the Acts, any term of a contract exempting from all or any of the provisions of Section 12 of the Act shall be void.

Section 13 of the 1893 Act implies a condition that goods will correspond to their description.

Section 14 implies a condition that the goods supplied are of merchantable quality and reasonably fit for their purpose. Where the buyer examines the goods before the contract is made, any defects which the examination ought to have revealed will however negate this implied condition. Clearly in the online environment, goods cannot be examined before purchase and so the presumption of merchantability will usually apply.

Section 15 of the 1893 Act implies a term into contracts for sale by sample that the bulk shall correspond with the sample in quality.

Under s 11 of the 1980 Act, any statement likely to be taken as indicating that a right or the exercise of a right conferred by, or a liability arising by virtue of, sections 12–15 of the

SOGAs is restricted, is an offence unless the statement is accompanied by a clear and conspicuous declaration that the contractual rights which the buyer enjoys by virtue of sections 12-15 are in no way prejudiced by the relevant statement. Any attempt to exclude statutory liability under the SOGAs should therefore be carefully considered.

1.4.7 Council Regulation No. 44/2001 on Jurisdiction and the Recognition and Enforcement of Judgments in Civil and Commercial Matters

Council Regulation No 44/2001 on Jurisdiction and the Recognition and Enforcement of Judgments in Civil and Commercial Matters came into force on 1 March 2002. While a detailed consideration of the Regulation is beyond the scope of this chapter, there are a number of provisions which are of particular significance to electronic contracts.

Article 23 of the Regulation retains the pre-existing position that the parties to a contract should be allowed choose the governing jurisdiction of their contract and acknowledges that this choice of jurisdiction will be exclusive unless otherwise agreed. The Regulation requires that such a jurisdiction clause be in writing (which includes electronic writing), or evidenced in writing or in a form that accords with international trade or commerce practices or in a form which is consistent with practices developed between the parties.

Article 15 of the Regulation allows consumers to sue in their own domicile in circumstances where:

> '... the contract has been concluded with a person who pursues commercial or professional activities in the Member State of the consumer's domicile, or by any means *directs such activities to that Member State* or to several countries, including that Member State, and the contract falls within the scope of such activities.' (emphasis added)

There has been a lot of debate as to the effect of Article 15 on consumer-focused internet sites. While the 'country of origin' principle was adopted by the E-Commerce Regulations (see above), Article 15 of the Regulation appears to dilute the effect of the country of origin principle in the context of consumer websites. The extent to which a website would be deemed to be 'directing' activities to a state has yet to be judicially decided. It is not clear, for example, whether an Irish website which fulfils orders from another EU Member State would be deemed to be directing its activities to that Member State or whether a more proactive stance by the supplier would be required to entitle the consumer to litigate in his or her country of domicile.

1.5 Conclusion

Advising an online enterprise on its contracts is more than just a Terms and Conditions drafting exercise. With the emergence of ecommerce specific legislation in Ireland, solicitors cannot properly advise online merchants without also actively reviewing their clients' websites and sales processes to ensure that the relevant terms and conditions are well drafted, enforceable and admissible.

CHAPTER 2

LEGAL ISSUES FOR START-UP TECHNOLOGY COMPANIES

Rob Corbet

2.1 Introduction

The purpose of this chapter is to bring together the primary legal areas which are of particular relevance to a solicitor advising a start-up company involved in technological innovation. The chapter will focus on practical suggestions to provide the best legal advice to start-up ventures reflecting their limited resources.

2.2 Overview

Most of the relevant areas of law will have been covered by students in the PPC 1 course. Therefore, the course is designed to weave together the following issues:

- company formation;
- raising Finance and the legal documentation required (including Heads of Agreement and Subscription and Shareholder Agreements);
- preparation for and conduct of a legal due diligence exercise;
- intellectual property protection;
- promoters' warranties;
- employment and service agreements for key personnel;
- share option schemes; and
- commercial contracts.

2.3 Incorporating a company

Incorporating a company and trading with limited liability offers the opportunity to reduce the personal risk of the entrepreneur in commencing trade.

As the reader will be aware, there is a myriad of company law which dictates the requirements as to how to establish and conduct business through a corporate body in Ireland. For example, there are different rules attaching to partnerships, public limited companies or branches of overseas companies. However, usually a promoter of a business proposition will opt to trade via a private limited company, which acts as a vehicle of limited liability for conducting business and attracting investment.

2.3.1 Primary information required to incorporate a company

The main information required to incorporate a company in Ireland includes the following:

- whether the company is to be a single member or a multi member company and the authorised share capital;
- the name and address of the shareholders(s);
- the number of shares they are to hold;

- the exact activity of the Company (for the principal objects clause);
- the registered office of the Company;
- with regard to the directors of which there must be a minimum of two (usually at least one must, in the absence of an appropriate bond, be an Irish resident), they must provide the following information:
    (i) full name;
    (ii) date of birth;
    (iii) home address;
    (iv) nationality;
    (v) occupation;
- list of current and past directorships over the last ten years detailing company number, company names, place of incorporation and date of appointment and resignation;
- name and address of company secretary;
- the place in the State where it is proposed to carry on the activity;
- the place in the State where the central administration of the company will normally be carried on.

For information on how to complete the Companies Registration Office company incorporation documentation you should consult your materials from your Company Secretarial Management chapter.

There are important tax consequences resulting from how any company is structured, and tax planning is a central concern before committing to any particular shareholding or corporate structure.

Note also that in the case of start-ups, as with any other new clients, solicitors have very clear obligations to 'know their clients' in accordance with applicable anti-money laundering legislation, and readers are encouraged to consult the Law Society's Guidance Notes for Solicitors on Anti-Money Laundering Legislation for further information on this critical topic. Often the point of initial company incorporation can provide a good opportunity to obtain the underlying client identification documentation.

2.3.2 Choosing a name

In choosing a company name, you should ensure that the name is available from the Companies Registration Office before your client incurs any expenditure on marketing the name. The company's promoters should be advised to avoid using a name that could be confused with another company or brand in Ireland or elsewhere. Given that the promoters are unlikely to have sufficient resources at this point to conduct formal trade mark searches, they should at least conduct internet searches against the proposed company and brand names to satisfy themselves that the name is not already in open commercial use. If the start-up is well funded, consideration should be given to filing trade mark applications in the key target markets. The promoters should also take steps to register the appropriate internet domain names, whether with the IE Domain Registry (for Ireland) or with other registries such as those who provide .co.uk, .com and .net registration services.

2.3.3 Duties of company directors and secretaries

The Office of the Director of Corporate Enforcement (ODCE) has produced a number of Information Books regarding the duties of companies, company directors, company secretaries and shareholders. These documents are easy to read and should be brought to the attention of the company's promoters (see www.odce.ie). In many cases the promoters of the company will not have any previous experience in acting as a company director or secretary and it is important that they are informed of the key obligations prior to joining the company's board. The ODCE documents provide a useful tool to assist solicitors in discharging their duties to advise the company promoters about their main responsibilities.

For those law firms and company formation agents who subscribe to the Ten Day Incorporation Scheme (Fe Phrainn), the Companies Registration Office (CRO) has made it an additional condition of membership of the Scheme that the relevant ODCE Information Books must be provided to all new directors and company secretaries.

2.3.4 Drafting the memorandum and articles of association

For information on drafting the company's initial Memorandum and Articles of Association, readers should refer to their materials on Company Secretarial Management.

2.3.5 Founding shareholders and directors

In most cases the company will be formed by the initial promoters, who are unlikely to number more than a few. In the absence of any seed capital, the promoters are unlikely to have sufficient resources to engage a solicitor to draft complicated shareholder agreements. Therefore the solicitor will not be thanked for producing costly and complicated documentation at this point and it would be unwise to do so in the absence of a very clear agreement as to how legal costs will be met.

In any event, once third party investment is obtained, it is likely that the promoter's initial shareholder arrangements will be revoked and replaced by a new agreement that reflects the (usually) preferential rights attaching to the investor's shareholding (see further below).

2.4 Raising finance

2.4.1 The business plan

Any investor will require a comprehensive and convincing business plan to be in place before he, she or it will commit any funding. The potential investor is likely to make its initial decision to invest or not to invest on the back of the statements and projections contained in the business plan, and will therefore often ask the founders of the company to warrant the accuracy and completeness of the business plan as part of any fund-raising. Promoters should therefore avoid using inaccurate and overly optimistic statements, as these are liable to cause difficulty at a later stage.

As the business plan and other sensitive information will be circulated to potential investors, promoters should ensure that any communications between the company and the potential investor are subject to a Non-Disclosure Agreement (NDA). NDAs may operate one way or mutually depending on the likely flow of the confidential information. Obviously, professional advisers such as solicitors and accountants are under professional obligations of confidentiality and would not usually be required to sign a NDA.

When you first meet with the promoters of a start-up company, ascertaining the status and quality of its business plan will give some indication as to whether or not the company has potential to succeed. While you are not qualified to assess the quality of the proposed venture, it can be informative to look at issues such as financial projections (if for no other reason than to assess whether or not legal fees have been considered as a projected expense!). In deciding whether or not to act for the company, you will need to assess the company's ability to meet their fees, and in making this decision it should be borne in mind that the vast majority of start-up companies do not succeed.

2.4.2 Potential sources of finance

While the promoters of a start-up company will usually invest their own or borrowed money and resources in getting the company started, this is unlikely to be sufficient to bring the company to a self-financing state, and third party investment will usually be required to help the company establish or develop its customer base.

The nature of the legal documentation required to conclude a capital investment in the company will depend on a number of variables. In particular, the amount of finance being raised and the nature of the investor will be determining factors in the commercial and legal terms which will apply to the proposed deal.

For example, if the company is eligible for Enterprise Ireland funding, the investment may be by way of grant and/or equity, and Enterprise Ireland will produce its standard documentation for execution by the Company. Similar arrangements exist in relation to the Shannon Free Airport Development Company or local county enterprise board funding. Most technology-focused start-up companies will be eligible for Enterprise Ireland funding and the promoters should pursue this option, as if funds become available from EI they are likely to be on more favourable terms than if the funds emanate from an institutional investor from the private sector.

Many technology companies can also qualify for Business Expansion Scheme (BES) status with the Revenue Commissioners. If so, subject to the BES rules, the company may be able to raise finance from qualifying private individuals who will be entitled to tax relief on their investments. However, it is important to check the position carefully with the Revenue Commissioners as the BES rules are regularly changed and, at the time of writing, they are the subject of a European Commission review.

Another interesting Revenue scheme is the Seed Capital Scheme (SCS). Under the SCS, employees who leave employment to invest in certain new businesses and take up employment in these businesses can claim a refund of tax paid for the previous 6 years. Again, however, the promoters of the company should check their eligibility for SCS relief directly with the Revenue Commissioners (www.revenue.ie).

Another source of finance is venture capital funds (VCs) which specialise in investing in early stage companies. There are dozens of such funds in Ireland which are constantly on the look-out for attractive investment opportunities among high-potential technology companies. However, prior to committing to an investment, a VC will be careful to conduct financial and legal due diligence on the target company.

If a company is fortunate enough to be able to choose from a number of investors, the company should determine the type of investor that is the best fit for the company. The primary factors that are likely to influence this decision include the amount of equity to be given to the investor and the level of control to be conceded by the company's founders.

The type of funding will also be relevant. Some investors may require a dividend yield in the course of the investment, whereas others will rely on a capital return at the point of exit, or both. These issues in turn will have an impact on the future financing of the business.

2.5 Heads of agreement

Given the time it can take to conclude an investment agreement, it is common for the parties to enter into a Heads of Agreement prior to the commencement of formal due diligence. The usual purpose of a Heads of Agreement (often referred to as a 'Term Sheet' or 'Memorandum of Understanding') is to provide a non-binding overview of the primary terms of the proposed deal. However, if not properly drafted, a Heads of Agreement can inadvertently create a binding legal agreement, and you should advise your clients accordingly.

It is not a good idea to try to include too much legal detail in the Heads of Agreement: that is the purpose of the Subscription and Shareholders Agreement. However, some of the issues which a typical Heads of Agreement might include are:

- amount of proposed investment;
- form of investment eg 'A' Ordinary Shares, Cumulative Redeemable Convertible Preference Shares, etc;
- basis of valuation;
- rights attaching to investor's shares eg dividends, liquidation, voting, further funding, veto rights on certain company decisions etc;
- specifying that the investment will be subject to satisfactory completion of due diligence and the execution of a formal Subscription and Shareholders' Agreement;
- pre-conditions regarding key personnel employment, key man insurance etc;
- proposed completion date;
- exclusivity period to conclude negotiations; and
- which provisions are non-binding and which provisions are binding (eg confidentiality and exclusivity).

Another provision which is often included in a Heads of Agreement is an obligation on the company to pay some or all of the investor's legal fees relating to the investment. If the company has sufficient bargaining power, this should be resisted.

It can be useful from the promoters' point of view to seek to include some key provisions in the Heads of Agreement to assist their negotiating position when it comes to drafting the Subscription and Shareholders Agreement. For example, the promoters may wish to make it clear that only very limited personal warranties will be given on completion. However, raising contentious issues at the Heads of Agreement stage can be detrimental if it leads to protracted negotiations or a breakdown in the relationship with the proposed investor, so this is a matter that needs to be approached delicately to avoid collapsing the deal.

2.6 Due diligence

Whether or not a Heads of Agreement is entered into by the investor, there is likely to be a period prior to the drawdown of the investment funds where the investor will wish to satisfy itself regarding the legal and financial state of the company. The extent of any due diligence exercise will depend on many factors, not least of which is the nature of the investor, and the size of the investment. However, unlike in due diligence exercises for established companies, a start-up company will not have a history of several years trading, and the promoters should seek to ensure that the due diligence exercise should therefore be as defined and contained as possible to keep to the deal time frame and to keep costs to a minimum.

If the company has a broad advance knowledge of the legal issues that are likely to arise in the course of a due diligence, this will allow the company's promoters to anticipate and deal with the legal issues more efficiently and therefore remove some of the obstacles to concluding the deal.

The key issues which are likely to be of central interest to a potential investor conducting a due diligence exercise would include the following:

- full details of all current and past shareholders, directors and secretaries. The investor will be keen to satisfy itself that the company is in compliance with the ever increasing corporate governance requirements and the company secretary

should be advised to ensure that all Revenue and Companies Registration Office filings are up to date;
- audited and management accounts and any financial reports;
- details of any related companies;
- details of all staff and their employment and service contracts, including pension entitlements, share option schemes and all fringe benefits;
- details of all liabilities and contingent liabilities of the company;
- details of all property owned, occupied or used by the company;
- details of all insurance policies held;
- details of all major customers;
- standard terms and conditions and all material commercial contracts;
- all intellectual property rights and computer equipment and software which is owned, licensed or required by the company;
- all licenses or registrations required to be held eg Data Protection registrations, Central Bank authorisations, environmental licences etc;
- details of any current, pending or threatened litigation; and
- clarification of all tax matters.

Management should anticipate the needs of the investor by gathering and compiling, in as orderly a way as possible, the appropriate information at an early stage. Failure to disclose material facts may result in legal liability for the company or the company promoters arising from a breach of warranty claim.

2.7 Intellectual property

The organisation and protection of intellectual property is a key consideration where investment in technology companies is concerned. Given that normally start-up technology companies have little in the way of tangible assets, potential investors will scrutinise the protection, value and strength of the company's intangible rights. If there are any rights associated with the business which are capable of registration, such as trade marks, domain names or patents, full details of any applications and registrations should be disclosed during the due diligence process. Remember however that disclosing any potentially patentable products or processes could endanger their patentability, which again emphasises the importance of concluding a NDA with any potential investor conducting a due diligence exercise.

Frequently, the founders of the company seeking investment will have commenced or completed the registration of some intellectual property rights, such as trade marks or domain names, in their own personal names. On incorporation of the company, these intangible assets should be transferred to the company at an early stage so as to be as tax effective as possible.

The company and its directors will be expected to confirm that the intellectual property underlying the venture does not infringe any third party intellectual property rights. This is a particular concern if the promoters have left their previous place of employment to set up a potentially competing operation. Remember that the copyright in any software or other intellectual property generated in the course of the promoters' previous employment will usually vest automatically in their former employer, and any assignment will be required to be in writing. There can be difficult decisions to be made by the promoters as to the extent to which their know-how gained in their previous employment can be freely used as against trying to exploit intellectual property which is legally owned by their former employer. It would be prudent to remind the promoters that they will probably be required to personally warrant the company's ownership of the intellectual property underpinning their venture during any fund-raising, and that any short-cuts in this area could lead to litigation against the company and/or against themselves for infringement of third party IP rights.

2.8 Warranties

In relation to any issues that arise during the diligence process, investors will almost certainly insist on obtaining warranties from the founding shareholders of the company. These warranties can lead to personal liability for the founders. However, it is standard practice for founders to negate or qualify the effect of warranties by providing a disclosure letter to accompany any final subscription or shareholders agreement. It is also prudent for the promoters to cap their potential liability under any warranty claims, often by reference to the value of their shareholding after the investment.

When acting for a start-up company, it is important that you make it clear to the promoters that you are advising the company and not the promoters. Given that there will be significant personal consequences for the promoters arising from any investment or employment arrangements with the company, you should advise the promoters to take independent legal advice before signing up to any employment, shareholders or other agreements which produce legal effects for the individuals. This is particularly important where the promoters are required to provide personal warranties in the Subscription and Shareholders Agreement.

On a related note, it can be very frustrating when acting for a start-up company when the solicitors for the investor produce their standard reams of investment documentation notwithstanding that the proposed deal relates to a small investment in a new company. When advising an investor in a start-up company, you should bear in mind the level of the proposed investment and the fact that the company has little or no trading history. To this end, rather than producing pages and pages of warranties, it can save an enormous amount of negotiating time if the investor's advisers focus on the key issues particular to the proposed investment rather than producing office precedent documentation that was originally designed for large scale investments in long-established companies. For example, if the company has no employees prior to completion, a warranty to this effect should be the extent of cover required for the investor, rather than a couple of pages requiring disclosure of non-existent PAYE records, pension documentation, employee share option schemes etc.

2.9 Subscription and shareholders agreements

The main document that formalises the deal in an equity investment is typically a Subscription and Shareholders Agreement. This will go hand in hand with changes to the company's Articles of Association. Both of these documents will set out the terms on which the investment is made, but will also control and regulate the future relationship between the parties, such as how decisions are taken on a daily basis and the level of control an investor wields.

The investor and the founders should attempt to deal fairly in the documents with their differing needs in areas such as the transfer of shares and how future funds are to be raised. In considering exit mechanisms, it may be in everyone's interest to include so-called 'drag along' or 'tag along' rights in the event of a third party offer for shares. These should endeavour to allow everyone to exit at the right price, if that is the ultimate goal. Provision may also be made for an alternative exit strategy, such as that increasingly elusive Initial Public Offering (IPO).

Another main concern for the promoters of the company will be the extent to which the investment will dilute their existing shareholding, and the extent to which the investor will be protected from future dilution. Usually there will be specific and detailed provision for the exercise of pre-emption rights in the Subscription and Shareholders Agreement to address this issue, and the company should remain conscious of the position under the Companies Acts and the Articles of Association in this regard.

2.10 Service agreements

The investor will be anxious to lock key personnel into the company by ensuring that appropriate employment or service agreements are entered into on or before completion of any investment. In addition to the standard terms of employment, given that the key personnel are likely to be shareholders in the company, the issue arises as to whether or not the key staff should be incentivised to remain in the company. For example, the investor may seek to have a penalty for 'bad leavers' whereby a portion of the promoter's shareholding will revert to the company or the investor in the event that the promoter leaves the company within a defined number of years after the investment. There are employment law and company law implications to 'bad leaver/good leaver' provisions which you should consider carefully in this context. In particular, note the restrictions under the Companies Acts on a company buying its own shares.

2.11 Employee share option schemes

Another method of incentivising staff is to create an employee share option scheme. Under a share option scheme, employees are given the right, in exchange for a nominal payment, to acquire shares in the company at a price set at the date of grant of the option. Normally, a share option scheme will provide that options may only be exercised within a specified period from the date of grant eg between 3 and 7 years after the option has been granted. The scheme may also provide that the options will only become exercisable on the achievement of certain individual or corporate performance targets. The scheme will normally provide that the options will lapse in certain circumstances, such as termination of employment. Where an employee's employment is terminated involuntarily, the scheme will usually provide that the options will not lapse automatically on the termination of his employment but may be exercised for a limited period thereafter.

Share option schemes and structures can be complicated documents with complex tax implications for the company and the recipients of the options. As with all legal services for start-ups, the client needs to make an informed decision as to the expense it wishes to incur in setting up any employee share schemes and advice should be tailored accordingly.

2.12 Commercial contracts

Regardless of whether or not a start-up technology company is raising finance, it will need to ensure that any commercial contracts it enters into are legally binding. Examples of the types of contracts that are likely to arise include the following:
- software development agreements;
- software licence agreements;
- strategic partnership agreements with established technology companies;
- beta testing agreements to test the company's software products;
- hardware maintenance agreements;
- software support agreements;
- web development and hosting agreements;
- online terms and conditions of sale (if the company is selling over the internet); and
- equipment purchasing agreements.

Obviously the terms of any particular agreement will need to reflect the commercial intent of the parties and drafting skills will need to be exercised accordingly.

It is worth noting, however, that in their haste to generate sales as quickly as possible, many start-up companies will tend to enter into very informal arrangements in their early years, and this can lead to problems down the line. In particular, any commercial arrangements regarding the licence, sale or use of the company's intellectual property should be properly documented. Similarly, clients should be advised that a failure to properly record the commercial and legal terms of any transaction in writing is likely to lead to difficulties in getting paid.

2.13 Useful sources of information

Some useful sources of information which are relevant to this chapter can be found at the following websites:

Enterprise Ireland:	www.enterprise-ireland.com
Irish Patents Office:	www.patentsoffice.ie
Department of Enterprise, Trade and Employment:	www.entemp.ie
Irish Software Association:	www.software.ie
Irish Internet Association:	www.iia.ie
Revenue Commissioners:	www.revenue.ie
Companies Registration Office:	www.cro.ie
Office of the Director of Corporate Enforcement:	www.odce.ie
Society for Computers and Law:	www.scl.org

CHAPTER 3

DOMAIN NAMES – REGISTRATION AND DISPUTES

Jeanne Kelly

3.1 What is a domain name?

Domain names are generally defined as the human-friendly form of internet addresses. A domain name corresponds to a series of numbers comparable to a telephone number. Each internet address is unique and corresponds to one specific place on the Net. The advantage of using a name rather than a series of numbers is that it is easier for people to remember a word than to recall a string of numbers.

The number can also be moved to a new machine if necessary but the domain name remains the same. The Domain Name System (DNS) is the international system that co-ordinates the allocation of domain names. The DNS records are updated to reflect the change. ICANN is the Internet Corporation for Assigned Names and Numbers and it is this organisation that runs the DNS. It has 13 computers, known as root servers, throughout the world.

The DNS is hierarchical and is divided into four levels. Reading from right to left, each level is separated by a dot. The part after the last dot (eg .com) is the top level domain (TLD).

3.1.1 Top level domains

3.1.1.1 *Generic top level domains*

These are divided into two-letter country codes according to the ISO 3166 standard (such as .ie for Ireland, .ca for Canada, etc).

Then there are three-letter generic top level domains (gTLDs) of which there are six originals and several new ones. The originals are:

- .com   for commercial organisations;
- .org   for non-profit organisations;
- .net   for internet network providers;
- .edu   for educational institutions (full-time, degree awarding);
- .mil   for military establishments; and
- .int   for international treaty organisations such as the United Nations.

New ones include:

Name	Status
.info	Fully operational and live
.biz	Fully operational and live
.pro	Fully operational and live

- .name — Fully operational and live
- .aero — Operational, run by SITA (Société Internationale de Télécommunications Aéronautiques SC)
- .museum — Operational
- .coop — Operational
- .cat — Operational
- .jobs — Operational
- .mobi — Operational
- .travel — Operational
- .asia — Start up phase
- .post — Under negotiations
- .tel — Not yet operational

3.1.1.2 Country code top level domains

If, for example, you wish to register your domain name as '.be' for Belgium, you must go to the registrar for Belgium and follow its rules for registration. It may be that their rules require a connection to the country whereas in the case of .com the rule was traditionally 'first come first served'. The country code top level domains (ccTLDs) are administered independently of one another, but the practices and procedures of many of them display similar characteristics. There are currently 243 ccTLDs in the database of the World Intellectual Property Organization (WIPO). WIPO has recently launched a database portal where one can carry out online searches for country code top level domains.

Included among the ccTLDs is the recently developed '.eu' which has been in existence since March 2005. This domain, created and administered, unsurprisingly enough, by the European Union, was created on foot of Regulation 733/2002. The '.eu' address appears to be an ongoing success story, with over 2.4 million registered domains at the time of writing.

3.2 How do domain name disputes arise?

Cyber squatting is the term generally given to the practice of pre-emptively registering the trademark of a third party as a domain name. Cyber squatters use the first come, first served nature of some of the domain name systems to register names of trademarks, famous people or businesses with which they have no connection. Since the registration process is extremely simple, cyber squatters can buy varieties of names and offer them for sale directly to the company involved or at prices that are far in excess of the cost of registration.

Often, they retain the site to divert business from their competitors or to defame them. The concept of defamatory or parody sites is a relatively recent one. High profile cases include sites related to Wal-Mart and Chase Manhattan Bank, both in the US. In some of these cases, a protest site in the US which criticised a major brand name was found to be a legitimate protest site.

3.3 How did WIPO become involved in resolving these disputes?

It was decided with the increase in disputes and the increasing commercial value of domain names that something would have to be done to ensure uniformity of dispute resolution. Harmonising national laws in almost 250 countries would take too long, as would writing an international treaty on the subject. WIPO, after extensive consultation with its members, published a report containing recommendations dealing with domain name disputes, out of which came the Uniform Domain Name Dispute Resolution Policy (UDRP) outlined below. It came into effect in December 1999 and under it, WIPO is the domain name dispute resolution provider. At the end of 2001, 60% of all the cases filed under the UDRP were filed with WIPO. In addition, a number of ccTLDs have designated WIPO as their dispute resolution provider.

Domain name disputes in the new gTLDs are subject to the UDRP. In the start-up phases or 'sunrise' phases for these gTLDs, WIPO is also administering specific dispute resolution policies. It should be noted that many of the new gTLDs which are restricted to certain purposes also provide special proceedings to resolve disputes concerning compliance with their respective registration restrictions.

3.4 What is the UDRP?

The ICANN UDRP works in the following way. If a trademark holder considers that its trademark has been breached by another domain name being registered it may initiate a proceeding under the UDRP. The respondent must submit to the proceeding. The complainant must specify the domain name in question, the respondent who registered it and the grounds for complaint. Such grounds can include the way in which the domain name is identical to or similar to the trademark, why the respondent should be seen as having no legitimate rights in respect of the domain name, and why the domain name should be considered as having been registered in bad faith.

The respondent is then given the opportunity to provide a defence and WIPO appoints a panellist who determines if the domain name should be transferred.

The panellists are neutral and highly qualified, and the procedure is both fast and relatively inexpensive. A domain name case filed with WIPO is generally concluded within two months, whereas conventional trademark litigation can take many years with higher costs. Costs generally do not exceed US$5000 even if WIPO appoints more than one panellist, and may be as low as US$1500.

3.4.1 Are the results binding?

A domain name is either transferred or the complaint is denied and the respondent keeps the domain name. There are no monetary damages applied and no injunctive relief is possible under the UDRP. A court appeal is possible within 10 days. However, in practice, this is quite rare. Case law of the UDRP is emerging and is searchable online under a number of headings, so you should be able to find a case similar to any being presented to you by your clients.

3.4.2 Ireland: .ie

The ccTLD '.ie' used to be administered by a department within UCD and is now run by IE Domain Registry Ltd, which is an independent company. It is expected to be run under the auspices of the Commission for Communications Regulation (ComReg) in the future.

In January 2002, the IE Domain Registry introduced a set of rule changes which relaxed the rules for obtaining an '.ie' registration, including the following:

- generic names are now allowed;
- domains of two characters are allowed (cannot be only two letters);
- you must still have a real and substantial connection with Ireland, but now this is referable to the 32 counties, therefore Northern Irish clients can now register '.ie' in addition to '.co.uk', which was not possible before;

- sole traders can now apply under their trading name under the 'personal trading name category'.

3.5 What about .com?

The .com TLD is administered by VeriSign and was previously administered by Network Solutions Inc. It sells domain names, often through brokers, on a first come, first served basis and has been the most successful of all the gTLDs.

3.6 Emerging UDRP case law

As we have seen, the three main things a complainant must show in a successful UDRP action are as follows:

- the domain name is identical or confusingly similar to a trademark or service mark in which the complainant has rights;
- the domain name holder has no rights or legitimate interests in the domain name; and
- the domain name was registered and is being used in bad faith.

The UDRP provides no guidance on how to prove or disprove the question of confusing similarity; presumably it is in the eyes of the beholder. As new cases have been brought, additional examples of facts or conduct satisfying each of the three factors have emerged.

To prove that the domain name holder (the respondent) does have a legitimate interest in the domain name (the second factor), the UDRP provides a non-exclusive list of three circumstances that are sufficient to demonstrate the respondent's right to the domain name:

- the respondent can demonstrate that before it received any notice of the complainant's rights, it had used or planned to use the domain name in a legitimate manner;
- the domain name corresponds with a name by which the respondent is commonly known; or
- the respondent is making a fair, non-commercial use of the domain name.

For the third factor, the UDRP provides four non-exclusive examples of bad faith use and registration:

- circumstances indicating that the respondent has registered or acquired the domain name primarily for the purpose of selling, renting, or otherwise transferring the domain name registration to the complainant who is the owner of the trademark or service mark, or to a competitor of that complainant, for valuable consideration in excess of the respondent's documented out-of-pocket costs directly related to the domain name; or
- the respondent has registered the domain name in order to prevent the owner of the trademark or service mark from reflecting the mark in a corresponding domain name, provided that the respondent has engaged in a pattern of such conduct; or
- the respondent has registered the domain name primarily for the purpose of disrupting the business of a competitor; or
- by using the domain name, the respondent has intentionally attempted to attract, for commercial gain, internet users to its website or other online location by creating a likelihood of confusion with the complainant's mark as to the source, sponsorship, affiliation, or endorsement of the respondent's website or location or of a product or service on the respondent's website or location.

3.7 The emerging principles

3.7.1 Standing

The standing issue concerns the rights a complainant must assert in order to proceed under the UDRP. Before the UDRP was adopted, Network Solutions Inc (NSI) held a monopoly on the registration of domain names. Under NSI's dispute resolution policy, a trademark owner could only object to the registration of a domain name if it possessed a prior valid US trademark registration on the Principal Register (or a comparable foreign registration) for a mark identical to the domain name. Common law trademark rights, registrations on the Supplemental Register, and State trademark registrations were irrelevant under NSI's policy.

Under the UDRP, by contrast, the complainant must only show that the disputed domain name is identical or confusingly similar to a mark in which it has rights. The UDRP does not specify what type of rights are required. Several of the 25 most cited cases have addressed this issue, and it is now clear that the successful complainant need not possess a registered mark.

In the two cases in the top 25 involving personal names, *Julia Roberts v Russell Boyd* Case No D2000-O210 WIPO and *Jeanette Winterson v Mark Hogarth* Case No D2000-0235 WIPO, both panels concluded that the complainants' common law rights in their own names were sufficient to bring an action under the UDRP. The complaints did not need to have a trademark or service mark registered with a government authority in order to invoke the UDRP. This is important because few individuals hold trademark registrations for their names.

3.7.2 Bad faith

The three most cited cases all address the issue of bad faith, the third element under the UDRP, and the most difficult to establish. The decision in *Telstra Corporation Ltd v Nuclear Marshmallows* Case No D2000-O003 WIPO is far and away the most cited case to date. The complainant in *Telstra* was the largest provider of telecommunication and information services in Australia and owned more than 50 Australian trademark registrations (and numerous foreign registrations) containing the term 'telstra'. The respondent, owner of the domain name telstra.org, did not file an answer to the complaint. The respondent had provided an Australian post office box address to the domain name registrar. Numerous attempts by the complainant to contact the respondent at this address were unsuccessful, and no record of the business name 'Nuclear Marshmallows' existed within Australia's company name register. The panel quickly found that the domain name was identical or confusingly similar to the complainant's trademark and that the respondent had no rights or legitimate interest in the *Telstra* name.

The panel then turned to the issue of bad faith. It first concluded that the UDRP requires the complainant to prove that the domain name was registered in bad faith and that it is being used in bad faith ie, that the bad faith had to exist at the time the domain name was registered and must have continued thereafter. Bad faith registration was found based on two facts:

- the respondent deliberately attempted to obscure its identity when registering the domain name; and
- the complainant's marks were so well known that it was inconceivable the respondent was not aware of them at the time the domain name was registered.

The difficult issue for the panel in the *Telstra* case, and the point for which it is most frequently cited, was bad faith use of the domain name. The respondent's activities did not fall into any of the four evidentiary illustrations listed in the UDRP. In fact, the respondent had not made any use of the domain name at all. There was no website connected to the domain name, nor was there any evidence of advertising, promotion or display of the domain name, nor had the respondent made any offer or attempt to sell the domain name. The panellists nevertheless found that there is a distinction between 'undertaking a positive action in bad faith' and 'acting in bad faith', and that the latter could be satisfied by inaction or passive holding where there was no possible use the respondent could have made of the domain name that would have been legitimate. As a result, the inaction of the respondent was not a bar to the complainant ultimately obtaining ownership of the domain name.

The second and third most cited cases, *Educational Testing Service v TO EFL* Case No D2000-0044 WIPO and *Talk City* Case No D2000-0009 WIPO, also addressed the question of proving bad faith. In *TOEFL,* the panel found that a general offer to sell a domain name constituted use and registration in bad faith, where the value that the domain name holder sought to secure from the sale was based on the value of the complainant's trademark. Bad faith use and registration was found in *Talk City* based on the respondent's having registered and used the *talk-city.com* domain name and other domain names corresponding to well known internet companies in order to misdirect traffic to its site.

Other factors in the top 25 cases that were found to constitute evidence of bad faith are:

- using complainant's mark to route users to a pornographic website:
  Ingersoll-Rand Co v Frank Gully Case No D2000-0021 WIPO;
- offering to sell the domain name and failure to make a good faith use of the domain name for two years following registration:
  Mary-Lynn Mondich Case No D2000-0004 WIPO;
- ownership of more than 40 domain names, many of which were well known product names. Similarly a note in the WHOIS record (ie information about or related to a domain name registration record) stating 'This domain is for sale' was sufficient evidence of bad faith, where the same legend was contained in the records for other domain names registered by the same respondent. These cases demonstrate clearly that it is extremely difficult for a respondent to prevail under the UDRP if it is attempting to profit by dealing in domain names in which others have legitimate interests.

In *Veuve Cliquot Ponsardin v The Polygenix Group Co* Case No D2000-0163 WIPO, the fame of the *Veuve Cliquot* mark was found to be so great that its very use by someone with no connection with the product was sufficient to suggest opportunistic bad faith. Finally, it should be noted that a domain name can be 'so obviously connected with the complainant' and its services that its very use by someone with no connection with the complainant suggests opportunistic bad faith. (*Deutsche Bank AG v Diego-Arturo Bruckner*, WIPO D2000-0277.)

3.7.3 Confusing similarity

The UDRP does not require that a complainant prove a likelihood of confusion between its mark and the respondent's domain name. It merely requires that the mark be identical to, or confusingly similar to, the domain name, with or without evidence of marketplace confusion.

The requirement of identicalness was expanded to include 'virtual identity' in *CBS Broadcasting Inc v LA Twilight Zone* Case No D2000-0397 WIPO, where the panel found that the addition of a hyphen in the domain name 'twilightzone.net' rendered the domain name virtually identical and confusingly similar to the complainant's 'twilight zone' mark.

In *General Electric Co* Case No D2000-O394 WIPO (cited 20 times in the CBS Broadcasting case), the complainant had registered the service marks 'GE Capital' and 'GECAL'. The respondent had registered the domain names 'gecapitaldirect.com' and, 'gecaldirect.com'. The panel found that the addition of the generic term 'direct' to the complainant's marks could not avoid a finding that the respondent's domain names were confusingly similar to those marks.

3.7.4 Legitimate rights or interests

In order to force the transfer or cancellation of a domain name, the complainant must prove that the respondent has 'no right or legitimate interests in respect of the domain name. Of the 25 most cited decisions, seven have been frequently cited in relation to a respondent's legitimate rights or interests in the domain name.

Paragraph 4(c) of the UDRP lists three non-exclusive circumstances in which the legitimate right to a domain name may be demonstrated. These are:

- use of, or preparations to use, the domain name or a name corresponding to the domain name in connection with a *bona fide* offering of goods or services before any notice of the dispute;
- public familiarity with respondent by the name, even in the absence of trademark or service mark rights; or
- a legitimate non-commercial or fair use of the domain name, without intent for commercial gain to misleadingly divert consumers or to tarnish the trademark or service mark at issue.

3.8 Recent .ie disputes

Adidas v Varga and Petho (Case No. DIE2006-0004)/B&S Limited v Varga and Petho (Case No. DIE2006-0005)

In these cases the disputed domain names were 'adidas.ie' and 'buy-sell.ie'. The respondents had a history and practice of registering well known trademarks and country names as domain names and counted among their collection 'nike.ie', 'ipod.ie', 'googel.ie', 'googol.ie', 'economist.ie', 'england.ie', 'belgium.ie' and 'estonia.ie'. Prior to the institution of proceedings, each of these famous domain names resolved to the respondent's own website 'eubrowser.ie'. However, after the service of a cease and desist letter in relation to the Adidas.ie domain, a homepage was put up for the 'Advanced Detailed Internet Directory and Search'; a purported search engine! The Claimants were Adidas AG, the sportswear giant, and B&S Ltd, publisher of the magazine 'Buy and Sell'.

The respondents had successfully registered all of the disputed domain names as business names with the Companies Registration Office before seeking to register them as domain names. The panel held this to be irrelevant as it was done simply to fulfil the requirements for .ie registration. Moreover, the .ie Dispute Resolution Policy (a modified version of UDRP) expressly provides that business name registration does not give any right or legitimate interest in the corresponding domain name.

The panel had little difficulty in ordering that the disputed domain names be transferred to the complainants. The domains were clearly identical or misleadingly similar to the well known trademarks or protected identifier of the complainants.

When considering the respondents' purported rights or legitimate interest in the domains, the panel had regard to the general conduct of the respondents; inferring from the respondents' failure to explain the registration of numerous famous names that the portfolio was not intended to be used for legitimate purposes.

Finally, when considering the question of bad faith, the panel noted (in the *Adidas Case*) that it would have to consider why the respondent registered the disputed domain name and whether they did it to target the complainant in some way. Having regard to the pattern of registration of well known marks and the fact that the respondents must be presumed to know the complainants' brands, it was held that the domain names had been deliberately chosen and registered so as to divert traffic to the respondents' primary website, allowing the respondents to profit from the goodwill accumulated by the complainants. Thus, the panel ordered the transfer of the domain names to the complainants.

Electricity Supply Board (ESB) v Lislyn Retail Limited (Case No. DIE 2003-0001)

Here, the dispute was over the domain name 'shopelectric.ie'. The complainant, the ESB, had, since 1968, sold electric appliances throughout the Republic of Ireland in retail stores which traded under the registered trademark 'shop electric'.

However, the respondent, which had no connection with the complainant had, for over thirty years, operated a network of electrical stores throughout Northern Ireland which traded under the name 'Shop Electric'! The respondent had further registered the style 'shop electric' as a trademark under Northern Irish law.

The panel held that the respondent was entitled to use the domain name and refused to order its transfer to the ESB. Noting that '.ie' was the country code for the island of Ireland, not just the Republic of Ireland, the panel concluded that the Lislyn Retail had 'legitimate rights in the 'shop electric' name due to the undisputed long use and the existence of trademarks in Northern Ireland.' This case demonstrates that where two persons or entities have a legitimate claim to a domain name, a first come, first served system still operates.

Hutchinion 3G v Mahon (Case No. DIE2005-1)

One of the more controversial decisions handed down by the panel in recent years saw the respondent, an amateur photographer, ordered to transfer the domain name 'three.ie' to the complainant, a communications giant best known in this jurisdiction for operating the '3' mobile service. The facts of this case are quite complex and merit discussion at length.

In July 2002, the respondent registered the disputed domain name and placed an 'under construction' notice on the site. In December of that year, the complainant's trademark agent emailed the respondent offering to purchase the domain for €1000. The Agent did not reveal who he was acting for. The respondent refused, noting that his costs to date exceeded €1000. He further pointed out that he was hoping to launch the site fully in early 2004 and that a temporary site, www.three.ie/temp, had been established.

The temporary site welcomed visitors and stated that the site was set up by amateur photographers to sell their photographs. It noted that the name 'three.ie' had been chosen in reference to the three primary colours.

The respondent's solicitors contacted the complainant's agent. Noting that their client had spent considerable time, money and effort in setting up the website, and that the entire marketing campaign was based on the idea of three primary colours they offered to sell the domain name for €5000. At this stage, the identity of the complainant had been successfully identified.

The complainant's agent refused this offer and accused the respondent of acting in bad faith. A counter offer of €2000 was made. The respondent refused and stated that in light of the derisory nature of the previous offer and allegations made against him he would not be prepared to sell the site to the complainant. The complainant subsequently made an offer of €5000 which was ignored.

The three.ie site was later launched by the respondent with three photographs offered for sale. The website was branded THREE.IE in capitals, adjacent to which was a white circle with short horizontal wavy lines coloured red, green and blue.

The panel noted that the most prominent feature of the complainant's trademark was the word 'THREE in block capitals and with minimal stylized effect'. As a result, the domain name was held to be confusingly similar to this trademark.

It was further held that the respondent had no legal rights or legitimate interests in respect of the domain name as he had failed to demonstrate that prior to being put on notice of the complainant's interest in the domain name, he had made good faith preparations to use it in connection with a business. It was held that the registration of the business name 'three.ie' with the CRO and correspondence entered into between the complainant and his web host over technical issues regarding the site did not amount to good faith preparations.

Finally, it was held that the domain name had been registered and used in bad faith. The primary reason for this appears to be that the respondent applied for the business name two weeks after media reports mentioned the complainants's intention to expand into the Irish market (it was not proven that the respondent was actually aware of these reports). It was also noted that the logo on the respondent's website was remarkably similar to the complainant's trade mark (which was issued after the respondent acquired the domain name) and that the respondent had failed to effectively develop the photography business venture. The panel dismissed the three primary colours explanation for the website as 'a clever rationale' and concluded that the website was no more than an attempt to justify the registration of the domain name. The panel consequently ordered that the domain name be transferred to the complainant.

CHAPTER 4

PRIVACY AND DATA PROTECTION

Philip Nolan & Rossa McMahon

4.1 Introduction

Privacy and data protection are areas of increasing popular and commercial concern. The retention and processing of vast amounts of personal information by commercial entities, made possible by developments in information technology, coupled with the damage that can be caused by the misuse of personal information has resulted in an extensive regulatory framework being put in place to safeguard personal information. Moreover, invasive media conduct has lead to a number of high profile cases being brought for invasion of privacy. Legislative reform in this area has also been proposed in the form of the Privacy Bill 2006 which seeks to create a statutory civil action for breach of privacy, although as of late 2007 the progress of the Bill had effectively been suspended.

This chapter will focus primarily on issues of data retention and protection as these will be most frequently encountered in practice.

4.2 Privacy as a constitutional and human right

4.2.1 Introduction

Privacy is a constitutional and human right. It is expressly protected by Article 8 of the European Convention on Human Rights (ECHR) and has been held by our courts to be an unenumerated constitutional right inherent in the Christian and democratic nature of the State. It is also recognised by Articles 7 and 8 of the Charter of Fundamental Rights of the European Union (which will be elevated to the same legal standing as an EU Treaty by the Reform Treaty, if passed by all Member States), Article 12 of Universal Declaration of Human Rights 1948 and Article 17 of the International Convention on Civil and Political Rights 1966.

4.2.2 Privacy under the Constitution

The right to privacy was first recognised in Ireland in the seminal decision in *McGee v Attorney General* [1974] IR 284 where Walsh J stated that 'it can scarcely be doubted in our society that the right to privacy is universally recognised and accepted with possibly the rarest of exceptions.' In *Kennedy v Ireland* [1988] ILRM 472 Hamilton P (as he then was) expanded and explained the nature of the right. Borrowing from American constitutional law he adopted Justice Brandeis's definition of the right to privacy as 'the right to be left alone' and noted that 'the nature of the right must be such as to ensure the dignity and freedom of an individual ... in a sovereign, independent and democratic society.' However, it was held that the right to privacy is not an unqualified right. Its exercise may be restricted by the constitutional rights of others, by the requirements of the common good and is subject to the requirements of public order and morality.

4.2.3 Privacy under the ECHR

On foot of Article 8 of the European Convention on Human Rights (ECHR), which guarantees protection for private and family life, the European Court of Human Rights has developed a substantial jurisprudence protecting the right to privacy. In *Von Hanover v Germany* [2004] ECHR 294 the court noted that 'private life ... includes a person's physical and psychological integrity. [The right to privacy] is primarily intended to ensure the development, without outsider interference, of the personality of each individual in his relations with other human beings.' The court went on to expressly note the risk posed to this right by modern data processing, suggesting that 'increased vigilance in protecting private life is necessary to contend with new communication technologies which make it possible to store and reproduce personal data.'

The court has also stressed that the right to privacy does not stop at the office door but applies to all aspects of life. In *Niemitz v Germany* [1992] 16 EHRR 97 the court noted that 'there appears ... to be no reason why [the right to privacy] should be taken to exclude activities of a professional or business nature.'

4.2.4 Data Protection in practice, the Constitution and the ECHR

The role of data protection and privacy law is to balance the expectation and right to privacy of the citizen against other competing rights and interests. Thus, when considering data protection and privacy legislation, practitioners should bear in mind the existence of the ECHR and the constitutional right to privacy, especially having regard to the fact that the actual scope and meaning of legislative provisions will be construed with regard to this right.

Section 2 of the European Convention on Human Rights Act 2003 provides that a court, in interpreting and applying any statutory provision or rule of law, shall, insofar as is possible, subject to the rules of law relating to interpretation and application, do so in a manner compatible with the State's obligations under the ECHR. Furthermore, the Data Protection Commissioner (the Commissioner) is, as an organ of the State, obliged by s 3 of the 2003 Act to perform his functions in a manner compatible with the ECHR.

Likewise, where a legislative provision is open to two or more possible interpretations, one of which is constitutional while the other is not, then the court, under the double construction rule, shall assume that the Oireachtas intended the constitutional interpretation (*McDonald v Bord na gCon (No 2)* [1965] IR 217).

4.3 The Data Protection Acts

4.3.1 Introduction

In order to balance the right of organisations to gather data with the right of individuals to control the content and use of their personal data, the storage and processing of personal data is regulated under the Data Protection Act 1988 (the Act) and the Data Protection (Amendment) Act 2003 (the 2003 Act) (together referred to as the Acts). The 2003 Act transposes into Irish law the provisions of Directive 95/46/EC on the protection of individuals with regard to the processing of personal data and on the free movement of data, and amends many of the provisions of the Act.

4.3.2 Data controllers

4.3.2.1 *What is a data controller and what is personal data?*

Section 2 of the Act, as amended by s 3 of the 2003 Act, sets out a number of principles with which all 'data controllers' are required to comply. Data controllers are defined as persons who, either alone or with others, control the content and use of personal data. The Acts also impose certain obligations on data processors, which are defined as entities that process data on behalf of data controllers (excluding employees of data controllers).

Personal data includes automated and manual data (data that is recorded as part of a structured filing system) relating to a living individual who is or can be identified from the data or in conjunction with other information which is in the data controller's possession or which is likely to come into such possession. Prior to 24 October 2007, most of the rules set out below only applied to manual data created after the passing of the 2003 Act. However, the rules apply to all manual data as of 24 October 2007.

4.3.2.2 *Which data controllers are subject to the Acts?*

Section 1(3B)(a) of the Act, as amended by the 2003 Act, provides that the Acts only apply in respect of data controllers that process personal data if:

(a) the data controller is established in Ireland and the data controller processes data in the context of that establishment; or
(b) the data controller is neither established in Ireland nor in any other State that is a contracting party to the European Economic Area Agreement but makes use of equipment in Ireland for the purpose of the data otherwise than for the purpose of transit through the territory of the State.

4.3.3 Duties of data controllers

4.3.3.1 *Duty to Secure Data*

What is the nature of the duty?

Data Controllers must take appropriate security measures against unauthorised access to, or unauthorised alteration, disclosure or destruction of, personal data, particularly where the processing involves the transmission of data over a network and against all other forms of processing.

Section 2C of the Act, as inserted by s 3 of the 2003 Act, provides that data controllers must put in place appropriate security provisions for the protection of personal data, having regard to the current state of technological development, the cost of implementing security measures, the nature of the personal data and the harm that might result from unauthorised processing or loss of the data concerned. Data Controllers and Processors are also obliged to take all reasonable steps to ensure that their employees, and other persons at the place of work concerned, are aware of, and comply with, the relevant security measures.

The Commissioner has issued guidelines about the procedures that should be put in place by data controllers to try to ensure compliance with section 2C. Although these guidelines are advisory (not binding) in nature, they offer a good outline of the basic security precautions that should be put in place.

The Commissioner suggests that placing a password on a computer is the minimum acceptable measure to prevent unauthorised access to data. However, to be effective, a password must be kept secure and be reviewed and changed if necessary. Moreover, computers should be locked when they are not in use. Ideally, users should only have access to data which they require in order to perform their duties, and firewalls should be installed by all data controllers. Anti-virus software should be in place and kept up to date and staff should be advised not to open email attachments from unexpected sources. Encryption systems may offer a high degree of protection but, as no industry standard exists, different encryption systems will not be interoperable, this should be borne in mind when sending encrypted data to the a third party.

The Commissioner has further noted that it is pointless having an access control system and a security policy if the system cannot identify potential abuses. Consequently, a system should be able to identify the user that accessed a file, as well as the time of the access. A log of alterations made, along with the author/editor, should also be created. The Commissioner has noted that remote network access and wireless networks are potential weak points in network security. Thus, the need for such systems should be carefully considered on security grounds rather than solely on ease of use. Laptops, due to their risk of theft, should be limited in the amount of sensitive data they contain. Any system where back up copies of the data are held should be subject to the same security precautions as the main system. Finally, the Commissioner has noted the importance of taking the simple steps of having good physical security at the data storage premises and ensuring that staff are aware of their responsibilities.

Is there an obligation to disclose breaches of data security?

Practitioners advising clients with US based operations should note that US law imposes more onerous security obligations on data controllers, requiring them to disclose the fact that a security breach has taken place. These disclosure rules are referred to as the *Data Security Breach Notification Laws*. These obligations have no equivalent under Irish or European data protection law, neither of which imposes any positive obligation to report personal data security breaches to data subjects. It should be noted that these breach notification laws are state-based, not federal in nature, and thus may vary between jurisdictions. However, many of the states have modelled their rules on the original Californian security breach notification law, SB 1386.

SB 1386 obliges entities that do business in California to notify Californian resident data subjects of instances of unauthorised acquisition of computerised data which compromises the security, confidentiality or integrity of their personal information. This notification is required to be carried out 'in the most expedient time possible and without unreasonable delay.' The obligation to notify data subjects of a security breach arises where the subject of the unauthorised acquisition in unencrypted, computerised personal data includes the data subject's first name or initial and last name, and one of the following:

- Social Security number;
- driver's licence or Californian identification card number; or
- financial credit card number or any PIN or access codes for these.

These obligations should be of concern to Irish practitioners as they appear to be extra-territorial in effect, applying not only to Californian companies but rather to 'any persons or business that conducts business in California.' This far-reaching provision could possibly require a company which is incorporated in, and physically present in this jurisdiction, to notify Californian residents of security breaches when it is doing business in California by way of internet sales.

It does not appear that this disclosure requirement will be incorporated into Irish or European Law. In a 2006 European Commission Communication on the Review of the EU Regulatory Framework for electronic communications networks and services (COM (2006) 334 final), that institution suggested that 'providers of electronic communication networks and services' should be required to notify the relevant national regulator of any breach of security which has lead to the loss of personal data and/or interruptions in the continuity of service-supply and to notify their customers of any breach of security leading to the loss, modification or destruction of, or unauthorised access to, customer personal data. This approach is very limited and would only apply to ISPs, network operators and certain other electronic communication operators. Thus, it appears that for the time being, data compromise disclosure is not a legal obligation under Irish law, but clients with US operations should be made aware of their obligations under US law.

Security breaches in practice

Personal data is valuable; that is why it is collected and processed. However, this asset can quickly become a liability in the event that the data is compromised, occasioning both financial loss to the company and potential loss of customer good will. A US based study by the Ponemon Institute has suggested that the average cost of a data breach is $182 per compromised record and the average cost per data breach incident is $4.8m. Security breaches have caused significant difficulties for several large companies in recent years, most notably The TJX Companies Inc which saw its 45 million entry strong customer database accessed by outside sources and Choicepoint, which was fined $15m by US regulators for failing to secure data.

Data Security and Data Processor Contracts

Section 2C provides that if a data controller uses a third party to process data, the processing of such data should be covered by a contract which contains certain prescribed terms. This contract should stipulate at least the following:

- the conditions under which the data may be processed;
- the minimum security measures that the data processor must have in place; and
- some mechanism or provision that will enable the data controller to ensure that the data processor is compliant with the security requirement (this might include a right of inspection or independent audit).

Since various commercial arrangements entail a personal data processing component, an increasing number of commercial contracts need to have provisions along the lines set out above.

4.3.3.2 *Other duties imposed on data controllers*

A data controller must also comply with the following obligations in relation to personal data held by them:

(a) The personal data must be obtained and processed fairly. Fairness needs to be judged by reference to the purpose for which the information was obtained. Section 2(5)(b) of the Act states that data shall not be regarded as having been obtained unfairly by reason only that its use for any particular purpose was not disclosed when it was obtained, provided the data is not used in such a way that damage or distress is likely to be caused to any data subject. In addition, s 2D of the Act, as inserted by s 3 of the 2003 Act, provides *inter alia* that in order for data to be processed fairly, the data controller that obtains the personal data from the data subject shall, as far as practicable, provide or make available to the data subject at least the following information:
- the identity of the data controller;
- the name of the person nominated by the data controller for the purposes of the Acts;
- the purpose or purposes for which the data is intended to be processed; and
- certain other relevant information.

(b) Personal data must be accurate and, where necessary, kept up to date. Section 1(2) of the Act defines inaccurate data as data that is incorrect or misleading as to any matter of fact.

(c) Personal data must be held only for one or more specified, explicit and legitimate purposes. Thus, collecting information about people routinely and indiscriminately, without having a legitimate purpose for doing so, will result in a breach of this obligation.

(d) Personal data must not be further processed in a manner incompatible with that purpose or those purposes. An example of incompatible processing would be where information expressly collected for one purpose, such as a political petition, was then used for marketing (Commissioner Case Study 5 of 2006).

(e) Personal data must be adequate, relevant and not excessive in relation to that purpose or those purposes for which it was collected or further processed. The Commissioner suggests that the guiding principle is that no more information than is necessary for the purpose should be collected from the data subject. This obligation is often breached by financial institutions who, for business reasons, seek information about customers opening accounts (such as their employment status and salary) that is not necessary to either operate the account or to comply with the bank's anti-money laundering obligations (Commissioner Case Study 7 of 2005).

(f) Personal data must not be kept for longer than is necessary for that purpose or those purposes. This obligation is frequently breached where personal information given to a company for a specific contractual purpose is used, after the discharge of the contract, for marketing purposes (Commissioner Case Study 4 of 2006).

4.3.3.3 *Non-compliance with duties*

Non-compliance with the principles set out in s 2(1) of the Act does not automatically constitute a criminal offence. However, it may lead to a complaint being made by a data subject to the Commissioner, who may in turn take action by issuing an enforcement notice pursuant to s 10(2) of the Act. However, the data controller may be liable under ordinary common law principles such as the law of confidence, contract law or the law of tort where the data controller fails to comply with its obligations as set out in section 2 of the Act. Furthermore, subject to certain limitations, a person who has suffered loss as a result of non-compliance with the data protection principles may recover damages in tort against the data controller.

4.3.4 The use of personal data for marketing purposes

Section 2(7) of the Act provides that where personal data is kept for the purpose of direct marketing and the relevant data subject requests in writing that the relevant data controller cease processing the data for that purpose, then generally the data controller must within 40 days accede to such request.

In addition, s 2(8) provides that where a data controller intends to process personal data which it holds for the purposes of direct marketing, then the data controller shall inform the relevant data subjects that they may object, by means of a request in writing to the data controller (and free of charge), to such processing. This provision creates a positive obligation on all data controllers to inform data subjects that are being targeted for direct marketing purposes of their right to object to such use of their personal data.

4.3.5 The processing of personal data

Section 2A of the Act provides that personal data shall not be processed by a data controller unless the data controller complies with its obligations under section 2 (outlined in **4.3.3** above) and provided that at least one of the pre-conditions contained in section 2A(1) is satisfied. This provision sets out a series of pre-conditions to the processing of personal data.

In this regard, it should be noted that 'processing' is defined as performing any operation or set of operations on the information or data, whether or not by automatic means. The definition gives a non-exhaustive list of examples of processing which includes obtaining data, recording data, collecting data, storing data, altering or adapting data, retrieving data, consulting data, using data, disclosing data or blocking, erasing or destroying data. When this broad definition of processing is read in the context of the rule that processing cannot take place unless one of the pre-conditions in s 2A(1) is satisfied, it would appear that virtually no dealings in personal data can be carried out by a data controller unless one of the pre-conditions contained in this section is satisfied. The first pre-condition contained in section 2A provides that data may be processed where the data subject has given their consent to such processing.

4.3.6 The processing of sensitive personal data

Section 2B of the Act contains additional pre-conditions, one of which must be satisfied prior to the processing of sensitive personal data. Sensitive personal data is defined as including data concerning racial or ethnic origin, political opinion, religious belief, trade union membership, mental or physical health, sexual life or data concerning the committing of an offence or proceedings in relation to an offence. The first of these pre-conditions provides that the 'explicit' consent of the data subject be given before a data controller can process sensitive personal data.

4.3.7 The rights of data subjects

4.3.7.1 *Right to be informed of data being kept*

Section 3 of the Act provides that where a person suspects that another person is keeping personal data relating to them, they may write to that person requesting that they be informed as to whether any such data is being kept. If the other person is keeping such data, then the data subject must be given a description of the data and the purpose for which it is kept. This must be done within 21 days of the request having been made.

4.3.7.2 *Right to prevent data being used for the purpose of direct marketing*

This right is discussed at **4.3.4** above.

4.3.7.3 *Right of access*

Section 4 of the Act confers upon the data subject a right of access to the data in the possession of the data controller. It provides that where the data subject makes a written request, the data controller must inform the data subject whether they hold personal data relating to the data subject and supply them with a detailed description of such data and additional information concerning the data.

4.3.7.4 *Right of blocking or erasure*

Section 6 of the Act, as amended by the 2003 Act, gives the data subject a right to have their personal data in the data controller's possession rectified, erased or blocked if the data controller fails to comply with its duties under the Act. The data controller has 40 days to accede to such request.

4.3.7.5 *Right to prevent processing where it might cause damage or distress*

Section 6A of the Act, as amended by the 2003 Act, provides that an individual is entitled at any time, by notice in writing served on a data controller, to request the data controller to cease or not to commence processing of that individual's personal data where such processing is likely to cause substantial damage or distress which is or would be unwarranted. There are certain public interest exceptions to this right of data subjects.

4.3.7.6 *Rights of data subjects concerning automatic processing of data*

Section 6B of the Act, as amended by the 2003 Act, provides that a decision which produces legal effects concerning a data subject or otherwise significantly affects a data subject may not be based solely on the processing by automatic means of personal data where such processing aims to evaluate personal matters such as work performance, credit worthiness, reliability or conduct. This right is subject to a number of exceptions.

4.3.8 The transfer of personal data outside of the EEA

4.3.8.1 *Introduction*

Section 11 of the Act, as amended by the 2003 Act, contains a number of restrictions on the transfer of personal data by a data controller to a country or territory outside of the European Economic Area (EEA). It provides that such a transfer may not take place unless that particular country or territory ensures an adequate level of protection for the privacy of its data subjects in relation to the processing of their personal data. The provision enables the European Commission to make findings as to when a particular country or territory satisfies this adequacy requirement.

The provision goes on to give the Commissioner wide powers to issue orders, 'prohibition notices', preventing the transfer of personal data from the state.

Interestingly, the Commission is of the opinion that the US fails to offers an adequate level of privacy protection; thus there is a general prohibition on the transfer of personal data between the EEA and the US. This can cause considerable difficulties in practice and several ways have been developed to overcome these problems.

4.3.8.2 *What is the transfer of personal data out of the EEA?*

Data will only be counted as personal if individuals can be identified from it; if the information is anonymous then the prohibitions on transfer will not apply.

Data is not transferred if it merely passes through the territory of a State en route to its ultimate destination. In *Bodil Lindqvist v Kammaraklagaren* (C-101/01) the ECJ drew a distinction between uploading personal information onto a server, which was accessible from the internet, and the actual transfer of data. Merely uploading information onto the server does not amount to a transfer of personal data, even though it can be accessed, via the internet, from outside the EEA. However, if this data were *actually* accessed by a person outside of the EEA, then a transfer of data will be deemed to have taken place.

4.3.8.3 *Does the recipient State have an adequate level of data protection?*

When a data controller is planning a personal data transfer to a country outside the EEA, best practice is to first check whether the country is on the European Commission's approved list. If the country is on the list then the data transfer can go ahead. If it is not then additional steps will need to be taken so as to ensure the security of the data.

The view of the Commission as to whether a country has an adequate level of data protection is definitive, and cannot be second guessed by national authorities or data controllers. If neither the EU nor any national data authority (ie the Commissioner and his counterparts) have expressed any view as to the adequacy or otherwise of the protection standards in any State then, in theory at least, the data controller is able to form their own opinion as to the standards in the recipient State. However, the Commissioner strongly recommends that this approach not be taken, as if the Commissioner takes a different view of the protections afforded by the recipient State, a prohibition notice may issue, thereby preventing the transfer from going ahead.

4.3.8.4 *The safe harbour principles*

There are a number of ways to transfer data to 'unapproved' states. If the controller is seeking to transfer the data to the US, then it may be wise to ascertain if the data importer has subscribed to the 'Safe Harbour Principles' and, if they have not so subscribed, encourage them to do so. The Safe Harbour scheme allows US companies to voluntarily adopt standards of data protection comparable to those in the EU. This scheme is not available to all industries. For example, telecoms and financial services are not covered by the scheme. The scheme itself is actually administered by the US Department of Commerce. Thus, if a company breaches the principles, enforcement action will be taken by the US Federal Trade Commission and not by EU bodies or national data protection authorities. Data subjects suffering prejudice have the right to seek redress under the adjudication regime chosen by the participant under the scheme.

4.3.8.5 *Model contracts*

When exporting to a state other than the US, or to a US controller which is not a member of the Safe Harbour Scheme, the exporter may be able to provide an adequate level of legal protection by means of a special EU-approved model contract. These offer a straightforward means for data controllers to comply with their obligation to ensure 'adequate protection' for personal data transferred outside of the EEA. However, it should be noted that the EU does not allow the parties to vary the model contractual clauses on substantive issues, and as such some have criticised these clauses as being too rigid. There are two types of contracts, one for data controller to data controller transfers and another for data controller to data processor transfers.

Data controller to data controller contracts require a data exporter to ensure that, prior to transfer, the processing of the data has been done according to applicable law. Restrictions are imposed on the manner in which the data importer can process the data. Moreover, the data importer must submit their data protection facilities for audit by the data exporter or as may be required by the data protection authorities. If a breach results in a data subject suffering damages both the data importer and the data exporter are jointly and severally liable for the breach unless both parties can prove that neither of them is responsible. It should be noted that under these clauses, the data subject is a third party beneficiary who can enforce the terms of the contract.

Data controller to data processor contracts again require the data exporter/controller to ensure that the processing of the personal data, prior to transfer, has been done in accordance with applicable law. The data controller is also required to ensure that the data processor has adequate technical and organisational measures in place to protect the personal data. The data importer/processor must ensure that adequate technical and organisational security measures are in place to protect the data. Furthermore, they are only permitted to process the data according to the applicable law and pursuant to instructions they received from the data controller. In contrast to the data controller to data controller contracts, the data controller is solely liable for any breach occasioning damage to the data subject, regardless of who is at fault. The data processor will only assume liability where the controller has been declared bankrupt, disappeared factually or ceased to exist.

As noted above, these model clauses were seen by many as too rigid, especially having regard to the manner in which they apportioned liability in the event of a breach. This has led to the development of 'Alternative Model Clauses'. Under these clauses each party is liable for its own breach. However, it should be noted these alternative provisions also allow national data protection authorities to suspend the data flow under a number of circumstances (under the original Model Clauses, the national authorities could only intervene where there was evidence that the transfer would create an imminent risk of great harm to the data subject).

4.3.8.6 *Binding corporate rules*

If the data is being transferred within a multinational corporation with operations both inside and outside the EEA, the use of Binding Corporate Rules (BCRs) may offer an alternative mechanism for international transfers within the organisation. These rules are legally enforceable data protection codes of practice. Their main advantage is that they can be drafted to meet the unique cultural business and organisational requirements of the organisation. It is the organisation, and not the regulator, that determines how the system operates. The regulator ensures that EU data protection standards have been adopted across the organisation; however, how exactly organisation achieves these standards is a matter for its own discretion. The ongoing nature of BCRs also makes them appealing to multinationals as it removes the need to execute model contracts on an *ad hoc* basis every time a personal data transfer needs to be made.

The use of BCRs has been gaining momentum since the US-based General Electric Company (GE) saw its BCRs approved by the UK's data protection authority, the Information Commissioner's Office, in December 2005. GE's BCRs set down minimum standards with regard to the protection of information about GE employees. These standards must be applied worldwide by all parts of the GE group. In June 2007, Philips adopted a BCRs scheme to enable it to share personal information about its clients and customers across the organisation. BCRs have also been adopted by Daimler Chrysler and the Bank Austria Creditanstalt. It should be noted that BCRs are not without their difficulties, as data protection requirements are complex and can very between jurisdictions. Thus, corporations wishing to use BCRs must submit their proposed rules to the data protection authority of each state from which they wish to transfer the data.

The BCR must set out the data protection requirements that are to be in place and how these will be achieved, the manner in which the BCRs can be amended, how complaints are to be handled and how compensation shall be provided in the event of a breach. BCRs must be legally binding. This means that the BCRs are binding on all members of the organisation and may be enforced by data subjects who are third party beneficiaries. The actual legal manner in which the BCR is made binding can vary but the most common approach would be to simply execute relevant contracts to that effect. When designing and considering BCRs, practitioners should have regard to their multinational character and issues of conflicts of law which may arise as a result. Indeed the Commission's Article 29 Data Protection Working Party (WP 74) has noted that the legal enforcement of unilateral commitments or contracts is extremely complex and may involve a disproportionate effort from data subjects.

4.3.8.7 *Other derogations and exceptions*

Finally, it should be noted that s 11(4) of the Act sets down certain derogations and exceptions which will allow the data transfer to go ahead notwithstanding the fact that protection to be afforded to that data cannot be guaranteed by law. The Commissioner recommends that these exceptions be seen as final options which should only be used when the above procedures are not truly practical and/or feasible.

These exceptions include where the data subject has consented to the transfer, where the transfer is necessary for the performance of a contract between the data subject and the data controller, where the transfer is necessary for reasons of public interest or under some international obligation of the State or where the transfer is necessary in order to prevent personal injury or damage to the health of the data subject.

These exceptions tend to be interpreted quite strictly. Consent in this context refers to 'unambiguous consent;' this consent must be freely given and informed. The UK's Information Commissioner's Office (ICO Guidance 1) has suggested that consent is only sufficient where the individual knows and understands what he is agreeing to, gives consent explicitly and freely, has been told the reasons for the transfer and, if possible, the countries involved and is made aware of the particular risks to the personal data which may be caused by the transfer. This approach was recently confirmed by the EU Commission's Article 29 Working Party in its report on the SWIFT Controversy (Opinion Number 10/2006).

4.3.8.8 *The SWIFT controversy*

Light has been recently thrown on the operation of these data protection rules by the numerous reports resulting from the recent controversy surrounding SWIFT, a Belgian financial messaging service which facilitates monetary transfers. SWIFT is a key part of the international financial infrastructure and is used by over 7,800 financial institutions. At the material time, SWIFT stored its messages in two operation centres, one in the EEA and one in the US. The messages contained personal information such as the name of the payer and the payee. Following the terrorist attacks of September 2001 the US Department of the Treasury issued subpoenas requiring SWIFT to provide access to the message information held in the US. SWIFT complied with the request. This led to an investigation by the Belgian Privacy Protection Commissioner, the Article 29 Working Party and the European Data Protection Supervisor.

The Belgian report concluded that SWIFT had made an error of judgment in providing the information to the US authorities and suggested that in circumstances such as this the company should have informed European authorities of the situation, allowing a solution to be worked out at an international level. The report noted the international precedent set by the Passenger Name Record (PNR) situation, where such a compromise was worked out diplomatically, and suggested that this is the correct approach to be taken in future cases. The European Data Protection Supervisor agreed with, and supported, the findings reached by the Belgian authorities.

The Article 29 Working Party report rejected SWIFT's argument that the consent of the data subject had been obtained. SWIFT's argument that the transfer was necessary for the performance of a contract was similarly rejected. The working party noted that in order to sustain such an argument a necessity test must be satisfied: there must be a substantial connection between the data subject's interest and the performance of the contract. The report went on to reject the argument that the transfers were needed on public interest grounds. This exception would apply only to public interest issues within the EEA, not a state outside the EEA. The report also noted that the financial institutions which use SWIFT had, as data controllers, a legal obligation to ensure that SWIFT fully complies with data protection law to ensure the protection of their clients.

4.3.9 Registration with the Data Protection Commissioner

Section 16(1) of the Act, as amended by the 2003 Act, contains a requirement for data controllers and data processors to register with the Data Protection Commissioner. The Data Protection Register is established and maintained by the Data Protection Commissioner.

Prior to 1 October 2007, there was no general obligation on data controllers and processors to register. Rather, data controllers and processors were only required to register if they fell into one or more express categories. Section 16 of the Act, as amended by the 2003 Act and which was commenced from 1 October 2007, takes a very different approach to the original section 16. From that date, the legislation imposes a far more extensive obligation for processors and controllers to register. Registration is now compulsory where a data controller holds or processes personal data on computer and is:

- a government body or public authority;
- a bank, financial or credit institution;
- an insurance undertaking (not including brokers);
- a person whose business consists wholly or mainly in direct marketing;
- a person whose business consists wholly or mainly in providing credit references;
- a persons whose business consists wholly or mainly in collecting debts;
- an internet access provider;
- a telecommunications network or service provider;
- a person processing personal data related to mental or physical health (e.g. a health professional);
- a person processing genetic data;
- a person whose business consists of processing personal data for supply to others, other than for journalistic, literary or artistic purposes.

Many organisations which previously were required to register, such as not-for-profit organisations, elected representatives, educational institutions and lawyers, are no longer required to do so, unless they also fall under a category which is required to register. However, any data controller or data processor who is required to register but who fails to do so is guilty of an offence. Practitioners should thus take great care when advising in this area, and consider the Acts alongside the Data Protection Act 1988 (Section 16(1)) Regulations 2007, as well as any orders relating to registration made by the Minister for Justice, Equality and Law Reform or the Data Protection Commissioner.

Members of the public can inspect the Register free of charge and may copy entries in the Register. The Register can also be searched on the Commissioner's website. Applications for registration are made in writing to the Commissioner using application forms supplied by the Commissioner, which are available on the Commissioner's website. Registrations last for a period of one year and, at the end of the year, the entry must be renewed or removed from the register.

4.4 The Electronic Communications Regulations 2003

Directive 2002/58/EC on the processing of personal data and the protection of privacy in the electronic communications sector (known as the Communications Data Protection Directive or the CDPD), has been transposed into Irish law as the European Communities (Electronic Communications Networks and Services) (Data Protection and Privacy) Regulations 2003 (SI 535/2003).

This legislation replaces Directive 97/66/EC (the Telecommunications Data Protection Directive). The European Communities (Data Protection and Privacy in Telecommunications) Regulations 2002 which transposed the 1997 Directive into Irish law has been accordingly revoked.

The centrepiece of the 2003 Regulations is Regulation 13, which restricts the ability to use publicly available electronic communication services to send unsolicited communications or to make unsolicited calls for the purpose of direct marketing. In particular, it provides that:

(a) the use of automatic dialling machines, fax, email or SMS (text messaging) for direct marketing to individuals is prohibited, unless the subscriber's consent has been obtained in advance;

(b) the use of email, SMS text messaging, automatic dialing machines or fax for direct marketing to non-natural persons or businesss is prohibited if the subscriber has recorded its objection in the National Directory Database or has informed the sender that it does not consent to such messages;

(c) the making of telephone calls for direct marketing to the line of a subscriber is prohibited if the subscriber has recorded its objection in the National Directory Database or has informed the sender that it does not consent to such messages.

A marketer who acts in breach of these provisions commits an offence and is liable to be prosecuted by the Commissioner. The first prosecution of this sort saw 4 A's Fortune Limited convicted of violating Regulation 13(1)(b) (Commissioner Case Study 11 of 2005). Here, the company called certain mobile phone numbers briefly, with the intention that the recipients would not have adequate time to answer. The recipient's phone would record a 'missed call'. When the recipient dialled this number a pre-recorded message was played in which callers were invited to phone a premium rate number in order to avail of an offer to claim €50 credit for use in 4 A's Fortune game. Under the legislation a marketer faces a potential fine of up to €3,000 per message sent. However, in this case a fine of €300 per message sent plus costs of €1,000 was handed down. What is interesting is that over 165,000 calls were made, but prosecutions were only entered on foot of five of these. The Commissioner has pointed out that prosecutions can only be made where there is no consent for the recipient to receive such call. Therefore, prosecutions can only be made in relation to specific complaints from individuals.

Marketers should be advised to take care to ensure that a purported consent for the purposes of Regulation 13 is properly given. This is an issue especially for promotions done in public houses and nightclubs. As the Commissioner has wryly noted, 'because of the nature of [these] venue[s] certain patrons might not be in a proper condition to give consent to the use of their personal data (Commissioner Case Study 12 of 2005).'

4.5 The Data Retention Directive 2006

Directive 2006/24/EC on the retention of data generated or processed in connection with the provision of publicly available electronic communication services (known as the Data Retention Directive) requires the providers of publicly available electronic communications services to retain traffic and location data on both legal and natural persons and any related data necessary to identify the subscriber or related user. It does not require the retention of the actual content of electronic communications. The stated purpose of this directive is to assist in the investigation, detection and prosecution of serious crime. This data must be retained for between six months and two years and, during this period, must be available to the competent national authorities in specific cases. On the expiry of the data retention period the retained data must be destroyed.

The retained data is subject to pre-existing data protection law. The Directive also lays down certain minimum security principles that should be followed to secure the data. The retained data must be subject to the same security and protection as data on the network, provision must be made to protect the data against unlawful or accidental destruction, loss or alteration or unauthorised storage processing access or disclosure. Furthermore, only specially authorised personnel are permitted to have access to the data.

This Directive should be operable as part of the laws of the Member States by 15 September 2007. However, the Irish government has launched a challenge to the ECJ challenging the legal base for the enactment of the Directive which may delay its transposition into Irish law. The Directive is also being challenged in the Irish courts by Digital Rights Ireland Limited, an Irish civil liberties organisation.

4.6 Privacy and data protection in the workplace

4.6.1 Data protection standards in the workplace

Employers have a considerable and legitimate interest in monitoring their employees' internet and email usage in the workplace. Not only is the internet a business resource paid for by the employer, but an employer can be exposed to various types of legal liability as a result of online misconduct by their employees, including, but not limited to, copyright infringement, inadvertent contracts, harassment, defamation, and, in extreme cases, vicarious liability for child pornography (s 9(1) Child Trafficking and Pornography Acts 1998–2004).

Despite these risks to employers, no special data protection or privacy regime exists in relation to the workplace; employees are entitled to the full protection of the Data Protection Acts in an employment context. Specifically, the collection, use or storage of information about workers, the monitoring of email or internet access or their surveillance by video cameras involves the processing of personal data and, as such, data protection law applies to the processing. The online activities of employees gain further protection by virtue of s 98(1) of the Postal and Telecommunications Services Act 1983. This provides, *inter alia*, that any person who:

  (a) intercepts or attempts to intercept; or
  (b) authorises, suffers or permits another person to intercept; or
  (c) does anything that will enable him or another person to intercept

telecommunications messages being transmitted [by a licensed telecommunications operator] or who discloses the existence, substance or purport of any such message which has been intercepted or uses for any purpose any information obtained from any such message, shall be guilty of an offence.

'Telecommunication message' is not defined in the Act. However, having regard to s 6 of the Interpretation Act 2005, which requires the court, when interpreting a statute, to have regard to, *inter alia*, changes in technology, it seems highly probable that email would be seen as falling under the scope of the s 98(1).

The effect of these provisions is to rule out any covert or surreptitious monitoring by an employer of their employees' email or internet usage except in certain narrowly defined situations, particularly the prevention, detection and investigation of criminal offences (s 5(1) of the Data Protection Act 1988, as amended).

It should be further noted that any covert monitoring of an employee would not only amount to a breach of these statutory provisions, but could also amount to a breach of the ECHR. In *Copland v UK* [2007] ECHR 253 the European Court of Human Rights found that the UK, the applicant's employer, had violated her right to respect for her private life and correspondence under Article 8 of the Convention by monitoring her telephone calls, email, correspondence and internet use in the workplace. The monitoring was done covertly without the applicant's knowledge or consent.

It should be noted that the court did accept that monitoring employees communications at the place of work could be seen as permissible and 'necessary in a democratic society' in certain situations in pursuit of a legitimate aim. However, the court declined to specify the circumstances where it would be permissible to do so.

4.6.2 Acceptable usage policies

In practice, the conflict between employees' privacy and data protection rights and employers' business and legal interests is solved by means of Acceptable email and Internet Usage Policies.

In these policy documents the employer sets out a readily accessible, clear and accurate statement of company policy regarding the use, confidentiality and monitoring of email and internet facilities in the workplace. Employees must consent to these policies in advance. This is generally done by making observance of the company policy a term of each employee's contract of employment. Alternatively each employee may be required to sign a document stating that they have been provided with, read, understood and accepted the company's email and internet policy.

The limitation of the employee's right to privacy set down by the policy should be proportionate to the likely damage to the employer's legitimate interests. The Data Protection Commissioner has stated that proportionality in this context means that 'the processing of personal data, in view of its specific purpose, should be appropriate and be the minimum necessary to achieve the stated purpose and that these be weighed against the intrusion on the employees' privacy rights (Commissioner Case Study 1 of 2005).' It appears that what is proportional will greatly turn on the facts of the individual case. In one case before the Commissioner, the use of a biometric time keeping, attendance and access system was held to be a proportionate response to security concerns in a public institution with valuable public assets under its control (Commissioner Case Study 1 of 2005). In a situation where there such security concerns were not present it is debatable if the use of such a biometric system would be considered proportionate.

The Article 29 Working Group (Working Paper 55) suggests that the usage policy should contain the following information:

- the extent to which company facilities can be used for private use;
- the reasons and purposes for the surveillance;
- the details of any surveillance measures taken;
- details of any enforcement procedures outlining how and when workers will be notified of breaches of internal policies and be given the opportunity to respond to any claims against them.

If an employer wishes to change from a relaxed regime in which use of email for private purposes is tolerated to a more restrictive regime involving monitoring by an employer, the Commissioner advises that the employer should notify employees in advance of the change in policy, and further allow an opportunity to employees to delete any such material from the employer's email system *(Annual Report of the Data Protection Commissioner,* 1999, at 33).

CHAPTER 5

IT CONTRACTS

Philip Nolan & Rossa McMahon

5.1 Introduction

According to IDA Ireland, over 800 software companies operate in Ireland, employing around 32,000 people and contributing to 10% of Ireland's exports. Leading US and European software companies have established large operations in Ireland over recent decades and have located their research and development functions in Ireland, attracted by the availability of a highly skilled workforce and the attractive corporation tax rates. As a result of the significant presence and influence of the leading US and European software companies in Ireland, indigenous Irish companies have also become established and leading players in the international software marketplace over the last few years.

The development of the Irish software industry has necessitated the development of a specialist area of law dealing with software licensing, IT law, internet law, telecommunications law and other related areas. This chapter will focus on software licensing law in particular. Drawing on existing principles of Irish contract law and Irish copyright law, software licensing has evolved over recent years into a discrete area of law. However, the rules governing software licensing in Ireland continue to be underpinned by a series of key legal principles.

This chapter is divided into three components. First, this chapter considers a number of preliminary issues which must be understood in order to fully comprehend the mechanics of a software licence agreement. Secondly, this chapter will examine some of the key legal principles which underpin software licensing in Ireland. Thirdly, this chapter shall take a practical look at the key components of a software licence agreement.

5.2 Preliminary issues

5.2.1 What is software?

Software or computer programs consist of a set of statements or instructions used directly or indirectly in a device in order to bring about a certain result. It is a 'recipe' to guide electronic circuitry to perform complex sequences of operations.

From the corporate user's point of view, software is whatever is necessary to produce, in conjunction with hardware and the user's business data, the results which the user requires from a computer system.

Software is usually written by a programmer in the form of 'source code'. This consists of a sequence of symbolic statements in a computer language. However, in order to be used in a computer, source code must be translated into 'object code' that can be directly used to govern operations in a computer.

5.2.2 What is a software licensing agreement?

A software licensing agreement is an agreement that authorises someone to do something with software which would otherwise be an infringement of copyright. The party that grants this authorisation is known as the licensor and the recipient of this grant is known as the licensee. The crucial distinction between a Software Sale Agreement, which is often referred to as a Software Assignment Agreement and a Software Licensing Agreement is that the former passes title in the software while the latter does not.

5.2.3 Why is software licensed and not sold?

Generally, software is licensed rather than sold in order to maximise profits and return on the resources invested in developing the software. When software is sold or assigned the legal title in the software passes to a third party, and therefore, the proprietary rights in the software move to a third party, making it impossible for the original developer to continue to deal in the software or sell it for profit. By merely granting a licence to a user to use the software and by placing various restrictions on that licence, the software developer is able to control the use of the product.

5.2.4 Difficulties with the software licence concept

Depending on the terms and conditions of a software licence, there is occasionally a risk that a software licence may be interpreted by the courts as effectively amounting to a sale or assignment of the software. Such an interpretation of a software licence can lead to numerous difficulties from the licensor's perspective. First, this can mean that the ownership of software may unintentionally transfer under such an Agreement. Secondly, since the licence is deemed to be a sale of a proprietary item, a charge to stamp duty may also arise.

In order to minimise the risk of a court adopting such an interpretation, the terms 'sale', 'purchase' and/ or 'purchaser' and related terms should generally be avoided in a software licence agreement. Additionally, the grant of a licence to use software in perpetuity may, depending on the other circumstances of the Agreement, also lead a court to infer that a so-called software licence amounts to a software sale agreement. The Irish courts' commitment to considering the substance of a legal agreement over the form of a legal agreement (which is evident from the law distinguishing a lease from a licence) means that the label attributed to a software agreement is less important than the actual substance of the agreement in this regard.

5.2.5 Types of software licensing agreements

There are numerous different types of software licence agreements. The following is a brief (and non-exhaustive) description of some of the more popular types of software licence agreements.

5.2.5.1 *Bespoke software licence agreements*

This type of licence agreement is entered into between the licensor and the licensee when the licensee commissions a software developer to design and develop a particular piece of software to carry out a particular function or functions. Unlike 'off-the-shelf' or packaged software, these agreements are normally individually negotiated between the parties since certain parts of the agreement (in particular, the description of the bespoke software) will be unique to the particular Agreement.

5.2.5.2 *Shrink-wrap licence agreements*

'Off-the-shelf' or packaged software is commonly sold by way of shrink-wrap licence agreements. Normally this involves software being distributed on a CD-ROM which is wrapped in a document containing the terms and conditions of the licence agreements. The important differences between a shrink-wrap licence agreement and a signed bespoke licence agreement is that shrink-wrap agreements are generally unsigned and are not normally individually negotiated between the parties. The shrink-wrap licence agreement's terms and conditions are normally the standard terms and conditions of licence of the licensor. Invariably, shrink-wrap licence agreements are more susceptible to being challenged than a signed software licence agreement since recipients of the software may occasionally argue that the terms and conditions contained on the wrapping were not properly incorporated into the software contract.

The main difficulty of such licences from an enforceability perspective is that they generally cannot be read prior to purchase.

5.2.5.3 *Click-wrap licence agreements*

There are generally two types of click-wrap licence agreements. First, often when software programs are downloaded from the internet, the user is often required to read the terms and conditions of the software licence and click 'I agree' on a box which appears at the end of the terms and conditions of the licence. The second type of click-wrap licence is where the licence is an intrinsic part of the purchased software and during the installation process a similar box will open asking the user to click 'I agree' after the user has scrolled through the terms and conditions of the licence. As with shrink-wrap licences mentioned above, click-wrap licences are more susceptible to challenge than Software Licence Agreements which are signed prior to the transfer of software. Browse-wrap agreements, under which the user of a website or software is deemed to have accepted the terms of an agreement by using that website, are similarly susceptible to challenge.

5.2.5.4 *Open-source licence agreements*

The concept of open-source software licensing is becoming increasingly popular. Open-source software licensing is a far less restricted model for the licensing of software than the traditional more restrictive licences. A licensor of open-source software is required to grant users various rights in the software before the licensor can be certified as 'open-source'. Applications such as the Linux operating system, the OpenOffice.org productivity suite and the Firefox web browser have become extremely popular open-source software solutions.

Open-source software is unique in that licensees are guaranteed certain rights including:

- the right to make copies of the program and to distribute those copies;
- the right to have access to the software's source code which enables licensees to further develop the software solution; and
- the right to make improvements to the program.

Open-source software licensing enables various individuals and companies to collaborate in developing software. In order to become a supplier of open-source software the licence must not restrain the licensee from selling or giving away the licensed software. Additionally, any open-source licence must allow for modifications and derived works to be made by the licensee and must allow them to be distributed under the same terms as the licence of the original software. Open-source software should not contain restrictions on the types of users of the software or the types of products for which the software might be used.

5.2.5.5 *Software escrow agreements*

The term 'escrow' refers to the holding on deposit by a third party of confidential material on certain terms as to its release or control and use. Software escrow agreements are occasionally put in place in conjunction with software licence agreements in order to protect the licensee. Generally, when software is licensed to users, the users do not receive a copy of the source code of the software. Without the source code, the users of the software may be able to use the software but are often unable to rectify the software in the event of problems or bugs arising in relation to the software. Typically, this does not pose a problem for the software user since the software supplier often supplies a support and maintenance service after the original licence of the software. Thus, the supplier of the software will often provide free upgrades and 'bug fixes' for its software.

Often, escrow agreements are designed to deal with a situation where a supplier of the software ceases to or becomes unable to supply support and maintenance services (for example, in the event of a liquidation of a corporate software supplier). Essentially, it provides that the source code of the software will be placed in escrow at the time when the software is originally licensed. A software escrow agreement normally involves the licensor, the licensee and the third party who holds the software in escrow. This agreement will normally provide that in the event of certain circumstances arising, such as the bankruptcy or liquidation of the licensor, then the licensee will be entitled to gain access to the source code for particular purposes.

Software escrow agreements can be categorised as software licence agreements since they typically require the software licensor to transfer by way of licence a copy of the source code to the software being licensed to the escrow service provider. This escrow service provider will hold a copy of this source code and will only release it to the licensee in the event of a bankruptcy or liquidation of the licensor or in the event of a failure by the licensor to support and maintain the licensed software or in accordance with any other release events described in the escrow agreement.

5.2.5.6 *Turnkey software agreement*

Often when complex software solutions are being commissioned by companies or institutions (possibly in conjunction with the purchase of hardware), the parties will enter into a turnkey software agreement or an integrated turnkey hardware and software agreement. These agreements break the process of supplying software down into a number of phases and the successful completion of each phase by the software supplier is a condition precedent to the parties proceeding to the subsequent phase of the agreement.

A typical turnkey software agreement might contain an initial phase where the software supplier does a study of the requirements of the proposed purchaser of the software solution. The second phase might entail the supplier designing and testing a prototype of the required software solution. In technical terms, this is often described as the 'proof of concept' procedure. In the event of the successful testing of the prototype software solution, the parties might then proceed to the third phase which involves the software supplier developing the comprehensive software solution, and the final phase of a typical turnkey project normally entails the installation, implementation and testing of the software solution.

5.3 Legal principles that underpin software licensing

5.3.1 Principles of contract law

The supply of software will always involve at least one contract between the supplier and the end user. However, there may be more than one contract involved in situations where the creator and licensor of the software licenses the software to a supplier who in turn sub-licenses it to the end user. Thus, the fundamental rules of contract law will invariably apply to a software licence agreement. These include the common law rules concerning the valid incorporation of the terms and conditions of an agreement into a binding contract between the parties. For this reason shrink-wrap, click-wrap and browse-wrap licences are occasionally challenged on the basis that the terms and conditions contained in such licences are not properly incorporated into the contractual relationships.

In terms of regulated contract law, the Irish sale of goods legislation (ie the Sale of Goods Act 1893 and the Sale of Goods and Supply of Services Act 1980) are also of note in the context of software licensing. Without a carefully worded contract, various terms and conditions may be implied into the software licence agreement between the parties as a result of the sale of goods legislation.

In the event that the software licence agreement is between non-consumers (what is commonly referred to as a business-to-business or B2B Agreement), then it is possible to contract out of most of the terms and conditions implied by the sale of goods legislation.

The vexed question as to whether the sale of software is the sale of a good or the supply of a service has not been addressed in the Irish courts to date. Interestingly, the Consumer Protection Act 2007, which in part implements Directive 2005/29/EC on unfair commercial practices into Irish law, at a stroke includes 'computer software' in the definition of 'goods' in s 2(1). This should not necessarily be taken as the final word on the categorisation of software, however, as consumer law will always tend toward greater protection for the consumer and, in these circumstances, it will generally make sense for consumer software to be considered a good. In addition, it has been argued by certain commentators that digital content suppliers should assume that the European Communities (Protection of Consumers in Respect of Contracts made by means of Distance Communication) Regulations 2001 apply to them notwithstanding the uncertainty over the goods/service nature of software, as courts tend to interpret consumer protection measures generously in favour of the consumer.

Thus, it is advised that B2B Software Licence Agreements entered into in Ireland should explicitly exclude the provisions of the sale of goods legislation which imply terms into contracts for the sale of goods (ie ss 13, 14 and 15 of the 1893 Act) and the implied terms concerning the supply of services (ie s 39 of the 1980 Act) when one is acting for the supplier or licensor of the software.

The English Court of Appeal has considered the issue as to whether licensing of software is the sale of a good or the supply of a service in the case of *St Albans City and District Council v International Computers Ltd* [1996] All ER 481. In that case, the court indicated that, where software was supplied on disks, then the actual disks used to carry the software were to be treated as goods within the meaning of the sale of goods legislation whereas the actual computer programs contained on the disks were not to be treated as goods.

Thus, when software is downloaded from the internet for a fee or transferred by a supplier via email to an end user rather than sold on a CD-ROM then such a contract might be regarded as a contract for the supply of services as opposed to a contract for sale. However, this position has not been tested yet in the Irish courts, and it is by no means clear if *St Albans* would be followed in this jurisdiction. As Green and Saidov (JBL, 2007, Mar 161-181) point out, there is no convincing reason why software should be excluded from the statutory protection afforded to other items subject to sales. They further argue that software actually has a tangible, corporeal form (ie bits on a CD's surface, magnetic switches on a hard drive or a series of electrical pulses transmitted through circuitry) and that it should consequently be seen as a 'good'.

Even if the Irish courts acted in accordance with the *St Albans* case, provisions such as s 39 of the Sale of Goods and Supply of Services Act 1980 would still be of relevance since it would still imply certain conditions into a software licence agreement concerning the quality of the services. As mentioned above, the parties may agree to exclude the application of such statutorily implied terms.

In this context, it should be noted that any term purporting to exempt a party from the terms implied by the sale of goods legislation (except a term purporting to contract out of s

39 of the Sale of Goods and Supply of Services Act 1980) shall be void where the buyer deals as a consumer. However, in most other cases, a term contracting out of the sale of goods legislation may be enforceable to the extent that such contracting out is shown to be fair and reasonable.

5.3.2 Principles of intellectual property law

5.3.2.1 *Copyright law*

At the core of every software licence agreement is the concept of copyright. Under the Copyright and Related Rights Act 2000 (the 2000 Act), the developer of a computer program shall have a copyright in such a program which shall subsist until 70 years after the death of the programmer (s 24 (1) of the Act). The Copyright and Related Rights Act 2000 specifically identifies computer programs as being beneficiaries of copyright protection. Thus, every instance of software licensing entails the licensing of a copyright.

In essence, the software owner's copyright is a right to prevent anyone from copying their software without paying something for it. Since the use of software requires copying to occur, then any user of software must have permission to use and thereby copy such software. A software licence agreement authorises someone to do something with software which would otherwise be an infringement of copyright.

The 2000 Act provides that the copyright in a computer program shall lie with the author who is defined as 'the person who creates the work', or in the case of a program which is computer generated, the person who undertakes the necessary arranging for the creation of the work.

Importantly, the 2000 Act goes on to provide that the copyright in computer software does not extend to the ideas and principles underlying any element of a work. In other words, only the physical expression of the work is protected. In the UK case of *Navitaire Inc v Easyjet Airline Company and BulletProof Technologies Inc* [2004] EWHC 1725 (Ch) the High Court rejected protection for the 'business logic' behind a software package, where the alleged infringer had not literally copied the source code but had reproduced its functionality. The protection sought essentially amounted to protection for the 'look and feel' of the software package. It remains to be seen whether the Irish courts would follow a similar line of reasoning, but such a conclusion is possible given the lack of protection for the ideas and principles or procedures and methods of operation underlying the work.

The owner and author of a computer program possesses a number of exclusive rights under the 2000 Act. These include the rights to:

- copy the program;
- make the program available to the public;
- make an adaptation of the program; and
- authorise or license others to use in whole or in part any part of the computer program.

Sections 80–82 of the 2000 Act specify certain acts which may be performed by lawful users of a computer program. These permitted acts include the right of a lawful user to make a back-up copy of the program (s 80 of the 2000 Act). Therefore, a person who purchases a piece of software will have a statutory right to make a copy of software and store such copy in case the original copy is damaged or destroyed.

The 2000 Act goes on to provide that it is not an infringement for a licensee of software to translate, adapt, arrange or alter a computer program and to copy such, where these acts are necessary to achieve interoperability of an independently created program with another program. However, any such copying, translating, adapting or arranging must only occur in order to achieve interoperability (s 81 of the 2000 Act). In other words, section 81 entitles a lawful licensee of a computer program to de-compile a program to gain knowledge of its working and, in particular, of its interfaces so that compatible non-infringing products such as applications, programs and peripheral devices can be used in conjunction with the licensed software.

Section 82 of the Act goes on to provide that licensed users of software shall also have the right to translate, adapt, arrange or alter the software program in order to correct any errors in the software.

The 2000 Act has created a series of penalties for misusing software. They include the following:

- the deliberate or negligent misuse of software is a criminal offence (s 140);
- the courts have the power to order that a copy of a work (including software), the author of which knew or had reason to believe was an infringing copy, be delivered up to the copyright owner (s 142);
- a judge of the District Court has the power to issue a warrant authorising a member of An Garda Síochána to enter and search the premises specified in the warrant, if the District Judge has reason to suspect that an offence under s 140 has been or is about to be committed (s 143).

A copyright owner will also of course be free to pursue civil remedies in respect of alleged software piracy. Remedies would include injunctive relief to prevent any further use of illegal copies and an account of profits made from illegal use by the defendant of software.

These new tough anti-piracy measures are to be welcomed. The injurious effects of infringing software copyright often extend far beyond the licensor of the software. Software copyright infringement is known to increase exposure to software viruses, corrupt disks and other defective software.

5.3.2.2 *Patents in software*

Despite the fact that computer programs are expressly excluded from patentability (s 9(2) of the Patents Act 1992, implementing Art 52(2) of the European Patents Convention 1973), it should be noted that they are only excluded 'as such', ie in their capacity as computer programs *per se*. But the provision has been interpreted to mean that an invention consisting of a computer program plus something else (eg plus hardware) may be patentable. It is not unusual to obtain a patent in this type of situation for what may be called computer-related inventions. Sometimes, this type of software is known as 'furnace'.

Notwithstanding the express wording of s 9(2) of the Patents Act 1992, certain patents in software have issued from the Irish Patents Office. The European Patents Office (EPO) has issued guidelines concerning the patentability of such inventions. These indicate that a computer-related invention is patentable if the contribution that the invention makes to the known art is of a technical character. The EPO and its Technical Board of Appeal have set out guidelines which help determine patentability. These include the following provisions:

(a) If the alleged invention overcomes a technical problem, it is patentable. In this, some real technical problem must be addressed and overcome.

(b) If what is claimed to be the inventive element (the new contribution) of the alleged invention when separated from the conventional elements of the alleged invention is determined to be technical, the alleged invention is patentable. This test looks at the patent issue not so much from the point of view of what technical problem is overcome but rather from the point of view of what new technical effect is produced by the invention.

The differences between the two tests may be more apparent than real in that both tests, when applied, are likely to lead to the same outcome.

Unsuccessful attempts have been made to harmonise the patenting of software at European level. The Commission and Council proposed a scheme under which a 'computer aided invention' would be patentable where it made an inventive step which amount to a technical contribution which was susceptible to industrial application (Council Common Position 20/2005). However, this scheme was rejected by the Parliament. Although there has been continuing debate about the desirability or otherwise of Europe-wide software patents, further legislative reform in this area does not appear to be forthcoming.

5.3.3 Trademarks

Trademarks are applicable to software products in the same way that they applicable to other goods and services.

Therefore, in drafting a software licence agreement, it is important to broadly define the intellectual property rights in the software to include any registered or unregistered trademarks in such software. Thus, the licensee of the software will acquire a limited licence to use the registered trademark which might form part of the software program being licensed.

5.3.4 Database rights

Part V of the Copyright and Related Rights Act 2000 implements the provisions of EC Directive 96/9 on the legal protection of databases. These new provisions create a new type of intellectual property rights known as 'database rights', which aim to protect an individual's investment in a database. Essentially, this database right is a right to prevent unlawful extraction of data from a database. Thus, an electronic database generated by computer software may benefit from at least two types of intellectual property rights, ie the contents of the database may be protected by copyright while the creation of the database itself may be protected by a database right.

5.4 Other relevant legal principles

Needless to say, numerous other areas of law may impact upon the licensing of software. This chapter does not propose to exhaustively analyse every type of law which might have an effect on a software licence. However, it is important to note that there exists a significant body of consumer protection legislation, which may be of importance in drafting or reviewing software licences where one or more of the parties to the software licence agreement is a consumer. In particular, the following might be noted.

5.4.1 The European Communities (Unfair Terms in Consumer Contracts) Regulations 1995 (SI 27/1995)

The European Communities (Unfair Terms in Consumer Contracts) Regulations 1995 provide that unfair terms in consumer contracts shall not be binding on the consumer. In addition to defining what constitutes an unfair term, Schedule 3 to the 1995 Regulations contains many examples of unfair terms. Thus, in drafting or reviewing any consumer software licence agreement, it is important to take into account the 1995 Regulations and, in particular, to check the examples of unfair terms contained in Schedule 3 to the 1995 Regulations against the clauses contained in the consumer software licence agreement in order to determine whether any of the last-mentioned clauses might be deemed to be unfair.

5.4.2 European Communities (Protection of Consumers in Respect of Contracts Made by Means of Distance Communication) Regulations 2001 (SI 207/2001)

The European Communities (Protection of Consumers in Respect of Contracts Made by Means of Distance Communication) Regulations 2001 apply to consumer contracts which have been entered into between the parties where the parties to the contracts did not meet face to face. Without going into too much detail, it should be noted that in the event that software is distributed via some type of distance selling model (eg through online sales), then it is possible that these Regulations will apply to such a sale. This means that the contracts between the licensor and the licensee will have to comply with certain important requirements set out in the Distance Selling Regulations. However, there are certain exceptions to the Distance Selling Regulations in relation to the sale of certain types of software. Thus, these Regulations will have to be carefully considered in order to ascertain their application to a consumer software licence agreement.

5.4.3 Export control and the Wassenaar Arrangement

Ireland has been attracting high technology companies, including software design companies, for a number of years. Generally, there are no legal restrictions on the establishment of design and manufacture facilities for encryption-related software in Ireland. However, encryption products and software are regarded by some as akin to military products due to the high degree of security which they can provide for many types of communications and information systems. Consequently, a number of countries, spearheaded by the US, have jointly attempted to control the export of certain types of encryption products. As a result of these international efforts to control encryption technology as well as other technology which may be used in a military context, the Wassenaar Arrangement came into existence.

Established in July 1996, the Wassenaar Arrangement is an alliance of 40 countries which maintains unified export controls on conventional arms and dual-use goods (ie goods which have both civilian and military uses) and technologies including computer systems and information security technology. Ireland was one of the founding members of the Wassenaar Arrangement.

The Wassenaar Arrangement is an arrangement and not a treaty and therefore is not directly binding on the 40 states which are party to it. Under the Wassenaar Arrangement, a comprehensive list of military and dual-use products has been compiled, which is updated occasionally. The framework for implementing the Wassenaar Arrangement into EU law is contained in Council Regulation EC/3381/94, and the Irish Government incorporated the first list of dual-use products into Irish law pursuant to this Regulation by passing the Control of Exports Order in 1996. A number of EU Council Decisions have amended the original list of military and dual-use goods which have been applied by the government in implementing Irish export control policy. Regulation EC/3381/94 has been repealed and replaced by Council Regulation EC/1334/2000, which provides for effective control of exports of dual-use items and technology. In this regard, four further pieces of legislation have been introduced, the Control of Exports Order 2000 (SI 300/2000), the European Communities (Control of Exports of Dual-Use Items) Regulations 2000 (SI 317/2000), the European Communities (Control of Exports of Dual-Use Items (Amendment)) Regulations 2002 (SI 512/2002) and the Control of Exports Order 2005 (SI 884/2005). The 2005 Order repealed and replaced the 2000 Order. There have been a number of amendments to Council Regulation EC/1334/2000 to allow for the changes to the list of dual-use products under the Wassenaar Arrangement.

If an exporter, based in any state which is a member of the Wassenaar Arrangement, intends to export any product which appears on the list of military and dual-use products compiled under the Wassenaar Arrangement, then such an exporter will have to comply with that state's export control regime before it may export such a product.

The list of dual-use products subject to the Irish export licensing regime is divided into two categories: dual-use goods which are not highly sensitive and dual-use goods which are highly sensitive. Irish exporters will be required to apply for an export licence when exporting highly sensitive dual-use goods anywhere outside the State or when exporting dual-use goods which are not highly sensitive to destinations outside the European Union and certain exempted countries including Australia, Canada, Japan, New Zealand, Norway, Switzerland, and the US.

Export licences are not required for the movement of dual-use goods which do not come within the category of highly sensitive within the European Union or the exempted countries. The only obligation on exporters in these circumstances is to indicate on the relevant commercial documents that the goods are subject to control if exported outside the European Union. However, such exporters of dual-use goods (not highly sensitive) to other EU Member States must comply with certain notification and record maintenance obligations.

The first time that an exporter sends controlled dual-use goods (not highly sensitive) to an EU country or to one of the exempted countries he must notify the Department of Enterprise, Trade and Employment export licensing unit in writing of his name and the address where his export records may be inspected. This notification must be made before, or within 30 days of, the first such export.

Exporters are also obliged to keep detailed records of transactions concerning the export of controlled dual-use goods. Such records must be kept in respect of all transfers of dual-use goods including non-highly sensitive dual-use goods. They must, in particular, include commercial documents such as invoices, transport and other dispatch documents which enable identification of the description of the goods, the quantity of the goods, the name and address of the exporter and the consignee, and the address of the end-user. Such records must be kept for at least three years from the end of the calendar year in which the export took place.

If, on the other hand, an Irish exporter intends to export dual-use goods which fall into the highly sensitive category anywhere outside Ireland, then he must apply for an export licence irrespective of their destination. Category 5, part 2 of the list of dual-use products is entitled 'information security' and designates products listed therein as highly sensitive. These provisions deal with encryption technology and provide that encryption software and hardware will generally require an export licence where it is being sold outside the State. However, there are a number of specific exemptions contained in this section in addition to a general exemption for encryption technology which meets a number of conditions.

The general exemption is contained in the cryptography note attached to the list of dual-use products and which has recently been amended. According to this general exemption, encryption products are not subject to export control when accompanying their user for their user's personal use. Alternatively, there is also a list of criteria which goods must satisfy to benefit from an exemption. The main criterion is that goods are generally available to the public by being sold, without restriction, from stock at retail selling points.

It should be noted that the limitations on exports discussed above are due to be expanded so as to impose limits on the brokerage of military and dual use goods, including software with military applications. Section 3 of the Control of Exports Act 2008 empowers the Minister to issue orders regulating or prohibiting brokerage as defined by Article 2 of Council Common Position 2003/486/CFSP. Article 2 defined brokerage as 'negotiating or arranging transactions that may involve the transfer of items on the EU Common List of military equipment from a third country to another third country.' Buying, selling or arranging the transfer of such items that are in the broker's ownership from a third country to any other third country will also amount to brokerage.

5.5 Software licence agreements

5.5.1 Introduction

Having considered some preliminary issues concerning software licence agreements and having considered some of the principles that underpin the area of software licensing, it is now appropriate to consider some of the more important terms and conditions which would regularly appear in a software licence agreement. These are discussed below.

5.5.2 Definition of software

It is critical to carefully and precisely define and describe the nature of the software which is being licensed in any software licence agreement. Often this is achieved by setting out a brief description of the software in the definitions section of the agreement, with a more comprehensive and detailed description of the software and its functionality in the schedule to the software licence agreement.

5.5.3 Licence grant

Often the actual grant of the licence by the licensor to the licensee to use the software is the first operative provision of a software licence agreement. The licence grant is one of the most important provisions in any software licence agreement. Since the owner of software in a software licence agreement intends to retain its proprietary rights in the software, it is important that the licence grant does not purport to transfer title in the software and that it consists of merely granting a licence to the licensee permitting the licensee to use the software in accordance with certain terms and conditions. Thus, the grant of a licence in a software licence agreement is normally accompanied by a series of limiting and restricting provisions. These tend to describe the purpose for which the licence is granted and the uses to which the software may be put.

The licence grant might specify limitations and restrictions including the following:

- The exact purpose for which the software is being granted. For example, software may be licensed only for use in a particular project or for use with certain other specified software.
- The period for which the licence is granted should also be specified. The duration of the licence will vary depending on the particular circumstances of the agreement. Occasionally, software is licensed on a perpetual basis which raises certain questions as to whether the software has been licensed or assigned. In this regard, the licensor may consider granting a perpetual licence to the licensee to use the software which is revocable by the licensor in the event that the licensee breaches some of the terms and condition of the licence agreement.
- The licence should also specify whether the software is being granted on an exclusive or on a non-exclusive basis. Generally, with 'off the shelf' or package software, the licence grant will be non-exclusive, since there will be many users of the software. However, with large-scale projects where bespoke software is being developed, the licence granted may be on an exclusive basis. From a drafting perspective, it is critical to specify whether the grant should be exclusive or non-exclusive, since granting a licence on a non-exclusive basis will permit the licensor to continue to grant licence of the software to other third parties, whereas an exclusive grant will prevent the licensor from doing such.

- The nature of the rights being granted to the licensee should also be expressed. For example, in the event that the software licence is a licence to an end-user, then the rights granted might simply be the rights to use a copy of the software, whereas in the event that the software is supplied to a distributor, the rights granted might include rights to distribute and sub-license the software in addition to rights to reproduce copies of the software.
- The licence may also specify limitations on the licensee's actions regarding the licensed software in terms of a territorial restriction or in terms of a particular computer system or location. For example, a distributor might be granted a licence to sub-license the software within the territory of the State while an end-user software licence agreement may restrict the rights of the user to load the software onto a single computer or a single network or a single server.
- The licence should also specify the number of copies of each program which the licensee is allowed to install. A site licence or a company licence may give a user the right to use the software throughout a company's computer network or alternatively, there may be a restriction on the number of users that can use the software.
- The licence should also specify whether it is transferable or not. Normally software licence agreements might provide that the licensed rights cannot be transferred to another party without the licensor's permission.
- The licence should also specify whether the object code or the source code or both is being supplied to the user. When acting for a licensor, you may want to restrict the subject matter of the grant to the object code of the software.
- The licence may also contain a prospective grant of rights of the user to receive and use all updates, enhancements and user documentation which may be supplied by the licensor during the term of the licence.
- It is also quite common for software licensors to prohibit licensees from examining, maintaining or amending the licensed software. In IT terminology the licensor will probably want to prevent the licensee from reverse engineering, de-compiling and/or making copies of the software in order to protect its proprietary rights in the software. However, in light of the provisions of ss 80–82 of the Copyright and Related Rights Act 2000, which are discussed in 3.2.1 above, it is possible that broadly drafted restrictions on de-compiling and copying of software may not be effective. Sections 80–82 of the 2000 Act confer certain rights on software licensees including the right to de-compile software in order to enable it to operate with another program. Similarly, ss 80–82 of the 2000 Act permit lawful end-users of software to make a back-up copy of the software and similarly permit end-users to copy or adopt software in order to correct errors.

5.5.4 Payment pursuant to a software licence agreement

The provisions for payment in a software licence agreement tend to vary depending on the type of licence. In the case of the sale of packaged consumer software, there may be a one-off licence fee payable at commencement. In other cases, such as the sale of packaged business software, there is usually an initial fee but, unlike consumer software, there will often be a recurrent annual fee as well. That fee may be classified as a licence fee or maintenance and/or upgrade fee or both.

5.5.5 Warranties and undertakings

Warranties are statements of fact about the software which the licensor may provide, with untruth constituting breach of contract entitling the aggrieved parties to contractual remedies. Generally, software suppliers are reluctant to provide significant warranties in relation to software and the fitness for the purpose of the software due to the inevitable teething problems associated with the installation and operation of software.

The most common type of warranty which a supplier might provide in a software licence is that the software will conform with its description either in the licence agreement or in the schedule to the agreement. Invariably, such warranties are accompanied by a time period during which the warranty will apply and after which the warranty shall cease to have effect. The utility value of such a warranty from a licensee's perspective depends on the nature of the description of the software. Thus, if the description and the functionality of the software in the schedule to a software licence agreement are quite detailed, then the warranty that such software will conform with its description should be of some value.

5.5.6 Intellectual property, warranty and indemnity

Since software consists of intellectual property rights and in particular copyright, there is always a risk that the licensor may be purporting to license software pursuant to a software licence agreement which the licensor does not properly own. It is important that a software licence agreement contains a warranty from the licensor to the effect that the software being supplied pursuant to the licence agreement does not infringe any third party intellectual property rights.

In order to reinforce this warranty and to increase the levels of legal protection for the licensee, it is also useful to back-up the warranty with an indemnity from the licensor to the effect that the licensor will indemnify the licensee for all costs, expenses, losses, liabilities and claims incurred or suffered by the licensee should any third party successfully take an action against the licensee because the latter's use of the software infringes certain intellectual property rights of that third party. This indemnity provides a measure of security to the licensee when operating the software.

The intellectual property indemnity is not a blanket indemnity and the licensor is entitled to exclude certain activities from the protection of the indemnity. Equally, the licensee may seek to extract a more comprehensive indemnity from the licensor which might cover negligent acts and omissions of the licensor and/or breaches by the licensor of the agreement. This is a matter for negotiation between the parties.

5.5.7 Exclusion and limitation of liability

As with all IT agreements, the allocation of risk between the parties is a critical part of a software licence agreement. Generally, risk is managed in a number of ways and these include the excluding of certain types of liability and the limiting or capping of liability. In particular, it will be important for the licensor of the software to carefully delineate its risk and exposure under the software licence agreement. This is due to the inevitability that software can give rise to errors or bugs and occasionally defective software can cause serious problems to computer systems. Thus, when acting for the licensor of software, it will be critical to ring-fence the risk of the licensor.

Due to the risk of defective software causing knock-on effects to the computer system in which it is installed, a licensor should attempt to exclude its liability for consequential, indirect, incidental and economic loss which might arise from the relevant software.

Due to a number of recent cases in England, the line between direct loss and indirect loss has become somewhat blurred. Therefore, in addition to excluding consequential, indirect, incidental and economic loss, it is also prudent for the licensor to go one step further and to enumerate precisely what the licensor means by these expressions. Thus, if the licensor does not intend to be responsible for any loss of profits of the licensee arising from the supply of defective software, then the licensor should explicitly state that the concept of consequential and indirect loss does not include loss of profits.

In addition to excluding certain types of loss, the licensor may also want to place an overall cap on its liability under the software licence agreement. Since the licensor may successfully limit consequential and indirect loss, the cap on liability normally applies to the direct losses which might flow from a breach of the software licence agreement by the licensor or arising from the licensor's negligence. During negotiations concerning software licence agreements, the actual financial cap on the licensor's aggregate liability under the agreement invariably becomes one of the most contentious issues.

5.5.8 Other issues arising in software licence agreements

The issues discussed above concerning software licence agreements are not exhaustive. They are simply an outline of some of the important components of a software licence agreement, depending on the requirements of the parties to a software licence agreement. The parties may also want the software licence agreement to address issues such as the support and maintenance of the software after its installation, the testing and acceptance of the software, the obligations of the licensor concerning the software (including the obligation to install, test and supply upgrades) and numerous other issues.

CHAPTER 6

COMMUNICATIONS LAW

René Rosenstock

This Chapter describes the sector-specific regulatory regimes governing the electronic communications and postal sectors.

6.1 Introduction and background

Until the 1990s there was no competition in telecommunications in Ireland. Telecom Éireann (as it was then known) enjoyed a statutory monopoly. Although it was managed as a company, Telecom Éireann was ultimately controlled by a Government Minister, who in various incarnations over the years was the equivalent of the current Minister for Communications, Marine and Natural Resources (the Minister).

The opening up of the electronic communications sector to competition has its origins in the programme at EU level to liberalise certain sectors of the economies of EU countries where previously Member States had enjoyed exclusive rights conferred by national laws. Such exclusive rights existed in areas such as transport, energy, postal services and telecommunications. Through the range of legal instruments at its disposal, principally Directives and Regulations made pursuant to Articles 3, 10 and 86 of the Treaty establishing the European Community (the EC Treaty) the EU Commission has sought to facilitate new entry in to these sectors. New entry should introduce competition in the provision of services to consumers, resulting in improved quality and greater variety of services at lower prices. From this, significant collateral benefits flow in terms of the competitiveness of the EU, resulting in sustained and new investment and the stimulation of enterprise in (and beyond) the electronic communications sector.

Ideally, legislators in market oriented economies would wish to be able to rely on market forces alone to achieve these aims and to use competition law to address any market failures associated with monopoly and oligopoly. However, it is generally accepted by policy makers and economists that some utilities networks (or at least parts of them) may constitute what are known as 'natural monopolies'. A natural monopoly may be said to exist where a single firm can serve a market at lower cost than any combination of two or more firms. In essence, natural monopolies exist because of economies of scale and economies of scope. Because of the inherent nature of some sectors, such as electronic communications, specific regulatory intervention is considered necessary to address market failures and to provide the impetus for competitive market conditions.

The public service monopoly environment began to change in the 1980s. In certain Member States, some market reforms started to occur much earlier. In particular, the Conservative government in the United Kingdom under Margaret Thatcher embarked on a radical programme of privatisation of state industries. This resulted in British Telecommunications, for example, becoming a publicly quoted company in 1984. In the same year, following several years of anti-trust proceedings by the United States Federal Government, AT&T (which had never been under State ownership) was split into seven independent regional companies known as the 'Baby Bells'.

Article 86 of the EC Treaty gives the EU Commission power to require the removal of special or exclusive rights granted to undertakings by Member States where other Treaty rules are broken as a result. In the telecommunications sector, the EU Commission decided that allowing certain public enterprises special and exclusive rights to produce telecommunications equipment, or to provide telecommunications services and operate networks, breached competition and internal market rules under the EC Treaty. A succession of Directives abolished these exclusive rights and required Member States to permit the provision of competing services. In addition, Articles 2 and 95 of the EC Treaty provide the basis for harmonising measures in order to further the goal of the Internal Market.

In Ireland, the Office of the Director of Telecommunications Regulation (the ODTR) was established in 1996. Etain Doyle was appointed as the Chairperson of the ODTR on 1 July, 1997 and served until 2002. The ODTR was granted most of the powers previously exercised by the Minister, and it oversaw the initial phases of market liberalisation under a series of EU Directives then in force. In 2002, the Commission for Communications Regulation (ComReg) was established in place of the ODTR.

6.2 Key concepts and terms in electronic communications regulation

In addition to the concepts of liberalisation and natural monopoly already referred to, an appreciation of some other concepts and terms is useful for an understanding of electronic communications regulation.

The main *aim of sector specific regulation* in electronic communications is to correct the market failures brought about by monopoly and to facilitate conditions that are conducive to effective and efficient competition emerging. Regulators are intended to give the necessary spur to competition and to nurture the 'green shoots' of competition as they emerge. The aim is not to protect inefficient competitors, but to promote and protect efficient, sustainable competition to the ultimate benefit of consumers. Sector specific regulators should, ideally, 'regulate themselves out of existence,' so that eventually, reliance on competition law, enforced by competition authorities, is sufficient to address competition problems *ex post*, when they arise. In the interim, new market entrants need regulatory support and certainty to gain access on reasonable terms to the networks of incumbent operators, until such time as they deploy their own networks. This aim is also articulated by the *ladder of investment* theory, which suggests that new entrants will initially enter the market with offerings based on wholesale inputs from the incumbent operator. Over time however, the new entrants will gain market share and a customer base, and have the certainty to be able to invest in building out their own networks.

Regulatory policy and regulation in practice aspires to being *light handed*. Regulators should aim to minimise and eliminate unnecessary bureaucracy in order to ensure that the least onerous, costly and detailed form of regulatory rules are selected. Regulators should in appropriate cases, exercise forbearance from regulatory intervention.

Sector specific regulators differ from competition authorities in that generally, they intervene *ex ante* (ie before the fact) to address, for example, structural problems in a market. Competition agencies on the other hand usually (but not in the case of proposed mergers) operate *ex post*. They investigate (and perhaps attempt to punish) an alleged breach of competition law after the fact. Competition agencies frequently have only one or isolated interactions in relation to a particular sector, whereas sector specific regulators have an ongoing role in monitoring the behaviour of firms in the industry and enforcing compliance with the rules that they establish.

Economic regulation of networks is particularly concerned with *access pricing*, ie determining a 'fair' or 'reasonable' price that third party operators should pay a monopoly network operator to interconnect with or to use its network. There are a variety of methods to set access prices to a network, and different objectives related to each. In determining access prices, the task of a regulator is highly complex not only because it must understand the costs that the telecommunications firm incurs in running its business, but because it must also seek to protect and create *investment incentives*. Investment incentives are particularly relevant in the context of access regulation. If the access price is set too low, the incumbent firm may have no incentive to invest in its network, service quality, etc, as it may be under-recovering its costs. Inefficient entry by the new entrant may also be encouraged. If on the other hand, the access price is set too high, new entry may be deterred; entrants may not believe they will be able to operate a profitable business. Regulators have to set investment incentives so that the monopoly (more usually the dominant) operator's infrastructure is replicated by competitors wherever this is technically feasible and economically efficient. In this manner, competitors should be able to move up the ladder of investment.

Former state run telecommunications operators were established as *vertically integrated* firms. This means that they owned and controlled the capital and assets through most of or the entire supply chain, from the manufacture of the upstream wholesale inputs to the sale of downstream retail goods or services. In general, vertically integrated utilities enjoy a monopoly at the wholesale level and unless mandated to provide access to other operators at a reasonable cost (so that they can provide retail services) will probably never do so (or at least not on a non-discriminatory basis). Vertical integration can offer huge advantages in terms of efficiencies (such as reduced transaction costs and co-ordination) and economies of scope.

However, if a firm has *significant market power* (SMP) and is also vertically integrated, it may have the ability and incentive to leverage that SMP to the detriment of competition, by effectively excluding competitors or making it more difficult for them to survive commercially. Many firms, to some degree or another, enjoy market power. It is only, however, where that market power is significant, such that the firm can act without regard to its competitors or customers, that it may attract the attention of regulators or competition agencies. SMP is discussed further below.

Utilities regulation is not solely concerned with identifying and controlling SMP. It also has social goals such as the provision of a *universal service*. The universal service refers to the provision of a defined set of basic services to all end-users, regardless of their geographical location at an affordable price. In describing those services as 'basic', it should be noted that what is basic is a somewhat dynamic concept because of technological innovation. In the telecommunications sector, the policy makers at EU level realised that in a liberalised market, operators might not wish to provide some services to users in certain areas, where they might not consider it commercially attractive. It was therefore agreed to maintain a 'safety net', to ensure that a set of basic telecommunication services would always be available at a determined quality and an affordable price, even if the market might not provide them.

Technological neutrality refers to the fact that similar or identical services may be delivered via different technologies. Thus, broadband (high speed internet) may be delivered over different technologies including traditional copper fixed lines, fibre optic cables, wireless mobile networks, cable networks or satellite networks. The principle may also be applied to the provision of a universal service. Thus, if broadband were part of a universal service requirement, one could apply the principle of technology neutrality as regards the means by which broadband is to be provided. The principle is also intended to ensure that regulators do not discriminate between competing technological platforms in a manner that would undermine investment in any of them. A technology neutral approach is therefore required for assessing SMP, in that regulators should take into account the development of services using future technologies where their emergence and deployment by established or new entrants might pose a credible threat to a SMP operator. Moreover, in imposing obligations to address SMP, regulators must also adopt a technologically neutral approach. In either case, the regulator should not discriminate in favour of a particular technology.

Related to technological neutrality and technological innovation is the term *convergence*. Convergence may be described as the assimilation or coming together of different media. Because of convergence, a packet-switched network, such as the internet, can be used to transmit digitised voice signals (voice over internet protocol or 'VoIP') in competition with traditional fixed line voice telephony services. Another manifestation of convergence is the availability of voice, data, broadband and VoIP services on a single mobile handset. Convergence also encompasses bundling of services, eg 'triple play' where one provider provides the consumer with a fixed line phone, TV and broadband service. Convergence is also relevant to market definition (see further below) as the boundaries between different technologies become blurred. Fixed and mobile technologies, for example, are beginning to converge. A single handset can now provide a traditional fixed line telephony service but also switch to mobile functionality (and tariffs) when used outside of the home.

Technology markets such as those for electronic communications services are characterised by relatively *rapid technological innovation* and even disruptive technological innovations, which can impact on the competitive environment. VoIP, for example, which is a relatively new technology, is perceived as a significant threat to the core revenue streams of incumbent telecommunications firms from traditional fixed line voice telephony. Innovation is contributing to increasing convergence of technologies and media.

Sometimes a goal of sector specific regulation is to address another market failure, that of *information asymmetries*. A classic example of an information asymmetry is that of the market for second hand cars where the buyer lacks the specialised information that would enable him or her to make an informed and optimal choice about whether or not to purchase the car. The market response may be to offset the asymmetry by offering full or limited warranties. In telecommunications markets, consumers may also lack information regarding price and quality, and may also lack bargaining power. Sector specific regulators may respond by requiring businesses to be transparent in the information that they provide and to require them to provide contracts to consumers that contain certain protections. These consumer welfare enhancing goals are related to and compliment the competition law goals of regulators. In the model of a perfectly competitive market for example, consumers (buyers) are said to have perfect information about providers of goods and services (sellers).

6.2.1 Policy making and collaboration

High level policy formulation in the electronic communications sector occurs largely at an EU level. The EU Commission is central to policy formulation and the enactment of legal instruments that reflect the policy aims. However, the Minister, because of his power to issue policy directions to ComReg, retains a degree of input in to the formulation of policy in Ireland that is by no means vestigial.

One of the policy aims of the EU Commission is to create consistency throughout the EU. Operators need to be assured that their investments can be planned in a regulatory environment that is stable, consistent and predictable throughout the single market. To this end, processes have been devised permitting collaboration among the different regulators across the EU and between the regulators and the EU Commission. Collaboration is intended to play a key role in achieving the necessary coherence within the regulatory process at EU level. For example, the different EU regulators frequently meet as the European Regulators Group to discuss the formulation and implementation of detailed policies. The EU Commission requires regulators to submit proposals in respect of findings of SMP on operators, and retains a right of veto in respect of such findings. The EU Commission also maintains a close vigil on obligations/remedies that regulators propose to address operators' SMP. In this manner, greater coherence is achieved.

At domestic level, ComReg further develops and implements policy. ComReg's functions and regulatory tasks often bring it in to close co-operation with other regulatory bodies, notably the Competition Authority, the Data Protection Commissioner and and the National Consumer Agency.

6.3 The legal framework

The following section addresses the provisions of electronic communications sector specific legislation that are most relevant in practice. Provisions that are considered less relevant are not specifically addressed.

6.3.1 The Communications Regulation Act 2002

Section 6 of the Communications Regulation Act 2002 (the Act of 2002) established ComReg as the National Regulatory Authority (NRA) in Ireland with statutory responsibility for the regulation of electronic communications networks, electronic communications services and postal services. ComReg replaced the ODTR and assumed its functions. The Act of 2002 is mostly concerned with matters relating to the establishment and administration of ComReg, rather than substantive issues such as control of market power, or appeals from regulatory decisions. However, s 10 is important. It describes ComReg's functions as follows:

> '(a) to ensure compliance by undertakings with obligations in relation to the supply of and access to electronic communications services, electronic communications networks and associated facilities and the transmission of such services on such networks;
>
> (b) to manage the radio frequency spectrum and the national numbering resource;
>
> (c) to ensure compliance by providers of postal services with obligations in relation to the provision of postal services;
>
> (d) to investigate complaints from undertakings and consumers regarding the supply of and access to electronic communications services, electronic communications networks and associated facilities and transmission of such services on such networks; and
>
> (e) to ensure compliance, as appropriate, by persons in relation to the placing on the market of communications equipment and the placing on the market and putting into service of radio equipment.'

ComReg's acts and decisions must be related to its functions.

Section 12 transposes Article 8 of Directive 2002/21/EC (see further below) into domestic law. It sets out a number of objectives for ComReg and thereby informs ComReg in relation to the proper exercise of its powers.

In addition, s 11 is significant in that it provides that ComReg shall be independent in the exercise of its functions. ComReg's statutory independence is buttressed by the fact that under s 30, it is funded not from the Government Central Exchequer, but by means of a levy on providers of electronic communications services and on providers of postal services. Other regulators, such as the Commission for Aviation Regulation and the Commission for Energy Regulation are funded in a similar manner.

6.3.1.1 *Regulatory impact assessment*

Under s 13(1) of Act of 2002, the Minister is empowered to give such policy directions to ComReg as he or she considers appropriate, to be followed by ComReg in the exercise of its functions. ComReg is obliged to comply with any such direction. Ministerial Policy Direction No 6 of 2003 obliges ComReg to conduct regulatory impact assessment (RIA) before imposing obligations on undertakings in electronic communications markets.

RIA aims to determine the impact of new regulatory obligations on all stakeholders. ComReg must therefore first consider the impact of proposed decisions, as they may impose a significant burden or cost on stakeholders. Appropriate use of RIA ensures that the most effective approach to regulation is adopted. RIA should set out the various options under consideration (including the option of doing nothing) and should assess their respective advantages and disadvantages. RIA should also attempt, as far as possible, to quantify the costs of decisions for the regulated, for ComReg, and for society in general and it should contain a cost benefit analysis.

6.3.2 The Communications Regulation (Amendment) Act 2007

The Communications Regulation (Amendment) Act, 2007 (the Act of 2007) was passed on 21 April, 2007. The Act of 2007 enhances ComReg's powers in a number of areas by amending the Act of 2002 and extends its statutory functions and tasks by amending the Competition Act, 2002 and the Electronic Commerce Act, 2000. The most notable amendments to the Act of 2002 brought about by the Act of 2007 are as follows:

- Section 6 considerably strengthens ComReg's information gathering powers and provides for criminal liability in the event that an undertaking fails to comply with an information requirement.
- Section 7 provides for the protection of whistleblowers making an appropriate disclosure to ComReg of information about the conduct of undertakings in the provision of an electronic communications network or service or an associated facility.
- Section 10 entitles ComReg to serve notices requiring persons to appear before it to give evidence, or to produce documents for examination, if ComReg believes on reasonable grounds that a person may be able to give evidence, or to produce a document, that relates to a matter concerning the performance or exercise of any of ComReg's functions or objectives. It is an offence, triable summarily by ComReg, if a person fails to comply with or to cooperate in relation to such a notice.
- Section 13 prohibits an undertaking overcharging for services not provided. Contravention of s 13 is an offence triable summarily. In the alternative, ComReg may invoke a civil procedure and apply to the High Court for an order to restrain repeated or apprehended contravention.
- Part 4 makes very significant amendments to the Competition Act, 2002. These are addressed further below.
- Part 6 of the Act of 2007 allows the Minister to enter in to a contract for the operation of the emergency call answering service (ECAS).

6.3.3 The Framework Regulations

Directive 2002/21/EC is transposed into Irish law by the European Communities (Electronic Communications Networks and Services) (Framework) Regulations 2003 (SI 307/2003) (the Framework Regulations).

Directive 2002/21/EC and the other EU and Irish legislative enactments are referred to below as the '2003 regulatory package'. The aims of the 2003 regulatory package is to create a harmonised framework for the regulation of electronic communications networks and services, to promote competition, entry and investment in the electronic communications sector, to guarantee the provision of a universal service and to promote the interests of consumers.

6.3.3.1 *Definitions and scope*

The Framework Regulations contain key definitions, transposed directly from Directive 2002/21/EC such as 'electronic communications network', 'electronic communications service' and 'undertaking'. Together, these definitions to a great extent define the scope of regulation. The definitions are interlinked and overlapping. In order to come within the scope of regulation, the activities of an operator would need to satisfy these definitions.

Because of the convergence of the telecommunications, media and information technology sectors, the EU Commission decided that all transmission networks should be covered by a single regulatory framework. The 2003 regulatory package is not only directed towards telecommunications networks and services, but all electronic communications networks and services. This includes fixed and mobile telecommunications networks, cable or satellite television networks and even electricity networks (if they are used for electronic communications services).

It should be noted that the *content* of services delivered over electronic communications networks, eg broadcasting content or financial services, is outside of the ambit of regulation. Therefore, ComReg has no role in matters such as determining what websites are deemed acceptable, the price that a mobile phone operator wishes to charge its subscribers to download a game, or the content of a text message sent between two subscribers over a mobile phone network.

6.3.3.2 *Independence of NRAs*

Article 3(1) of Directive 2002/21/EC obliges Member States to guarantee the independence of NRAs by ensuring that they have no links with providers of electronic communications networks or services. That is not to say that the central Government of a Member State is prohibited from providing an electronic communications network or service. If it does, it must however ensure effective structural separation of the regulatory function from activities associated with ownership or control of organisations providing electronic communications networks, equipment or services.

6.3.3.3 *Transparency and consultation*

In order to foster transparency, accountability and better informed decision making, Regulation 19 of the Framework Regulations obliges ComReg to consult publicly in relation to measures that have a significant impact upon an electronic communications market. In doing so, ComReg must provide reasons for its proposed measures and the relevant statutory power giving rise to them, and it must take into account any representations made to it before adopting the proposed measures as final.

6.3.3.4 *Appeals*

The 2003 regulatory package aims to ensure proper accountability and an effective appeals mechanism is vital in this respect.

Prior to the coming into force of the Framework Regulations, most regulatory decisions of ComReg were subject only to judicial review under Order 84 of the Rules of the Superior Courts. A number of decisions by the ODTR and ComReg relating to the price that could be charged for access to the local loop were challenged in this manner by *eircom,* although these proceedings were all subsequently settled by the parties. Certain decisions were however capable of being appealed, notably those pertaining to licensing under the pre-2003 licensing regime. In *Orange Communications Ltd v Director of Telecommunications* [2000] 4 IR 136, the High Court overturned the ODTR's decision to award a mobile telecommunications licence to the mobile operator, Meteor on the grounds of unreasonableness and bias. The High Court's decision was however subsequently reversed on appeal to the Supreme Court in *Orange Telecommunications Ltd v Director of Telecommunications Regulation (No 2)* [2000] 4 IR 159.

Because of Article 4 of Directive 2002/21/EC, Member States are obliged to provide for an effective appeal mechanism in respect of the decisions of NRAs. Even by definition, judicial review (as known in Ireland) would hardly fulfil this requirement. Accordingly, Part I of the Framework Regulations established the Electronic Communications Appeals Panel (the ECAP) and provided for a merit based appeal in respect of ComReg's decisions. The ECAP has now been abolished (see further below) but the few rulings it made are still of interest. Part I of the Framework Regulations bore some similarities to the models for appeal regimes in for example, the electricity sector and the aviation sector. Significantly however, the appeal mechanism under the Framework Regulations was not restricted to only certain categories of decisions by ComReg.

Part I of the Framework Regulations set out the framework for administering and determining appeals and the powers of the ECAP, but was silent with respect to certain matters. Many of these matters were left to the ECAP to rule upon. In relation the standard of review to be adopted, the ECAP's preliminary ruling in *Hutchinon 3 G (Ireland) Ltd* [Decision No 02/05] effectively established a standard of review that lay somewhere in between the standard that applies in *de novo* appeals and the standard known as 'curial deference' that usually applies where a decision of an expert public body is judicially reviewed. The ECAP ruled that there must be a 'significant error or errors' made by ComReg that would have a bearing on a decision in order for the decision to be vitiated – the error or errors must not be trivial but equally, such errors need not go to the root of the decision.

The ECAP delivered a number of other rulings in relation to procedural matters such as discovery, confidentiality and evidence that may be relied upon in appeals. It should be noted that in the United Kingdom the Competition Appeals Tribunal (the CAT) was established to hear appeals from decisions of the Office of Fair Trading (the OFT) and other regulators, including ComReg's equivalent, OFCOM. The decisions of the CAT are particularly relevant for sector specific regulators in Ireland and the Irish Competition Authority.

In practice, certain decisions of ComReg (particularly those relating to market analysis and SMP) can be very contentious. Where an operator is found to have SMP, it may be legally obliged to alter its commercial behaviour and its commercial freedom may be significantly curtailed, notably through the imposition of price controls – typically at the wholesale level. Because such control of SMP may operate to the advantage of new entrants and competitors, it is perhaps not surprising that operators found to have SMP may view this as a threat to their profitability. Given the control that regulators can exercise and the effect that this can have on the regulated entity, regulators are now put to a very high standard of proof when making decisions relating to SMP. On a number of occasions ComReg has had its decisions in respect of SMP challenged before the ECAP.

The most notable decision of the ECAP was *Hutchison 3 G (Ireland) Ltd v Commission for Communications Regulation* [Decision No 02/05]. That appeal, concerned ComReg's designation of the appellant with SMP on the market for mobile voice call termination.[1] ComReg had also designated the other mobile operators (Vodafone, O2 and Meteor) with SMP. The ECAP annulled that part of ComReg's decision that designated Hutchison (which trades as '3') with SMP. It ruled that ComReg had over-relied on Hutchison's 100% market share and that it had failed to thoroughly analyse issues in relation to countervailing buyer power – issues that could have meant that Hutchison had *no* SMP. Significantly, the ECAP appeared to draw upon a series of decisions in which the European Court of Justice had annulled merger decisions of the EU Commission and had been critical of a lack of thoroughness in the EU Commission's analyses.

Another case, heard not before the ECAP but in the Commercial Court (ie the commercial list of the High Court) was *Smart Telecom Ltd v Commission for Communications Regulation* (29 July 2005, unreported, McKechnie J). That case concerned the award of a licence to Smart Telecom to operate a 3G mobile telephony service. Smart Telecom was already providing a calls and broadband service and following a 'beauty contest', in which *eircom* and Meteor were placed second and third respectively, ComReg awarded the licence in question to Smart Telecom. However, ComReg withdrew the licence because of the unacceptability of the bonds being proffered as security by Smart Telecom for the fulfilment of its licence obligations. Smart Telecom contested the decision, arguing that the award of the licence constituted a contract between it and ComReg and that ComReg had acted unlawfully and unreasonably in withdrawing the licence. The Court ultimately upheld ComReg's decision, based on evidence that Smart Telecom had not procured the requisite bonds in the manner sought by ComReg and that ComReg had in all respects acted reasonably with Smart Telecom in relation to the matter.

Smart Telecom was at that time, also embroiled in a commercial dispute with *eircom*. This led to *eircom* terminating the provisions of its interconnection agreement with Smart Telecom and ultimately to Smart Telecom ceasing to provide residential call services (although remaining active in the broadband market).

6.3.3.5 *The Framework (Amendment) Regulations, 2007*

The European Communities (Electronic Communications Networks and Services) (Framework) (Amendment) Regulations 2007[2] (the Framework (Amendment) Regulations 2007) provide for the abolition of the ECAP. A user or undertaking affected by a decision of ComReg may lodge an appeal to the High Court in respect of it. The High Court has the power to affirm, or set aside in whole or in part a decision of ComReg. It may also remit a decision to ComReg for it to be determined again. At the time of writing, no appeal has yet been ruled upon by the High Court.

6.3.3.6 *Market definition and analysis*

The 2003 regulatory package assigns certain tasks to NRAs. One of its key tasks is market analysis and it is perhaps the cornerstone of regulation.

Prior to the coming into force of the Framework Regulations, telecommunications operators would be designated with SMP by the ODTR (ComReg's predecessor) where they were found to have a market share of 25% or more of a particular market. This method of measuring market power was considered crude and mechanistic. Under the Framework Regulations, SMP has now become aligned with the competition law concept of dominance derived from Article 82 of the EC Treaty. Therefore, under Regulation 25 of the Framework Regulations an undertaking has SMP:

> '... where the Regulator is satisfied that, in relation to any relevant market, such undertaking (whether individually or jointly with others) enjoys a position which is

---

[1] When a call is made to a mobile phone, whether from a fixed line or from a mobile on another network, the call passes from the originating operator to the terminating operator. The terminating operator charges a fee for connecting the call to its customers; this is known as a termination charge. The termination charge is paid by the originating operator and passed on to the caller in the retail price it pays for a call.

[2] SI 271/2007.

equivalent to dominance of that market, that is to say a position of economic strength affording it the power to behave to an appreciable extent, independently of competitors, customers, and, ultimately, consumers.'

In economic terms, dominance, or 'the position of economic strength affording ... power to behave to an appreciable extent, independently' is frequently said to be synonymous with the ability to raise the prices for the relevant good or service above the competitive level.

Under Regulation 26 of the Framework Regulations, ComReg is obliged to define relevant markets in accordance with competition law principles. Markets must be defined having regard to relevant case law of the European Court of Justice and decisions of the EU Commission and must use standard and accepted tools of economic analysis. In this respect, the task of NRAs represents a confluence of law and economics.

The Framework Regulations are complemented by two further legal instruments, which play a key role in directing the procedure for the analysis. Firstly, the Recommendation on Relevant Markets[3] comprises a list of 7 different markets which, because of their structures and characteristics, the EU Commission views as being susceptible to *ex ante* regulation by NRAs throughout the EU. While under EU law a Recommendation does not have the same binding legal force as a Directive or a Regulation, NRAs are obliged to take the 'utmost account' of the Recommendation on Relevant Markets by Directive 2002/21/EC (which itself is binding as to the result to be achieved) and the Framework Regulations. NRAs do however have discretion to depart from the Recommendation on Relevant Markets where national circumstances would dictate differently, but they must comply with a special procedure in order to do so.

As competition and convergence develops, it is expected that the range of markets identified as being susceptible to *ex ante* regulation will in the future, be reduced further. Traditional fixed line telephony for example has thus far been defined as a separate market to mobile telephony or VoIP. However, if VoIP becomes increasingly able to compete with traditional fixed line voice telephony, NRAs may choose to define a market that includes both VoIP and traditional fixed line voice telephony. In such a scenario, the incumbent operators may be less likely to have SMP and existing regulation might have to be removed.

The second legal instrument that complements the Framework Regulations is the SMP Guidelines[4]. The SMP Guidelines provide guidance to NRAs, by reference to the case law of the European Court of Justice as to (i) how markets should be defined; (ii) how SMP is measured and found; and (iii) how the 'mischiefs' arising from SMP may be addressed through the suite of remedies available to NRAs.

In practice, market definition begins by applying the *Small but Significant and Non-transitory Increase in Price* (SSNIP) test. One attempts to identify the smallest market in which a hypothetical monopolist could impose and sustain a small but significant non-transitory increase in price (5–10%) – this is the relevant market. The essence of the exercise lies in identifying the relevant competitive constraints on a given product or

---

[3.] EU Commission Recommendation of 17 December 2007 on Relevant Product and Service Markets within the electronic communications sector susceptible to ex ante regulation in accordance with Directive 2002/21/EC of the European Parliament and the Council of 7 March 2002 on a common regulatory framework for electronic communications networks and services. The Recommendation on Relevant Markets updated an EU Commission Recommendation of 11 February 2003 that had listed 18 different markets susceptible to ex ante regulation. The reduction in the number of markets now listed reflects the gradual trend towards the removal of ex ante regulation and reliance on competition law, because markets are perceived as being more competitive by the EU Commission.

[4.] Commission guidelines on market analysis and the assessment of significant market power under the Community regulatory framework for electronic communications networks and services (2002/C 165/03).

service. Such constraints may either come from the demand side (consumers) or the supply side (producers). Demand-side substitutability is used to measure the extent to which consumers are prepared to substitute other services or products, for the service or product in question. On the demand side, one must ask whether in response to a small, but significant price increase of product A, consumers would switch to product B. If the answer is no, then the market boundary has been identified and the product market is defined as product A. If the answer is yes, then the market definition comprises at least products A and B, but one must extend the analysis to product C and perhaps further, until the market boundary is identified. Supply-side substitutability indicates whether suppliers, other than those offering the product or services in question, are likely to switch their line of production within a reasonable timeframe and offer the relevant products or services, without incurring significant additional costs.

To define the limits of the geographic market, one proceeds in a similar way to assessing demand and supply-side substitution in response to a price increase. The relevant geographic market is the area in which the undertakings concerned are involved in the supply and demand of the relevant products or services, in which area the conditions of competition are distinguishable from neighbouring areas where the conditions of competition are appreciably different.

Once the relevant product and geographic market has been defined, the object is to then determine whether or not there is an operator that has SMP on the relevant market. SMP is assessed in accordance with competition law principles. A number of factors must be examined to determine whether or not there exists an operator with SMP. Typically, one begins by measuring the market share of different operators in the market under consideration. There is a considerable body of case law of the European Court of Justice to the effect that high market shares equate with dominance (or for the purpose of this discussion SMP). It has been held that market shares of 70% or more give rise to a presumption of dominance. However, with the increased influence of economics and the discipline that it has brought to bear on the practice of competition law, the relative importance of market shares has declined somewhat. It is probably safer to now describe the measurement of market share (at least with respect to the electronic communications sector) as a helpful and suggestive initial 'screening device'.

One of the most important additional factors to be examined is whether or not there exist high and persistent barriers to entry in to the relevant market. If entry is relatively easy, then this might tend to weaken the potentially dominant operator's position of strength in the relevant market. Furthermore, if there are strong buyers in the market that can exert sufficient countervailing buyer power on the potentially dominant operator, this might also offset any SMP that they would otherwise have. The assessment of SMP must be prospective, in that ComReg must look ahead to estimate whether technological innovation or new market entry would mean that a position of SMP observed today is not durable in the short to medium term.

It is important to be aware that the behaviour of the operator in a particular market is not especially relevant to assessing SMP. In this regard, SMP is not predicated on a finding of abuse of dominance under Article 82 of the EC Treaty, or under s 5 of the Competition Act 2002 (although there is some case law to the contrary in Article 82 cases). The premise for *ex ante* regulation is that a position of SMP affords an undertaking with the economic *ability* and *incentive* to distort or undermine competition in the market. As such, NRAs seek to guard against potential problems occurring in advance, by imposing behavioural remedies on the SMP operator.

The Framework Regulations also introduce the possibility of *two or more* undertakings being found to have a position of joint SMP (or 'collective dominance'). Collective dominance is a relatively new concept in EU competition law. In order to maintain a finding of collective dominance in a market, a competition authority or regulator must demonstrate that the necessary criteria for such a finding are fulfilled. *Airtours v Commission* [2002] ECR II-2585 sets out the relevant legal test as follows:

1. Each member of the dominant oligopoly must have the ability to know how the other members are behaving in order to monitor whether or not they are adopting the common policy. There must, therefore, be sufficient market transparency for all members of the dominant oligopoly to be aware, sufficiently precisely and quickly, of the way in which the other members' market conduct is evolving.
2. The situation of tacit coordination must be sustainable over time, that is to say, there must be an incentive not to depart from the common policy on the market. It is only if all the members of the dominant oligopoly maintain the parallel conduct that all can benefit. The notion of retaliation in respect of conduct deviating from the common policy is thus inherent in this condition.
3. To prove the existence of a collective dominant position to the requisite legal standard, it must be established that the foreseeable reaction of current and future competitors, as well as of consumers, would not jeopardise the results expected from the common policy.

6.3.3.7 *Dispute resolution*

Regulation 31 of the Framework Regulations makes provision for persons to submit disputes to ComReg where they relate to an obligation of an undertaking. ComReg must adjudicate upon a dispute within four months once it accepts it. The procedure does not preclude either party from bringing an action before the Courts and is without prejudice to the right of appeal.

6.3.4 The Authorisation Regulations

Directive 2002/20/EC is transposed into Irish law by the European Communities (Electronic Communications Networks and Services (Authorisation) Regulations 2003 (SI 306/2003) (the Authorisation Regulations).

The Authorisation Regulations replace the previous system of individual licensing with general authorisations (while a special scheme for attributing frequencies and numbers continues to exist). The provisions of the Authorisation Regulations cover authorisations for all electronic communications networks and services, whether they are provided to the public or not. They only apply to the granting of rights to use radio frequencies if the use involves the provision of an electronic communications network or service, normally for remuneration.

The overarching objective is to reduce regulation in this area to a minimum. The provision of electronic communications networks or services may only be subject to a general authorisation. There is no *ex ante* licensing mechanism. The undertaking concerned may be required to submit a notification, but the exercise of the rights under the general authorisation is not dependent upon an explicit decision by ComReg, or any other administrative act by it.

A distinction is made between the conditions applicable under the general authorisation and those linked to the rights to use radio frequencies and numbers.

The general authorisation and the rights of use may only be subject to the specific conditions listed in the Annex to the Directive 2002/20/EC. Consistent with the principle of light handed regulation and the desire to reduce red tape, no other conditions may be imposed.

6.3.5 The Access Regulations

Directive 2002/19/EC is transposed into Irish law by the European Communities (Electronic Communications Networks and Services) (Access) Regulations 2003 (SI 305/2003) (the Access Regulations).

6.3.5.1 *Negotiation of interconnection and access*

Regulation 1 of the Access Regulations defines 'access' as:

> '... the making available of facilities, services or both facilities and services, to another undertaking, under defined conditions, on either an exclusive or non-exclusive basis, for the purpose of providing electronic communications services ...'

Access is a very broad term encompassing many things; even the specific elements set out in the above definition are not exhaustive. Interconnection for example, is a form of access. 'Interconnection' is defined as:

> '...the physical and logical linking of public communications networks used by the same or a different undertaking in order to allow the users of one undertaking to communicate with users of the same or another undertaking, or to access services provided by another undertaking...'

Interconnection is fundamental in a liberalised electronic communications market. The ODTR was very preoccupied with ensuring interconnection and at 'cost oriented' rates during the early period of regulation. Under the Access Regulations, operators have a right to negotiate interconnection with other operators. The operator, with whom interconnection is requested, also has a corresponding obligation to negotiate interconnection.

6.3.5.2 *SMP obligations*

Regulations 9–14 of the Access Regulations address SMP obligations that may be imposed at the wholesale level and describe both the conditions for their imposition and the types of obligations that may be imposed. In order for SMP obligations to be imposed, an undertaking must first be found to have SMP, otherwise SMP regulation is forbidden. If SMP is found, ComReg must impose at least one of the SMP obligations available to it in order to address that SMP. A SMP operator at the wholesale level may be obliged to:

- provide access on reasonable terms to its network to other operators;
- ensure transparency with respect to tariffs and conditions for access by amongst other things, publishing those tariffs and conditions;
- ensure that it does not discriminate in relation to the provision of access and wholesale inputs;
- comply with price control obligations. ComReg has considerable flexibility with regard to the forms of price control it may choose to impose;
- maintain separated accounts. The purpose of separated accounts is principally to ascertain whether or not discrimination is occurring and whether prices comply with any price controls;
- maintain cost accounting systems.

The selection and design of SMP obligations is a complex matter. As a prerequisite to ComReg imposing SMP obligations, it must demonstrate by reasoned analysis that a SMP obligation is necessary, appropriate, justified and proportionate. The need for SMP obligations must be linked to identifiable competition problems that could arise in the market being regulated. This involves an examination of the economic ability and incentives that exist for SMP operators to engage in anti-competitive behaviour. Other considerations include the need to maintain investment incentives in the industry generally. ComReg must also follow detailed procedures relating to consultation with the public, the EU Commission and other NRAs.

For a number of years, competing operators have, as a result of SMP access obligations imposed by ComReg, been able to purchase a wholesale line rental product from *eircom*. This allows them to provide a retail line rental product to their subscribers. Operators can also purchase a product from *eircom* allowing them to offer carrier pre-selection. This is a facility allows customers to opt for certain defined classes of call to be carried by an operator selected in advance (and having a contract with the customer), without having to dial a routing prefix or follow any other different procedure to invoke such routing. This has enabled competing operators to provide subscribers with calls and line rental at lower prices and with a single bill. ComReg has also mandated access in the market for wholesale broadband access, which enables competitors of *eircom* to provide a retail broadband product to their subscribers. Operators other than *eircom* are therefore now able to provide 'bundles' that include line rental, calls and broadband access. As their brand recognition and customer base develops, the ladder of investment theory suggests that new entrants will develop competing infrastructure and move up the value chain.

6.3.5.3 *Local loop unbundling*

Local loop unbundling (LLU) is also a SMP obligation. It is a specific form of access to *eircom's* network. The local loop is sometimes referred to as the 'last mile' of an incumbent operator's telecommunication network. LLU essentially involves the provision to competing operators of access to individual subscriber lines so that in theory, the costs to that operator do not include any other access network or overhead costs. LLU therefore gives a competing operator access to customers via the local loop. It gives the operator the ability to compete in terms of price, quality and differentiation of service. Importantly, it also offers an incentive to operators to commit investments to developing their own infrastructure. Although there are competing technologies that can provide broadband (cable, wireless, mobile and satelite) LLU has for a long time been seen as key to increasing competition in the sector and increasing broadband uptake in Ireland. LLU has been one of the most fractious issues on the regulatory agenda since the inception of sector specific regulation. Successive decisions of ComReg in relation to LLU have been judicially reviewed and appealed by *eircom* since 2000.

In 2005, for example, ComReg issued a decision notice which required *eircom* to respond with information regarding the impacts associated with the implementation of certain access seeker requirements associated with the provision of LLU. Subsequently, having formed the opinion that no satisfactory response had been provided by *eircom*, ComReg issued an 'urgent' enforcement direction under the Access Regulations, which was then challenged by *eircom* by way of judicial review in the High Court. In the judicial review, *eircom* was successful. Essentially, the judicial review concerned a net, rather technical point of law. The judgment confirmed that a direction of ComReg is not enforceable within the permitted appeal period of 28 days, in view of the subject's right of appeal and his right to seek a suspension of the decision, pending the outcome of that appeal as provided for by Article 4 of Directive 2002/21. The Court arrived at this view notwithstanding the fact that the Framework Regulations had expressly provided that 'urgent' directions were not capable of being appealed.

While some progress has since been made in relation to LLU, it has been slow. Undoubtedly a seismic shift is needed if more significant progress is to be made. One radical solution that has been mooted is that of structural separation, ie that *eircom* would split, or be split, into its separate wholesale and retail arms, resulting in two businesses under separate ownership. In such a scenario, *eircom* would no longer be vertically integrated. Functional separation, not involving a change of ownership, is another possibility. Either of these potential solutions would certainly take considerable time and the correct model of structural or functional separation would need to be carefully designed. In theory, proper structural separation, with separate ownership and control of the businesses and their assets, could remove the economic incentive by *eircom* to engage in discrimination at the wholesale and retail levels. In purely simple terms, a separately owned wholesale business would (presumably) have an incentive to maximise its revenues by providing access (at an acceptable price) to all comers. It is not clear if, or how, such structural separation might come about. Specific legislation would need to be enacted to empower ComReg to order structural separation. *eircom* under its current owners, Babcock and Brown, has itself suggested that, under the right circumstances, it may wish to structurally separate (voluntarily) and that this might suit its business and commercial model.

6.3.6 The Universal Service Regulations

Directive 2002/22/EC is transposed into Irish law by the European Communities (Electronic Communications Networks and Services) (Universal Service and Users' Rights) Regulations 2003 (SI 308/2003) (the Universal Service Regulations).

The Universal Service Regulations set out obligations that may be imposed on SMP operators and the universal service provider. They also impose obligations on providers of publicly available telephone services (PATS) generally.

6.3.6.1 *The universal service*

Member States must ensure that basic telecommunications services are made available to all users in their territory, regardless of their geographical location, at a specified quality level and an affordable price, and are required to designate one or more universal service provider(s) in the State for this purpose.

The ODTR designated *eircom* as the universal service provider in the State in April, 1999 and subsequently by ComReg on 25 July, 2003. On 25 July, 2006, *eircom* was again designated by ComReg as the universal service provider in the State for a period of four years, ending on 30 June, 2010.

As the universal service provider, *eircom* is obliged by ComReg to:

1. provide access to end users at a fixed location that supports local, national and international calls, facsimile communications and data communications at data rates sufficient to permit functional internet access;
2. (a) provide to end-users (ie consumers) a comprehensive printed directory of subscribers, free of charge and updated at least once a year, based upon information supplied to it in accordance with the national directory database;
   (b) keep a record (to be known as the national directory database) of all subscribers of publicly available telephone services in the State, including those with fixed, personal and mobile numbers who have not refused to be included in that record and allow access to any information contained in such a record to any such other undertaking or any person in accordance with terms and conditions approved by ComReg;
3. ensure that public payphones are provided to meet the reasonable needs of end-users in terms of geographical coverage, the number of telephones, and the quality of services;
4. provide a range of specific services to disabled end-users;
5. adhere to the principle of maintaining affordability for universal services and ensure that universal services are provided at geographically averaged prices so that they are available to all consumers at the same price throughout the country; and

6. take certain measures aimed at helping end-users to control their expenditure.

Broadband is not currently an element of the universal service (although functional internet access is). Directory inquiry services are also not within the ambit of the universal service as ComReg is of the view that, currently at least, the market is adequately delivering these services.

6.3.6.2 *Financing of universal service obligations*

The provision of a universal service can, potentially, involve the provision of some services to some end-users at prices that depart from those resulting from normal market conditions. Directive 2002/22/EC provides that, where necessary, Member States should establish mechanisms administered by national regulatory authorities for financing the net cost of universal service obligations, if it is demonstrated that the obligations can only be provided at a loss or at a net cost.

Regulation 11(1) of the Universal Service Regulations allows an undertaking designated as having universal service obligations to seek to receive funding for the net costs of meeting those obligations by, in the first instance, submitting to ComReg a written request for such funding.

If it is found by ComReg, on the basis of a net cost calculation, that there is an unfair burden on the undertaking designated as having universal service obligations, the Universal Service Regulations require that the net cost be apportioned among providers of electronic communications networks and services. Thus, in theory at least, industry could be required to meet some or all of the net cost of providing a universal service by in effect, having to make payments to *eircom*. To date however, ComReg has not made any finding that a net cost arises for *eircom* as the universal service provider, or that such a net cost represents an unfair burden on *eircom*.

6.3.6.3 *SMP obligations on retail markets*

SMP obligations may only be imposed on retail markets where ComReg is satisfied that obligations at the wholesale level would not achieve its objectives. Obligations must also be proportionate and justified. ComReg may under Regulation 14 impose obligations such as retail price control, obligations not to show undue preference to end users, obligations not to charge excessive prices, obligations not to inhibit market entry or restrict competition by setting predatory prices and obligations not to unreasonably bundle services.

6.3.6.4 *Consumer provisions*

Consumer protection aims and competition policy aims are linked and complimentary. A poorly informed consumer may not be able to make optimal choices. Service providers with market power may be in a position to exploit this and it is therefore important to remove information barriers and switching costs. The Universal Service Regulations seek to protect consumers from information asymmetries and other consumer problems that arise. They complement existing consumer protection legislation, eg the European Communities (Protection of Consumers in Respect of Contracts Made by Means of Distance Communication) Regulations 2001.

Under reg 17, an undertaking that provides to end-users connection or access, or both connection and access to the public telephone network must do so in accordance with a contract. Consumer contracts must contain certain information including:

- the services provided, the service quality levels offered and the time for the initial connection;
- the types of maintenance service offered;

- particulars of prices and tariffs;
- the duration of the contract, conditions for renewal and termination of services and of the contract;
- any compensation and refund arrangements if service quality levels are not met;
- procedures for settling disputes.

Under reg 18, ComReg has the power to take various measures aimed at ensuring transparency and the publication of adequate information in relation to prices and service quality levels. ComReg also operates a website (www.callcosts.ie) to assist consumers in choosing the electronic communications service that suits their budgets and needs.

6.3.6.5 *Number portability*

An important competition tool is the power of the ComReg to oblige operators to allow subscribers to retain their phone number when switching to a different operator. Unless subscribers can do this, switching is made very unattractive. Accordingly, under reg 26 of the Universal Service Regulations, ComReg has the power to require operators to provide 'number portability' (in relation to both fixed line and mobile service providers).

6.3.7 The Data Privacy Regulations

Directive 2002/58/EC is transposed into Irish law by the European Communities (Electronic Communications Networks and Services) (Data Protection and Privacy) Regulations 2003 (SI 535/2003). These Regulations replace the European Communities (Data Protection and Privacy in Telecommunications) Regulations, 2002.

Amongst other things, these Regulations make it illegal for persons to send unsolicited direct marketing electronic communications without the consent of the recipient. The Regulations cover unsolicited communications sent in a variety of ways, including by e-mail or mobile phone text message.

The Regulations impose criminal and civil liability in respect of breaches and ComReg and the Data Protection Commissioner have shared responsibility for enforcement.

6.4 Enforcement

6.4.1 Civil liability

A civil enforcement procedure is available to ComReg in respect of non-compliance by undertakings with 'obligations' (either imposed directly by statute or created by ComReg) or 'directions' (issued by ComReg) under the different sets of Regulations comprising the 2003 regulatory package.

As it is a civil procedure, proof of non-compliance in accordance with the civil standard of proof is required, ie proof on the balance of probabilities. This is of course lower than the criminal standard of proof of beyond reasonable doubt and, in theory, is easier to satisfy. The onus is on ComReg to prove non-compliance. There are no presumptions in the legislation that shift the onus of proof.

6.4.1.1 *Outline of the procedure*

The civil procedure under the Access Regulations is replicated in the other sets of Regulations comprising the 2003 regulatory package.

Regulation 18 of the Access Regulations involves ComReg applying to the High Court for an order to compel compliance with an obligation or a direction under the Access Regulations.

The procedure operates as follows:

1. ComReg makes a finding of non-compliance. This is not as straightforward as it sounds and as a general proposition, the 'finding' must amongst other things, be evidence based, observe the principles of natural justice and comply with all relevant statutory procedures.
2. If ComReg finds that a person has not complied with an obligation, or a direction under reg 17, ComReg notifies the person concerned and gives them an opportunity to state their views or remedy any non-compliance. The period is either one month after issuing the notification or a shorter period if that is agreed with the person, or a longer period if that is specified by ComReg (in the case of repeated non-compliance).
3. After the period referred to above has elapsed and if ComReg is of the opinion that the person concerned has not complied with the obligation or the direction, ComReg may apply to the High Court for such order as may be appropriate to compel compliance. The Court may grant or refuse the order and if it compels compliance must stipulate a reasonable period for same. As a matter of statutory construction, what is 'reasonable' will usually depend on the surrounding circumstances.
4. Under reg 18(5) the Court may make such interlocutory order as it deems appropriate. An interlocutory injunction is of course only a temporary order pending the full hearing. In order to obtain an interlocutory injunction the Court must be satisfied that there is a serious issue to be tried. Relief is only granted if the 'balance of convenience' lies in so granting it and where damages would not be an adequate remedy for the applicant. The Courts are slow to grant mandatory injunctions (injunctions ordering the direct performance of a positive act) on an interlocutory application. The jurisdiction of the Courts to grant injunctions is discretionary and is also subject to the maxims of equity (which may assist a party in either defending or bringing an application for an injunction).
5. Regulation 18(7) introduces 'civil fines'. It is a matter for ComReg to actually apply for civil fines to be imposed, but it is ultimately the decision of the High Court as to what amount should be payable. In deciding what amount (if any) should be payable, the Court is required to consider the circumstances of the non-compliance, including:
    - its duration;
    - the effect on consumers, users and other operators;
    - the submissions of ComReg on the appropriate amount;
    - any excuse or explanation for the non-compliance.

As a 'double jeopardy' safeguard, the use of the reg 18 civil enforcement procedure precludes the bringing of criminal proceedings under the various Regulations, or under s 44 of the Act of 2002. The mere service of a notification of non-compliance however, does not preclude the possibility of criminal enforcement proceedings.

6.4.1.2 *Urgent directions*

ComReg may under reg 18(10) dispense with the one month period of notification that normally applies and issue a direction requiring immediate compliance if ComReg has evidence that the non-compliance:

> '... will in the opinion of the Regulator create serious economic or operational problems for undertakings or for users of electronic communications networks or services ...'

Under reg 18(12), ComReg may apply to the High Court in a summary manner for an order compelling compliance with a direction under reg 18(10). The power under reg 18(10) is arguably a quite exceptional one and in that case, it would have to be construed narrowly.

6.4.2 Section 39 of the Act of 2002

Part 3 of the Act of 2002 sets out certain powers of enforcement for ComReg. Section 39 provides for the appointment of 'authorised officers' who enjoy extensive 'search and seizure' powers. Thus, they may enter premises connected with the provision of electronic communications services and remove and retain books, documents or records for further examination. Such authorised officer powers are found in enactments regulating diverse areas of the economy. The powers are also similar to the so called 'dawn raid' powers of the Irish and other European competition authorities and can be a very effective method for obtaining evidence in furtherance of compliance investigations.

6.4.3 Criminal liability

Section 44 of the Act of 2002 introduced the concept of 'on the spot fines' in respect of criminal offences and these can be imposed where ComReg has reasonable grounds for believing that a person has committed an offence. The fine is €1,000 and notice must be served. If payment is made there is no prosecution.

One of the most significant initiatives of the Act of 2002 was to substantially increase the penalties that could be imposed for a breach of a condition in their licences. Pursuant to s 45 of the Act of 2002, an undertaking was liable on summary conviction, to a fine not exceeding €3,000 or on conviction on indictment, to a fine not exceeding €4 million or 10% of turnover in the previous financial year, whichever was the greater. However, these provisions were subsequently repealed when the Framework Regulations came into force in 2003.

Although the various Regulations created a variety of summary criminal offences that may be prosecuted by ComReg, the level of fines that may be imposed was limited to €3,000. This is because of the provisions of s 3(3) of European Communities Act 1972 which prohibits the creation of indictable offences in Regulations made under that Act. In addition, there was no criminal liability for a breach of SMP obligations imposed by ComReg.

6.4.4 Increased criminal liability and penalties

To address the perceived deficiencies in relation to criminal liability, new Regulations were made by the Minister under s 14 of the Act of 2007. It may be noted that those Regulations are not subject to the prohibition on the creation of indictable offences (as with Regulations made pursuant to s 3(3) of European Communities Act 1972) bacuse they are made pursuant to an Act of the Oireachtas and s 14 of the Act of 2007 expressly allows for the creation of indictable offences. Accordingly, the Framework Regulations, the Access Regulations, the Authorisation Regulations and the Universal Service Regulations have all been amended so as to provide for increased civil and criminal liability[5]. Breaches of SMP obligations for example, are now criminal offences. Offences committed by corporations and tried on indictment now attract a fine of €5,000,000, or 10 per cent of the turnover of the corporation (if its turnover is more than €5,000,000).

[5.] See the Framework (Amendment) Regulations 2007 (SI 271/2007) (referred to previously) the EC (Electronic Communications Networks and Services) (Access) (Amendment) Regulations 2007 (SI 373/2007); the EC (Electronic Communications Networks and Services) (Authorisation) (Amendment) Regulations, 2007 (SI 372/2007) and the EC (Electronic Communications Networks and Services) (Universal Service and Users' Rights) (Amendment) Regulations, 2007 (SI 374/2007).

6.5 Competition law and administrative law

6.5.1 Competition law

In the United Kingdom, ComReg's equivalent, OFCOM enjoys concurrent competition law powers under the Competition Act 1998. That is to say, it enjoys the same powers as the OFT and may exercise them when it is best placed to do so. It may also make 'market investigation' references to the Competition Commission under the Enterprise Act 2002.

ComReg applies competition law principles, *ex ante* in its specific sector. However, until 2007, that was the extent of ComReg's competition law remit. ComReg did not have full competition law powers (although sector specific regulation was always without prejudice to the powers of the Competition Authority). Thus, ComReg could not for example investigate anti-competitive agreements or cartel activity in the electronic communications sector. In addition, its ability to pursue abuses of dominant positions in the sector was quite limited. For some time, there had been debate in Ireland about whether to confer powers on ComReg similar to those enjoyed by OFCOM in the UK. Now, since the passing of the Act of 2007, ComReg has concurrent competition law powers in the electronic communications sector (but *only* in the electronic communications sector) by virtue of the amendments made to the Competition Act 2002 under Part 4 of the Act of 2007.

ComReg now has the power to investigate breaches of s 4 and s 5 of the Competition Act 2002 (and breaches of their equivalents under Articles 81 and 82 of the EC Treaty). Under s 4 of the Competition Act, 2002, all agreements between undertakings, decisions by associations of undertakings and concerted practices which have as their object or effect the prevention, restriction or distortion of competition in trade in any goods or services in the State or in any part of the State, are prohibited and void. Section 5 of the Competition Act, 2002 prohibits the abuse by one or more undertakings of a dominant position in trade for any goods or services in the State, or in any part of the State. ComReg has the power to initiate criminal proceedings in respect of an offence committed under ss 4 and 5 of the Competition Act 2002 (and Articles 81 and 82 of the EC Treaty). Summary criminal proceedings and proceedings on indictment may be instigated by ComReg in respect of such offences. ComReg is also entitled under s 14 of the Competition Act, 2002, to initiate civil proceedings in the High Court in respect of an agreement, decision or concerted practice which is prohibited under s 4, or an abuse of dominant position which is prohibited under s 5 (or by Articles 81 or 82 of the EC Treaty). ComReg may seek certain reliefs from the Court, including those of declaration and injunction.

It should be noted that the Act of 2007 provides for cooperation between ComReg and the Competition Authority with respect to the carrying out of ComReg's functions in the electronic communications sector. In addition, the Act of 2007 creates an express double jeopardy protection in relation to proceedings that may be initiated by either body against an undertaking in respect of the same matter.

While legislative amendments would be required for ComReg to structurally separate a SMP operator (such as *eircom*) such powers arguably already exist where an abuse of dominant position has been proved by ComReg. In that regard, if the Court decides that an undertaking has, contrary to s 5, *abused* its dominant position, it may, either at its own instance, or on the application of ComReg or by order either:

'(a) require the dominant position to be discontinued unless conditions specified in the order are complied with, or

(b) require the adjustment of the dominant position, in a manner and within a period specified in the order, by a sale of assets or otherwise as the Court may specify.'

As well as the SMP Guidelines previously referred to, useful guidance in relation to the application of competition law to the electronic communications sector is contained in the Commission Guidelines on the *Application of EEC Competition Rules in the Telecommunications Sector* (91/C 233/02) and the Commission Notice on the *Application of the Competition Rules to Access Agreements in the Telecommunications Sector* (98/C 265/02). In addition, in 2005, the EU Commission published its '*DG Competition Discussion Paper on the Application of Article 82 of the Treaty to Exclusionary Abuses*'. This contains an excellent explication of the economics and law relating to 'exclusionary' abuses such as predatory pricing and margin squeezes, tying and unreasonable bundling, which are particularly relevant in the electronic communications sector.

6.5.2 Administrative law

Although as previously noted there exists a specific appeal regime in respect of decisions by ComReg, certain decisions of ComReg may also be subject to judicial review. Judicial review is a means whereby the various organs of Government and administration in the State may be held accountable in respect of their decisions and whereby the legality of those decisions may be scrutinised by the Courts. The grounds for judicial review are fluid and overlap and while they cannot be neatly reduced to a list, they fall broadly under four heads:

- illegality (or the *ultra vires* ground);
- unreasonableness and irrationality;
- procedural impropriety, including breach of natural justice;
- legitimate expectation.

Each of the above heads might be expanded to include further grounds. For example, a failure to give reasons for a decision, or the making of decision affected by bias might constitute a breach of natural justice. Equally, a duty to give reasons might be expressed in a statute and a failure to comply with that statutory duty would be *ultra vires*.

ComReg is subject to the full range of administrative law duties, a number of which are given specific statutory expression. Section 12(3) of the Act of 2002 for example, provides that ComReg 'shall seek to ensure that measures taken by it are proportionate' having regard to its statutory objectives. Regulation 19 of the Framework Regulations requires ComReg to observe specific consultation procedures before making certain decisions that have a significant impact on markets for electronic communications. In addition, ComReg is subject to express statutory obligations requiring it to maintain the confidentiality of information (including commercially sensitive information) it receives from industry stakeholders.

6.6 The postal sector

As with other network industries in Ireland, the postal sector was historically a vertically integrated monopoly owned by the State.[6]

Responsibility for the national postal service resided in the old Department of Posts and Telegraphs. An Post was established as a statutory corporation with limited liability under the Postal and Telecommunications Services Act 1983 (the Act of 1983). The statutory monopoly was enshrined in s 63 which gave 'exclusive privilege' to An Post in the provision of postal services. The Minister for Posts and Telegraphs was the principal shareholder and also responsible for the regulation of the sector. The principal objects of

---

[6.] In the postal sector, the upstream end of the vertically integrated monopoly would be the post offices and the sorting offices and the retail end would be at the collection and distribution of mail points.

An Post are set out in s 12(1)(a) and (b) of the Act of 1983. They include the provision of a national postal service within the State and places outside the State and, so far as the company considers reasonably practicable, satisfying all reasonable demands for such services throughout the State. Under s 13(1)(a), An Post has a duty to ensure that charges for services are kept at the minimum rates consistent with meeting approved financial targets. The Minister has a general power to issue directions to An Post under s 110.

In *Attorney General and Minister for Posts and Telegraphs v Paperlink Ltd* [1984] ILRM 373, the statutory monopoly held by the Minister for Posts and Telegraphs was challenged. The defendant, a courier company claimed that the monopoly conferred by s 34(2) of the Post Office Act 1908 infringed its constitutionally protected right to earn a living. This challenge was ultimately unsuccessful. In the case of *Procureur de Roi v Corbeau* (Case C-320/91 [1993] ECR I-2533) the European Court of Justice held that it was contrary to Article 82 (then Article 86) of the EC Treaty, for national legislation to confer on the national postal service the exclusive right to carry and distribute mail, or to prevent an operator from offering services outside the conventional postal service, in so far as those services do not compromise the economic equilibrium of the service of general economic interest performed by the holder of the exclusive right. The Court stated that it is for the national court to consider whether the services in question in the main proceedings meet those criteria. The rule enunciated in this case is not an automatic prohibition on monopolies, but includes an assessment of whether the monopoly goes further than is necessary to fund the universal service requirement.

Section 63 of the Act of 1983, which conferred the statutory monopoly on An Post was repealed in 2000.

6.6.1 Role of ComReg in postal regulation

The ODTR was designated as the independent NRA for the postal sector on 27 September 2000, when Directive 97/67/EC (see below) was transposed into national law. While ComReg is today the independent NRA for the postal sector in Ireland, the Minister may also give policy directions to ComReg under s 13(1) of the Act of 2002.

Under s 10(1) of the Act of 2002, it is one of the functions of ComReg to ensure compliance by providers of postal services with obligations in relation to the provision of postal services. Section 12 of the Act of 2002 provides that one of the objectives of ComReg is to promote the development of the postal sector and in particular the availability of a universal postal service within, to and from the State at an affordable price for the benefit of all users. As in the electronic communications sector, regulation is funded by a levy on providers of postal services under s 30 of the Act of 2002.

6.6.2 The Postal Regulations

The European Communities (Postal Services) Regulations 2002 (the Postal Regulations) gave effect to Directive 97/67/EC, as amended by Directive 2002/39/EC.

The overall purpose of the Postal Regulations is to establish common rules for the development of a liberalised postal services market in the EU. The intention is to guarantee, at community level, the provision of a minimum level of universal service, while at the same time, progressively opening up the sector to increased competition.

6.6.2.1 *Universal service obligation*

The Postal Regulations use the 'universal service' concept to ensure that services provided in remote areas of the Community do not suffer as a result of the opening up the sector to increased competition. It defines the type of service which can be reserved for universal service providers. Postal services in remote areas have to be kept at an affordable level. If a universal service obligation imposes an inequitable financial burden, Member States may require other providers to make obligatory financial contributions to support the universal service.

Regulation 4 designates An Post as a universal service provider and the Minister may designate one or more additional postal service providers as a universal service provider having an obligation to provide all or part of the universal service.

Regulations 4 and 5 define the type of postal service that everyone has the right to receive. It covers letters up to 2 kilogrammes, postal packages up to 20 kilogrammes, registered and insured items. Universal service providers must guarantee one clearance, and subject to derogation, one delivery to the address of every natural or legal person in the State five days a week.

6.6.2.2 *Postal service authorisations*

Under reg 7, postal service providers with an annual turnover of €500,000 or more must apply to ComReg for a postal service authorisation.

6.6.2.3 *The reserved area*

Member States are allowed to reserve parts of the universal service to the universal service provider. For example, in Ireland correspondence weighing up to 50 grammes is reserved. The Postal Regulations reserve to An Post the provision of services within the maximum limits laid down by the Postal Regulations. Charges for services within the reserved area may only be increased with the agreement of ComReg.

6.6.2.4 *Quality standards*

Member States are responsible for establishing service quality standards for domestic postal services. At community level, the European Commission, assisted by an advisory Committee composed of representatives of the Member States, sets out the quality requirements for cross-border mail services. Independent performance monitoring is carried out by external bodies.

6.6.2.5 *Transparent cost accounting*

The Postal Regulations assume that the costs of meeting the universal service obligation will be funded by cross-subsidisation. Cross-subsidisation refers to the practice of covering the cost of offering some services through excess revenues earned from other services. For example, unprofitable mail delivery in rural areas could be subsidised through revenues from profitable mail delivery in urban areas. It is not necessarily a breach of competition law to cross-subsidise, but may be so where the undertaking engaging in the practice is dominant in a particular market. Typically, the dominant undertaking concerned will offer the services in the competitive market at low prices, while maintaining overall profitability by charging above-cost prices in the market in which it enjoys a monopoly or market power. The Postal Regulations outline the accounting procedures to be followed to prevent cross-subsidy from the reserved area to services in the competitive area, except insofar as is necessary to cover the additional costs of the universal services.

The extent to which there can be cross-subsidy between and within services is set out in the EU Commission's 1998 'Notice on the Application of the Competition Rules to the Postal Sector and on the Assessment of Certain State Measures Relating to Postal Services.'

6.6.2.6 *Judicial review*

If ComReg refuses the grant of a postal service authorisation, the applicant may appeal that decision within 28 days to the High Court. Other decisions by ComReg in the postal sector cannot be appealed before the High Court (or the ECAP) but would ordinarily be subject to judicial review under Order 84 of the Rules of the Superior Courts.

6.6.3 Directive 2008/6/EC

Further reform of the postal sector is being driven by the EU. Continued reform is seen as essential for the viability and quality of postal services, given the increasing dominance of the different means of electronic communication that are now available. Directive 2008/6/EC of the European Parliament and Council amending Directive 97/67/EC with regard to the full accomplishment of the internal market of Community postal services ('Directive 2008/6/EC') entered in to force across the EU on 20 April 2008. Directive 2008/6/EC must be transposed in to national law by Member States no later than 31 December 2010. Two of the most significant changes brought about by Directive 2008/6/EC are as follows:

- In relation to the universal service, Member States will be able to ensure its provision by means such as public tendering by postal service providers. If the provision of the universal service represents a net cost to a service provider (s) Member States may make provision for service providers to be compensated from public funds, or a compensation fund; funded by a levy on service provider (s).
- In relation to 'downstream access', Member States will be obliged to ensure that transparent, non-discriminatory access conditions are available to elements of postal infrastructure or services provided within the scope of the universal service. This includes access to the postcode system, the address database, post office boxes, delivery boxes, information on the change of address service, the re-direction service and the return to sender service.
- IMember States will be obliged to provide for a right of appeal from decisions of NRAs.

At the time of writing, Directive 2008/6/EC has not yet been transposed in to Irish law by the Minister. However, in 2008, the Minister completed a public consultation in advance of the transposition of Directive 2008/6/EC which posed a series of detailed questions in relation to the future provision of postal services and the transposition of Directive 2008/6/EC.

6.7 Broadcasting and spectrum

6.7.1 Broadcasting

One of the markets identified by the Recommendation on Relevant Markets is the national market for provision of national analogue terrestrial broadcasting transmission services for the provision of television content. RTÉ Networks Limited (RTÉNL) is a wholly owned subsidiary of RTÉ. It owns and operates the only such broadcasting transmission network in the State. RTÉNL is the only participant on the relevant market. In April, 2004, RTÉNL was designated by ComReg as having SMP in the following markets:

- the wholesale market for provision of national analogue terrestrial broadcasting transmission services for the provision of radio content to end-users; and
- the wholesale market for provision of national analogue terrestrial broadcasting transmission services for the provision of television content to end-users.

A number of *ex ante* obligations were imposed on RTÉNL by ComReg to address its dominant position and to guard in advance against potential abuses of its dominant position. However, an obligation to actually provide access to its network was not imposed upon RTÉNL.

6.7.2 Spectrum

Spectrum is regarded as a critical but finite economic resource. As such, ComReg's policy is aimed at the optimal allocation and use of spectrum. Given its statutory remit under s 10 of the Act of 2002, ComReg has a central role regarding the proper management and use of spectrum.

The legislative framework until 2003 comprised of the Wireless Telegraphy Acts 1926–1988. The 2003 regulatory package does not replace that framework but takes precedence over it. Since 2003, licensing of wireless electronic communications services and networks under those Acts must be in accordance with the requirements of the Authorisation Regulations.

In broadcasting, ComReg's role is limited to spectrum management and assignment issues. Broadcasting policy is decided by the Minister and content issues are regulated by the Broadcasting Commission of Ireland and the RTÉ Authority.

Included in the 2003 regulatory package is the Radio Spectrum Decision 676/2002/EC. Its aim is to promote competition, the interests of the citizen (universal service, consumer protection, privacy, dispute resolution) and the single market. A dynamic and adaptable spectrum policy is important in the context of convergence. While on the one hand, ComReg needs to ensure that no harmful interference is caused by spectrum usage, it also seeks to liberalise spectrum management by removing unnecessary regulatory constraints. An innovative spectrum policy can encourage new investment in research and development and the commercialisation of various applications, using, for example, liberalised or exempt spectrum. There has been increasing interest in the use of market based approaches to spectrum management, as opposed to the more 'command and control' type approach prevalent in most countries. This has opened up the possibility for 'spectrum trading' which ComReg and other NRAs are carefully studying.

It is anticipated that in the next few years, new legislation relating to the regulation of the electronic communications sector will be enacted which will impact on spectrum and other areas. This includes the already published Communications Regulation (Amendment) Bill 2007, a new Radiocommunications Act (which will replace the Wireless Telegraphy Acts 1926–1988) and a new Broadcasting Act.

6.8 Conclusion

Although much progress still needs to be made in certain areas such as LLU, the last decade has witnessed dramatic changes in the Irish electronic communications sector. Instead of a single, vertically integrated, state monopoly provider, there are now multiple players competing in the provision of varied and innovative services and signs of emerging competition in certain markets. These changes may be seen as the result of liberalisation, regulation, technological innovation and market forces. In the postal sector, significant changes may occur in the next few years with the implementation of Directive 2008/6/EC.

CHAPTER 7

COMPUTER CRIME IN IRELAND

Andy Harbison & Pearse Ryan

7.1 Introduction

Computer development since the mid-1980s has been so rapid, and information technology is today so all-pervasive, that it is sometimes forgotten how recently technologies taken for granted as part of modern life were even invented. The internet, developed in the mid-to-late 1970s, was only opened to public use in 1991. The World Wide Web, now ubiquitous, was only invented in 1993. In a sense, it is only in this new century that information technology has come into its own, and individuals, organisations and businesses learned to use it to its full potential.

Regrettably, in parallel with its development as a technology for both business and leisure, IT has also developed as a means of committing crimes and inflicting harm on others. Computers have been used for destructive purposes as long as they have existed. The public has long been familiar with phenomena such as computer viruses and worms (which were essentially first developed in the early-to-mid 1980s), and computer hacking. However, the recent proliferation of IT has led to the development of new varieties of criminal and culpable activity. Recent years have seen the development of new forms of malicious software, such as 'spyware' and 'Trojan' programs, new techniques used for computer-based extortion such as 'denial-of-service' attacks and 'data napping', and new methods for carrying out large scale fraud, from simple confidence trickery (called 'social engineering' by its practitioners) to sophisticated, large-scale email 'Phishing' scams. We can expect criminal activity to continue to develop as technology develops.

Nor is the use of information technology by offenders limited to computer-centric offences like hacking and virus-writing. Computers are now so ubiquitous and all-pervasive that many investigations, which at first glance appear to have little or nothing to do with computers, can turn on computer-based evidence. It has been said that the expression 'computer fraud' is now rather outdated. Because the vast majority of modern financial and accounting systems are computer based, it is a rare fraud in today's world that does not involve some manipulation of computer systems. Generally, there is a distinction to be drawn between those crimes which are unique to computers and those which are facilitated by the use of computers. The former are essentially new crimes, while the latter are traditional forms of crimes in a new context – for example, a threat made by email.

A useful illustration of the broad relevance of computer based evidence concerns the investigation of 2001 murder of Ms Mary Gough. In this well-publicised case, Ms Gough was murdered by her husband, Colin Whelan, who then faked his own suicide and fled to Spain, where he was later identified and extradited back to Ireland. The key evidence in the case was found on Mr Whelan's work computer. It was found that he had been using internet search web-sites to research methods of killing his wife. It was also found that he had used the computer to establish and manage life insurance policies covering his wife. To quote from the newspaper coverage – 'He may have been a computer analyst, but

Whelan either forgot or did not realise that the gardai could trace his every movement in cyberspace.'

We can see, then, that even where computers are not used to directly commit an offence, they can still retain crucial evidence. People use computers to research crimes, identify victims, communicate with conspirators, disperse proceeds and track the ongoing investigation of their offences in the media. Computer evidence can be used to track individuals' movements, determine the timelines of their actions, uncover their financial details, and even gain insights into their thought processes.

The investigation of computer crimes and the recovery of computer-based evidence in cases like those discussed above is the remit of the computer forensics specialist. Computer forensics is the application of computer science and legal procedure to identify evidence in criminal, civil and administrative cases. From its beginnings in the late 1980s the discipline has accumulated a large body of legal precedent and broadly accepted best practice which has led to computer forensics today being routinely used in criminal and civil proceedings in this as well as most other developed countries.

The purpose of this chapter is to summarise the kinds of computer crimes commonly seen affecting individuals and organisations using computer technology. It will consider the legal issues associated with computer crime, and in particular how they apply to criminal and civil law. The chapter will briefly discuss, in a non-technical way, how modern computers and data storage devices actually record information, and how that information can be extracted for use in legal proceedings. It will consider the kinds of data that can accumulate on computer hard drives that may be of value to legal professionals. The chapter will conclude with a brief discussion of proper computer forensic procedures and the methods that must be employed in handling computer data to ensure that it remains evidentially reliable. Chapter 8 deals with the separate issue of Electronic Discovery, an example of the use of the computer in a traditional legal environment, where the environment has had to evolve to cater for the realities of the new world.

7.2 Computer-specific fraud

The development of information technology has resulted in the emergence of a wide variety of threats directly affecting computers and their users (as opposed to those where computers are used less directly in the planning or commission of an offence). These threats vary in severity from simple nuisance to seriously disrupting a victim's daily life, often inflicting significant personal distress and financial loss. We examine below the most common forms of computer based crime.

7.2.1 Unsolicited bulk commercial emails – 'spam'

In May 2007, it was estimated that unsolicited bulk emails were estimated globally to constitute in excess of 75% of email traffic on the internet. In Ireland, the situation is somewhat less severe, yet over 60% of emails received by companies can be designated as 'spam'. Certain internet service providers in the United States now report that over 90% of emails received over their networks are spam.

The distribution of spam is a lucrative business, although in recent times legal barriers have made it more difficult in developed countries. In May 2007, a large proportion of the spam transmitted in the world originated in the People's Republic of China, although the point of origin of spam can change exceptionally quickly. (In August 2006 less than 20% of world spam originated in China; in December 2006 over 40%, a figure which reduced again in early 2007 to around 20%). Most computer users have experienced spam at some time or another.

At a superficial level, most spam appears to be an attempt to sell some form of product to the recipient of the email, often of highly dubious quality and/or origin. The underlying principle behind spam is that originally stated by PT Barnum: 'There's a sucker born every minute.' While it is unlikely that any particular individual would respond to a spam email, a tiny proportion will be sufficiently ill-advised to reply. If a distributor of spam (referred to as a 'spammer') can send enough emails to enough recipients, sooner or later a significant group of recipients will be credulous enough to respond, making the process worthwhile to the spammer.

The vast quantity of spam on the internet is a reflection both of the fact that sending spam remains highly profitable, and the fact that as people throughout the world become more aware of spam, the proportion who will respond to any single spam email has reduced, thereby increasing the number of emails spammers must send to receive each 'successful' response.

Spam has become a significant issue both for individuals and companies. Immense disruption and financial loss is caused by spam simply as a consequence of the sheer quantity being transmitted. Companies must either purchase and deploy ever higher capacity data communications links simply to accommodate this additional useless traffic, or outsource the problem to a third party application service provider who essentially acts as the companies' gatekeeper for all email, an example of a new business model deriving from the peculiarities of the internet. Companies and service providers must invest in increasingly sophisticated 'spam filtering' software on their email connections to prevent the majority of such emails getting through. A proportion of spam messages will, nevertheless, evade spam filtering and arrive at users email accounts, where users must spend time removing them, affecting their productivity.

More worryingly, an increasing quantity of spam has malicious software attached, which represents a direct threat to any person opening such a message. Spam is also regularly used as the basis of fraudulent confidence (or 'phishing') schemes, discussed below. As the sending of spam becomes increasingly restricted, senders have begun to operate outside the law. Spam is now commonly sent from networks of computers (so-called 'botnets') previously compromised through hacking or viruses. Essentially, the compromised computer acts as a conduit and not just recipient of spam. In this way individuals and companies can become implicated in spamming without being aware that it is actually originating from their computers.

In Ireland, the sending of unsolicited mails is restricted by the European Communities (Electronic Communications Networks and Services) (Data Protection and Privacy) Regulations 2003 (SI 535/2003). The Regulations make it an offence to use or cause any publicly available electronic communications service to be used to send an unsolicited communication for the purpose of direct marketing by means of email to a subscriber, unless notified by that subscriber that for the time being he or she consents to the receipt of such a communication, an effective 'opt-in' standard.

The Regulations also prohibit the sending of email for the purposes of direct marketing, which disguises or conceals the identity of the sender on whose behalf the communication was made, or without a valid address to which the recipient may send a request that such communication shall cease.

Summary proceedings for an offence under these Regulations may be brought and prosecuted by the Data Protection Commissioner. Furthermore, a person who suffers loss and damage as a result of a contravention of the requirements of these Regulations by any other person shall be entitled to damages from that other person for that loss and damage. You can see that the Regulations are telecoms and data protection based, reflecting the evolving role of the Data Protection Commissioner. You can also see, however, that the Regulations are unlikely to stem the tidal wave of non-jurisdiction based spam.

7.2.2 Maliciously developed software – 'malware'

Maliciously developed software, commonly referred to as 'malware', is software designed to alter the operation of a computer, usually to the user's disadvantage, which is transmitted and installed without the user's informed consent. It comes in a number of forms, the best known and longest standing being the 'Virus' or 'Worm' program. In the 1980's and 1990's, malware was typically identified as a form of computer vandalism, a means for technically gifted but misguided individuals to amuse themselves or gain kudos among their peers. In recent years malware has become increasingly associated with commercial, illegal and organised criminal activity.

The increasing proportion of technically unsophisticated home users has resulted in a profusion of malicious software, as well as the development of a number of new malware types. The more common varieties of malware include:

(a) *Adware:* Adware is software that causes advertising to pop-up on the user's screen. Typically, this kind of malware is downloaded unintentionally, although it can be deliberately installed as part of the licensing agreements of certain freely distributed ('freeware') software. Typically, the presence of adware on a computer constitutes little more than a nuisance, only becoming a problem when multiple instances of the software, all running simultaneously on the computer, affect its performance.

(b) *Spyware:* Spyware is more insidious than Adware. It is malicious software that collects information about the computer's user without their informed consent. The least intrusive can, for example, collect information about a user's browsing habits so that accompanying Adware software can target them more effectively. The most damaging spyware software can collect personal information stored on a user's computer, monitor and record users typing (so called 'key logging') and pass this information to third parties.

Spyware software can find its way onto computers in a number of ways. Like Adware it can be installed with software. It can also be installed when users visit certain websites. Typically the software is installed either without the user's knowledge or through deception (for example, it is often installed under the guise of 'web-acceleration' software.

A large proportion of Spyware software is intended to perform activities that would be in breach of most developed countries' data protection and privacy legislation and certainly in breach of the obtaining and fair processing principles set out in EU Directive 95/46/EC. In more severe cases, its presence on a computer can lead to users suffering 'identity theft,' ie impersonation and misuse of their credentials, typically for the purposes of financial fraud. The use of anti-Spyware software, which is regularly updated by the user and the avoidance of web-sites not trusted, are two of the main tools to guard against Spyware.

(c) *Viruses and Worms:* These two terms are increasingly used interchangeably, although in strict terms they differ. By definition, viruses are spread unintentionally by user action, while worms spread without user intervention.

Because they require user intervention to spread, viruses are closely associated with computer-to-computer communication. In the early days of personal computing, viruses were typically transferred from computer to computer on floppy disks. Since the development of the internet they have become most closely associated with email and messaging applications. The second writer was first introduced to viruses in the mid-1990s when negotiating a contract with a certain well known Swedish IT provider, a draft of which sent via email caused mass-infection to the recipient. Today, it would be hoped that the recipient's firewall software should catch the majority of infected emails and attachments, although anti-virus software is only as good as the last update.

Worms typically take advantage of programming faults or other weaknesses in the software of internet facing computers. Web server computers have been seen as the most common target of computer worms, both because they exist in large numbers on the internet and because, for technical reasons, they are relatively difficult to secure. However, worms have been seen affecting other applications. The first recorded computer worm, the 'Morris Worm' of 1988, affected the mail software on computers, and the highly destructive 'Slammer' worm of 2003 affected the SQL database application.

Large scale, destructive, internet worms have become less common in recent years. To some extent this reflects a greater attention to computer security by software developers and computer users. Regrettably, it also a symptom of the increasing use of computer vulnerabilities by organised criminals. Rather than attempting to cause general mayhem (as in the case of 'Slammer', 'Code Red' and other worms) criminals use such vulnerabilities to compromise computer systems to their own purposes. Modern worms and viruses typically have sophisticated 'payloads' which can:

- disable antivirus software;
- search for confidential information for the purposes of identity theft;
- install key-logging software or other eavesdropping software;
- enable 'backdoor' or 'trojan horse' software (which allows the virus writer to gain remote access to the infected computer);
- allow for the distribution or storage of illegal material;
- install remote control (or 'bot') software which can allow the virus writer to use the computer for distributing spam or carrying out denial of service attacks (see **7.2.4** below); and
- repeatedly make the computer's modem dial premium-rate telephone services ('dialler' payloads).

Recently, viruses have been found that continuously download new versions of themselves to keep ahead of anti-virus software. Others are 'polymorphic' and change their structures to evade detection and deletion.

At the time of writing, software vendors were reporting a recent trend that showed that the number of new virus and worm payloads was increasing at a much higher rate than the number of actual attacks. This indicates that criminals are increasingly tailoring their attacks to their targets, and to the specific purposes to which they want to put any compromised computers.

7.2.3 Legal issues arising from malware

It is exceptionally difficult to track-down and prosecute the developers and distributors of malware. The reputable Center for Education and Research in Information Security (CERIAS) at Purdue University estimates that fewer than 20 malware developers have ever been successfully traced and prosecuted worldwide. However, this is not by far the only legal exposure arising from malware infection.

Disputes can arise over the liability of persons who have suffered loss or damage as a consequence of malware infection. Issues arise over the liability for financial fraud originating in, for example, malware-based identity theft or the installation of dialler software. A number of disputes have arisen in other jurisdictions as to the liability of the various parties in such circumstances.

The presence of backdoor or trojan horse software has famously been used in this and other jurisdictions to invalidate computer based evidence – the so-called 'Trojan Defence'.

In one exceptional UK case (*Crown v Caffrey*) this defence was successfully employed, despite the fact that no such malware was in fact found on the evidential computer in question. The Court found that Mr Caffrey, a highly experienced computer 'hacker', could be the victim of specialised and difficult-to-detect malware software.

Finally, there has been some discussion in the common law world that the operators of business networks, whose computers are compromised by malware and used to cause loss or injury to others, may be liable for damages to the injured party, particularly where reasonable measures have not been taken to secure the malware-infected computers in the first place. In a common law jurisdiction, the normal principles of the law of negligence would apply, albeit in a highly technical and fast evolving environment. Just what constitutes 'reasonable care' in this environment would not be a clear cut decision. The network operators have well worn arguments at this stage relating to their status as a mere conduit for user communication. This area will bring those arguments into a very technical environment.

7.2.4 Denial of service

A number of Irish companies have been the victims of denial of service attacks in recent years. Such an attack involves knocking-out the internet connections of the victim by one of a number of means. The most effective mode of attack (and therefore the most commonly employed) is the so-called 'Distributed Denial of Service' attack, where the attacker disables the victim's internet links by overloading them with spurious connections, usually from networks of previously compromised computers ('botnets', discussed at **7.2.1** above), thereby preventing legitimate users connecting to them. Another common form occurs when a hacker discovers a weakness in the victim's internet connections which, when attacked, will cause them to fail.

The principal targets of such attacks are companies who carry out some or all of their business on the internet. The motive can be simple vandalism, politically inspired or, increasingly commonly, as a means of extorting money from the victim. In a recent well publicised attack, a number of internet betting sites were subjected to a Denial of Service attack before a series of major sporting events, with the threat that customers of the sites would be prevented from using them until the attackers were paid a sum of money.

Denial of Service attacks are prevented by ensuring that any vulnerable site has sufficient capacity on standby to prevent it being overloaded, among other more sophisticated techniques. You can see that such business continuity planning carries a cost component, the most straightforward of which is a large volume of potentially unused storage capacity.

Business interruption is the main commercial risk issue here. From the legal perspective, the major threat to the user or company is that they, as victim of such an attack, will have their computer compromised and used as part of an attacking 'botnet'. In cases where the compromised computer was not adequately protected, then, there have been some suggestions that a victim might incur some kind of vicarious liability. The writers are not aware of any case law in this area, but going back to basic principles of the law of negligence, assuming an injured party can succeed on the nexus point, a claim would seem capable of success in the right circumstances. However, again, the arguments would likely turn on quite technical points, most likely the extent to which the victim of malware had taken reasonable precautions to protect itself and others.

7.2.5 Unauthorised access – 'hacking'

Hacking is not as serious a problem in Ireland as it is in other countries, although it remains an issue. The principal mode of hacking seen in Ireland remains simple credential theft, ie stealing or guessing another user's password and using it without authorisation to gain access to restricted information. More sophisticated hacking attacks have become quite rare in recent times, mostly because the computer vulnerabilities employed by skilled hackers to attack computers are now used by malicious software writers in their viruses, forcing computer administrators to close such loopholes far more quickly than they would have in the past. Also, as computer crime has become more developed, and as organised criminals have moved into the area from other fields, it has become increasingly clear that there are more lucrative and less time-consuming methods of making money, such as spamming, phishing and virus writing.

Over 80% of successful hacking attempts are now targeted at the computers which run websites. Website applications are often not written to the same standards as other commercial software, and web-server software is intrinsically more vulnerable to attack than other types. In addition much valuable data, such as personal details and credit card numbers, can be stored on such computers. A large proportion of website attacks are simply carried out for the purpose of vandalism, the principal motive being for the attacker to gain kudos among his hacking peers.

Hacking is dealt with under the Criminal Damage Act 1991. This rather old piece of legislation essentially grafted an offence of criminal damage in the computer context into a piece of legislation originally intended to deal with criminal damage to tangible property. The Act framed computer crime as a form of criminal damage and essentially criminalises criminal damage to data and programmes (s 2), as well as unauthorised access to data (s 5). The Act is discussed further at **7.4.1** below. Historically there have been few successful prosecutions in Ireland for hacking per se, although a number of successful cases have been taken with respect to frauds originating in hacking activity.

At time of writing, the European Union is preparing a directive that will require any company or organisation in the EU that loses customer details to information theft or hacking to promptly inform the affected persons. This directive is likely to be the cause of considerable legal activity in future years.

7.2.6 Identity and credential theft – 'phishing, vishing and pharming'

Phishing is a form of confidence trickery (or 'social engineering') that has become very common in recent years. In it simplest form, the victim is sent an email, purportedly from their bank or some other internet service. Typically these emails will state that there is something wrong with the user's account, and that it is imperative that they immediately connect to the internet site in question to correct matters. The email will typically contain a link, which supposedly will allow the user to connect directly to the site in question.

In reality, the link will not connect to the real site, but to a facsimile of the site created by the fraudster. The victim enters their username, password and other credentials (usually including their credit card or bank account details) into the fake site. The fraudster can then use these credentials to commit fraud against the victim, running up charges on their credit card, accessing and emptying their bank account, even, in extreme cases, using their credentials to take out loans.

In the case of credit cards, the victim is not usually liable (if the credit card is not present in a fraudulent transaction, the burden of losses falls on the vendor). In attacks against bank accounts the picture is more complicated, with some banks fully refunding customers their losses, others refusing compensation and others handling losses on a case by case basis. In reality, there is no consistency across either the banks or the type of incident.

In Ireland, phishing attacks against online banking services are typically orchestrated by domestically based criminals. Money transfer restrictions mean that stolen funds can only be transferred to other Irish bank accounts, which makes it difficult for foreign criminals to retrieve the funds once transferred. It is common, however, for these domestic criminals to 'outsource' the emailing and website elements of the crime to foreign criminals for a percentage of the proceeds.

The phenomenon of phishing is too recent to have legal precedent in Ireland or, as far as the writers are aware, in any major common law jurisdiction. There have been, as yet, no legal cases taken in Ireland; however as losses increase (banking losses in Ireland alone were estimated to be well over €2 million in 2006 alone) it is likely that there will be significant legal consequences.

Since their first appearance in 2002, Phishing attacks have become increasingly sophisticated. Perpetrators have used weaknesses in browser software to make their e-mails and fraudulent sites appear increasingly convincing. Another approach occasionally used is to redirect victims from the real website to the fraudulent one by means of a hacking attack, a technique known as 'pharming' a website. Another approach is to use malware software to redirect or override the browsing software to pass a user's credentials to the fraudster. Finally a recent variant of phishing attacks relies on the fraudster making voice contact with the victim over mobile phone, and under false pretences persuading them to provide them with their credentials (an approach know as 'vishing').

While the effects of such attacks can be lessened through proper website design and bank procedures, the most effective countermeasure against hacking is user education. User education has the additional advantage of lessening the exposure of banks and other internet service providers to legal action in the event their clients are the targets of phishing attacks.

7.2.7 Computer hijacking

Computer hijacking has become a major illegal industry in recent years. In the past, hackers went to considerable lengths to compromise single computers. Recently, however, hackers have been able to compromise large numbers of computers at the same time, usually through the use of malware programs called 'Trojan Horses' or 'Trojans'. Typically, the hacker will not use the Trojan to take full control of the computer, but instead will use it to obtain a part of the computer's functionality for their own use. Modern computers are so fast that even if the true user detects that their computer has slowed down to some degree (because of the presence of the Trojan) the deterioration will probably not be significant enough for them to take action to investigate or correct it. In this way a hacker can accumulate networks of hundreds or thousands of compromised computers.

A single computer compromised in this way is referred to as a 'bot' or a 'zombie'. A collection of compromised computers is called a 'bot net' and the hacker running them a 'bot herder'. As discussed at **7.2.1** above, bot nets are increasingly used for distributing spam, and carrying out Denial of Service attacks. Bot herders will typically sub-contract their services to other criminals for a fee or share of the proceeds of a crime.

7.2.8 Other forms of computer fraud

As discussed above, as well as being used directly to commit offences, computers can also be used to aid offenders in researching, committing and covering up their actions. The most common forms of computer misuse (as determined by a recent Information Systems Security Association (ISSA) survey) are:

- *The use of computers to access inappropriate websites and material on the internet* has become a significant issue for business and organisations. The experience in Ireland is that the material most commonly accessed from the internet consists of pornographic images and media. It has been estimated that over a third of internet websites contain some amount of pornographic material. While the accessing of pornographic material is not a criminal offence, save in relation to child pornography, it is a matter which the prudent company would wish to manage and control, in this case typically by way of an outright prohibition. Employee access to this material can give rise to claims of sexual harassment and other liability issues for the company – which are primarily employment law issues. Access to illegal material – child pornography – is outside the scope of this chapter and is primarily a criminal matter. The company employment contract should allow for the application of IT use policy documentation, which can deal with inappropriate and illegal use of employer IT resources.

- *Access to gambling*, humour and sports web-sites can also be an issue.
- *Excessive use of the internet and World Wide Web*, in particular where excessive access adversely affects employee productivity. Again this is primarily an employment law issues.
- *Harassment and bullying* by means of email and electronic communications has also been a serious issue. There is a perception that harassing or threatening messages can be sent to victims by means of anonymous, untraceable web-mail accounts (Hotmail, Google Mail and Yahoo Mail are all examples of webmail). In fact, it is often possible to trace emails such as these to source.
- *Theft of property, including intellectual property,* has become a critical issue in recent years. The development of high-capacity portable data storage devices, such as USB pen drives, has made it almost trivially easy to copy large quantities of data from almost any computer. Any device with substantial amounts of on-board memory can be employed for data theft. A recent phenomenon, for example, is the use of portable digital music players to remove data from computers, a practice referred to as 'podding' by its practitioners. Again, company IT use policy documentation should deal with downloading of company data.
- *Financial fraud*, as discussed above, is now mainly performed using computer systems.

While the above issues are dealt with by different legislation and legal procedures, they have in common the fact that they all must to a greater or lesser extent be investigated using computer forensic techniques. This is because in all case some or all of the key evidence in the case is likely to reside on computer systems.

Recent research by UCD and the ISSA has shown that in Ireland computer fraud is generally detected:

- *By accident,* usually reported by a member of staff, a customer or supplier. Over 65% of frauds are detected this way.
- *More rarely by automated detection tools,* although these are of more use against computer-specific frauds rather than computer-enabled ones. The known existence of such tools and back-up procedures does tend to dissuade the would be wrongdoer.
- *Audit,* although fewer than 20% of frauds are identified in this way. It is a common misconception that audit is primarily intended to detect frauds, when in fact its main usefulness is generally prevention. Again, the known existence of an audit and review programme does tend to prevent the occurrence of computer crime and, in particular, fraud.
- *Data analysis* has been shown to be highly effective in other countries, but is not often used in Ireland. Consequently, few computer frauds are detected this way. There are IT challenges in implementing sophisticated data analysis.

7.3 Reaction to discovery of computer fraud

If you suspect computer fraud:

- Don't panic; gather a support team (legal, audit, human resources, public relations, IT, etc).
- Implement a pre-existing contingency plan, which ideally should form part of the overall corporate contingency planning. Where this does not exist, promptly, then, compile at least an outline plan. Consider if the company will want to 'contain and eradicate' the incident or 'investigate and prosecute'.
- Start documenting: Who? What? Where? When? How? Proper documentation is crucial in recovering from a computer fraud and in any legal action that may follow.
- Identify who will 'own' the investigation. Who has responsibility for managing the investigation team and final approval on tasks.
- Agree what the investigation should attempt to accomplish and determine when the investigation can be concluded.
- Limit information of the incident to people with a need-to-know. Determine if there is to be notification to the Gardaí.
- Gather evidence 'legally' (see **7.7** and **7.8** below).
- Where necessary consult security specialists and legal advisors.

A fraud contingency plan should have senior level approval, should be communicated in general terms to staff, and included within corporate training, noting that there will be an element of secrecy in relation (at least) to the reaction element of the plan. In terms of administering the plan it is recommended that responsibilities be assigned to key personnel, especially in relation to reaction matters, which would include the preservation of evidence of fraud, maintenance of confidentiality, reporting upwards within the plan structure and (perhaps) taking an initial decision as to whether to report the incident to the Gardai. The contingency plan should be regularly reviewed and updated. Where appropriate, a financial recovery policy should be included within the contingency plan.

As part of a corporate policy of fraud prevention and as part of good corporate governance, it is recommended that companies:

- implement a fraud detection/prevention programme, as mentioned below; and
- attempt to avoid criminal investigation by avoiding fraud.

A criminal prosecution, which is a matter for the law enforcement agencies of the State rather than a company, will invariably bring bad publicity and make demands on the time of corporate officers and staff. However, in certain circumstances, referring the matter to the Gardai is necessary. The key elements of corporate anti-fraud planning are:

- detect;
- react;
- prevent.

7.4 Computer fraud and the law

All of the examples of corporate computer misuse discussed above can be seen as forms of computer fraud. Computer fraud is the manipulation of a data processing system, without the consent of its owner, to:

- obtain money;
- obtain property;
- obtain information;

- gain an advantage of value; or
- cause a financial loss.

The legal issues associated with computer fraud can be broken down between the criminal and civil law. Fraud has a specific meaning in criminal law, as there is no fraud committed under criminal law unless and until a criminal offence can be identified and proven. Also, it is true to say that not all dishonesty is a crime. Companies should be aware of the position under both criminal and civil law, in order to put in place appropriate detection, preventive and reactive planning to reduce the risk of an event of corporate fraud occurring. The key maxim is that prevention is better than cure. The cure tends to be technically challenging, time-consuming and costly, without any real guarantee that it will not recur. Hence, the importance of focusing on the prevention and detection elements of corporate contingency planning.

7.4.1 Criminal law

Fraud is not a specific criminal offence of itself. Rather, fraud is an umbrella term which includes criminal offences such as conspiracy, larceny, obtaining by false pretences and various breaches of the Companies Acts 1963—2006. The most relevant statutes in the area of computer fraud are the Criminal Damage Act 1991 (the 1991 Act), discussed at **7.2.5** above, and the more recent Criminal Justice (Theft and Fraud Offences) Act 2001 (the 2001 Act).

(a) The 1991 Act at s 2(1) introduced the offence of damage to property, defined as:

'a person who without lawful excuse damages any property belonging to another intending to damage any such property or being reckless as to whether any such property would be damaged shall be guilty of an offence.'

Property includes data, and damage to data includes the addition, alteration, corruption, erasure, or movement thereof, or introduction of a virus therein, which causes damage. It shall be noted that the offence requires the absence of *'lawful excuse'* and, in addition, requires the accused to act with intent or recklessness. Interestingly, the concept of damage is not tied to harmful effect, although in reality, given the imperative to succeed in prosecution, the prosecution services will likely require its existence. Differing penalties apply on summary conviction or on indictment (meaning trial by jury). On summary conviction the penalties are a fine of up to €1,270 or imprisonment for up to 12 months, while on indictment, the penalties are a fine of up to €12,700 or imprisonment for up to 10 years, or both.

As with most criminal legislation, the 1991 Act introduced a range of offences. Section 3 of the 1991 Act introduced the offence of threatening to damage property and s 4 introduced the offence of possession of anything with intent to damage property. Both carry the same penalties as a s 2 offence. Section 5 then introduced the offence of operation of a computer with intent to access data without lawful excuse. The offence is defined as follows:

'A person who without lawful excuse operates a computer within the State with intent to access any data kept either within or outside the State, or outside the State with intent to access any data, kept within the State, shall, whether or not he accesses any data, be guilty of an offence.'

The penalties on summary conviction are a fine of up to €6,349, or imprisonment for up to three months. The penalties are light and therefore the offence has in the past not been perceived as a serious offence. However, it is the offence which, prior to the introduction of the 2001 Act, was typically relied on by the law enforcement agencies. It can be seen that either (or both) the perpetrator and the data may be located either inside or outside the State. It is also worth noting that the required intention must be to access any data and not necessarily specific data and that the accused need not succeed in accessing data.

(b) The law in relation to computer fraud has been updated and augmented with the introduction of the 2001 Act. The 2001 Act introduced a number of new offences into Irish law, the most important of which arises under s 9, which states:

> 'A person who dishonestly, whether within or outside the State, operates or causes to be operated a computer within the State with the intention of making a gain for himself or herself or another, or of causing loss to another, is guilty of an offence.'

This section introduced the concept of '*dishonesty*' into Irish computer-related offences. The perpetrator can be located either inside or outside the State and is required to act dishonestly, meaning '*without a claim of right made in good faith.*' The operation of a '*computer*' is required. The 2001 Act is technology neutral in not defining the term, reflecting a general legislative tendency to allow for technology development.

Section 9 of the 2001 Act requires the presence of intent, which could relate to the unauthorised access of another's computer or, alternatively, authorised access of a computer for unauthorised purposes (bad faith use). The intention must be to make a gain, whether for themselves, or another, or, alternatively, to cause a loss to another. Therefore, for example, the section would not cover a straightforward hacking incident, being information based, where no gain or loss arose (the 1991 Act unauthorised access offence may apply here). As per s 2(3), the terms gain and loss 'are to be construed as extending only to gain or loss in money or other property.' Section 9 is a more serious offence than existed under the 1991 Act. It is an indictable offence, carrying a potential fine of unspecified amount, or maximum of 10 years imprisonment, or both.

7.4.2 Garda Bureau of Fraud Investigation

The Garda Bureau of Fraud Investigation (GBFI) has national responsibility for:
- money laundering;
- computer crime;
- commercial fraud;
- cheque and credit card fraud;
- counterfeit currency.

Its objectives are as follows:

- to establish if criminal activity exists;
- to refer the file to the Director of Public Prosecutions (DPP) who decides whether to prosecute the suspect.

The average time for adjudication in a computer fraud criminal case is:

- District Court — minor offence — 12 to 18 months;
- Circuit Court — serious offence — two to four years.

The approach taken by the GBFI is as follows:

- obtain statements (days/weeks);
- investigate environment of alleged fraud;
- seize evidence – documents and computers;
- conduct forensic analysis;
- possible examination of company accounts;

- identify/detain/interview suspects;
- identify what was stolen/obtained via fraud;
- determine intent or 'mens rea';
- determine whether a criminal or a civil matter;
- prepare file, refer to DPP.

7.4.3 Common law

The listing of common forms of computer crime and, in particular, fraud, at **7.2.7** above, points to the many types of computer fraud that could be committed by people within an organisation. Fraud should be treated by companies in the same way as any other business risk, meaning that the risk should be scoped, a proactive approach taken to risk management, corporate plans should be implemented and procedures put in place to prevent, detect, and react to corporate fraud. Finally, the company should check its policies of insurance. A corporate fraud alert plan covering the key issues of detection, reaction, and prevention, would include a fraud prevention plan (prevention), together with a fraud contingency plan (detection and reaction).

7.4.4 Civil remedies against wrongdoers

Issues which arise in relation to possible corporate civil remedies against wrongdoers, whether employees or external to the organisation, include:

- lower burden of proof;
- proper procedures (interviews, search, seizure);
- adequate documentation;
- proper control of 'evidence';
- time-consuming;
- litigation — costly;
- Gardaí investigation may facilitate civil recovery (although not the role of the Gardaí).

7.5 Computer forensics

Computer forensics is defined as the application of computer science and legal procedures to identify and collect evidence in a criminal or civil matter.

The searching of computers and retrieval of evidence from them is more technically complex than it might first appear. Unless it is done under strictly controlled conditions, the simple act of viewing or retrieving data from computers can alter the data itself or the dates and time stamps associated with it. Although the data can often be found and recovered, it may have little evidential value in criminal or civil proceedings.

Fortunately, there now exist multiple ways to search computers and recover data using both freely available and commercial software, including shareware. Computer forensics tools and associated procedures are intended to ensure that the data recovered from the computer will comply with the rules of 'best evidence' and be admissible in any subsequent legal proceedings. Most reputable computer forensics specialists in Ireland now use procedures consistent with guidelines set out and maintained by the UK Association of Chief Police Officers (ACPO).

7.6 Computer evidence

Among other techniques, computer forensics exploits the file system of computer operating systems to recover 'evidence'. Modern computer file systems are largely still based on technologies developed in the 1960s and are a good deal less efficient than might be expected. They tend to retain large quantities of information, even after it has been deleted.

Common computer data storage systems are often described using the analogy of an 'inefficient library'. For data stored on the hard drive:

- the file system identifies where to store documents and images in area called sectors (analogous to library shelves) and clusters (analogous to library bookcases) in the hard drive;
- the file system then assigns an entry (an index card) for each document or image in a recording system called a file system table (card catalogue);
- when you 'delete' a file, the file system only removes the file table entry. It does not eliminate the document or image; in the library analogy a note is made on the 'index card' (file table entry) to state that both the card and the space it references to are now free for reuse. The file itself 'out on the shelves' is not erased or rewritten until the space is reused, possibly weeks or months later. Consequently, the 'deleted' file can often be recreated.

Furthermore, when a file is saved, and the file system stores the new file, document or image on top of the old data, the new file saved may not be as large as the old file was previously on the disk. In such circumstances the new file will not completely overwrite the old file, leaving traces of the old file behind. Consequently, the 'old' data can often be recovered. Technically, this old data is referred to as 'slack' data.

Another source of useful data can be found in the user's material that computer browsing software, such as Internet Explorer or Firefox, leaves on a computer hard drive as it operates. It is not well known that browser software stores the material it downloads from the internet on the computer hard drive, a process known as 'caching'. The browser software does this in case a user decides to return to an internet site at some later stage. Rather than download the same material again from the internet, a relatively time-consuming process, the computer can instead quickly retrieve the same data from the hard drive. A consequence of this is that material searched for or viewed by a user on any computer can persist on that computer for months, and can be retrieved without difficulty.

Browsers also typically store the history of a user's internet browsing for long periods of time. These records will show the web-address of every page the user visited, including the search terms entered into internet search engines such as Google or Yahoo. Analysis of these records has become a very powerful investigative tool, as seen in the Gough case discussed at **7.1** above.

Evidence can be obtained in the following locations:

- intact files;
- browser remnants;
- deleted files;
- internet history files;
- unallocated space (space containing deleted material);
- email and webmail remnants;
- slack data. (deleted material stored alongside existing files);
- instant messaging files,
- registry entries (which can show the files and application most recently used on a computer, among much else);
- system logs;
- swap files (which can occasionally store material which, in theory, was never stored by the user to the hard drive);
- security logs;
- hidden and encrypted files;

- application logs;
- temporary files.

Often but not always, the following can be recovered:

- hidden files;
- damaged or corrupted files;
- deleted files;
- password-protected files;
- some encrypted files;
- email and webmail correspondence;
- evidence of web browsing;
- internet chat data.

7.7 Proper computer evidential practice

Evidence is a key risk area which applies to both criminal and civil law. In both cases, the prudent advice upon becoming aware of an incident of computer fraud or misuse is to:

- Locate any evidential computers.
- Secure all evidential computers and the area around them.
- Document the area – photograph the front and back of the computer including any network connections and peripheral devices.
- Save any data on the screen to a diskette. For more skilled specialists, freely obtainable forensics disks such as E-Defense' Helix will download detailed information from the evidential computer.
- Secure the suspect's computer and work area.
- Disconnect the suspect's computer from the network/modem.
- If the computer is turned on, as a general rule, follow the standard shutdown sequence as opposed to cutting power to the device. Sometimes, if the computer is in a 'locked' state there may be no alternative to cutting the power, however.
- Remove the suspect's computer access to other appropriate systems; ie remote access dial-up, internal network, specific applications, etc.
- Check the current time of the computer's internal clock. Note any difference to the actual time. An accurate time can be obtained from the radio time signal or from the telephone speaking clock.
- Write protect all diskettes and removable media.
- Catalogue all electronic devices that the potential fraudster had access to.
- Document the 'chain' of control of the evidence. Be aware of the criminal burden of proof ('beyond reasonable doubt'). Small objects such as hard drives, floppy disk and CDs can be secured in a sealed envelope, with a signature across the seal;
- Never examine the original computer media – hard drive or diskettes. Always conduct your analysis on a forensically valid copy of the original.
- Be aware that the ability of the alleged wrongdoer to cover their trail could jeopardise the case (both civil and criminal).
- Do not conduct interrogations without all the facts, as well as due consideration of employee rights, abuse of which could jeopardise the case. In general terms, Irish law places so many restrictions on interviews with employees that they are of limited usefulness in terms of gathering evidence, although they can alert the wrongdoer to the seriousness of the situation.
- In relation to manual records and documents, original documentation should be exhibited where possible and there will be a requirement to prove documentary information (who made what entries, when and why), which is an evidential

requirement. This can boil down to an issue for security experts and forensic analysis. It is worth noting that CCTV can constitute admissible evidence.

7.8 Best evidence — in a 'paperless' society

(a) Manual records and documents:
- Originals where possible.
- Must prove who made entries and when.

(b) Computerised records:
- Irish courts have historically relied on a very broad definition of what constitutes a document.
- Issue for computer forensic experts to prove.
- Section 30 allows authenticated copy or fax of document.
- CCTV included within computerised records.
- Civil law evidence — rules of superior courts.

(c) Governing law — s 5(1) of the Criminal Evidence Act 1992 admits computer records in criminal trials:
- Information contained in a document admissible if it:
  — was compiled in ordinary course of a business;
  — by a person with personal knowledge of the matters dealt with.
- Information in non-legible form reproduced in legible form admissible if:
  — reproduced in the normal operation of the system concerned;
  — document includes computerised reproduction in permanent form of any information stored in non-legible form.

7.9 Summary

Computer crime is a fast moving and ever expanding area of the law. While the traditional area of fraud has become computer enabled, the computer, itself and in particular, the networking potential of the computer, has produced a slew of computer specific crimes. It can be seen that the statutory basis for combating computer crime is quite out of date now, and written in broad terms.

In particular, as the law currently stands, the criminal law requires the shoehorning of specific actions into the narrow categories of damage to property (1991 Act) or a form of dishonesty (2001 Act). Given its prevalence in modern life, computer crime is arguably a new form of criminal activity, requiring specific legislation, with a specific intellectual foundation. There are limits to the extent to which new wine can be forced into old bottles.

CHAPTER 8

ELECTRONIC DISCOVERY

Andy Harbison & Richard Willis

Richard Willis would like to acknowledge the research assistance provided by his colleague, Conor McClements, during the writing of this chapter.

8.1 Introduction

Electronic discovery refers to discovery in civil litigation which deals with information in electronic form. In the great majority of cases this information is stored either on computer hard drives or data storage media, such as floppy disks, CD ROMs or Backup Tapes.

The exponential increase in the use of computers that has occurred since the late 1980s has meant that a large proportion of cases, where discovery of documents is an issue, involve electronic discovery. A 2003 study by the University of Southern California at Berkeley found that in excess of 93% of documents used in modern businesses are computer generated. Of these, more than 35% were never printed. Over 70% of emails are never printed. Bearing these findings in mind, it is clear that any process of legal discovery that relies solely on printed documents must necessarily exclude large quantities of relevant material.

Another consequence of the profusion of computers in modern businesses that is also driving electronic discovery is the vast increase in relevant material which must be considered in any conventional discovery. Twenty years ago when desktop computers and printers were less common, substantially less material was committed to paper. Typing was a relatively ungainly method of committing material to paper. Today, most computers have word-processing software installed as standard and it is expected that the average user will be able to use it. This has led a to a great deal more information being committed to paper or its electronic equivalents, and has meant that material which in the past would not have been recorded in detail or retained is now readily recoverable from computers or electronic archives. While this has been a boon to the effective maintenance of records and to the management of organisations, it has made the amount of material to manage in legal procedures increase in proportion, to the point where many modern legal cases require the analysis of hundreds or thousands of documents.

Email has added to this burden. In the past, the principal mode of communication within and between organisations was the telephone, which rarely resulted in a permanent record. Today, email is a common form of communication, and produces a potentially permanent record of every transaction (often to the considerable disadvantage of the organisation retaining them).

Electronic discovery has been the norm in other common law jurisdictions for a number of years, most notably the US and Australia. Electronic discovery was employed in the US as early as the mid-1980s, in the investigation of the Iran Contra scandal during the Reagan presidency. The practice became widespread in the aftermath of the Enron scandal, where large numbers of paper documents were deliberately destroyed, forcing investigators and litigators to rely on electronic versions.

Recent years have seen a growing body of precedent in this area in other jurisdictions. Amendments to the UK Civil Procedure Rules – CPR 31 Section 2A (October 2005), and to the US Federal Rules of Civil Procedure (December 2006), have placed electronic discovery procedures on a more formal basis.

Furthermore, in other jurisdictions where electronic discovery is widely used, legal professionals have long since come to the realisation that if documents are generated electronically, and retrieved electronically (as discussed in the chapter on Computer Crime in Ireland, and below), they must necessarily be analysed and managed electronically if the people dealing with them are not to be overwhelmed. This has lead to the development of a number of sophisticated analysis and case management systems which, while not in common use in Ireland at the time of writing, will likely soon be arriving on these shores (as discussed in detail below).

To date, electronic discovery orders are not as common in Irish courts as they are in other jurisdictions. It has been specifically used in a number of high profile High Court cases which had substantial electronic discovery components. However, it is observed that the number of cases requiring electronic discovery is increasing in Ireland, and it is to be expected that, like other jurisdictions, electronic discovery will become the norm in Irish cases sooner rather than later.

This chapter will briefly examine the processes used in electronic discovery, and how they differ from conventional discovery. It will look at the Irish law on electronic discovery and will consider some of the legal issues that arise in that context. It will then proceed to consider the rules governing electronic discovery in other common law jurisdictions. Finally, it will consider some of the issues and pitfalls that await litigators in electronic discovery, and how Irish legal professionals might deal with them.

8.2 The process of electronic discovery

8.2.1 Evidence handling

Electronic discovery relies on computer forensic procedures to copy computer hard drives and media and then search for relevant data from them. The techniques used in electronic discovery and computer forensics typically differ only in the scope and depth of the electronic search process. A typical computer forensic investigation may only involve the analysis of one or two computers or devices, but may require in-depth investigation of the data thereon, including the technical analysis of system files, data remnants and other complex procedures.

Electronic discovery will normally involve the analysis of more computers, typically one or two for every individual involved in an organization. The Enron investigation, for example, involved the copying of hundreds of different computers. However, these computers will be searched in far less detail than in a complex IT forensics investigation. Electronic discovery is predominantly concerned with documents, and will rarely require detailed analysis of the underlying computer system or the recovery of highly remote or fragmentary data.

The same evidence handling standards apply to both, however (these are discussed in the chapter on Computer Crime in Ireland). Under normal conditions, opening a document on a computer will alter it. While such alterations may not be visible, they can be significant, destroying metadata (discussed below) and possibly rendering the document useless as evidence. Hence, all analysis should be carried out on forensic copies of the original documents, so as to preserve their evidential value.

8.3 Categorisation of electronic data

In discussing electronic discovery, most electronic data can be considered as falling into one of four categories:

- active data;
- archival data;
- hidden data;
- forensic data.

8.3.1 Active data

Active data includes the day-to-day files saved on the computer hard drives as part of normal operation. The word-processing files, spreadsheets and databases visible in the folders (directories) of a computer in normal operation would all be considered active data, as would the email messages in the mailboxes of the various users of the computer. Active data can also includes the valuable browser cache and log files discussed in the chapter on Computer Crime in Ireland.

8.3.2 Archival data

Archival material is backed up to tape, floppy disk, CD-ROM or other storage media. While data stored on Floppies, CDs and USB devices are usually recovered without too much difficulty data stored on tape is far more problematic. This is because the data on tape is usually stored in a compressed format, and also must be transferred onto some other storage media before it is analysed. A modern business or organisation might easily have Terabytes (equivalent to billions of printed pages) of material archived onto backup tapes.

Discovery requests which include material from archive storage have caused a lot of problems in other jurisdictions, largely because recovering data from archive typically costs considerably more than recovery from computer hard drives. Nevertheless, it can be (and has been) argued that the sole purpose of archive data is to be recovered, so discovery respondents can hardly complain if counterparties request it. Considerable precedent exists in other jurisdictions on this matter, but it is too complex to be considered here. However, an analysis of the seminal case of *Zubulake v UBS Warburg* (2003) 217 FRD 309 will familiarise the reader with many of the most important issues.

8.3.3 Hidden data

Hidden data includes compressed, password-protected and encrypted data. It also includes any deleted data on an evidential hard drive or storage device which is still intact and readily recoverable (as discussed in the previous chapter). It should be noted that objections have been made in a number of cases to the use of deleted material, despite the fact that with modern technology it is as readily accessible as active data to forensic specialists.

8.3.4 Forensic data

Forensic data is often used in IT forensic investigations, but much less commonly used in electronic discovery. Forensic data is hidden data that may have been degraded over time by the normal operation of the computer. The principal problem with forensic data is that it is usually only recoverable by skilled specialists. Such data is often fragmentary, making it time-consuming and expensive to recover. In other jurisdictions, judges have typically only permitted forensic discovery of materials under special circumstances, for example where a key document is known to have been deleted, or where events under contention have occurred a long time previously.

Data can also be described as being either Accessible or Inaccessible. Accessible data does not require extraordinary (and typically expensive) measures to recover it, inaccessible data does.

By definition, most, if not all active data is accessible, and quantities of hidden data are also accessible. Archival data stored on CDs, USB Devices and Floppy Drives can usually be recovered without too much difficulty, and would be considered accessible.

Forensic data is usually considered inaccessible, as is archival data stored on tape. Hidden files protected by encryption and/or password would normally be considered inaccessible in cases where encryption keys and passwords have not been provided. As discussed above, forensic data is only recovered in exceptional circumstances. In other jurisdictions, the applicability of tape archives to discovery is usually decided on a case by case basis.

8.4 Identification of relevant data

Once the appropriate data has been recovered from electronic storage, it is usually brought together on a single large computer so that it can be searched for relevant material. Most electronic documents can be searched in their original format without modification. Email files occasionally require some manipulation because they are often stored in compressed form, which is not immediately searchable. Additionally, email attachments are stored in an encoded form, as standard, and must also be converted to a form that can be conventionally searched.

Paper documents can be converted to electronic form through scanning. They can be stored in a computer searchable form by means of a technology called 'optical character recognition' (OCR). This technology is now well established and quite reliable. Typically, an OCR version of the document will be stored with a graphical copy (usually in Tagged Image File Format (TIFF)), so that, in case of doubt, the original version can be checked.

Problems still exist with video and sound recordings, and with handwritten documents. In these cases, manual transcription to electronic format is still the only practical option.

The most common means of searching for relevant files is through the use of software which scans the data for keywords or search terms. Some of these search programs are highly sophisticated, and will automatically look for synonyms, close spellings and other variants on terms entered. Most will also allow for logical searches, allowing the analyst to combine search terms, to run search terms on subsets of the available data or to run new searches on documents identified by earlier searches. The most sophisticated tools will, among many other functions, allow the analyst to manage the entire case electronically, to remove duplicate files and emails and to discover all documents related to an original.

8.5 Presentation of evidence

In Ireland, documentary evidence is usually still adduced in court in printed form unless otherwise agreed between the parties or ordered by the court. In other jurisdictions, such as Australia and the US, court rules specifically permit evidence to be adduced in its original electronic form.

8.6 How much data ...

Legal professionals sometimes underestimate the amount of data that exists on a computer's hard drive. Before deciding to handle a discovery using conventional paper-based techniques, it is worth considering just how much data is stored on even a single computer. The complete works of William Shakespeare can be stored in a file smaller than 10 Megabytes (a byte is analogous to a single written letter, character or digit). A single CD ROM disk can store enough documents in Microsoft Word format to fill 10 to 15 lever arch files (taking an average of 375 pages per lever arch file). It has been estimated that the entire contents of the 7 million books in Trinity College Library is equivalent to slightly less than 3 Terabytes of data (3000 Gigabytes or 3 Trillion letters or digits). By the end of 2007, it will be possible to store this data, without compression, on three conventional hard disk drives. At current rates of development, by 2009 it should be possible to store the store all the data on a single hard drive.

If someone were to print all the data stored on the 80 Gigabyte hard drive (most commonly found in evidential computers at time of writing) on standard A4 paper, the resulting stack would be over 3 kilometres high. Of course, only about 7% of the data on a modern computer would ever be printed, but this would still leave a stack of paper 210 metres high – taller than the Empire State Building in New York. It should also be borne in mind that while the average workstation computer might not contain 80 Gigabytes of printable data, the average email-server computer, in use in most Irish businesses, would.

If this data is printed out (potentially a costly and time-consuming process) the legal professional dealing with it loses any realistic chance of searching it, or even reading it all properly. It is for this reason that electronic discovery methods are being employed more and more.

8.7 Metadata

Almost every program run on modern computers, word processors, spreadsheets, email systems, internet browsers etc collects large amounts of background data called metadata (strictly speaking, metadata is data which describes other data). A lot of this metadata is created to help the programs work more efficiently or to provide additional functionality to the user. Metadata has been accepted as part of documentary evidence before in Irish courts and has proved to be of considerable value.

Microsoft Word word-processing documents have long been known for the amount of metadata they contain. Inside a typical Microsoft Word document you can find metadata detailing:
- the name of the document's creator;
- the name of its last editor;
- its time of creation;
- its time of last modification;
- its time of last printing;
- the number of times it was edited;
- the location it was saved in the last 10 times (and thereby, usually, who was in possession of it at various stages of drafting);
- the name it was saved with, at each location; and
- material the user thought they had deleted from the document.

It should also be considered that in normal operation, Word will regularly make background copies of any documents being worked on, then save these copies to the computer without the user's knowledge. The consequence of this is that disclosure requests of documents in their electronic form can give you their previous drafts, their editing history, and all their previous owners, even fragments of the older documents upon which it is based. In comparison, conventional paper-based discovery will only produce final drafts.

At the time of writing, many Irish legal practices still print Word documents received, then scan them back into electronic form as a TIFF format file, losing most, if not all, of the metadata in the process. Similarly, the standard procedure for dealing with emails is to print them out, when emails contain almost as much potentially useful metadata as Word documents.

8.8 Legal issues

In Ireland, s 9 of the Electronic Commerce Act 2000 allows for the introduction of evidence in Electronic Form:

> 'Information (including information incorporated by reference) shall not be denied legal effect, validity or enforceability solely on the grounds that it is wholly or partly in electronic form, whether as an electronic communication or otherwise.'

Section 2 defines 'information' in the context of the Act:

> '"Information" includes data, all forms of writing and other text, images (including maps and cartographic material), sound, codes, computer programmes, software, databases and speech.'

The lack of a definitive definition in the Irish Superior Court Rules of what constitutes a 'document' for the purposes of discovery raises a number of issues in relation to discovery of electronically held information.

The seminal English case of *Derby & Co Ltd v Weldon (No 9)* [1991] 2 All ER 901 (subsequently approved in a number of cases including *Victor Chandler International v Customs & Excise* [2000] 2 All ER 315) laid the foundations for discovery beyond the traditional paper-based method. In his judgement, Vinelott J stated that;

> '... no clear dividing line can be drawn between digital tape-recorded messages and the database of a computer on which the information which has been fed into the computer is analysed and recorded in a variety of media in binary language ... if I am right in my conclusion that the memory or database of the word processor is the original document, the court must have power to permit the party seeking discovery to inspect the word processor's memory by reading from the console or screen, or taking hard copy in any case where there is real doubt whether the printouts supplied comprise a complete and accurate copy of all relevant and non-privileged information stored on the word processor's memory.'

First, the extent of any discovery must be re-examined when considering electronically held documentation for discovery purposes. In the modern business environment, files are more often than not created on computers and amended on a continuing basis. They may never in fact be printed and constitute a document in the traditional 'paper' sense. The Irish courts, cognisant of this, quite rightly require email and other computerised information to form part of the orders for discovery. However any party seeking discovery is required to 'verify that the discovery of documents sought is necessary for disposing fairly of the cause or matter or for saving costs' in accordance with SI 233/1999.

But at what point does information constitute a document for the purposes of discovery? Need every saved version of a document be included, or simply the most recent? Do auto-save or back-up versions have to be included in discovery to indicate 'train-of-thought' or, because they are purely computer-generated images of a document, is there an argument to say that the lack of human element negates their relevance?

Secondly, if a file is deleted by the system in the normal course of business or by its creator, can that document be said to continue to be within the power, possession or custody of the creator and therefore create an obligation to discover same?

These issues lie at the heart of the discovery process in litigation in Ireland. The lack of any recent revision of the Court Rules in this jurisdiction can lead to uncertainty in the discovery process. The consequences for failing to comply with the stringencies of discovery can result in the striking out of a party's claim or defence and associated orders as to costs. With the stakes so high, clarification is required. An examination of the practice in other common law countries may offer some assistance.

8.9 Discovery in Ireland

Under the discovery procedure, the parties are obliged to discover any documents that are of relevance to the litigation as sought by a party to the proceedings. The basic purpose of the discovery process is to seek to ensure that both parties are aware, before trial, of the case they have to meet. To that end the documents to be discovered must be 'relevant', and within the 'possession, power or custody' of a party.

Precisely because there is no definition of 'document' set out in the Irish Superior Court Rules, the Irish Courts have adopted a very flexible attitude to its definition. Essentially a document constitutes any written thing (whether in hard or soft copy) capable of being evidence. It has thus far been defined to include:

- any document in writing (including letters, minutes, emails, etc);
- maps, drawings or graphs;
- photographs and x-rays;
- tapes or CDs;
- film or videotapes;
- computerised information.

In furtherance of this, Mr Justice O'Sullivan in the case *McGrath v Trintech Technologies Ltd & Trintech Group PLC* (2003) 10331 P, ordered the plaintiff to discover '...emails, instantaneous messages (Yahoo), logs etc... all entries... in the plaintiff's electronic diary including emails to himself and others, instantaneous messages (Yahoo), logs etc' extending to backup data. The order was given on the defendants' undertaking that they would instruct and pay for an independent expert to, firstly, reconstitute documents contained on hard drives of the two company laptop personal computes which were the property of the defendant companies but which were currently in the possession of the plaintiff; and second, to make hard copies of the said documents and send them with the two said laptops to the plaintiff's solicitor. Furthermore the defendants gave an undertaking not to communicate with the said independent expert except to discharge fees.

8.10 The position in the UK

Under the Civil Procedure Rules (CPR) 1999, 'document' was until more recently defined in sufficiently broad terms to encompass material such as databases and discs holding information in electronic form. CPR Rule 31.4 states:

'In this Part–

'document' means anything in which information of any description is recorded;

'copy' in relation to a document, means anything onto which information recorded in the document has been copied, by whatever means and whether directly or indirectly'.

According to the Cresswell Report on 'Electronic Disclosure' of 6 October 2004, at p 8:

'This definition of 'document' is a very wide one and clearly covers computer databases and emails, word processed documents, imaged documents and metadata held on computer databases. It also covers electronically recorded communications and activities such as instant messaging on on-line systems (eg MSN Messenger) and multi-media files (eg. voicemail and videos).'

The Creswell Report looked to the discovery orders in *Marlton v Tectronix UK Holdings* [2003] EWHC 383 (Ch) which built upon the judgement of Vinelott J *I Derby & Co Ltd v Weldon (No 9)* [1991] 2 All ER 901 in coming to this conclusion.

Most notably however, the Cresswell Report states:

'Whilst active data (ie data directly accessible on the desktop PC) should be readily accessible and it is not usually difficult to carry out a key word search for relevant information, the other forms of data are less accessible. In the case of residual data (ie material deleted from the users active data and stored elsewhere on the database) it may even be argued that it is not within a party's control within the meaning of CPR 31.8. Even if it is to be regarded as being within a party's control, the cost and burden of retrieval (often with the assistance of an expert) means that applications for such disclosure needs to be properly justified and confirmed.'

A subsequent Practice Direction to CPR 31 was issued on disclosure and inspection. It clearly follows the recommendations of the Creswell Report by stating that the normative order is to make 'standard discovery', requiring the party to make a reasonable search for documents. The extent of any search will depend on the circumstances of the case, but is governed by the overriding principle of proportionality (rule 1.1(2)(c)).

The Practice Direction clearly states at paragraph 2A.1 that the definition of document 'covers those documents that are stored on servers and back-up systems and electronic documents that have been 'deleted'. It also extends to additional information stored and associated with electronic documents known as metadata.'

The reasonableness of any search required by Rule 31.7 is dependant upon:

- the number of documents involved;
- the nature and complexity of the proceedings;
- the ease and expense of retrieval of any particular document;
- the significance of any document likely to be found.

Beyond normative disclosure, a party may apply for specific disclosure in accordance with Rule 31.12. Such an application must be supported by evidence, and the court in deciding to make such an order will have regard to all the circumstances of the case.

8.11 The position in Australia

In Australia, under the Federal Court Rules, Order 1 Rule 4, the term 'document' is understood to include 'any record of information which is a document within the definition contained in the Dictionary in the Evidence Act 1995 and any other data stored or recorded by mechanical or electronic means.'

The Dictionary in the Evidence Act 1995 provides that 'document' means any record of information including anything on which there are marks, figures, symbols or perforations having a meaning for persons qualified to interpret them.

Thus in a number of cases such as *London Economics (Aus) Pty Ltd v Frontier Economics Pty Ltd* [1999] FCA 932 and *Wimmera Industrial Minerals Pty Ltd v RGC Mineral Sands Ltd* [1998] FCA 299, the Australian courts have ordered disclosure of electronic records such as computer files and CD ROMs even if same files or discs contain information not relevant to the case (see *Sony Music Entertainment (Aus) Ltd v University of Tasmania* [2003] FCA 532 at 49–54). In the Sony Music case the courts held that 'document' will be construed in a wide approach which encompasses the electronic storage media, rather than the more specific construction of reference to where each item of information is recorded.

According to the Cresswell Report, such an interpretation is consistent with that given in the English case of *Derby & Co Ltd v Weldon (No 9)* [1991] 2 All ER 901 (paras 2.4–2.6).

8.12 The position in New Zealand

New Zealand is generally lagging behind other countries such as the US and Australia in relation to the use of electronic evidence. Each party to commercial litigation has the right to compel every other party to provide a list of all documents 'relating to any matter in question in the proceeding' which are, or have been in the possession, custody or power of the party providing the list of documents. The New Zealand courts have recognised that if parties maintain electronic data and communications for business purposes, they will be obliged to produce same information in discovery, provided it is both relevant and reliable.

Salmon J in the case of *SP Bates & Assoc Ltd v Woolworths (NZ) Ltd* (15 November 2002), HC, Auckland, CL15/02, held at p 3: 'It is, of course, clear that computer records, no matter how difficult they are to access, are prima facie discoverable if they are relevant in any way to the issues raised in the pleadings. In that respect there is no difference between hard copy records and computer records.'

Rule 3 of the HC Rules contains an expansive definition of 'document'. It states:

> ''Document' means a document in any form whether signed or sealed or initialled or otherwise authenticated by its maker or not; and includes –
>
> > Any writing or material:
> >
> > Any information recorded or stored by means of any tape-recorder, computer, or other device; and any material subsequently derived from information so recorded or stored:
> >
> > Any label, marking, or other writing that identifies or describes any thing of which it forms part, or to which it is attached by any means:
> >
> > Any book, map plan graph, or drawing:
> >
> > Any photograph, film, negative, tape or other device in which one or more visual images are embodied so as to be capable (with or without the aid of some other equipment) of being reproduced:'

8.13 The position in the USA

As with Ireland, Australia and the UK, the Federal Rules of Civil Procedure which define the scope of discoverability, do not define 'document'. Rule 34(a) does however allow discovery of:

> 'documents (including writings, drawings, graphs, carts, photographs, phone records, and other data compilations from which information can be obtained, translated, if necessary, by the respondent through detection devices into reasonably usable form), or to inspect and copy, test or sample any tangible things which constitute or contain matters within the scope of Rule 26(b) and which are in the possession, custody or control of the party upon whom the request is served.'

Rule 34 obviously permits the discovery of electronic documents, but Rule offers no assistance to the extent of such discovery, ie whether it should cover data such as cookies, temp files and residual data (for a discussion on same see S Scheinden and J Rabkin,

'Electronic discovery in Federal Civil Litigation: Is Rule 34 up to the task?' 41 BCL Rev 327 (1999-2000)). Case law development in this regard remains incoherent and strongly fact dependent. In *Byers v Illinos State Police* 53 Fed R Serv 3d 740 (ND Ill May 31, 2002), Magistrate Nolan J stated:

> 'Computer files, including emails, are discoverable... However, the Court is not persuaded by the plaintiffs' attempt to equate traditional paper-based discovery with the discovery of email files... Chief among these differences is the sheer volume of electronic information. Emails have replaced other forms of communication besides just paper-based communication. Many informal messages that were previously relayed by telephone or at the water-cooler are now sent by email. Additionally, computers have the ability to capture several copies (or drafts) of the same email, thus multiplying the volume of documents. All of these emails must be scanned for both relevant and privilege. Also, unlike most paper-based discovery, archived emails typically lack a coherent filing system. Moreover, dated archival systems commonly store information on magnetic tapes which have become obsolete. Thus, parties incur additional costs in translating the data from the tapes into useable form.'

8.14 General conclusions

In light of the foregoing jurisdictional analysis, some tentative suggestions can be made in relation to the extent of discovery, whether this includes deleted files, and the related cost of any such recovery.

8.14.1 The extent of discovery

Electronic data and documents are potentially discoverable under common law Rules of Civil Procedure in various jurisdictions. To that end organisations must properly preserve electronic data and documents that can reasonably be anticipated to be relevant to litigation.

The obligation to preserve electronic data and documents requires reasonable and good faith efforts to retain information that may be relevant to pending or threatened litigation. However the Sedona Principles: 'Best Practices Recommendations & Principles for Addressing Electronic Document Production' – A Project of the Sedona Conference Working Group on Best Practices for Electronic Document Retention & Production, January 2004, state that it is unreasonable to expect parties to take every conceivable step to preserve all potentially relevant data.

8.14.2 Discovery of deleted files

According to the Sedona Principles (USA), as approved of by the Cresswell Report (UK), and likely therefore of relevance to this jurisdiction:

> 'The primary source of electronic data and documents for production should be active data and information purposely stored in a manner that anticipates future business use and permits efficient searching and retrieval. Resort to disaster recovery back-up tapes and other sources of data and documents requires the requesting party to demonstrate need and relevance that outweigh the cost, burden, and disruption of retrieving and processing the data from such sources. Absent a showing of special need and relevance a responding party should not be required to preserve, review, or produce deleted, shadowed, fragmented, or residual data or documents.'

As such, unless material to the dispute resolution, 'there is no obligation to preserve and produce metadata absent agreement of the parties or order of the court.'

Deleted file forms can therefore be discoverable if relevant and reasonable to a dispute. In the US, deleted computer files have been held to be documents for the purposes of discovery under Rule 34 Fed Rules of Civil Procedure in the cases of *Antioch Co v Scrapbook Borders Inc* 210 FRD 645 at 652 (D Minn 2002); *Simon Property Group LP v mySimon Inc* 194 FRD 639 at 640 (SD Ind 2000); *Zubulake v USB Warburg LLC* (2003) 217 FRD 309; and *Rowe Entertainment Inc v The William Morris Agency Inc* 205 FRD 421, 431 (SDNY 2002).

8.14.3 The cost of recovery of deleted information

In *Zubulake v USB Warburg LLC* (2003) 217 FRD 309, it was held that where discovery is ordered of materials that have been deleted and reside only on back-up discs, the courts consider the solution to be 'cost-shifting: forcing the requesting party, rather than the answering party, to bear the cost of discovery.'

8.15 Problems for the litigator

8.15.1 Spoliation

It is the nature of electronic evidence that is far easier to alter and destroy than conventional data, hence the availability of special IT forensic procedures sometimes used in its collection. However, business and organisations destroy large quantities of data every day, often without realising it, and much of this data may be of relevance in legal cases.

For example, most well-run organisations back up their data to tape every evening or every weekend. These tapes are not retained indefinitely, but are reused, usually on a monthly basis. This means that any data older than a month may be destroyed by being inadvertently overwritten. If the data on backup tapes is seen as being relevant to an ongoing discovery, this routine action can be (and in the US has been) interpreted as destruction of evidence – spoliation in US terminology.

Another common cause of spoliation is email management. Email users are typically assigned a limited amount of hard drive space in which to store their emails and are encouraged to delete older ones. Some email systems automatically delete older emails (often in an attempt to limit legal exposure arising from email traffic, or in response to data protection regulations). Unfortunately, emails are often of high value as evidence in legal cases and their unwarranted destruction can be seen as deliberate spoliation.

At the very least, such loss of data will be frowned upon by the court. In extreme cases where key data has been carelessly destroyed US courts have applied severe sanctions (see *Zubulake v UBS Warburg*). Federal Rules in the US now dictate that counsel have a responsibility to make the management and IT specialists of their clients aware of the possibility of evidence destruction through routine data management processes, and state that legal representatives may now be subject to sanctions where they are felt not to have met that responsibility adequately.

8.15.2 Privilege

Another issue that causes problems in many Irish legal cases is the fact that computers containing evidence of relevance to discovery may also contain material that is subject to legal privilege. This fact often renders it impossible for one side in a case to discover the entire contents of a computer, whether or not such a discovery request might be considered reasonable. Another issue that often arises, particularly in employment cases, is that an individual might retain privileged material on a computer (usually a laptop) that is the possession of their employer. This fact can cause difficulty for an an employer retrieving a computer that is rightfully theirs.

Irish courts have dealt with such issues in different ways. One solution involves the use of an independent IT forensics specialist to examine the computer and either remove the privileged material, or perform searches on it for terms specified by the parties to the case. Documents recovered as a result of such searches can be checked for privilege before being handed to the party requesting discovery.

8.16 Document management systems

8.16.1 The way forward

Modern businesses and organisations accumulate vast quantities of data in many different formats. It can be extremely difficult to assess where all this data is stored in the event of litigation. Many US law firms now spend a great deal of time assisting their client in 'litigation preparedness' – helping them in advance to identify where their company stores data that may be of relevance in a legal case. Many large companies in Ireland are implementing or considering implementing sophisticated documentation management systems for the very same reason.

8.17 Conclusion

The definition of 'document' for the purposes of discovery is widely construed globally. Electronic disclosure must be 'relevant' and 'reasonable'. The discovery of metadata and deleted, or partially deleted, files can be said to go beyond what is reasonable. However, having considered the nature and complexity of the proceedings, and the ease and expense of retrieval, a request for specific disclosure may not be unreasonable if the significance of a given document to litigation outweighs these factors.

CHAPTER 9

OUTSOURCING

Pearse Ryan

9.1 Introduction

This chapter will consider the legal and commercial aspects of IT outsourcing from an Irish law perspective. The text will primarily focus on legal issues associated with IT outsourcing, recognising that outsourcing is, by its very nature, a commercially-driven process (see Figure 1 below for a summary of outsourcing pros and cons and figure 2 for a summary of customer and supplier requirements).

From both a legal and a commercial perspective, outsourcing is a delicate balancing act between the generally conflicting pressures on the two sides of the negotiating table. The eventual aim of both parties is the same, namely to construct a mutually beneficial deal which will stand the test of the contractual term, which tends to be lengthy. However, what constitutes an acceptable deal may well look very different from the viewpoint of each party at the commencement of the negotiating procedure.

One of the main challenges facing lawyers involved in IT outsourcing is to assist their client in, first, clearly stating their position, and, secondly, negotiating from that position to a position which, while not capturing 100% of the client's requirements, does capture the client's essential requirements. Two of the main attributes required of a lawyer working in the area of IT outsourcing are perspective and balance, especially bearing in mind that the time period from initial tendering to conclusion of a large-scale IT outsourcing contract is often substantial, with a period of up to six months, and in some cases up to 12 months, not being unusual.

Figure 1: Outsourcing overview

Pros	Cons
• cost savings – reduce capital and (possibly) current expenditure;	• cost savings risk – are cost savings achieved?
• improve service levels;	• service delivery and risk;
• service delivery innovation.	• reputation at risk – service delivery has impact on business;
	• strategic risk – loss of strategic direction.

It can be seen that the risks are very similar to the possible benefits of outsourcing – properly structuring the deal is an important aim for the customer, in order to manage and control the risks.

9.2 What is outsourcing?

Outsourcing is not a term of science but rather a term of art. Depending on one's perspective, outsourcing may be variously described as allowing another to control strategically important parts of one's business, or, alternatively, paying another to do the dirty work which a company no longer wishes to do in-house. Defining outsourcing is a notoriously difficult business, given the many varieties of outsourcing in existence. Outsourcing is essentially a long term relationship between a customer and a supplier, generally being in excess of three years and in large scale transactions often being for longer than 10 years. An essential feature of outsourcing is that the supplier takes on responsibility for delivering a specific range of services to the client on a contractual basis. The outsourcing contract is, therefore, central to the issue of concluding a successful outsourcing arrangement, by which is meant an arrangement which will meet the requirements of both parties over the contract term.

Figure 2: Customer and supplier requirements

- Customer requirements – adequate services, at adequate price.
- Supplier requirements – profit at reasonable levels.
- Incentives to perform services at and above contractual service levels.

9.3 Types of outsourcing

This chapter will focus on outsourcing in the IT environment. However, outsourcing is not restricted to the IT environment and large scale outsourcing will invariably involve an element of IT outsourcing. In the early days of the IT industry a practice arose of specialist providers of certain software solutions, typically payroll software, providing customers with a licence to use software on a centrally hosted basis, together with ancillary payroll functions, such as printing of payroll slips. The customer took a strategic view that it made sense to effectively outsource this function to an expert supplier who performs the function for a wide range of customers. As mentioned above, outsourcing is essentially a customer paying a supplier to perform a function which the customer decides is best performed by a third party. The reasons for taking such a view are numerous, but generally relate to availability of expert resources (a common problem with IT resources), and, perhaps most importantly, a wish to focus on core functions, leading to the contracting out, or outsourcing, of non-core functions to third party suppliers. As well as IT-related functions, other functions which are typically outsourced include management of property, catering, cleaning, and car fleet management.

Some years ago, the IT industry responded to a need from customers to contract out or outsource the management of their IT functions. This process became known as facilities management and is still a major part of the IT outsourcing market. More recently, the practice of corporate business processing outsourcing arose, where, typically large, companies outsource entire business process to third parties, which tend to involve a large IT-related component. For example, a company may decide to outsource its entire human resource, financial, or IT function, such functions previously having been performed by company employees. These functions, or business processes, are outsourced on a contractual basis to suppliers, with the contracts typically being concluded for lengthy terms.

A key element of strategic business outsourcing, including IT-related outsourcing, is the conclusion of a contract which, first, is clear in its terms as to what is being outsourced and, secondly, places on the supplier clear obligations in relation to the level at which contractual services will be performed. This issue of service levels, discussed below, is a key issue in the conclusion of outsourcing contracts and, more importantly, in ensuring a successful relationship between customer and supplier. A related issue, of particular importance to suppliers, is ensuring that the contractual standards are dearly understood within the customer organisation, such that supplier achievement of service levels is understood by the customer to constitute, first, supplier compliance with its contractual obligations and, secondly, more general supplier achievement of the spirit of the parties' relationship. A recurring problem in long term outsourcing arrangements is that, as well as technical service levels being measured on a recurring basis, general customer satisfaction with the level of service being provided by the supplier is also measured. It is difficult to avoid the existence of a gap between customer expectation and contractual service level, especially given the possible unrealistic expectations of customers as to the quality of services to be provided.

From the supplier's perspective, however, what is important is the achievement of contractual obligations, including service levels, rather than any generalised improvement in the quality of service available to the customer following outsourcing (see Figure 3 below for summary of service quality-related issues). It is perhaps asking too much of a lawyer to be able to bridge this gap. But it is important that the lawyer is aware of the potential for difficulties between the parties in this area, and that they help the customer in the inevitable learning curve between expecting to cure all ills with outsourcing and realising that the supplier will perform contractual services to contractual service levels, no more and no less. The issue of expectation versus reality is a core issue with IT outsourcing, but one which is more commercial than purely legal.

Figure 3: Focus on quality

> In order to focus on the delivery of quality the parties will agree to a Service Level Agreement, setting out the standard to which services shall be provided. Backing up this Service Level Agreement, the parties will agree that certain assets may be transferred from customer to supplier and, furthermore, may agree, and the law will dictate in the case of the Transfer Regulations (European Communities (Protection of Employees on Transfer of Undertakings) Regulations 2003 (discussed below), that certain personnel transfer from the employment of the customer to the supplier. The chief characteristics of outsourcing, as opposed to facilities management, might be summarised as follows:
>
> - agreement on service levels;
> - agreement on service credits;
> - (possible) inclusion within service levels of reference to strategic direction of corporate technology bas and improvements in corporate technology base;
> - medium to long term contract term;
> - transfer of assets from customer to supplier and (in some cases) from supplier to customer;
> - (possible) transfer of personnel from customer to supplier.

9.4 History of outsourcing

In the early days of outsourcing development as a business tool, many companies were understandably reluctant to outsource core functions, preferring to outsource peripheral functions such as cleaning, catering, or security services. However, as technology became more sophisticated companies realised that, in order to retain *state-of-the-art* technology levels within their organisations, there was benefit to be had in the contracting out of the technology base and technology-related services to specialist suppliers. Accordingly, the current technology outsourcing marketplace reflects the fact that many companies are no longer able to derive economies of scale by adopting a DIY approach to their technology operations. Companies see advantage *in* hiring a technology partner in order to stay ahead of the game, bound into the customer by way of an outsourcing relationship. It is unusual to find a large company which has not, to some degree, concluded outsourcing arrangements with a supplier.

At one end of the spectrum, companies will outsource specific IT-related functions, such as a helpdesk service or provision of a data centre, being discreet and well defined functions. At the other end of the spectrum are so-called 'end-to-end' outsourcing deals, in which a company's entire IT operation is outsourced, or business process outsourcing (BPO), involving core business processes, many of which, due to the nature of today's business, are IT driven. This second category is the direction in which the outsourcing market is moving.

Outsourcing as we now know it largely emerged in the 1980s as a response to economic downturn. Companies considered outsourcing as a way to reduce costs and move non-productive or non-core assets off the books and place them in a service provider's books, in return for payment of a recurring (typically annual) service charge. Typically, outsourcing is first considered by a business as a means of cost cutting and reducing internal cost. It is less common for companies to go to the outsourcing market for purely strategic reasons. From the customer's viewpoint, there is always a conflict between the desire for reduction of internal costs and strategic imperatives, such as implementation of new technology. Quite often, companies realise during the procurement process that the cost of procuring the entire range of services required, to the quality required, is outside their budget and, accordingly, what is actually procured is either a reduced scope service or service provided by reference to lower service levels than originally anticipated.

9.5 Best-of-breed versus end-to-end outsourcing

Initial experiences of outsourcing tended to focus on customers who outsourced particular functions to service suppliers, typically selected on a best-of-breed basis. This strategy required the customer to manage a number of *best-of-breed* suppliers across various outsourced business functions. More recently, a trend towards more concentration of outsourcing has emerged, which has gone hand in hand with the move to larger IT outsourcing contracts. Companies, and especially large companies operating across a number of jurisdictions, generally prefer to consolidate their outsourcing relationships among a simple or smaller number of suppliers. This *end-to-end* outsourcing requires companies to make a strategic decision to outsource key areas of the business, typically entire business functions, to a single supplier. This is an important decision for companies to make for a number of reasons, which include the high value of the contracts typically concluded, and, perhaps more importantly, the strategic nature of the relationship between customer and supplier going forward.

There is a risk that the customer can become dependent on the supplier to deliver anticipated cost savings and business benefits in order for the company to achieve its anticipated cost savings, business benefits, and strategic imperatives. The consequences of such a strategic relationship not living up to the expectations of the parties, and particularly those of the customer, are serious (see Figure 4 below for summary of outsourcing procurement and service delivery related processes).

Figure 4: Outsourcing processes

Typical phases pre-service commencement	Typical post-service delivery processes
• phase I – assessment and preparation • phase II – proposal and evaluation • phase III – due diligence • phase IV – contract development • phase V – contract initialisation	• solution process • financial process • human resource process • communication process • contract management process

9.6 Commercial drivers

Companies outsource for a large number of reasons, which include cost saving, access to the supplier's range of specialist skills and superior technology, a desire to tap into economies of scale which could not be achieved internally, and an need to focus management on core business activities. 'Focus' is a word much used in the outsourcing arena, with companies realising that by outsourcing non-core functions management is freed-up to focus resources on core profit-making activities. Key profit-making functions, such as sales, tend not to be outsourced, there being limits on what companies will entrust to third party suppliers on foot of contractual arrangements.

From a commercial viewpoint, one of the main disadvantages with outsourcing is that it can be difficult for companies to move back to an in-house service provision arrangement once a company has gone down the outsourcing road. One of the core reasons for this is that previously in-house skills and know-how have gone elsewhere. Some companies attempt to reduce this risk by requiring that company staff which have transferred to the supplier pursuant to the Transfer Regulations (discussed below) remain, either entirely or partially, allocated to the provision of services to the company. However, this is somewhat contrary to one of the main aims of outsourcing, namely the ability to tap into supplier expertise and achieve economies of scale by utilising supplier resources. Suppliers typically seek to provide services to customers based on the most economically advantageous model available to them, which in today's environment generally includes the moving of customers' outsourced functions, and in particular customers' back-office functions, to a supplier's location, which may be offshore, from which these services can be provided back to the customer in conjunction with the provision of similar services to other customers.

As mentioned below in relation to the Transfer Regulations, in circumstances of taking back in-house previously outsourced functions, customers are typically dealing with supplier employees at that point in time who differ from the personnel who originally transferred from the employment of the customer to the supplier on foot of the Transfer Regulations. There is, therefore, an issue for customers to address in compiling their outsourcing strategy, in order to ensure, insofar as possible, that following conclusion of an outsourcing contract they are not left entirely bereft of expertise in the areas outsourced.

Another key area which companies must address in order to successfully outsource is to outsource IT service provision, rather than IT strategy. Companies generally wish to retain control of their business-wide IT strategy. The supplier of outsourcing services is primarily focused on delivering services which have been contracted for, rather than seeking to develop an IT strategy for the customer. The supplier will, generally, provide no more or no less than that which they are contracted for and if this involves utilising old technology which is not in the best interest of the company then they may be contractually compliant in doing so. IT strategy is a key area which companies should consider prior to engaging in any outsourcing arrangement.

A key imperative for customers is the proper scoping of its requirements within the outsourcing contract, reflected in a number of service levels or key performance indicators (KPIs), backed up by adequate contractual assurances that the supplier will achieve these contracted levels. This assurance is typically obtained by way of a mixture of contractual warranties, service credits applicable to the service levels and, ultimately, the limitation of liability provisions. These issues are discussed in more detail below. A key issue which customers must consider is the balancing of strict contractual imperatives, which provide customers with at least contractual comfort and at most contractual assurance, with the need to build flexibility into contractual arrangements. It is difficult to balance both concepts, which are not entirely consistent. Vendors are keen to emphasise the 'partnership' nature of arrangements with customers, which is a concept which customers have generally been reluctant to embrace in the past. Customers tended to view references to 'partnership' as a supplier's attempt to reduce the contractual emphasis on concrete legal obligations and remedies for non-performance. However, as the outsourcing market has evolved and customers have come to accept the need to build flexibility into long term arrangements, there has been a greater tendency to acknowledge that a form of partnership is acceptable, so long as the arrangement balances the requirements of contractual flexibility and services performance to known service levels at a known service charge. This issue is discussed further below.

9.7 Outsourcing market

The European market for outsourcing continues to grow, largely fuelled by the rise of business process outsourcing, or BPO. Fears of an economic downturn have, it seems, had little effect on the outsourcing market, in part because outsourcing serves a valid purpose during a recessionary period, when the main rationale for outsourcing shifts from strategic acquisition of specialist services a more clear cut emphasis on costs savings (see Figure 5 below for summary Irish market statistics, courtesy of IDC, 2003. It can be seen that the Irish market is; expected to grow steadily, rather than spectacularly, over the next five years). What has materialised over the last few years is a vendor focus on public sectors of the outsourcing market, such as healthcare and the public sector. In addition, an interesting set of circumstances is unfolding, particularly in the UK, where the first wave of large scale outsourcing arrangements negotiated some years ago, largely in the public sector, are now coming up to either strategic review milestone or end of contract term. In particular, evidence from the UK does seem to point to a difficulty for the customer, in this case the public sector, in attracting competing bids from third party suppliers where the customer seeks to either re-negotiate an original outsourcing arrangement or put the opportunity back on the market, based largely on a belief that the incumbent is in such a strong position that a customer appointment of an alternative supplier is unlikely.

Recently, the UK Ministry of Defence (MOD) has invited bids for a 10-year IT outsourcing procurement, with an estimated value of €4 bn (Silicon.com – 26 June 2003). Contract scope would include numerous IT systems and close to 200,000 desktops worldwide. The MOD has shortlisted bidders, with the contract award planned for the first quarter of 2005, the first implementation stage planned for completion by early 2007, and full service delivery planned by 2008. It can be seen that the value of IT outsourcing transactions can be large and the service delivery complex.

In order to attempt to reduce risk in the long term outsourcing the MOD has included a number of structured requirements:

(a) consortium bidding – all short listed bidders are consortiums of at least four bidders – to reduce over-dependence and consequences thereon of one supplier failure;

(b) recurring service level management – including step-in rights in the event of failure to meet service levels;

(c) MOD to retain ownership of (at least) key IT infrastructure; and

(d) mixed economy of service provision by supplier and MOD staff – likely involving retention of staff who would otherwise transfer to the supplier under the Transfer Regulations.

It can be seen that the MOD has gone to some length to attempt to minimise what has emerged as a key customer risk in large-scale IT outsourcing, namely the level of dependency on the supplier. A number of these requirements are price-sensitive and may influence the charges payable by the MOD.

The Irish market is split between the public and private sectors. The private sector has developed in recent years, with a number of large indigenous companies having gone to the market. Recent examples are eircom and Bank of Ireland Irish Times, 15 July 2003, in relation to eircom, and 23 July 2003, in relation to Bank of Ireland), who have held discussions with suppliers, although at the date of writing no contracts have yet been concluded. Both transactions would be large scale and high value, involving an outsourcing of a large degree of internal IT functions, including staff transfer pursuant to the Transfer Regulations.

Other Irish companies have outsourced more specific IT functions, such as management of the desktop environment. To date, the Irish public sector has not engaged in any large-scale IT outsourcing, although there are some IT functions included within a number of recent public private partnership (PPP) procurements. Experience from abroad indicates that until the public sector enters the market with large scale transactions, it is likely that IT outsourcing will not substantially increase in Ireland, as following supplier ramp-up (ie increase) to meet the requirements of large scale public sector procurements, economies of scale tend to be available to the private sector.

Figure 5: Irish market statistics

Ireland IT services viewed by outsourcing engagement, 2002 and 2007			
	2002 Market Size ($M)	**2007** Market Size ($M)	Five-year CAGR
Outsourcing*	210	323	9.0%

* IDC's outsourcing engagement type comprises five activities: Application Management, IS Outsourcing, Network and Desktop Outsourcing, ASP, SISP (System Infrastructure Service Providers)

9.8 Outsourcing contract – key risk issues

It is worth remembering that to a large extent the contract is the outsourcing relationship, given that the scope of the contract will include not just service provision but also the management and the overall relationship between customer and supplier. It is important that the outsourcing contract be as broad in its scope, and as flexible in terms of managing the lengthy relationship between customer and supplier, as possible. The contract should deal with the issues of risk sharing, risk allocation, and liability, in addition to the basic issues of service delivery and management.

A typical IT Outsourcing Agreement would include detailed provisions in relation to the following areas.

9.8.1 Risk allocation

This area brings up consideration of issues of risk sharing versus risk allocation. The word 'partnership' is much used in relation to outsourcing, particularly by customers in the initial procurement stages. However, in essence, outsourcing is a purely contractual relationship between service supplier and service customer. Having said that, it is important to build in as much inter-working between the parties during the contractual term as is possible, in order to ensure that, first, there is a process in place to manage service issues and, secondly, there is a process in place to allow the parties to develop the scope of service provision on an ongoing basis. In negotiating an outsourcing contract, both the parties will have regard to the principles of 'risk versus reward'. Following negotiation, the risks will be apportioned between the parties in such a way that both parties accept that the contract reflects their obligations in relation to the services concerned and represents a fair allocation of risk. A contract which is unduly onerous to one side or the other will not be deemed a 'win-win' outcome and will, therefore, begin life at a disadvantage (see Figure 6 below for summary of risk allocation issues).

Figure 6: Risk allocation

- Objective of balance of risk/reward between parties.
- Accept that one-sided contracts are commercially poor deals.
- Mutual objective to achieve mutually commercially sensible deal.
- Both parties share common interest in contract which balances flexibility and evolution with certainty over contract term.
- Be aware of legal boundaries on what is 'fair and reasonable' within contract. Be aware also of the role of 'entire agreement' clauses in determining the scope of the parties' bargain.

Taking limitation of liability provisions as an example of contractual risk allocation, it is worth noting that the customer may well commence negotiations by reference to a limitation of liability cap which is either unlimited or fixed at a high level, calculated by reference to the maximum possible damage which the customer may suffer as a result of default by the supplier. The supplier will probably decline to provide such limitation figures on a number of grounds, which would include the fact that this figure exceeds the limits of their insurance coverage and that it bears no relationship to the reward to the supplier under the contract (based upon the risk versus reward formula).

In addition, the supplier will point out that all risk over and above what the supplier traditionally accepts and includes within its costs is price sensitive, and, therefore, increased liability will lead to increased costs. Following negotiations, it is usual that the customer accepts that, based upon the level of charges they are prepared to pay, a commercially reasonable limitation of liability figure can be agreed. This will typically involve the customer accepting a limitation of liability figure which is less than that originally required, but which the customer can accept based on a realistic assessment of the likely scope of loss or damage which the supplier may cause, bearing in mind its back-up and contingency planning. An element of this solution may be the inclusion of a customer ability to partially terminate the supply agreement in circumstances of supplier default, thus removing from the scope of supply those elements which the supplier has demonstrated itself to be deficient in providing.

9.8.2 Contract default and contract remedies

Prior to contract negotiations the customer should have formulated a range of preferred contractual remedies, intended to give the supplier an incentive to perform the services to contractual levels, as well as penalising the supplier in circumstances of failure to achieve contractual standards. Contractual remedies often include:

- agreed liquidated damages relating to implementation and service credits relating to delivery of services;
- the customer's ability to claim damages at large under contractual limitation of liability provisions;
- the customer's ability to trigger enhanced performance standards and/or terminate the contract, whether in whole or in part, for specific supplier default and more general supplier default;
- the customer's ability to claim injunctive relief for certain specified forms of loss or damage caused by supplier default.

Allied to a range of customer remedies are the contractual management and escalation provisions. As well as including a remedy in relation to specific supplier default it is important that the contract includes a process intended to ensure that such defaults do not occur again in the future and includes a process for managing problem resolution, including on a quick-fix and longer term basis.

Contract management procedures should link into contract dispute resolution procedures, which will generally include escalation within the ranks of the customer and supplier, together with reference to an overall steering group attended by both parties, and reference out to an external dispute resolution forum, such as mediation, an expert, arbitration, or the courts. Generally, in large scale outsourcing there are a number of remedies available to the parties, which will include the foregoing, together with clarification that in the event that parties fail to agree on the form of alternative dispute resolution, then the matter will fall to be addressed by the courts. In addition, contracts frequently allow either party to make direct reference to the courts in order to obtain injunctive relief or remedies in relation to a breach of confidential information and intellectual property rights (IPR), being matters most appropriately dealt with by the courts.

Of all the remedies available to the customer, the least attractive is the right of termination, which is very much a remedy of last resort. The consequences of termination can be serious, especially in relation to larger and more complex outsourcings. Termination will generally require a customer to either take the service back in-house, which is contrary to their business model, or, alternatively, contract with an alternative service provider (known as second generation outsourcing). From a customer's perspective, taking the service back in-house brings up issues in relation to the Transfer Regulations, together with quality of service going forward, while second generation outsourcing brings up issues in relation to procuring an alternative provider and conclusion of an acceptable contract in circumstances where the customer has reduced negotiating power. Generally, outsourcing agreements contain fairly comprehensive provisions in relation to post-termination obligations of either party, including supplier assistance to the customer and/or any alternative service provider in relation to a hand-over of service provision.

In relation to termination of the contract, it is generally advisable for customers to reserve the ability to terminate in whole or in part. Partial termination may be an appropriate remedy in circumstances where the supplier has proven itself to be deficient in delivery of a particular element of the outsourced service. Contract termination can be specific, by reference to particular measured service failures (generally defined as 'persistent service failure') or, alternatively, more general, by reference to terms such as 'material default' or 'material breach'. Definitions of persistent failure often operate on the principle of 'three strikes and you're out', allowing a supplier default a number of times, in relation to a single or number of service levels, before the definition of persistent service failure is triggered. However, the contract management process should provide a resolution and problem escalation process, intended to ensure that the cause of the failures is remedied before contract termination rights are triggered.

In relation to contract termination on foot of supplier material default or material breach, the parties may define the circumstances, in order to narrow down the other party's ability to terminate based on allegations of general service delivery failure or other contractual failure. From the customer's perspective a technical definition of circumstances giving rise to the right of termination, such as definitions of persistent service failure, together with a catch-all reference to material default or the material failure, is advisable in order to provide the customer with a broad range of remedies. Given the complex nature of IT outsourcing and their lengthy term, a specific definition of what might constitute a material default or material breach in all cases is probably impossible.

From the customer's perspective, it is important to consider issues relating to the supplier's ability to terminate for customer default. The supplier will probably require equally strict definitions of customer 'persistent service failure'.

Apart from the obligation to make payment of service charges, customers will argue that they have few service delivery-related obligations of such importance as to warrant reference to the termination clauses. In relation to the customer payment obligations, it is common to include a specific procedure, allowing the customer to place in escrow sums disputed under an invoice, with reference to the dispute resolution procedure, in order to resolve whether such amounts are payable. Given the serious consequences for the customer's business of termination of the Agreement by the supplier, customers tend to strenuously object to detailed provisions relating to their service-related defaults. Given that the supplier's main aim under the contract is revenue generation, most forms of customer default can be remedied by financial claim, rather than by contract termination.

9.8.3 Service levels and service credits

Allied to the key performance indicators identified by the parties in the contractual schedules will typically be financial remedies which apply if service thresholds are not met (see Figure 7 below for summary of service level measurement. Also, note that liquidated damages or service credit arrangements are often essentially limitation or exclusion of liability provisions, which are discussed below). Service credits tend to apply on an automated basis, rather than by reference to a process of negotiation and agreement. Service credits are typically provided by reference to either cash payments, credit against future invoices, or credits against other services from the supplier. The supplier's preference is that service credits not be payable in cash. Service credits are a limited remedy for the customer against the supplier. First, there are a number of KPIs or service levels against which it is technically difficult or inappropriate to apply service credits. For example, the KPI of customer staff satisfaction with the level of service, determined by conducting regular staff surveys, is not a KPI which generally attracts service credits.

Service credits are typically not acceptable by the customer as a sole remedy in relation to the particular supplier's failure, although the supplier will generally seek that they be provided on this basis. The customer will seek service credits to be provided as a first remedy, to be backed up by reference to the contract management procedure, in order to ensure that the particular default does not re-occur, and reference to definitions of 'persistent service failure', which ultimately allows for customer contract termination. Thus service credits are a first line remedy available to customers in circumstances of a supplier's failure to achieve KPIs/service levels.

Typically, service credits operate as a form of liquidated damages, reducing the service fee, in circumstances of service delivery failure. Generally, service credits are calculated by reference to a reduction in service fees, to reflect non-delivery of service, rather than as a method of customer compensation for loss or damage suffered as a result of service non-delivery. The contract service schedules will determine at what level service delivery is so deficient as to move from the service level/service credit measurement regime to considerations of contractual default, namely contractual limitation of liability and termination provisions

It is worth noting that service levels or KPIs can be measured against technical standards, such as resolving faults referred to an IT helpdesk within a set number of minutes, or, alternatively, by reference to broader industry norms, utilising benchmarking tools. Benchmarking is also an important element in overall contract management, tying into market norms in terms of cost of service delivery and use of new technology.

As *a quid-pro-quo* for conceding service credits, suppliers generally seek payment of 'reverse service credits' or 'service bonuses' for services which exceed contractual service levels/KPIs. Whether these are agreeable will depend on whether service in excess of *minimum* contractual standards is of commercial benefit to the customer.

Figure 7: Service level measurement

> - Bad service levels – reference to contractual termination and limitation of liability provisions.
> - Unacceptable service level – reference to contractual payment and service credit provisions.
> - Minimum acceptable service levels – reference to contractual payment provisions.
> - Target service levels (being in excess of *minimal* acceptable service levels) – possible reference to contractual bonus payment provisions.
>
> The above sets out a possible structure for contractual service levels, ranging from failure to perform service levels to achievement of contractual service levels, to achievement of higher target service levels. It is preferable to prompt the supplier under the contract to perform adequate service rather than create a scenario where the contract is vague as to service level commitments, leaving the customer only with the final solutions of contractual termination and reference to the limitation of liability provisions.
>
> It is advisable to simplify the service levels insofar as possible – concentrate on the what rather than the how. The how tends to be a matter for the IT supplier, while the what determines the output which the customer requires. What is outsourced is the customer business process, while what is best measured is the business output.

Service levels or KPIs are generally agreed between the parties either prior to contract signing or partially prior to contract signing and partially post-contract signing. There is risk to the customer in signing a contract with vague service levels/KPIs, in that they are in a weak negotiating position post-contract. Also from a legal perspective, issues relating to concluding an 'agreement to agree' should be considered. Generally speaking, the more detailed the service levels can be agreed pre-contract signing the better, from the customer's point of view. Typically, there is a comprehensive due diligence process undertaken by the supplier pre-contract signing, during which service levels/KPIs can be agreed. During the term of the contract service levels/KPIs should be reviewed by the parties on an ongoing basis, as part of the overall contract management procedure. It is not unusual for service levels to be revised on an annual basis, including by reference to external benchmarking in relation to service levels which are influenced by general changes in the overall IT marketplace. For example, a typical KPI would be ensuring value for money, which is influenced by issues of supplier cost of labour and infrastructure costs.

As mentioned above, service level management and review should tie into the overall contract management process. This process, in turn, should link into other vendor obligations and customer rights, including customer access to and use of measurement and monitoring tools, and audit rights. Audit rights are of particular importance where it is agreed between the parties that the customer has the ability to audit the profitability of the contract for the supplier. In this regard, customers may require that access to supplier financial records is provided on an 'open book' basis and that the supplier profit margin is limited to a set figure or percentage.

9.8.4 Limitation and exclusion of liability

As with all commercial contracts, suppliers seek to clarify the scope of their obligations to customers within contracts. This includes the use of detailed contractual provisions, together with detailed warranty provisions. The warranties in IT outsourcing transactions can be quite specific and invariably include exclusion of statutory and common law express and implied terms, insofar as legally permissible. Pursuant to the Sale of Goods and Supply of Services Act 1980, exclusion of certain forms of statutory implied terms in relation to the sale of goods and supply of services is permitted, some being permitted on an absolute basis and some on the basis of a 'fair and reasonable test' (see Chapter 6 for a discussion of the Sale of Goods and Supply of Services Act 1980 in relation to technology contracts). In a sophisticated environment customers generally do not seek to rely on general sale of goods legislation type references to supplies being of 'merchantable quality' or 'fit for purpose'. Both customers and suppliers prefer reference to express service levels/KPIs which clarify the scope of the rights and remedies of both parties.

In addition to exclusion of statutory and common law implied terms, parties will seek to limit their liability under the contract by express reference to limitation of liability figures and exclusion of liability in respect of indirect loss or damage, caused by the negligence or breach of contract of a party.

Detailed review of Irish law relating to exclusion and limitation provisions is outside the scope of this chapter. However, it is worth noting that the courts tend to take a pragmatic view of limitation of liability and exclusion clauses in sophisticated commercial arrangements such as IT outsourcing and apply a 'fair and reasonable test', as set out in Schedule 1 to the Sale of Goods and Supply of Services Act 1980.

There is no Irish or UK case law known to the author in relation to IT outsourcing contracts. However, there are useful UK precedents in relation to software licensing agreements. See Chapter 5 for a discussion of case law relevant to the supply of IT systems, which is helpful in establishing the principles which the courts could take to determine outsourcing disputes, as well as dealing in part with IT-specific issues which may be relevant in part to an outsourcing dispute. The principles set out in the IT cases and in particular in the software licensing cases discussed in Chapter 5 would be generally applicable to IT outsourcing. In the *St Albans* case (*St Albans City and District Council v ICI* [1995] FSR 686), the parties were found to have contracted on the basis of the vendor's standard written terms and conditions of business, despite a period of negotiation between the parties, based on the principles set out in the UK Unfair Contract Terms Act 1977 (UCTA). Ireland does not have equivalent legislation, although a number of the tests in relation to the reasonableness of limitation and exclusion clauses set out in UCTA are set out in the Irish Sale of Goods and Supply of Services Act 1980. In the *St Albans* case, the ICL standard terms and conditions failed the UCTA fair and reasonable test and as a result ICL was held to be unable to rely on its standard contractual limitation of liability.

Factors influencing the court's decision in relation to the reasonableness of this limitation clause were the substantial resources of the supplier, including the fact that it carried large amounts of commercial insurance. In the *South West Water* case *(South West Water v ICL* (1999) BLR 420) the contract was based on terms proposed by the customer. However, during the negotiation process ICL caused certain limitation and exclusion of liability provisions to be added, which derived from its standard form agreement. The court did not accept that the contract was 'negotiated' and, in this regard, would seem to have been concluded on the basis of the supplier standard terms, which is a factor relevant in determining reasonableness under UCTA. The court held that the contractual limitation of liability level of £250,000.00 was 'unfair, unreasonable and unenforceable.' This line of UK case law, while not of binding effect in Ireland, does indicate the requirement that exclusion and limitation of liability clauses be robust enough to withstand challenge on grounds of reasonableness, which is greatly assisted by the clauses having been adequately and fairly negotiated, such that both parties ultimately accept the clauses as, first, reflecting the negotiation procedure, and, secondly, adequately balancing risk and reward.

Almost invariably the exclusion and limitation of liability provisions will be one of the final provisions to be agreed during contract negotiations. The provisions are of key importance to both parties in the event of serious difficulties arising under the contract. Limitation and exclusion of liability provisions in IT outsourcing contracts tend to be structured involving the following components:

(a) Distinction between liability for direct loss of damage, being loss or damage to tangible property and other forms of direct loss or damage. This distinction reflects, first, the availability of large sums of insurance in relation to such loss and, secondly, the high value of loss or damage to tangible property. The limitation figures in relation to loss or damage to tangible property tend to be large and suppliers do not regard such figures as of the same magnitude of risk as the reference to other forms of direct loss or damage.

(b) In relation to supplier liability for direct loss of damage, other than direct loss or damage to tangible property, the suppliers tend to focus on this figure and it is not unusual for suppliers to commence negotiations by reference to a figure such as one quarter's service charge. Conversely, the customer will commence negotiations by reference to a figure calculated to fully protect the customer from the consequences of supplier default under the contract, which tends to be a large figure. During the negotiation process the parties will agree on a limitation figure which typically bears a relationship to the contract value. However, it is worth noting that a better relationship in circumstances of supplier default giving rise to customer loss or damage is not between the limitation of liability figure and the contract value but, rather, with the customer loss or damage suffered.

(c) Separate limitation of liability figures may be agreed, or uncapped liability agreed, in relation to certain specific forms of loss or damage, which could include fraud, breach of confidentiality obligations, breach of IPR obligations and breach of statutory obligations.

(d) In addition, there are certain types of liability which are not capable of exclusion or limitation under Irish law, which include liability for death or personal injury arising from negligence in certain circumstances, including product liability, and breach of certain of the implied warranties set out in the Sale of Goods and Supply of Services Act 1980 (see Chapter 6 for a discussion of the Sale of Goods and Supply of Services Act 1980 in relation to technology contracts).

(e) The contractual limitation of liability provisions may also include indemnity protection by one party to another in relation to certain heads of loss of damage, which, from the customer's perspective, might include IPR infringement, breach of confidentiality obligations, data loss or damage, virus infection, and breach of statutory obligations.

(f) The contractual limitation of liability provisions may be stated to apply on a 'per event' or 'in aggregate basis'. Alternatively, they may be calculated on a 'per year' or other recurring basis. From the customer's perspective 'per event' liability levels may be preferable, while the supplier may seek to limit its liability in aggregate over the contract term, for the purposes of quantifying contractual risk.

(g) The relationship between the liquidated damages or service credit regime in relation to, respectively, supplier delay in implementation of contractual services and failure to achieve contractual service levels/KPIs, and the contractual limitation of liability provisions, should be clarified. For example, it should be clarified whether recourse to the contractual liquidated damages and service credits applies on a 'sole remedy' basis, or whether the customer may have recourse to the contractual limitation of liability provisions while such sums are being paid or, alternatively, when the 'pot' for such figures is exhausted. Also, it might be clarified whether such figures operate as a deductable from the contractual of limitation of liability figures, in order to avoid any future argument on this point.

(h) As well as clarifying the supplier's contractual liability to the customer, it is advisable to clarify the customer's contractual liability to the supplier. The customer will seek to negotiate contractual limitations of liability which are substantially less than the supplier's limitations, based on the substantially reduced scope for the customer to cause loss or damage to the supplier. An exception is generally made in relation to customer payment obligations. Again, the 'risk-reward' matrix is relevant.

(i) The contract should deal with the exclusion of indirect consequential loss or damage, which is generally agreeable to both parties and applicable to both parties. What can be contentious is the reference to specific heads of loss or damage, such as loss of profits, and whether these are excluded on an *ab initio* basis, or rather in so far as they are indirect or consequential. The supplier will seek to exclude such heads of loss or damage *ab initio,* irrespective of whether they are direct or indirect. This essentially involves a supplier excluding from the scope of potential liability all forms of economic loss or damage, which is not to the customer's benefit, given that the main risk under the contract is, in fact, economic loss or damage. The UK *British Sugar* case indicates that unless the supplier indicates clearly whether economic loss or damage is being excluded *ab initio,* irrespective of whether it is indirect or direct, then the court may construe the exclusion clause to refer to such heads of loss or damage insofar as it is indirect or consequential only, thereby allowing the customer to seek to recover such loss or damage where direct, subject to contractual limitation of liability figures *(British Sugar plc v NEI Power Projects Ltd and Another* [1998] ITCLR 118). This can result in damages being recoverable for lost production. It should be noted that some vendors may accept liability for indirect or consequential loss or damage, provided that a clear cap is referenced, although this is unusual.

(j) The contractual 'entire agreement' clause is also relevant in relation to liability issues, in determining the scope of the parties' bargain. Both the Sale of Goods and Supply of Services Act 1980 (at s 46) and case law (*Thomas Witter Ltd v BP Industries Ltd* [19961 All ER 573) point to the need for such clauses to be reasonably drafted, with, in particular, an attempt to use such a clause as a shield to defend allegations of fraudulent misrepresentation likely to fail.

It is important to tie together all contractual limitation and exclusion of liability provisions in order to avoid uncertainty or ambiguity within the contract. Given the amount of supplier service delivery measurement and provisions dealing with late or defective delivery by suppliers, this can be a difficult task.

9.9 Employment law aspects of IT outsourcing

The Transfer Regulations (European Communities (Protection of Employees on Transfer of Undertakings) Regulations 2003 (SI 131/2003)) enact into Irish law the provisions of the EU Acquired Rights Directive, ie Council Directive 2001/23/EEC of 12 March 2001 on the approximation of the laws of the Member States relating to the safeguarding of employees' rights in the event of transfers of undertakings, businesses or parts of undertakings or businesses (the Directive). The aim of the Directive and, in turn, of the Transfer Regulations, is to ensure continuity of employment relationships and the protection of employees' rights within a business, irrespective of any change of ownership. The conditions which must be fulfilled in order for a transfer to qualify as a business transfer for the purposes of the Transfer Regulations fall to be determined by the Irish courts and the Employment Appeals Tribunal, in conformity with the case law of the European Court of Justice (ECJ).

The Transfer Regulations were not primarily enacted in order to deal with the consequences of outsourcing on employees, but, rather, apply generally to transfer of businesses which may, in certain circumstances, include transfer of that element of a business which is the subject matter of an outsourcing trans-action.

9.9.1 Transfer of a business

In deciding whether the Transfer Regulations apply, the primary consideration is whether there has been a transfer of a business. According to the ECJ, the basic test is:

(a) whether an identifiable, stable, and autonomous economic entity existed prior to the transfer;

(b) whether it has retained its identity and is still in existence following the transfer; and

(c) whether there is a change in employer, regardless of whether ownership of the business changes.

In order to ascertain whether such an economic entity exists and whether or not it has retained its identity, it is necessary to determine, having regard to all of the relevant facts and circumstances, whether the functions performed with the original employer are, in fact, resumed under the new employer. Other factors to be taken into account in making an overall assessment of the question of whether an economic entity has retained its identity include the following:

(a) the type of undertaking or business concerned;

(b) whether tangible or intangible assets are transferred, including value;

(c) whether any employees of the transferor are being offered employment by the transferee;

(d) whether customers and contracts are being taken over by or transferred to the transferee;

(e) the degree of similarity between the activities carried on before and after the transfer; and

(f) the period, if any, for which those activities are suspended.

All of the above factors are elements in the overall assessment which must be made and cannot be considered in isolation. For example, a transfer of property between the transferor and the transferee is not essential for an economic entity to have been transferred.

The Transfer Regulations will apply to a relevant transfer where there is a change in the person responsible for running the business or undertaking, regardless of whether ownership of the business or undertaking is transferred.

This is applicable to IT outsourcing transactions. The fact that the activity transferred is merely an ancillary activity of the transferor does not operate to exclude the transfer from the scope of the Transfer Regulations. For example, quite a number of business processes can be seen to be ancillary activities of the transferor and do not constitute core business.

The Transfer Regulations will apply to outsourcing, if the outsourced function is a stable economic entity, meaning an organised grouping of resources which has the objective of pursuing an economic activity, but may not apply if the activity of the entity being transferred is limited to the performance of a one-off task under a single contract of finite duration; however, such a limitation would not be common in practice.

9.9.2 Effect of the Transfer Regulations

If applicable, the Transfer Regulations ensure the following:

(a) The employees employed in the transferred business are entitled to continued employment with the transferee under the same terms and conditions of employment as those they enjoyed with the transferor. All employment rights and obligations, whether express or employed, with the exception of most aspects of pensions (mentioned below) are transferred.

(b) All employees are protected against transfer connected dismissals, whether occurring before or after the transfer. This does not prevent dismissals for economic, technical, and organisational reasons entailing changes in the workforce.

(c) Changes in the terms and conditions of employment of the employees by reason of a transfer are prohibited, even with the employee's agreement. If the employment is terminated by the employee because of substantial change in the working conditions, the employer may be deemed to be responsible for the termination.

(d) Both the transferor and transferee are obliged to fulfil requirements of information and consultation.

(e) All collective agreements, transfer and the recognition of trade unions continues. This is of particular concern where the transferee is a non-unionised business. The new employer will be obliged to recognise any trade union recognised by the transferor and will be obliged to abide by the terms of any collective agreement which forms part of the terms and conditions of employment of the employees of the transferor until the date of termination or expiry of the collective agreement or until the entry into effect or application of another negotiated collective agreement.

(f) Employment-related civil liability under contract, statute or common law also transfers to the business.

The Transfer Regulations do not apply in relation to employees' rights to old age, invalidity or survivors' benefits under supplementary company or inter-company pension schemes outside the Social Welfare Acts. In relation to discretionary benefits which the employees may have enjoyed pre-transfer, the transferee's obligations will be no greater or no less than those obligations which apply to the transferor and if benefits are discretionary then they will remain so, post-transfer. However, it should be noted that employees may be entitled to make a claim to the Labour Court seeking payment of any such benefits where payment was customary by the transferor.

It is worth noting that the requirements of data protection legislation may apply to the transfer of employee-related information from transferor to transferee, both at stages of initial contracting out and any second generation contracting involving a third party supplier.

9.9.3 Objection to transfer

Any employees who claim a right to be employed by the transferee will not be entitled to a redundancy payment from the transferor. If an employee objects to the transfer and opts not to avail of the protection of employment ensured by the Transfer Regulations, then that employee may, depending on the circumstances, be entitled to claim redundancy.

9.9.4 Affected employees

Only those employees who work exclusively or mainly in the part of the business to be transferred will be entitled to transfer to the employment of the transferee. Employees who are absent due to illness, secondment, leave of absence, or for other reasons, at the time of the transfer, continue to enjoy the relationship of employment during their absence. Their contracts of employment continue to exist and the rights and obligations of the transferor thereunder will be transferred to the transferee.

9.9.5 Transfer Regulations and IT outsourcing

There has been little case law in the area of IT outsourcing under the Transfer Regulations, despite the high value of the transactions and the often large number of employees transferring. However, in more labour intensive areas such as catering and cleaning, which are commonly outsourced in today's environment, there is quite an amount of case law which is useful by analogy.

Initially, there was uncertainty as to whether the Directive and Transfer Regulations were intended by the legislators to apply to outsourcing. Following a number of cases in the early 1990s, the high water mark of the broad application of the Directive was perhaps the ECJ case of *Schmidt* Case C-392/92 [1994] IRLR 302, where a German bank decided to contract out the cleaning of one of its branches, which was previously undertaken by one employee, Christel Schmidt. Frau Schmidt was offered additional monies to work for the contractors, but calculated that under her new duties she would be paid less per square metre, and therefore refused to accept the contractor's employment offer. She was dismissed by the bank and sought to challenge her dismissal on the basis of the Directive. The ECJ held that the Directive was capable of applying to these facts. Up to this point there was considerable debate as to whether the Directive did apply to outsourcing.

An important later case is the decision of the ECJ in *Suzen v Zehnacker Gebaudereinigung GmbH Krankenhaussemice* Case C-13/1995 [1997] ICR 662. This was a labour based transaction, in respect of which the ECJ held that where an activity is transferred from one contractor to another, then the Directive may apply if there was a transfer of assets or if the second contractor employed a substantial part of the employees formerly assigned by the first contractor to the activity. This decision refers to what is known as second generation outsourcing. Thus, for example, in circumstances where an outsourcing transaction is terminated, in whole or in part, and an alternative service provider contracted with, in respect of some or all of the terminated services, then the Transfer Regulations may apply. Prior to the *Suzen* decision, there had been doubt as to whether or not the Transfer Regulations would apply to second generation outsourcing, in circumstances where assets were not to transfer to the new service provider (eg software licences and hardware).

The *Suzen* decision was followed by a number of subsequent cases of relevance, both before the ECJ and in the UK before the Court of Appeal. A relevant UK Court of Appeal case is *RCO Support Services and Another v Unison and Others* [2002] EWCA *Civ* 464 (Court of Appeal). In this case, an NHS Trust wished to transfer in-patient care from one hospital to another, some miles apart. A contractor supplied cleaning services to the first hospital and argued that the UK implementation of the Directive, the Transfer of Undertakings (Protection of Employment) Regulations 1981 (SI 1794/1981), commonly known as TUPE, applied. The cleaning company holding the contract at the second hospital declined to take on the workers of the first contractor who provided services to the in-patient department, unless those staff applied for the positions to the second contractor and accepted new terms and conditions, being worse than those previously enjoyed. None of the staff applied and therefore none were taken on by the second contractor. The Court of Appeal held that a TUPE transfer had occurred, despite the fact that there was no transfer of assets of any significance and none of the relevant employees were taken on by the new employer. The court emphasised that whether or not staff transferred was merely one factor in an overall assessment of the facts in a particular case and the court should also take into account other factors. Following this case, it seems that, certainly in the UK, in labour intensive transfers, the Directive will probably apply.

The case law in relation to employee intensive activities and the Directive is not conclusive and there has been quite an amount of judicial opinion in the area, both at ECJ and at national court level. However, it is broadly accepted within the IT industry that the Directive will apply to IT outsourcing transactions where an organised group of resources which has the object of pursuing an economic activity is outsourced, and suppliers tend to proceed on this basis.

Part II: Intellectual Property

CHAPTER 10

PATENTS

Gerry Carroll, Aoife Murphy & Andrew Parkes

10.1 Patent law

A patent is a monopoly granted by the State in respect of an invention as an incentive to innovate.

Patent law is the creature of statute. Prior to the foundation of the Irish State, UK statutes applied. Since the foundation of the State, three Acts dealing with patents have been enacted: first, the Industrial and Commercial Property (Protection) Act 1927; next the Patents Act 1964, which repealed the patent provisions of the 1927 Act; and then the Patents Act 1992 (PA 1992) which repealed the 1964 Act. PA 1992 has been altered by the Patents (Amendment) Act 2006 (P(A)A 2006) which became law on 11 December 2006. P(A)A 2006 gives effect to the Agreement on Trade-Related Aspects of Intellectual Rights (TRIPs) and to amendments in the European Patent Convention (EPC 2000). It has come into operation in the parts derived from TRIPs and EPC 2000 but some other provisions are not in force at the time of writing, pending the adoption of new Rules. PA 1992 as amended by P(A)A 2006 is identified herein as PA 1992–2006

The 1992 Act is implemented by the Patents Rules 1992 (PR 1992) (SI 172/1992) and Patents (Amendment) Rules 2006 (PR 2006) (SI 142/2006), with the current fees being laid down in the Patents, Trade Marks and Designs (Fees) Rules 2001. Provisions of P(A)A 2006 arising from EPC 2000 have been brought into operation on 13 December 2007 by the Patents (Amendment) Act 2006 (Certain Provisions) (Commencement) Order 2007 (SI 761/2007). Other relevant secondary legislation includes:

- European Communities (Supplementary Protection Certificates) Regulations 1993 (SI 125/1993);
- European Communities (Supplementary Protection Certificates) (Amendment) Regulations 2001 (SI 648/2001);
- European Communities (Legal Protection of Biotechnological Inventions) Regulations 2000 (SI 247/2000);
- European Communities (Limitation of Effect of Patent) Regulations 2006 (SI 50/2006);
- European Communities (Patent Agents) Regulations 2006 (SI 141/2006);
- European Communities (Enforcement of Intellectual Property Rights) Regulations 2006 (SI 360/2006).

There are also three items of direct EC legislation:

- Council Regulation (EEC) No 1768/92 of 18 June 1992 concerning the creation of a supplementary protection certificate for medicinal products;
- Regulation (EC) No 1610/96 of the European Parliament and of the Council of 23 July 1996 concerning the creation of a supplementary protection certificate for plant protection products;

- Regulation (EC) No 816/2006 of the European Parliament and of the Council of 17 May 2006 on compulsory licensing of patents relating to the manufacture of pharmaceutical products for export to countries with public health problems.

Under the 1964 Act, patents were granted with a term of 16 years. Patents granted under PA 1992 are for a term of 20 years. However there is a provision for the grant of short term patents which have a term of 10 years.

Under the transitional provisions of PA 1992, the term of any patent which had been granted for 16 years under the 1964 Act and which was in force at the commencement of PA 1992 was extended to 20 years. However, during the final two years of the term of such a patent, it was not an infringement to make preparations for putting the invention into effect after the patent expired, provided that this did not include importation or marketing of the patented product. This exemption has been repealed by P(A)A 2006.

Some provisions of the 1964 Act may still be relevant eg a patent granted under the 1964 Act is revocable only in accordance with the provisions of the 1964 Act. All patents granted from 1 August 1992 onwards have been granted under the 1992 Act.

10.2   International conventions and agreements

10.2.1   Paris Convention for the Protection of Industrial Property 1883–1967

The International Convention for the Protection of Industrial Property (signed in Paris in 1883) provides that, as regards the protection of industrial property, each member country shall afford to nationals of other member countries the same protection as it affords to its own nationals and that the filing of an application for a patent in one member country gives a right of priority to the date of that application in respect of corresponding applications filed in other member countries within 12 months of that date. Ireland formally acceded to the Paris Convention in 1925.

10.2.2   Patent Co-operation Treaty 1970–2001

The Patent Co-operation Treaty (PCT) created an international system for lodging applications for the grant of patents. The applications are subjected to an International Search and (at the option of the applicant) an International Preliminary Examination. The applications are then sent to national or regional patent offices for completion of the grant procedure. Ireland joined the PCT in 1992.

10.2.3   European Patent Convention 1973–2000

The European Patent Convention (EPC) established a common system of law for the grant of patents in European countries (including some non-EC members), and led to the opening of the European Patent Office (EPO) in Munich and The Hague in 1977. An application to the EPO leads to the grant of a single European Patent, but this takes effect as a bundle of national patents, in selected States designated by the applicant. Ireland joined the EPC in 1992, and the law on patentablility in PA 1992 is derived from it. A revised text of the EPC was adopted in 2000 (EPC 2000) and entered into force on 13 December 2007.

10.2.4   Agreement relating to community patents, incorporating the Community Patent Convention (CPC) 1975–1989

This Agreement was an attempt by the then EC countries to provide that the European Patent granted by the EPO would have unitary effect in the Community. It has never entered into force but it is the source of the national law applied to granted patents in EU States, including Ireland.

10.2.5 Agreement on Trade-Related Aspects of Intellectual Property Rights 1994

The Agreement on Trade-Related Aspects of Intellectual Property Right (TRIPs) 1994 was annexed to the Marrakesh Agreement Establishing the World Trade Organization (the WTO Agreement). Among its aims is 'the provision of adequate standards and principles' concerning the availability, scope and use of trade-related IP rights. Articles 27–34 relate to Patents. P(A)A 2006 has given effect to certain provisions of the TRIPs Agreement.

10.3 Patentability

10.3.1 Patentable inventions

Section 9(1) of PA 1992–2006 provides that an invention in all fields of technology shall be patentable if it is susceptible of industrial application, is new and involves an inventive step. An invention is considered as susceptible of industrial application if it can be made or used in any kind of industry, including agriculture (s 14 of PA 1992).

Section 9(2) provides that any of the following shall not be regarded as an invention within the meaning of s 9(1):

(a) a discovery, a scientific theory or a mathematical method;

(b) an aesthetic creation;

(c) a scheme, rule or method for performing a mental act, playing a game or doing business, or a program for a computer;

(d) the presentation of information.

Section 9(3) provides that the provisions of s 59(2) shall exclude patentability of subject matter or activities referred to in that subsection only to the extent to which a patent application or patent relates to such subject matter or activities as such.

Section 10(1)(c) of PA 1992–2006 provides that a patent shall not be granted in respect of a method for treatment of the human or animal body by surgery or therapy and a diagnostic method practised on the human or animal body. Section 10(2) provides that the provisions of subsection 10(1)(c) shall not apply to products, and in particular substances or compositions, for use in any such method. Pharmaceutical compositions are, of course, the subject of many valuable patents. It is worth noting that although methods of medical treatment are excluded from patenting in Ireland (and other EPC countries), they can be patented in the US. The above provisions of s 10 of PA 1992–2006 are substantially the same as s 9(4) of PA 1992 before amendment.

It will be seen therefore that there are four basic requirements for patentability:

(a) there must be an 'invention' in a field of technology;

(b) the invention must be 'susceptible of industrial application';

(c) the invention must be 'new';

(d) the invention must include 'an inventive step'.

There is no definition of 'invention' in PA 1992 but s 9(2) contains a non-exhaustive list of things which are not to be regarded as inventions. Likewise, there is no definition of 'invention' in the EPC but Rule 27 of the Rules made under the EPC says the following:

'The description shall:

(a) specify the technical field to which the invention relates;

(b) ..... ;

(c) disclose the invention...in such terms that the technical problem....and its solution can be understood...'

These references to 'technical field' and 'technical problem' are taken as authority for requiring that an invention should have a technical character.

Some examples of patentable inventions include:

(a) machines and mechanical devices;
(b) electronic and telecommunications equipment;
(c) computer hardware and systems;
(d) computer-implemented inventions;
(e) pharmaceuticals and agrochemicals;
(f) biotech products and methods;
(g) manufacturing processes;
(h) methods for treating materials;
(i) improvements in any of the above.

10.3.1.1 *Biotechnological inventions*

A patent will not be granted for a plant or animal variety or an essentially biological process for the production of plants or animals, but may be obtained for a microbiological process or its products (s 10(2) of PA 1992). Special provisions for the biotech field are laid down in the European Communities (Legal Protection of Biotechnological Inventions) Regulations, 2000 (SI 247/2000).

10.3.1.2 *Computer-implemented inventions*

It will be noted that under s 9(3) of PA 1992 a computer program is excluded from patentability 'only to the extent to which a patent or patent application relates to such subject matter ... as such.' The equivalent exclusion in EPC, Art 52(3), is narrowly interpreted in the EPO. If the subject matter of an invention makes a technical contribution to the known art, patentability will not be denied merely on the ground that a computer program is included in its implementation. Program-controlled machines and program-controlled manufacturing and control processes should normally be regarded as patentable subject matter. Various ways of claiming protection for computer-implemented inventions are available, and it should not be assumed that computer software or business systems cannot be patented. The law has been under extensive discussion in Europe, both before and after the circulation of a draft EU Directive on the patentability of computer-implemented inventions, but this draft Directive was withdrawn. Also, the law in the US is different from that in Europe and permits patent claims to software and business methods. Even if a patent can only be obtained in the US, this may well be the most valuable market for the inventor. Meanwhile, the basic protection in Europe for computer programs per se is under copyright law.

In *Aerotel Limited v Telco Holdings & Others* [2006] EWCA Civ 1371, the English Court of Appeal handed down a judgment which it considered to be the test for what should properly be regarded as patentable subject matter for computer programs and business methods. The judgment is not in line with recent decisions of the EPO Boards of Appeal, which the Court of Appeal found to be flawed and contradictory.

The Court of Appeal approved the approach currently adopted by the UK Patent Office as a reformulation of the questions that had previously been used by the Court of Appeal in *Fujitsu* (*Fujitsu Appn* [1997] RPC 608):

1. To construe the claim properly.
2. To identify the actual contribution – has the invention really added to human knowledge?
3. To ask whether it falls solely within the excluded subject matter.
4. To check whether the actual or alleged contribution is actually technical in nature.

The Court of Appeal pointed to the contradictory decisions on patentable subject matters by the EPO Boards of Appeal and suggested that it was in line for the President of the EPO to use powers granted under EPC Art 112(b) to refer points of law to an Enlarged Board of Appeal. The Court had the support of the UK Patent Office in adopting this approach. The Court of Appeal noted that it had no powers itself to make a referral to the Enlarged Board of Appeal but Jacob LJ went on to outline four questions which it suggested the Enlarged Board of Appeal should consider:

(1) What is the correct approach to adopt in determining whether an invention relates to subject matter that is excluded under EPC Art 52?

(2) How should those elements of a claim that relate to excluded subject matter be treated when assessing whether an invention is novel and inventive under EPC Arts 54 and 56?

(3) And specifically:

   (a) Is an operative computer program loaded onto a medium such as a chip or hard drive of a computer excluded by EPC Art 52(2) unless it produces a technical effect? If so, what is meant by 'technical effect'?

   (b) What are the key characteristics of the 'method of doing business' exclusion?

10.3.2 Novelty and inventive step

Novelty and inventive step are different criteria. Novelty exists if there is any difference between the invention and the known art. There must first be novelty before there can be an inventive step.

Section 11(1) of PA 1992 provides that an invention shall be considered to be new if it does not form part of the state of the art. Section 11(2) provides that the state of the art shall be held to comprise everything made available to the public (whether in the State or elsewhere) by means of a written or oral description, by use, or in any other way, before the date of filing of the patent application. Where the invention is disclosed to the public before the date of filing of the patent application then the invention is said to be anticipated and a patent, even if granted, is likely to be invalid. 'The public' includes any person or organisation not in a relationship of confidentiality with the inventor(s) or their employers. It is crucially important, therefore, that a patent application is filed before any publication of the invention. In practice, this can cause particular problems for inventions arising from university research, where the pressure for early publication has to be balanced against the wish to obtain patent protection. Even an oral contribution at a conference can amount to disclosure.

Section 11(3) provides that in addition, the content of a patent application as filed, of which the date of filing is prior to the date of filing the Irish application and which was published under PA 1992 (or, by virtue of the transitional provisions, the 1964 Act) on or after that date, shall be considered as comprised in the state of the art. Thus, the novelty of a later application has to be judged against the content of an earlier unpublished application. However, the earlier application is not considered in deciding whether or not there has been an inventive step (s 13 of PA 1992)

Section 11(4) of PA 1992–2006 provides that the provisions of s 11(2) and (3) shall not exclude the patentability of any substance or composition, comprised in the state of the art, for use in a method for the treatment of the human or animal body or a diagnostic method, provided that its use for any such method is not already comprised in the state of the art. Therefore, a substance that is already known for a non-medical use can be patented when it is first found to be useful in a method of medical treatment ('first medical use'). In addition, new subsection 11(5) of PA 1992–2006 has been added to recognise the patentability of a known substance or composition for a specific use in a method of medical treatment or a diagnostic method, provided that the specific use is not known ('second or subsequent medical use').

An inventor faces the risk of anticipation on two fronts, first from independent inventors and secondly from those persons whose information comes from the same source as his own. In the latter case, a disloyal employee can disclose the invention to a third party, or a third party to whom the invention was disclosed in confidence can breach that confidence. In the absence of any statutory provisions, those disclosures would prejudice an application for a patent on the basis that the relevant invention was anticipated. Section 12 was enacted to give limited relief in such circumstances. The section relates to disclosures which are non-prejudicial. The section provides that, disclosures where occur not earlier than six months preceding the filing of the patent application and if the disclosure was due to, or in consequence of, a breach of confidence or agreement in relation to, or the unlawful obtaining of, the matter constituting the invention, such disclosures do not form part of the state of the art. The same applies if the applicant has displayed the invention at certain specified international exhibitions.

For the subject matter of a later patent to have been anticipated, the earlier invention must coincide with it exactly (*General Tire & Rubber Co v Firestone Tyre & Rubber Co* [1975] 1 WLR per Sachs LJ). In that case it was held that to determine whether an invention had been anticipated, the prior publication and the later claim are to be construed by a reader skilled in the art as at the respective relevant dates ie, the dates of publication. This means that, when construing an earlier document, the reader skilled in the art will be assumed to be skilled in the art as it was at the time of its publication and later technical advances are irrelevant (*Kirin – Amgen Inc v Transkaryotic Therapies Inc* [2002] EWCA Civ 1096, [2003] RPC 31). Similarly, the later claim would be construed in the light of the state of the art at its own date of publication.

10.3.3 Short-term patents (Pt III of PA 1992, ss 63–67)

Short-term patents are granted for a term of 10 years. An invention is patentable as a short-term patent if it is new and susceptible of industrial application, provided it is not clearly lacking an inventive step. This definition is intended to set a somewhat lower threshold of inventiveness for a short-term patent. No novelty search is required before a short-term patent is granted.

It is not possible to have a short-term patent and a full-term patent for the same invention. Where an application for a short-term patent and a full-term patent are filed by the same applicant in respect of the same invention, then the short-term patent, if granted first, shall be deemed void upon the grant of the full-term patent, or in the event that the application for the short-term patent is pending at the date of grant of the full-term patent then the application is deemed to be abandoned at that date.

A drawback of a short-term patent is that infringement proceedings may not be commenced without going through the procedure laid down in s 66. Section 66(1) provides that the proprietor must first request the Controller to cause a search to be undertaken in relation to the invention and a report of the results of the search to be prepared, and furnish a copy to the proposed defendant.

There is an alternative procedure under s 66(3), under which it is possible to submit the results of a search carried out in a prescribed foreign state (the UK or Germany), or under a convention (the EPC) or treaty (the PCT) in respect of the same invention.

Proceedings for infringement of a short-term patent may be brought in the Circuit Court irrespective of the value of a claim (s 66(4)).

There is an additional ground for revocation of a short-term patent, namely, that the claims of the specification of the patent are not supported by the description.

10.3.4 Supplementary Protection Certificates

On 2 January 1992, Council Regulation EEC/1768/92 concerning the creation of Supplementary Protection Certificates for medicinal products (SPC) was published. It was given effect in Ireland by SI 125/1993. The SPC recognises that the period of time between filing a patent application and obtaining regulatory approval to market a new medicinal product can mean that the effective period of patent protection is very much reduced. This placed European industry at a disadvantage when compared with other jurisdictions where patent term restoration provisions had been introduced.

A similar system of SPCs for plant protection products was introduced by Regulation EC/1610/96. No statutory instrument was required to bring it into effect in Ireland, as SI 125/1993 was considered to be sufficient.

Once an SPC has been granted it will not take effect until the end of the term of the basic patent. It confers the same rights as the patent but only in respect of the medicinal or plant protection product for which a marketing authorisation was issued. The maximum life of any SPC in Ireland is five years. The period of protection is equal to the period which elapsed between the date of the filing of the application for the basic patent and the date of the first marketing authorisation in the EEA reduced by a period of five years. In any event, the duration of the SPC in Ireland is not to exceed five years.

10.4 Ideas and know-how

Ideas are generally not patentable unless they have some potential industrial application. As already noted, s 9(2) of PA 1992 excludes such items as a discovery, a scientific theory, or a scheme for performing a mental act from being regarded as an invention. Know-how has been defined by Commission Regulation EC/240/96 as:

> 'A body of technical information that is secret, substantial and identified in any appropriate form'

It usually consists of industrial information or techniques likely to assist in the manufacture or processing of goods or materials, and of potential value to a competitor or licensee. Know-how may include something patentable but it often lacks an inventive step.

10.4.1 Patent v know-how

In deciding whether to apply for a patent or to retain secret know-how, various advantages and disadvantages must be balanced:

(a) Advantages of a patent:
- exclusive statutory right for up to 20 years;
- scope of protection defined;
- no need for secrecy after a full patent application has been made.

(b) Disadvantages of a patent:
- the invention is published after 18 months from the date of the first patent application;
- after the invention has been published, a patent may be refused or revoked because of lack of novelty or inventive step.

(c) Advantages of know-how:

- with good controls on confidential information, know-how may be kept secret for the whole working life of a product or process.
(d) Disadvantages of know-how:
- not protected if it gets into the public domain or if someone else devises it independently;
- lack of clarity as to what is protected;
- competitor may deduce it by analysing the product.

10.5 Applying for a patent

If a solicitor is consulted by a client about a new invention, it is usual to refer the client to a Patent Agent (these days generally practising also as a European patent attorney) for advice and, if appropriate, for preparation of a patent application.

10.5.1 Novelty searches

As a first step, a Patent Agent will usually recommend that a search should be carried out to check whether the invention appears to be new. Database searches can be done among previous patents, or in abstracts or full texts of technical literature. Most relevant prior art is often found in the inventor(s') own literature collection. However it is not obligatory to carry out a preliminary search. A decision may be made to wait for an official search report from a Patent Office after an application has been filed (eg, under s 29 of PA 1992).

10.5.2 Preparing a patent application (ss 18–22 of PA 1992)

A patent agent drafts a Specification, which should contain the elements set out in s 18(2) of PA 1992:

(a) A description of the invention, accompanied by drawings if appropriate to the type of invention concerned. The description must disclose the invention in a manner sufficiently clear and complete for it to be carried out by another person skilled in the technical field (s 19 of PA 1992).

(b) One or more claims, placed after the description. The claim or claims define the matter for which patent protection is sought. They should also be clear and concise and be supported by the description (s 20 of PA 1992). In practice the Patent Agent will draft a set of claims, starting with the broadest scope that can be justified by the novel contribution made by the invention, as compared to the prior art. Several aspects of the invention or a group of inventions (eg a product, process, apparatus, etc) may be claimed in one application, provided that they are so linked as to form a single inventive concept (s 21 of PA 1992).

(c) An abstract, which serves for use as technical information, eg for entry into databases for searching purposes. It is not to be used for interpreting the scope of patent protection sought.

10.5.3 Filing a first Irish patent application (s 18(1), (3); s 63(5) of PA 1992)

The Irish Patents Office is based in Kilkenny but also retains a filing office in Dublin. The initial application may be made for either:

- a short-term patent for 10 years (a short term patent can be granted quickly because there is no requirement for a search or evidence of novelty of the invention before grant); or

- a full-term patent for 20 years. In the case of a full-term patent, the applicant must either request an official search (s 29 of PA 1992) or submit evidence of search results or of the grant of a patent for the same invention in a prescribed foreign state (Great Britain or Germany), or under a convention (the EPC) or treaty (the PCT). The applicant must then amend the application in the light of the evidence relied upon (usually called the 'evidence of novelty') or must file a statement that no amendment is considered necessary (s 30 of PA 1992). When submitting such an amendment or statement, the applicant must be represented by a patent agent (Rule 93(2) of PR 1992).

10.5.4 Filing a first application elsewhere

Instead of starting with an application for an Irish patent, the applicant may decide to file a European application initially in order to get the results of a full EPO search at an early date. Alternatively, because of differences between European and US law, it may in some cases be sensible to send the first application to the US Patent and Trademark Office.

10.5.5 Claiming priority (ss 25–27 of PA 1992 and Art 4 of the Paris Convention)

During a period of twelve months after filing the first application, the applicant (or a successor in title) may make a subsequent application to patent the same invention and can effectively get the subsequent application back-dated to the first filing date, thus enjoying a right of priority over a later applicant. This can be done both in Ireland and in any country or region abroad which belongs to the Paris Convention or the WTO Agreement (s 25 of PA 1992–2006). The 12 month period should allow the inventor or other owner of the invention to investigate its commercial potential before incurring the expense of an international patent filing programme, although in practice the time runs very quickly.

10.5.6 Patenting an invention in Europe (European Patent Convention; s 118–124 of PA 1992)

It is possible to apply for national patents in individual European countries but translation of the text is generally required at the outset (except of course in the UK). Instead, an application at the European Patent Office (EPO) can be presented in English, can designate up to 34 States and can be extended to a further 4 States. The application is subjected to official search and examination at the EPO. If and when it proceeds to grant, the European Patent takes effect as a bundle of patents in the designated States. Under current arrangements, a translation is then required in most States, but the applicant can decide to abandon protection in a number of countries if the translation costs are too high.

Since Ireland joined the EPC in 1992, the majority of applicants from other countries have used the EPO route to obtain patent protection here. A European Patent designating the State is treated from its date of grant as a patent granted under the 1992 Act (s 119 of PA 1992). If the European Patent is not published in English (ie, is in French or German), an English translation must be filed at the Irish Patents Office within 6 months from the date of grant (s 119(6) of PA 1992 and Rule 83 of PR 1992).

Third parties have nine months from the date of grant to oppose a European patent at the EPO. If the patent is amended or revoked as a result of the opposition, the amendment or revocation has automatic effect in Ireland (s 119(4) of PA 1992).

10.5.7 Applying internationally (Patent Co-operation Treaty; s 127 of PA 1992)

As in Europe, it is possible to apply for national patents in countries in other parts of the world, such as the US, Canada, Japan, Australia, etc. However, an application under the

Patent Co-operation Treaty (PCT) can designate up to 138 States as well as regional patent offices including the EPO. The PCT application is subjected to an International Search and (at the applicant's option) to an International Preliminary Examination. Then, usually after two and a half years from the priority date, the application goes forward into national processing in individual countries and/or regional processing at the EPO and other regional offices, where patents are granted or refused. The PCT provides an international system for filing applications but does not establish an international patent.

10.6 Ownership of the right to a patent (ss 15–16, 79–80 of PA 1992)

Section 15 provides that any person may make an application for a patent either alone or jointly with another. Section 16 then provides that the right to a patent belongs to the inventor or his successor in title, but if the inventor is an employee the right to a patent shall be determined in accordance with the law of the state in which the employee is wholly or mainly employed or, if the identity of such state cannot be determined, in accordance with the law of the state in which the employer has his place of business to which the employee is attached. Section 16(2) goes on to provide that if two or more persons have made an invention independently of each other, the right to a patent for the invention shall belong to the person whose patent application has the earliest or earlier (as the case may be appropriate) date of filing, but the provisions shall only apply if the earliest or earlier application has been duly published under the PA 1992.

In Ireland ownership of employee inventions is determined by common law, which provides that an invention made by an employee belongs to an employer:

(a) if the invention is made in the course of the normal duties of the employee or in the course of duties falling outside his normal duties, but specifically assigned to him, and if the circumstances in either case were such that an invention might reasonably be expected to result from the carrying out of his duties; or

(b) the invention was made in the course of the duties of the employee and, at the time of making the invention, because of the nature of his duties and the particular responsibilities arising from the nature of his duties, he had a special obligation to further the interests of the employer's undertaking.

Unlike the UK, there is no statutory provision in Ireland which provides for compensation to employees in respect of inventions made in the course of employment.

10.6.1 Co-ownership of patent applications and patents (s 80 of PA 1992)

This section deals with co-ownership. Section 80(1) provides that where a patent is applied for by, or is granted to, two or more persons, each of those persons shall, unless an agreement to the contrary is in force, be entitled to an equal undivided share in common in the patent application or patent, as the case may be.

Section 80(2) provides, that subject to the provisions of the section where two or more persons are entered in the register as applicants for or proprietors of a patent, then, unless an agreement to the contrary is in force, each of those persons shall be entitled, by himself or his agents, to do in respect of the invention concerned for his own benefit without accounting to the others any act which would, apart from the subsection, amount to an infringement of the patent application or patent concerned.

Section 80(6) provides that nothing in s 80(1) or s 80(2) shall affect the mutual rights or obligations of trustees or of the personal representatives of a deceased person, or their rights or obligations as such. Accordingly the undivided share of a co-owner of a patent or an application devolves upon his personal representatives.

Sections 80(3), (4) and (5) cover certain dealings by a co-owner of a patent or patent application. Section 80(3) provides that a co-owner may not grant a licence or assign his share without the consent of all the other co-owners. Section 80(4) allows a third party to supply to a co-owner with means, relating to an essential element of the relevant invention for putting the invention into effect without being guilty of indirect infringement. Section 80(5) provides that where a co-owner sells a product covered by the co-owned invention, then the purchaser and any person claiming through him is entitled to deal with it in the same manner as if the product had been sold by a sole owner.

Section 79 of PA 1992 provides that subject to s 80 (which deals with co-ownership of patent applications and patents) the rules of law applicable to the ownership and devolution of personal property shall apply in relation to patent applications and patents as they apply in relation to other choses in action.

10.7 Infringement (ss 40–46 of PA 1992)

Before considering whether there has been infringement, it is first necessary to construe the claims of a patent. If the relevant product or process does not fall within the claims, properly construed, then there can be no infringement. The relevant date for construction of the patent is the date of publication of the specification.

The 1992 Act has statutory provisions relating to construction. Section 45(1) of PA 1992–2006 provides that the extent of the protection conferred by a patent shall be determined by the claims; nevertheless, the description and drawing shall be used to interpret the claims. Section 45(3) provides that the court shall have regard to the directions contained in the Protocol on the Interpretation of Art 69 of the European Patent Convention and set out in Schedule 2 of the Act. This endeavours to define a compromise position between strict and liberal interpretation 'which combines a fair protection for the patentee with a reasonable degree of certainty for third parties.'

Article 69 of the European Patent Convention and the Protocol to Art 69 (the Protocol) have been implemented into Irish law by s 45 of the Patents Act 1992 and the Second Schedule thereto.

In the recent decision of the High Court in *Ranbaxy Laboratories Ltd & Others v Warner Lambert Company* [2005] IEHC 178 and [2005] IESC 81, [2006] 1 IR 193, O'Sullivan J gave guidance with regard to the approach which a Court will take to issues of patent construction. While the matter was appealed to the Supreme Court, the Supreme Court did not demur in any way from the statements of the law contained in the judgment of O'Sullivan J. His judgment did not purport to contain an exhaustive identification of the relevant principles of construction but he did confirm that the principles which are applicable in Irish law are those set out in the standard English text books.

O'Sullivan J, having confirmed that the general principles of construction of a patent are found in the standard text books, went on to refer to two principles of construction (at p 11):

'(a) Construction is a question of law for the Judge: accordingly, evidence as to what a patent means is inadmissible and in particular evidence as to what the inventor or patentee (or his representatives) intended to mean is inadmissible. Support for the above could be found in any one of a dozen authorities. The following passage from the judgment of Staunton LJ in *Glaverbel SA v British Coal Corporation & Anor* [1995] RPC 225 at 268 is one of them:

'The interpretation of a patent, as of any other written document, is a question of law. That does not mean that the answer to it will necessarily be found in our law books. It means that it is for the Judge rather than the jury to decide, and that evidence of what the patent means is not admissible. In particular, evidence of the patentee as to what he intended it to mean should not be admitted, nor is direct evidence which is said to point to his intention. Compare the rule that the parties to a deed or contract cannot give evidence of what they intended it to mean.'

(b) Evidence will be received from witnesses 'skilled in the art' concerned. In *Catnic v Hill and Smith* [1982] RPC 183 at 242 Lord Diplock said that a patent specification is 'addressed to those likely to have a practical interest in the subject matter of his invention (ie, skilled in the art), being persons with practical knowledge and experience of the kind of work in which the invention was intended to be used.' Aldous LJ in *Lubrizol v Esso Petroleum* [1998] RPC 727 at 738 put it as follows:

> 'Patent specifications are intended to be read by persons skilled in the relevant art, but their construction is for the Court. Thus the Court must adopt the mantle of the notional skilled addressee and determine, from the language used, what the notional skilled addressee would understand to be the ambit of the claim. To do that it is often necessary for the Court to be informed as to the meaning of technical words and phrases and what was, at the relevant time, the common general knowledge; the knowledge that the notional skilled man would have.'

O'Sullivan J went on to elaborate on the role of the expert and quoted with approval from the judgment of Mummery J in *Glaverbel SA v British Coal Corporation* [1995] FSR 254, where it was made clear that whilst a relevant expert was entitled to give evidence of what the specification would have taught him and whether what was described in the specification could be carried into effect by workers skilled in the art, the opinion of the expert witness on the construction of the specification will not be admitted by the court. It was also noted that it is for the court and not an expert witness to construe the specification and the ambit of the claims made in it.

O'Sullivan J also accepted that the court in construing the patent may have regard to the surrounding circumstances as they existed at the date of publication of the specification. They would not include circumstances known only to the patentee or a limited class of persons, since every skilled addressee should be able to know what the patent means and therefore have equal access to the material available for interpretation. He also confirmed that the Court can admit evidence of meaning of technical terms.

P(A)A 2006, following the EPC 2000, adds a new provision with regard to 'Equivalents' in the Second Schedule of PA 1992–2006. For the purpose of determining the extent of protection conferred by a patent, due account shall be taken of any element which is *equivalent* to an element specified in the claims. There is no transitional provision to clarify whether this principle of interpretation can affect the continuation of a third party activity that did not infringe the patent before the operative date of the amendment.

Knowledge on the part of the infringer about the invention or patent is normally irrelevant. Whether or not the infringer intended to infringe is also irrelevant. It is not necessary for the patentee to suffer damage in order for there to be infringement.

The onus is on the plaintiff to prove infringement. He must provide sufficient evidence to establish infringement on the balance of probabilities. There is a statutory exception to this rule. Section 46 provides that if the subject matter of a patent is a process for obtaining a new product, the same product when produced by a person other than the proprietor or applicant, as the case may be, shall, in the absence of sufficient evidence to raise an issue as to whether the product was obtained by that or another process, be deemed to have been obtained by the process which is such subject matter.

Section 40 makes it clear that infringement only occurs if a person does specified things 'in the State' without the proprietor's consent. Section 117 declares that the Act applies to the waters in the portion of the sea which comprises the territorial seas of the State, the waters in all the areas of the sea to which the internal or inland waters of the State are extended by s 5 of the Maritime Jurisdiction Act 1959, and the waters in any area which is for the time being a designated area within the meaning of the Continental Shelf Act 1968.

10.7.1 Direct infringing acts (s 40 of PA 1992)

A patent, while it is in force, confers on its proprietor the right to prevent all third parties not having his consent from doing in the State all or any of the things following:

(a) making, offering, putting on the market or using a product which is the subject matter of the patent, or importing or stocking the product for those purposes;

(b) using a process which is the subject matter of the patent;

(c) offering, putting on the market, using or importing, or stocking for those purposes, the products obtained directly by a process which is the subject-matter of the patent.

It will be noted that the classic infringing acts are included ie, making a patented product and using a patented process. After manufacture, the list of infringing acts covers offering, putting on the market, using or importing or stocking a patented product or a product obtained directly by a patented process. Where patented goods pass down the distribution chain each person in that chain becomes an infringer in his capacity as offeror and putting the infringing product on the market. The ultimate recipient will be an infringer if he is a user.

10.7.2 Indirect infringement

Prior to the enactment of the PA 1992, the courts were reluctant to treat as a contributory infringer someone who assisted in preparations for infringing acts within the claims but did not himself perform those infringing acts. Only where the person who assisted in the preparations actually ordered the other party to infringe, or participated in a conspiracy or common design to secure performance or knowingly induced another person to perform, would any liability in tort be imposed.

Although the marginal note to s 40 refers to prevention of direct use of an invention, s 40(b) does cover a form of indirect infringement. It is an infringement to offer a process for use in the State knowing that the user will have no licence from the proprietor of the patent and that the use will be an infringement. Both the offer and use must be in the State and the knowledge of the person who offers the process is judged objectively, taking account of what is obvious to a reasonable person in the circumstances.

Section 41(1) provides that a patent while it is in force shall also confer on its proprietor the right to prevent all third parties not having his consent from supplying or offering to supply in the State a person, other than a party entitled to exploit the patented invention, with the means, relating to an essential element of that invention, for putting it into effect therein, when the third party knows, or it is obvious in the circumstances to a reasonable person, that the said means are suitable and intended for putting that invention into effect.

This subsection would cover the situation where the third party supplies a product in kit form to be assembled into an infringing article by the purchaser.

Subsection 41(2) provides that s 41(1) shall not apply when the means referred to therein are staple commercial products, except when the third party induces the person supplied to commit acts which the proprietor of a patent is enabled to prevent by virtue of s 40(1).

There is no definition of staple commercial products. It is assumed that the word staple is a reference to raw materials or other basic products commonly available. The purpose of the subsection is to protect the supplier of such products even if he has knowledge that they are to be put to an infringing purpose.

Section 44(3) provides that persons performing acts referred to in s 42(a), (b) or (c) shall not be considered to be parties entitled to exploit an invention pursuant to s 41(1).

The person or persons who actually perform the infringing act are liable to the patentee. A person can infringe a patent by making the article himself, or by his agent, or by his servant. The agent and servants themselves can infringe the patent, and actions can be brought against them individually but that does not absolve the person who employed them for that purpose.

Persons may be liable for infringement if their acts are such as would make them joint tortfeasors under the general law. Before a person can be said to be a joint tortfeasor, he must have acted in concert with another person in the commission of the tort.

10.8 Action for infringement

Section 85(7) of PA 1992 provides the sanction for non-registration of registrable documents eg, an assignment of a patent and an exclusive licence. A document in respect of which no entry has been made in the register under s 85(3) shall only be admitted in any court as evidence of title of any person to a patent application or share of or interest in a patent application or patent if the court so directs. Similarly, the holder of an exclusive licence may also be delayed in instituting an action under s 51.

Section 51(1) provides that an exclusive licensee has the like right as the patentee to take proceedings in respect of any infringement of the patent committed after the date of the licence, and in awarding damages or granting any other relief in the proceedings the court shall take into consideration any loss suffered or likely to be suffered by the exclusive licensee as a result of the infringement or, as the case may be, the profits derived from the infringement, so far as it constitutes an infringement of the rights of the exclusive licensee as such.

Section 51(2) provides, in proceedings taken by an exclusive licensee, that unless the patentee is joined as plaintiff in the proceedings he shall be added as a defendant provided that a patentee added as a defendant in pursuance of the subsection is not liable for any costs unless he enters an appearance and takes part in the proceedings. A sole licensee has no right to take an infringement action.

Section 95 gives power to the High Court in an action or proceeding for infringement or revocation of a patent to call in aid an assessor specially qualified in the opinion of the Court and try the case wholly or partially with his assistance.

Section 95(2) gives a similar power to the Supreme Court.

10.9 Remedies for infringement

Remedies for infringement include:

(a) Injunction;
(b) Damages and account of profits;
(c) Order for delivery up or destruction;
(d) Relief for infringement of partially valid patent;
(e) Certificate of Contested Validity;
(f) Costs;
(g) Publication of the judgment that patent has been infringed.

Under the terms of s 47 of PA 1992, in infringement proceedings a claim may be made for:

(a) an injunction restraining the defendant from infringing;

(b) an Order requiring the defendant to deliver up or destroy any product covered by the patent;

(c) damages;

(d) an account of profits derived by the defendant from the alleged infringement;

(e) a declaration that the patent is valid and has been infringed by the defendant;

Section 47(2) provides that the court shall not, in respect of the same infringement, both award the patentee damages and order that he shall be given an account of the profits.

The grant of an injunction is a discretionary matter and the court retains a discretion to refuse an injunction and award damages in lieu.

In *SmithKline Beecham and Others v Genthon BV and Others* [2003] IEHC 623, the High Court delivered an important ruling on the criteria for pre-trial injunctive relief in patent infringement proceedings in Ireland.

The plaintiffs marketed a drug in the State known as Seroxat. The plaintiffs had Irish registered patents which related to the drug. The defendants marketed a similar drug under the name of Mexolat. The plaintiffs sought an injunction to prevent the marketing of the defendants' drug, claiming that it was infringing their patent. The defendants contended that the plaintiffs' patents were invalid and opposed the granting of an injunction.

Mr Justice Kelly confirmed that the established three step test for pre-trial injunctions, which was originally set forth by the Supreme Court in *Campus Oil v Minister for Energy (No 2)* [1983] IR 88, [which in turn accepted the speech of Lord Diplock in *American Cyanamid v Ethicon* [1975] AC 396], was the correct statement of the law. Mr Justice Kelly also confirmed that the tests for the granting of pre-trial injunctions in patent cases were the same as in any other case and he made a number of significant comments on the application of the three step test to patent disputes.

Whilst Mr Justice Kelly refused to grant injunctive relief in this case he stressed that there was no hostility inherent or otherwise to the granting of interlocutory injunctions in patent disputes. He emphasised the evidence that must be produced by each side, in seeking to apply the criteria set out in *Campus Oil/American Cyanamid* in particular the second criterion, whether the plaintiffs would suffer irreparable loss if injunctive relief was refused.

He expressed the view that the plaintiffs had not, by reference to the complaints made, demonstrated that damages would not be an adequate remedy for them. He was satisfied that if the defendants wrongfully made inroads into the plaintiffs' market, a commercial loss would be suffered by the plaintiffs which could easily be compensated by damages. In addition, he noted that there was not the slightest suggestion that the defendants would not be in a position to meet any award of damages if the plaintiffs succeeded at trial. However, he gave comprehensive directions in relation to preparation for the trial with a view to ensuring an early trial date.

Until recently, in the UK, an injunction not to infringe a patent could not be effective after the patent had ceased to be in force. A post patent injunction was granted in the case of *Dyson Appliances Limited v Hoover Ltd* [2001] RPC 544. The injunction, granted to Dyson, was to restrain manufacture and sale of certain Hoover vacuum cleaners after the expiration date of a Dyson patent that would have infringed the patent when it was in force. This followed a finding in October 2000 that Hoover had infringed a patent in relation to groundbreaking technology. Until the decision, 'post-expiry' injunctions were seen to be at odds with the limited 20 year monopoly granted under the patent system. Dyson asked the court to prevent Hoover from manufacturing and selling any vacuum cleaners which would have infringed the Dyson patent (or alternatively to recommence selling their Vortex vacuum cleaner which had been held to infringe) for a period of 12 months after expiry of the patent.

The Judge ruled that in the absence of a post-expiry injunction Hoover would be able to recommence selling its Vortex cleaner soon after expiry of the patent as it had 'jumped the gun,' having already carried out all the necessary development work and obtained the requisite product authorisation[s]. Hoover's re-entry into the UK market would be boosted by the fact that the product had already been sold for about 18 months before Dyson secured its judgment. The Judge felt that Hoover should not be able to gain a 'springboard' by which it could compete with Dyson almost as soon as the patent expired. Furthermore, an accurate assessment of damages would be 'notoriously difficult' and therefore, 'prevention was better can cure.'

10.9.1 Damages and account of profits

A successful patentee is entitled to damages in respect of actual infringement of his patent or, at his option, an account of profits. The patentee is entitled to disclosure from the defendant to enable him to choose between damages or profits.

Damages are intended to restore the claimant to the position he would have been in but for the infringement – damages can be awarded not only for the lost sales of the patented item but also for goods commonly sold with the patented item ('convoyed goods', *Gerber Garment Technology INC v Lectra Systems Ltd* [1997] RPC 443). Where the claimant does not manufacture the innovation or license the patent to third parties the quantum of damages may be assessed by regard to a reasonable royalty rate (*Meters Ltd v Metropolitan Gas Meters* [1911] 28 RPC 157). A reasonable royalty rate would be that which a potential licensee not yet in the market would pay, disregarding the possibility of making non-infringing alternatives.

10.9.1.1 *Restriction on recovery of damages for infringement (s 49 of PA 1992)*

The courts have always been reluctant to award damages against a person who innocently infringes a common law right, but they have always been willing to grant injunctions to prevent continued infringement. Section 49(1) provides that in proceedings for infringement of a patent, damages shall not be awarded, and no order shall be made for an account of profits, against a defendant who proves that at the date of the infringement he was not aware, and had no reasonable grounds for supposing, that that patent existed, and a person shall not be deemed to have been so aware or to have had reasonable grounds for so supposing by reason only of the application to a product of the word 'patent' or 'patented' or any word or words expressing or implying that a patent has been obtained for the product, unless the number of the relevant patent accompanied the word or words in question. The requirement of reasonableness means that a defendant who copies a new product ought to enquire whether it is patented. The proviso to the subsection suggests that the courts will take a reasonable approach.

Section 49(2) provides that in proceedings for infringement of a patent the court may, if it thinks fit, refuse to award any damages or make any order in respect of any infringement committed during an extension period specified in a late request for renewal under s 36(3) but before the payment of the renewal fee and any additional fee prescribed for the purpose of that subsection.

Section 36(3) provides that where an amendment of a specification of a patent has been allowed under the Act, no damages shall be awarded in any proceedings for an infringement of the patent committed before the date of the decision allowing the amendment, unless the court is satisfied that the specification of the patent, as originally published, was framed in good faith and with reasonable skill and knowledge. The principle to be applied when assessing damages is that the plaintiff should be restored by monetary compensation to the position which he would have occupied but for the wrongful acts of the defendant, provided always that such loss as he proves is the natural and direct consequence of the defendant's act.

Section 51 provides that in awarding damages or granting any other relief to an exclusive licensee who sues as plaintiff, the court must take into consideration only the loss suffered or likely to be suffered by the actual exclusive licensee. If the exclusive licensee claims an account of profits in lieu of damages, the profits to be considered are those earned by means of the infringement so far as it constitutes an infringement of the rights of the exclusive licensee as such.

10.9.2 Delivery up or destruction

Section 47(1)(a) of PA 1992 gives power to the court to order that the infringing goods be delivered up to the patent owner or that they be destroyed. This is to ensure that the infringing goods are not retained in order to be placed on the market after the expiry of the patent. If such an order were not available then the infringer could profit after patent expiry from sale of goods that were manufactured at the time the patent was in force. Under the European Communities (Enforcement of Intellectual Property Rights) Regulations 2006 (SI 360/2006), paragraph 4, the court may also order destruction or recall of any material or implement principally used in the creation or manufacture of infringing goods.

10.9.3 Relief for infringement of partially valid patent

By s 50 of PA 1992, where in infringement proceedings a patent has been found to be only partially valid, relief may be granted in respect of that part of it which has been found to be valid and infringed, providing that the court shall not grant relief by way of damages or costs except in circumstances that are mentioned in s 50(2). Section 50(2) provides that where in proceedings for the infringement of a patent the plaintiff proves that the specification of the patent was framed in good faith and with reasonable skill and knowledge, the court may grant relief in respect of that part of the patent which is valid and infringed, subject to the discretion of the court as to costs and as to the date from which damages should be reckoned.

As a condition of relief, the court may direct that the specification be amended under s 38 or, in the case of a European patent designating the State, by limitation of the claims at the EPO (sub-s 50(4) of PA 1992–2006).

10.9.4 Certificate of contested validity

Section 52 provides that if in any proceedings before the court the validity of a patent to any extent is contested and the patent is found by the court to be wholly or partially valid, the court may certify the finding and the fact that validity of the patent was contested. Section 52(2) provides that where such a certificate has been granted then in any subsequent proceedings before the court for infringement of the patent or before the court or the Controller for revocation of the patent, a final order or judgment is made or given in favour of the party relying on the validity of the patent that party shall, unless the court otherwise directs, be entitled to his costs as between solicitor and own client. The purpose of this provision is to prevent a patentee from being put repeatedly to the expense of defending successive attacks on the validity of his patent.

10.9.5 Costs

In the usual way, a successful patentee in an infringement action would be entitled to his costs. As in any other court proceedings, costs are discretionary but usually follow the event.

10.9.6 Publication of judgment

Under the European Communities (Enforcement of Intellectual Property Rights) Regulations 2006 (SI 360/2006), paragraph 5, if a court finds that a patent has been infringed the court may order appropriate measures for the dissemination and publication of the judgment at the defendant's expense.

10.10 Defences and statutory exceptions to infringement

10.10.1 Consent of the proprietor of the patent

It is a pre-requisite of infringement under s 40 that the act complained of should be done without the consent of the proprietor of the patent. There is no requirement that this consent should be express and the normal rules of law will apply to determine whether consent is to be implied.

10.10.2 Euro-defences

Limitation of rights is dealt with under s 43 of PA 1992. The rights conferred by a patent shall not extend to any act which, pursuant to any obligations imposed by the law of the Treaty of Rome establishing the European Communities, cannot be prevented by the proprietor of the patent.

Acts which cannot be prevented fall into three broad areas: Arts 28–30 of the Treaty (formerly Arts 30, 34 and Art 36), Art 81(1) (formerly Art 85(1) and Art 82 (formerly Art 86).

A person who relies on the provisions of these Articles in defence to an infringement action is said to be relying on 'Euro-defences'.

In order to succeed in a Euro-defence, the defendant must establish a connection between the attempted enforcement of the patent rights and the alleged infringement of the Treaty.

> 'The nexus required is....that the exercise of the exclusive right as sought by the plaintiff in the pleadings would involve a breach of the Treaty' (*Ransburg-Gema AJ v Electrostatic Plant Systems Ltd* [1991] FSR 508, Ch, per Aldous J).

> 'It is sufficient that the existence of the intellectual property right creates or buttresses the dominant position which the plaintiff is abusing. The remedy contemplated by the court [in *Volvo v Veng*] is that the plaintiff may have to be deprived of the means of maintaining his dominant position' (*Pitney Bowes Inc v Francotyp-Postalia GmbH* [1991] FSR 72, Ch D, per Hoffmann J).

Patent rights raise particular difficulty under EU competition law. The EU has endeavoured to balance the rights of the patent owner which are monopolistic with free competition in a single market. A patent owner has, for a period of years, the right to use his invention or to sell the products covered by his patent. He has the right to dispose of the patent entirely or to license others to use the invention for the whole of the territory where the patent rights exist or a defined part of that territory. The existence of such rights and the terms upon which licences are granted may restrict competition.

The purpose of the EU internal market is to establish a single market among all EU Member States ie, one national market throughout the European Union. If intellectual property rights applied throughout the Union there would be no great difficulty in achieving this. Apart from the Community Trade Mark and Community Design, which cover the entire Union, intellectual property rights are essentially national. Therefore, as a matter of law a patent owner in one Member State may, in certain circumstances, prevent the importation of products covered by his patent lawfully marketed in another Member

State by suing for infringement of his patent and thereby obstruct the free movement of goods.

In resolving the conflict between national patent rights and free movement of goods the ECJ has relied on the principles under Arts 28 to 30 (formerly Arts 34 and 36). Article 28 prohibits all quantitative restrictions and measures having equivalent effect on imports and exports between Member States. The right of the owner of a national patent to bring an action against an importer *prima facie* constitutes a measure having equivalent effect. The right given by PA 1992 to the owner of a patent to bring an infringement action must therefore be justified under Art 30, which provides that the prohibition in Art 28 is subject to an exception if the measure in question is 'justified on grounds of ... the protection of industrial and commercial property.' In determining the extent of the protection offered by Art 30, the ECJ has drawn a distinction between the 'existence' and the 'exercise' of intellectual property rights and held that it is only the 'existence' of the right which is protected by Art 30 and that the 'exercise' of the right is subject to limitations arising from the rules of the Treaty.

The ECJ has also developed another important principle known as 'exhaustion of rights.' The ECJ has held that Arts 28–30 provide a complete defence to an infringement action if it is shown that the products in question have been previously marketed in another Member State by the proprietor of that right or with his consent. The previous marketing is said to have 'exhausted' the ability of the owner of the right to prevent the subsequent free circulation of the products concerned throughout the Union.

Under Arts 28–30, the effect of the rules on free movement of goods on actions for patent infringement may be summarised as follows:

(a) Articles 28–30 of the Treaty preclude the proprietor of a patent protected by the law of one Member State from suing for infringement to prevent the importation of a product that has been lawfully marketed in another Member State by the proprietor or with his consent. This is the 'exhaustion of rights' principle and applies even if the product is not patentable in the latter Member State.

(b) The effect of Arts 28–30 is not finally decided in the case of a direct sale into one Member State by a patent licensee or assignee in another Member State where the goods in question have not been previously marketed in the latter Member State.

(c) Articles 28–30 of the Treaty do not preclude the exercise of patent rights to prevent the importation into the European Union of goods originating in third countries.

(d) Articles 28–30 do not otherwise affect actions for infringement, unless it is shown that for some other reason the infringement action is not 'justified for the protection of industrial or commercial property rights,' or amounts to 'arbitrary discrimination' or a 'disguised restriction on trade between Member States' within the meaning of the second sentence of Art 36.

Under Art 81(1) (formerly Art 85 (1)), although intellectual property rights do not as such fall within Art 81(1), the bringing of an infringement action may contravene Art 81(1) where the infringement action tends to the partitioning of the common market and is brought as 'the object, the means or the consequence' of an agreement.

Under Art 82 (formerly Art 86), according to the recent case law of the Courts of Justice and of First Instance, the improper exercise of an intellectual property right is capable of infringing Art 82. However, for Art 82 to apply it is necessary to establish:

(i) a dominant position in a relevant product and geographic market in a substantial part of the common market; and

(ii) an abuse of that position in a manner likely to affect trade between Member States.

When considering how best to defend a patent infringement action, consideration should always be given as to whether it is possible to plead one or more of the Euro-defences. When the defendant is importing the patentee's own product from another EU Member State, consideration should first be given to whether the parallel import 'defence' is available. Consideration should then be given as to whether there are any agreements relating to the patent in suit which may be contrary to Art 81(1). Finally, consideration should be given to whether an Art 82 defence is available. In order to successfully plead such a defence the defendant will need to establish dominance in a relevant market, abusive conduct, a connection between the alleged abuse and the infringement action and connection between the abuse and an effect on trade between Member States. None of these matters are easy or cheap to prove.

The English Court of Appeal in *Intel Corporation v Via Technologies Inc* [2003] FSR 33 (p 574), reinstated certain defences under Arts 81 and 82, accepting that they were exceptional cases in which the exercise of an exclusive right might involve abusive conduct. It is not possible, however, from the authorities to date to categorise those types of allegations which would give rise to a successful defence. However, the mere refusal to grant licences either at all or on reasonable terms, is not of itself an abuse.

10.10.3 Infringement not novel

No relief could be obtained in respect of an invalid patent. If the defendant can prove that the act complained of was merely what was disclosed in a publication which could be relied on against the validity of the patent, without any substantial or patentable variation having been made, he has a good defence. This is the so called 'Gillette defence'.

10.10.4 Patent invalid

More generally, the validity of a patent may be put in issue by way of a counterclaim in infringement proceedings. The grounds of invalidity must be one of the grounds specified in s 58 of PA 1992 on which the patent could be revoked (see below).

10.10.5 Right to continue use begun before priority date

Under s 55, where a patent is granted for an invention, a person who, in the State, before the date of filing of the patent application or, if priority was claimed, before the date of priority, does in good faith an act which would constitute an infringement of the patent if it were then in force, or makes in good faith effective and serious preparations to do such an act, shall have the rights specified in s 55(2):

(2) The rights referred to in s 55(1) are the following:

(a) the right to continue to do or, as the case may be, to do the act referred to in s 55(1)

(b) if such act was done or preparations had been made to so do it in the course of a business—

    (i) in the case of an individual—

        (I) the right to assign the right to do it or to transmit such right on death, or

        (II) the right to authorise the doing of the act by any of his partners for the time being in the business in the course of which the act was done or preparations had been made to do it;

    (ii) in the case of a body corporate, the right to assign the right to do it or to transmit such right on the body's dissolution;

and the doing of that act by virtue of this subsection shall not amount to an infringement of the patent concerned.

(3) No right to grant a licence.

(4) Where a product which is the subject of a patent is disposed of by any person to another in exercise of a right conferred by s 55(2), that other and any person claiming through him shall be entitled to deal with the product in the same way as if it had been disposed of by a sole proprietor of the patent.

It is important to note that this prior user's right is restricted to the State and does not, for example, permit sale of the product in the United Kingdom if a corresponding patent is in force there but the prior use was not carried out there.

10.10.6 Right to continue use commenced while patent lapsed

Although a patent may lapse by reason of failure to pay renewal fees, s 37 of PA 1992 contains provisions for the restoration of the patent under certain circumstances. Section 37(7) provides that an order under the section for the restoration of a patent shall be subject to such provisions as are prescribed for the protection of persons who, during the period beginning on the date on which the patent lapsed and ending on the date of the order under the section, may have begun to avail themselves of the invention which is the subject of the patent. Rule 38 of the PR 1992 prescribed the provisions for the protection of such persons. Under P(A)A 2006 the effect of an order for the restoration of a patent is given statutory force under s 37(7) and (8). Similar provisions are also included: in s 35B to deal with the effect of reinstatement of a patent application under new s 35A; in s 110A for the effect of restoration of a patent application which was withdrawn in error; and in s 119A for the effect of restoration of a European patent designating the State where the English translation was not filed in time.

10.10.7 Private use

Section 42(a) of PA 1992 provides that the rights conferred by a patent do not extend to acts done privately for non-commercial purposes.

10.10.8 Experimental use

Similarly, under s 42(1), an act done for experimental purposes relating to the subject matter of the relevant patented invention will not be an infringing act.

10.10.8.1 *Trials of generic medicines*

Section 42 has been amended by the European Communities (Limitation of Effect of Patent) Regulations 2006 (SI 50/2006) made on 30 January 2006. These Regulations made under the European Communities Act 1972 give effect to EC Directives. The rights conferred by a patent have been limited so that they cannot stop acts done in conducting the necessary studies, tests and trials to fulfil the application requirements for a marketing authorisation for a generic or similar biological medicinal product for human use or for veterinary use.

10.10.9 Extemporaneous preparation on prescription

Section 42(c) provides that the extemporaneous preparation for individual cases in a pharmacy of a medicine in accordance with a medical prescription issued by a registered medical practitioner or acts concerning the medicine so prepared do not infringe.

10.10.10 Vessels, vehicles and air craft

10.10.10.1 *Ships*

The rights conferred by a patent do not extend to the use on board vessels registered in certain countries, other than in the State, of the invention which is the subject of the patent, in the body of the vessel, in the machinery, tackle, gear and other accessories, when such vessels temporarily or accidentally enter the territorial waters of the State, provided that the invention is used in such waters exclusively for the needs of the vessel.

The interpretation of the word 'temporarily' causes difficulty. The English courts have decided that a Dublin-based ferry which regularly served Holyhead was only ever 'temporarily' in the territorial waters of the United Kingdom and therefore although it fell within the valid claims of a UK patent it did not infringe the rights conferred by the patent – see *Stena v Irish Ferries* [2002] RPC 990 and [2003] RPC 668.

10.10.10.2 *Aircraft, hovercraft and vehicles*

The rights conferred by a patent do not extend to the use of the invention which is the subject of the patent in the construction or operation of aircraft or land vehicles of certain countries other than the State or of such aircraft or land vehicle accessories when such aircraft or land vehicles temporarily or accidentally enter the State.

10.10.10.3 *Breach of restrictive conditions*

Under s 83(4) the inclusion by the proprietor of a patent in a contract of any condition which by virtue of the section is null and void shall be available as a defence to an action for infringement of the patent to which the contract relates brought while that contract is in force.

Section 68(1) makes provision for the proprietor of a patent to apply to the Controller for an entry to be made in the register to the effect that licences under the patent are to be available as of right.

Section 68(2)(b) provides that where such an entry is made in the register, then if in any proceedings for infringement of the patent (otherwise than by importation of goods) the defendant undertakes to take a licence on terms to be settled by the Controller, no injunction shall be granted against him. And the amount (if any) recoverable against him by way of damages shall not exceed double the amount which would have been payable by him as licensee if such a licence had been granted before the earliest infringement.

10.11 Revocation

Section 57 of PA 1992 provides that any person may apply to the court or the Controller for revocation on the grounds set out in s 58. Section 57(5) provides that where there are proceedings with respect to a patent pending in the court under any provision of PA 1992 Act, then the revocation application may not be made to the Controller without the leave of the court.

Section 59 gives power to the court or the Controller to revoke where they consider the grounds for revocation mentioned in s 58 prejudice the maintenance of the patent.

The grounds for revocation in s 58 of PA 1992–2006 are:

(a) that the subject matter of the patent is not patentable under PA 1992;
(b) the specification of the patent does not disclose the invention in a manner sufficiently clear and complete for it to be carried out by a person skilled in the art;

(c) there has been unlawful extension of the disclosure;

(d) the protection conferred by the patent has been extended by an amendment which should not have been allowed;

(e) the proprietor of the patent is not entitled thereto.

Section 60 gives the power to the controller to revoke patents on his own initiative.

If a European Patent is under opposition at the European Patent Office (EPO), a petition to revoke the same patent before the High Court may be stayed because a decision by the EPO to revoke the patent would have automatic effect here under s 119(4) of PA 1992. Such a stay was granted by McCracken J in *Merck & Co Inc v GD Searle & Co* [2001] 2 ILRM 363, when the patent owners gave an undertaking not to enforce the patent by way of injunction pending final determination of the EPO.

In *Re Irish Patent No 52364* [2005] IEHC 114, a petition was presented to the Court by Merial Limited seeking an Order that a Supplemental Protection Certificate be revoked together with an Order for Costs. The Order for Revocation was made on consent. However, the respondent objected to the award of costs in favour of the petitioner and applied for costs to be awarded in its favour.

Mr Justice Kelly noted that an Order for Revocation of a Patent would usually include an Order for the respondent to pay the petitioner's costs. This is so even though an Order is made by consent and no previous notice of the intention to present a petition has been given to the patentee. He held that the failure to write a warning letter prior to the presentation of the petition seeking revocation of the Supplementary Protection Certificate was not fatal to the award of costs nor would such a warning letter have produced different results. Accordingly, he made the Order for Revocation of the SPC and the costs of the proceedings were granted in favour of the petitioner.

10.12 Amendment

A reference to amendment is included so that a client may be advised in general terms as to the possibility of amending a patent application (s 32 of PA 1992) and amending the patent specification after grant (s 38 of PA 1992). The rules governing amendment distinguish between alterations in the description of the invention and in the claims. The description must not be amended so as to introduce matter extending beyond that disclosed in the specification as filed (s 32(2) and s 38(3) of PA 1992) and the claims must not be amended after grant so as to extend the protection conferred by the patent (s 38(3) of PA 1992). If the claims are amended during application, they still have to satisfy the basic rule that they must be clear and concise and be supported by the description (s 20). Amendments which are wrongly admitted may provide a ground for revocation (s 58(c) and (d) of PA 1992). Where a specification is amended after grant under the provisions of s 38 the amendment is deemed always to have had effect from the date of grant of the patent. Amendment in the course of an application is frequent. Amendment after grant is much less frequent.

A patent specification defines the subject matter of the invention and by implication what people are free to do. Thus, there is a public interest in applications for amendment after grant. This public interest is reflected in the fact that the intention to apply for amendment must be advertised (s 38(1) and (2) of PA 1992). In addition, s 38(5) provides that 'any person' may oppose the proposed amendment.

The onus on an applicant for amendment is heavy and he must make full disclosure to the court or the Controller as the case may be. Any undue delay in making application for amendment can be fatal.

In *Re Matter of Irish Patent No 1121375* [2005] IEHC 441, Akzo Nobel N.V., in patent revocation proceedings brought by Norton Healthcare, sought leave pursuant to the provisions of s 38(2) to bring an amended claim which it would seek to rely upon in the event of certain of the original claims being condemned.

Mr Justice Kelly indicated that it did not appear to him to be impermissible. He went on to state that if such an amendment was permitted he was satisfied that an appropriate costs Order could address any inconvenience that might be suffered by the petitioner. In his view, the application for leave to amend should be brought timeously. He noted that the application would fall to be considered on the merits and he was of the opinion that the principles expressed by Aldous LJ in *SmithKline and French Laboratories Ltd v Evans Medical Ltd* [1989] FSR 561, had much to recommend them in consideration of such an application.

Patent amendment has been a problem in the UK and Ireland for several years. Amendment remained a discretionary matter, effectively requiring the patentee to make full disclosure of all relevant materials, even those that were privileged. Despite attempts by lower courts in the UK to ease the position, the Court of Appeal in the UK reaffirmed the court's wide discretion in *Kimberly-Clark v Procter & Gamble* [2000] RPC 422. The issue is of importance where litigation uncovers prior art which invalidates certain claims of the patent, but where the claims could be limited to overcome the prior art.

One of the changes agreed at the Munich Diplomatic Conference in Munich in November 2000 effectively overturns the problem in seeking amendment. The new Art 105a allows a patentee to apply to the EPO at any time to limit the European patent, providing the patent is not in opposition at that time. The examination will effectively only be on formalities and is expected to go through quickly. On entry into force of the revised EPC 2000, this will provide a valuable, pan-European, mechanism for the rapid amendment of claims.

In addition, the new EPC Art 138(3) makes it clear that patentees will have a right to limit the claims of their patents in any proceedings before national courts where validity of the patent is in issue. The court would no longer appear to be able to exercise any discretion in the matter. Section 38(7) introduced by P(A)A 2006 provides that in considering whether or not to allow an amendment after grant the court or Controller shall have regard to any relevant principles applicable under the European Patent Convention. This is applicable to amendment of either a patent granted under PA 1992 or a European patent designating the State.

10.13 Remedy for groundless threats

Section 53 of PA 1992 has relevance when you are consulted by a client who owns a patent which he believes is being infringed and he requests you write to the alleged infringer, or where you are consulted by a client who has received a cease and desist letter from a patent owner alleging he is infringing a patent. The purpose of the section is to give to a person who receives a threat of infringement proceedings a remedy to prevent the threats. It has long been recognised that a potential plaintiff can do damage by merely threatening to sue. A manufacturer or importer is particularly prone to damage where their customers are threatened and they capitulate to those threats.

Under s 53, if any person (whether or not entitled to any right in a patent) by circulars, advertisements or otherwise, threatens another person with proceedings for any infringement of a patent, a person aggrieved by the threats (whether or not the person to whom the threats are made) may bring proceedings against the person making the threats, provided that proceedings may not be brought for a threat to bring proceedings for infringement alleged to consist of making or importing a product for disposal or of using a process. If the threats and the plaintiff's status as a person aggrieved are proved, then the plaintiff can obtain relief unless the defendant proves that the acts in respect of which proceedings were threatened constitute or would constitute an infringement of a patent and the patent alleged to be infringed is not shown by the plaintiff to be invalid. The plaintiff may claim relief by way of a declaration, injunction and damages.

Mere notification of the existence of a patent does not constitute a threat of proceedings within the meaning of s 53. Additionally, under s 53(3), introduced by P(A)A 2006, proceedings may not be brought for a threat against a person who made or imported a product for disposal or used a process where the infringement is alleged to consist of doing anything else (eg, selling) in relation to that product or process.

10.14 Declaration of non-infringement

The Oireachtas recognised that the threat of patent infringement proceedings is an exceptional hindrance to trade and s 54 of PA 1992 is a specific statutory provision enabling a third party to seek declarations of non-infringement from the court. This is so regardless of whether the patentee has made any assertion of infringement. By this procedure third parties know where they stand before launching a new product or venture. The applicant must show that he has applied in writing to the proprietor or licensee for a written acknowledgement the effect of which, if given, would be similar to that of the declaration claimed, and has furnished him with full particulars in writing of the process or product in question, and the proprietor or licensee has refused or neglected to give such an acknowledgement.

The validity of a patent in whole or in part may not be called into question in proceedings for a declaration of non-infringement, and accordingly the making or refusal of such a declaration in the case of a patent shall not be deemed to imply that the patent is valid.

A declaration of non-infringement was refused by Mr Justice Clarke on 10 July 2007 in *Ranbaxy Laboratories Limited & Others v Warner Lambert Company,* mentioned at **10.7** above.

10.15 The role of a patent agent in patent litigation

A patent agent usually works with solicitors and counsel during patent litigation, in order to assist, *inter alia*:

(a) in interpreting the patent and investigating its validity;
(b) in providing background information about the technical field;
(c) in liaising with expert witnesses;
(d) in explaining specialist areas of patent law and practice, including European law and EPO practice;
(e) in participating in a 'confidentiality club' if evidence is made available to professional advisers only.

If a patent is found to be partially invalid and/or is amended during the litigation, the patent agent who drafted the original specification may be required to give evidence to satisfy the court that the specification was framed in good faith and with reasonable skill and knowledge (ss 49(3) and 50(2) of PA 1992).

10.16 Miscellaneous matters

10.16.1 Privileged communications of solicitors and patent agents

Section 94 of PA 1992 extends privilege to certain specified communications. A communication to which the section applies is privileged from disclosure in any proceedings (including a proceeding before the Controller or competent authority under the European Patent Convention or the Patent Co-operation Treaty) to the same extent as a communication between client and solicitor is privileged in any proceedings before a court in the State. The section applies to a communication between a person (or a person acting on his behalf) and a solicitor or patent agent (or a person acting on his behalf) or for the purpose of obtaining, or in response to a request for, information which a person is seeking for the purpose of instructing a solicitor or patent agent in relation to any matter concerning the protection of an invention, patent, design or technical information or any matter involving passing off.

Under s 106(7) of PA 1992, nothing in the Act shall be construed as prohibiting solicitors from taking such part in proceedings under the Act as has heretofore been taken by solicitors in connection with a patent or any procedure relating to a patent or the obtaining thereof.

10.16.2 Discovery

General principles are applicable to discovery in patent actions as much as in any others. Two detailed judgments have been given recently: by Kelly J in *Medtronic Inc & Ors v Guidant Corporation & Ors* [2007] IEHC 37; and by Finlay Geoghegan J in *Schneider [Europe] GmbH v Conor Medsystems Ireland Ltd* [2007] IEHC 63.

10.16.3 Action for disclosure

A person may be made a defendant in an action brought specifically to obtain discovery of the identity of infringers where that person (whether knowingly or not) 'has got mixed up in the tortious acts of others so as to facilitate their wrongdoing.' (*Norwich Pharmacal Co v Customs & Excise Commissioners* [1974] AC 133) The costs of the innocent defendant in providing such information will be borne by the plaintiff, as will the costs of proceedings if the defendant properly doubts whether he should have to provide such information and submits the matter for determination by the court. The plaintiff may, however, be able to recover such costs from the infringer in subsequent proceedings.

The European Communities (Enforcement of Intellectual Property Rights) Regulations 2006 (SI 360/2006), paragraph 3, expressly provides that a claimant may apply to the court for an order that information regarding the origin and distribution networks of goods or services which infringe an intellectual property (IP) right shall be disclosed by relevant persons, including *inter alia* a person found in possession of the infringing goods on a commercial scale which are used in activities that infringe an IP right.

The court has jurisdiction to order the disclosure of the name of a wrong-doer outside the jurisdiction even though such wrongdoing is under the laws of another country, provided it is shown that the transaction in which the defendant and the wrongdoer were involved related to the same subject matter. (*Smith, Kline & French Laboratories Ltd v Global Pharmaceuticals Ltd* [1986] RPC 394)

10.16.4 Compulsory licences

After three years from the grant of a patent, a third party may apply under ss 70–75 of PA 1992 for a compulsory licence on certain grounds, mainly related to alleged non-working of the invention. The grounds have been amended by P(A)A 2006 to conform with the TRIPs Agreement. In addition, Regulation (EC) No 816/2006 has introduced special measures for compulsory licensing of patents and SPCs concerning the manufacture and sale of pharmaceutical products, when the products are intended for export to eligible countries with public health problems. This implemented a decision of the WTO. For further details, see the Chapter on Life Sciences.

10.16.5 Customs & excise procedure

Council Regulation EC1 1383/03 concerns procedures for requesting national customs authorities to detain infringing goods including goods that infringe a patent. The procedure involves notifying the customs and excise authorities of details of the right being infringed and details of the import/export of the relevant goods together with a request that the goods be detained. The applicant must also give a full written indemnity to the customs & excise authorities with regard to the detention of the goods. SI 34/2005 implements the regulation in Ireland.

CHAPTER 11

TRADE MARKS

Maureen Daly & Louise Carey

11.1 Introduction

Trade mark law in Ireland is currently governed by the Trade Marks Act 1996 (the 1996 Act), (which implements the Trade Marks Harmonisation Directive 89/104/EEC), Council Regulation 40/94/EC on the Community Trade Mark (as amended) and the Common Law action of passing off.

11.2 What is a trade mark?

Put at its simplest, a trade mark is some type of sign which distinguishes the product or service of one manufacturer or service provider from another. Well known trade marks such as 'Flake' or 'Oxo,' 'Michelin Man character' etc are extremely valuable assets for the companies who own them. The key feature of a trade mark is that it is 'distinctive' of that product or service and no one else's product, so that it serves as a 'badge of origin' and as a type of guarantee to the consumer as to the origin of that product.

A great many people mistakenly believe that if a trade mark is not registered then it is not legally protected. This is not the case if the mark in question has been put to significant use in trade such that it has become well known and has thus accrued a 'reputation' and 'goodwill'. Such an unregistered trade mark will then be protected in Ireland by the law of passing off.

11.3 What type of mark can be registered?

According to s 6 of the 1996 Act, practically any kind of distinctive sign can be registered, provided it is capable of being represented graphically. Most commonly, trade marks consist of words, 'devices' (sometimes referred to as 'logos') and shapes. However, s 6 lists as possible trade marks: words (including personal names), designs, letters, numerals or the shape of goods or their packaging.

11.4 Where should a trade mark be registered?

Currently, there are four possibilities for registration, namely:

(a) a national filing at the Irish Patents Office, Hebron Road, Kilkenny;
(b) a filing at the Office for Harmonisation in the Internal Market (OHIM) in Alicante, Spain (Community Trade Mark);
(c) a Madrid Protocol filing;
(d) selective filings in individual countries.

The relative merits of each of these options are dealt with in the following sections.

11.4.1 Irish national filing

This is the cheapest option and is best suited to a proprietor whose mark is only used in Ireland. It is possible to apply in a single application to register one mark in several classes of goods or services by paying additional fees per additional class. Marks are classified according to the 'Nice Classification' (this can be accessed at the Patents Office website www.patentsoffice.ie). For example, a person might wish to protect a mark for use in regard to soft drinks, coffee and t-shirts, in which case the filing should be made in classes 32, 30 and 25. Provided an applicant has an Irish address they can file the application personally but a solicitor must be registered at the Patents Office as a Trade mark Agent in order to be able to process trade mark filings.

11.4.2 Office for Harmonisation in the Internal Market

The 1996 Act gave effect to the Council Regulation No 40/94 (the Regulation) on the Community Trade Mark. Since April 1996, applications have been filed at OHIM in Alicante, Spain to obtain 'Community Trade Marks' (CTMs). The principal advantage to this type of protection is that a mark can be protected in all Member States of the European Union by a single registration. However, as the registration system is an 'all or nothing' system, it means that it is not possible to hold a CTM registration excluding one or more European Union countries. Therefore, an earlier trade mark on one of the national registers in a European Union country or indeed on the Community Trade Mark Register itself can form the basis of an opposition before OHIM. If the opposition is successful, the applicant can either abandon the application, or alternatively convert it into a series of national applications which will still enjoy the same filing date as the original CTM application (see **11.4.4** below).

11.4.3 The Madrid Protocol

The 1996 Act also gave effect to the 'Madrid Protocol'. The Protocol was implemented by the Trade Marks (Madrid Protocol) Regulations 2001 (SI 346/2001) which came into operation on 19 October, 2001. The gist of this system is that once the trade mark owner is domiciled or is a national or has a real commercial base in a Protocol country (eg Ireland) and his mark is the subject of an application or registration in the home country (eg Ireland) (the 'basic application or registration'), the trade mark owner can choose or 'designate' in which of the Protocol countries the registration (known as an 'international registration') is to take effect. Since 1 October, 2004, the applicant can designate the CTM system. An application is filed at the Irish Patents Office and once examined as to formalities, it is forwarded to the International Bureau of the World Intellectual Property Organisation (WIPO) in Geneva. The WIPO office records the mark in its 'International Register,' and then notifies the mark to the Trade Mark Offices of each designated country. However, these designated country offices can refuse protection to the mark, and the trade mark owner can contest this refusal at the local office. Even if a country is deleted from the application, the international application will (notwithstanding this) proceed in respect of the balance of the countries designated by the applicant. The risk with a Madrid Protocol filing is that if the 'basic' application or registration fails or is cancelled within the first five years of the initial 10 year term of the international registration, then the latter also fails. However, if this occurs, the proprietor may convert the international registration into a series of national applications, which retain the date of filing of the international registration. Such a conversion must occur within 3 months of the loss of the international registration. After five years, the international registration is independent of the 'basic' application/registration.

11.4.4 Selective filings in individual countries

Frequently, traders use their trade mark only in Ireland and perhaps one or two other countries. In such a case, it may be cheaper and easier to file in each relevant country at the national Patents Office. The foreign country filings will then have to be done through local agents.

11.5 Who should do the filing of the application?

The trade mark owner or his authorised registered trade mark agent can file trade mark applications in Ireland. To file at the OHIM in Spain, the trade mark owner may appoint a registered representative to file the application. Irish trade mark agents are accepted as representatives by OHIM. The filing and prosecution of trade mark applications can in some circumstances be very straightforward, if no official objections on the mark's registrability is encountered and there is no third party opposition to the registration. However, dealing with official objections and oppositions requires a detailed up-to-date knowledge of the applicable statutory and case law.

11.6 Registrability

An important issue to be aware of, for the purposes of the registrability of a mark, is that a mark can be refused registration by the Patents Office on the basis of what are known as 'absolute' and 'relative' grounds. Each of these grounds will be examined separately below in order to understand the basis on which an application can be refused registration.

11.6.1 Absolute grounds

Under s 8 of the 1996 Act, an application can be refused registration by an Examiner at the Patents Office if the following criteria are not met:

(a) the mark is not a 'trade mark' as defined in s 6;
(b) the mark is devoid of any distinctive character;
(c) the mark consists exclusively of signs or indications which may serve in the trade to designate the kind, quality, quantity, intended purpose, value, geographical origin, time of production of goods or of rendering of services, or other characteristics of goods or services;
(d) the mark consists exclusively of signs or indications which have become customary in the current language or in the *bona fide* and established practices of the trade.

Notwithstanding the above criteria, an application for registration of a mark may still be accepted by the Patents Office even though it falls foul of (b)–(d) above. If the applicant can show to the satisfaction of the Patents Office that the mark has acquired a distinctive character as a result of substantial usage prior to the date of application, the trade mark application will be allowed to proceed.

In addition to the above, a mark cannot be registered if it consists exclusively of a shape which results from nature of the goods, a shape which is necessary to obtain a technical result or a shape which gives substantial value to the mark. Also, a mark cannot be registered if it is contrary to public policy or accepted principles of morality, or if it is of such a nature so as to deceive the public, for instance as to the nature, quality or geographic origin of the goods/services.

Also, a mark cannot be registered if its use is prohibited in the State by any enactment or rule of law (including Community Law) or if the application itself was made in bad faith. A mark consisting of or similar to a State emblem of Ireland cannot be registered, unless the requisite consent has been granted by the Minister. This protection for emblems also extends to those of a public authority, unless the requisite consent has been obtained. The national flag may only form part of a trade mark if its use is not misleading or offensive.

From each of the above objections, it is clearly evident that a mark cannot be registered if it is one that should be open to use by the public or indeed by other traders in the industry for which the mark is to be used. This protection also extends to marks that might be deceptive. Concern is also had for marks that are contrary to public policy or accepted principles of morality and examples of this would occur in situations where the marks would be likely to cause offence to a section of the public on the grounds of race, religious belief or even general matters of taste and decency.

11.6.2 Relative grounds

Relative grounds are raised by an examiner where there are earlier trade mark rights for which protection should be granted. There are three circumstances in which objections on relative grounds (which can be found in s 10 of the 1996 Act) will be raised and these circumstances are as follows:

(a) the trade mark is 'identical' to the earlier mark and the goods/services for which the mark is to be applied are also 'identical' to the goods/services for which the earlier mark is protected;

(b) the mark is 'identical/similar' to the earlier mark and the goods/services which protection is sought are also 'similar/identical or similar' to the goods/services for which the earlier mark is protected *and* there is a likelihood of confusion on the part of the public which includes the likelihood of association;

(c) a mark is 'identical/similar' to an earlier mark but the goods/services in respect of both marks are 'dissimilar' *but* the earlier mark has a reputation in the State (or in the case of a CTM, in the Community) and the use of the later trade mark without due cause would take unfair advantage of or be detrimental to the distinctive character or reputation of the earlier trade mark.

In addition to the above circumstances, a mark can be opposed by an earlier trade mark owner under s 10(4) of the 1996 Act, to the extent that he can prove that the use of the later mark would be prevented under the law of passing off or by the invocation of another earlier right. Obviously, during the course of a trade mark examination, this will not be raised by an examiner, because he would be unaware of the existence of such rights. However, in practice this provision is cited by an opponent who relies upon unregistered rights in opposition proceedings before the Patents Office.

Having looked at the basis on which an examiner can object to the registration of a trade mark, let us now look at the actual procedure for registering a mark in Ireland.

11.7 Procedure before the Patents Office

When an application for registration is filed at the Patents Office, it is assigned an official filing number. The information required for filing an application is:

(a) the name and address of the applicant;
(b) a representation of the trade mark;

(c) a statement of the goods/or services, in respect of which the mark is to be registered;

(d) an address for service in the State ie, the address of a Trade Mark Agent/solicitor.

Under s 40, if the mark has already been filed in a country which is a member of the 'Paris Convention' of 1883, and priority is claimed from that application (that is, the Irish application is filed within six months of that application), the filing date of the Irish application is deemed to be the date of the filing of the application in the Convention country.

Once filed, the application joins a queue of applications that await formal examination by an Examiner, which includes a search of the trade mark databases for similar earlier marks. If the Examiner has any question as to the mark's registerability, an official report will be issued and if the proprietor can address the questions to the satisfaction of the Examiner, the application will proceed to advertisement in the *Official Journal*, which is issued by the Patents Office to all Irish Trade Mark Agents and which is published. At this stage, third parties will have the opportunity to oppose the application, such opposition to be filed within three months of the date of advertisement. This deadline date is 'non-extendible'. If there is no third party opposition, the mark will proceed to registration upon payment of the registration fee.

The procedure indicated above is identical to the procedure for registering CTMs before OHIM. However, when CTM applications are being examined, they are only examined on 'absolute grounds'.

11.8 The duration of the registration

Registered trade marks (be they national Irish marks, Madrid Protocol marks or CTMs) are registered initially for a ten-year period but uniquely among intellectual property rights, this term can be renewed indefinitely for successive ten-year terms, on payment of a renewal fee (s 47). If a national mark is not renewed, s 48 provides for the possible late renewal or even restoration, if the mark has already been taken off the Register.

11.9 Limitation on rights

A trade mark registration will only remain valid to the extent that the mark is used by the owner in respect of the goods/services for which it was registered. Failure to use a mark will render the registration vulnerable to cancellation on the grounds of non-use. This attack will only arise after the mark has been registered for five years. Thereafter, a cancellation action can be instituted.

11.10 Effects of registration

The registration of a trade mark in Ireland gives the trade mark proprietor the exclusive right to use that trade mark in Ireland in respect of the goods/services for which it is registered (s 13 of the 1996 Act).

Accordingly, if another person uses that mark without consent, that usage will in general infringe the rights of the proprietor. Such rights arise from the date of registration of the mark, which is deemed to be the date the application was filed, although the legal proceedings for infringement of a national mark may not be brought before registration of the mark is published. A CTM proprietor has the right to sue from the date of publication of the registration of the CTM but damages can be claimed from the date of publication of the application.

Section 14 sets out the criteria for infringement of the registration. In summary, an infringement will occur where a mark, which is the same or similar to a registered mark, is used in relation to the same or similar goods or services as the registered mark. Section 14(2), which applies where there is not absolute identity between the marks and the goods or services, refers to the infringing use creating a 'likelihood of confusion...which includes a likelihood of association.' The interpretation of this has been scrutinised by the ECJ in a number of important cases (see *Marca Mode CV v Adidas AG and Adidas* C-425/98 [2000] ET MR 723). The upshot of these cases is that the concept of 'likelihood of association' is not an alternative to that of likelihood of confusion, but serves to define its scope.

Section 14(3) provides for infringement occurring where an identical or similar mark is used in relation to goods or services, which are not similar to those for which the registered trade mark is registered, provided the registered trade mark has a reputation in the State and the unwarranted use of the infringing mark takes unfair advantage of or is detrimental to the distinctive character or reputation of the registered trade mark. This is a new provision introduced by the 1996 Act.

11.11 What constitutes 'infringing use'?

Section 14(4) sets out examples of unauthorised acts, which will infringe a registered mark. The list is not exhaustive. Affixing the mark to goods or their packaging, selling goods or supplying services under the mark, importing or exporting goods under the mark, or using the mark on business papers or in advertising are all actions, which will be deemed to be infringements of the registered mark. Section 14(5) provides for a person who knowingly applies an infringing mark to labelling or packaging materials or to business papers or advertising materials to be deemed to be an infringer.

Section 14(6) radically changed the law by permitting 'comparative advertising'. This is where a trader compares his product to that of a competitor and in doing so explicitly refers to the competitor's product by its trade mark. This was not permitted in the past but is now allowed, provided it is in accordance with 'honest practices in industrial or commercial matters'.

11.12 Defences and exceptions to infringement:

(a) Use of another registered mark which is valid (s 15(1) and s 52(6) of the 1996 Act).

(b) Use of a person's name or address (s 15(2)(a) of the 1996 Act).

(c) Use of purely descriptive indications (eg, quantity, geographical origin) (s 15(2)(b) of the 1996 Act).

(d) Use of the registered mark to explain the purpose of another product, for example, an accessory made to fit a BMW car (s 15(2)(c) of the 1996 Act).

(e) Use of an earlier unregistered mark which applies in a particular locality, which has been in continuous use in relation to goods or services since before either the first use of the registered mark or its registration and the earlier mark applies only in that locality. This provision is aimed at permitting a limited form of geographical co-existence between an earlier local mark and a later registered mark.

(f) In general, infringement will not occur where the trade mark rights have been 'exhausted'. This occurs where the registered mark is put onto goods in another country in the European Economic Area (EEA) by the trade mark owner or with his consent, and which after the first sale, are resold and circulate from there into Ireland. The registered mark in Ireland cannot be invoked in that situation to stop the 'parallel importing' of the goods, unless the condition of the goods has been changed in some way since first marketing (s 16(l) and (2) of the 1996 Act). It should be noted that it is possible to use national trade mark rights to stop such parallel imports from countries outside the EEA (*Silhouette International Schmied GmbH and Co KG v Hartlauer* C-355/96 – [1998] ETMR 539, decision of 16 July 1998).

11.13 Infringement proceedings

These are covered exhaustively in ss 18–23 of the 1996 Act. The civil remedies available are:

(a) damages;
(b) an account of the defendant's profits;
(c) injunction;
(d) an Order for erasure, removal or obliteration of the infringing sign;
(e) an Order for destruction of the goods if erasure etc. is not possible;
(f) an Order for delivery up to the plaintiff of the infringing goods (this is subject to a six year time limit – see s 22);
(g) an Order for disposal (ie, destruction or forfeiture to a particular person).

Additional reliefs are available under the European Communities (Enforcement of Intellectual Property Rights) Regulations 2006 (see **11.24.5** below).

In most litigation concerning trade mark infringement, the pleadings will almost certainly claim damages, and as an alternative, an account of profits, and usually a permanent injunction. In addition to a prohibitory interlocutory injunction, orders such as a *Mareva* injunction, an *Anton Piller* order, a *Quia Timet* injunction and a *Norwich Pharmacal* order can be made in trade mark infringement cases.

Pursuant to s 25, the District Court has the power to grant a warrant for the search and seizure of infringing goods, and also to order their subsequent delivery up or destruction.

The Customs Authorities pursuant to the European Communities (Counterfeit and Pirated Goods) Regulation 1996 have the power to seize counterfeit goods at the behest of the trade mark proprietor, who has submitted evidence of ownership of the requisite intellectual property.

11.14 Section 24 – Groundless threats of infringement proceedings

Under s 24 of the 1996 Act, where a person threatens another with proceedings for infringement, the person aggrieved may apply to court for relief for groundless threats. This provision is not applicable where the infringement arises out of the application of the mark to the goods, the importation of goods to which the mark has been applied or the supply of services under the mark. Relief available to the complainant is an injunction to stop the threats from continuing, a declaration that the threats are unjustified, and damages sustained as a result of the threats.

If proceedings are instituted by the threatened individual, the registered owner will find himself losing the initiative and forced into defending costly litigation. Normally such a defendant will counterclaim for infringement. In such cases, the onus is on the registered proprietor to show that the threats are justified and that the acts complained of constitute infringement. If the plaintiff can prove invalidity or achieve revocation of the registration in any relevant respect, then there is an entitlement to the relief sought. However, the mere notification by a registered proprietor that his mark is registered or that an application for registration has been made, does not constitute a threat.

Therefore, care must be taken when writing 'cease and desist' letters. If it is certain that the infringing act is one of the three exceptions to the section, then the threat can be made, as the section does not apply. In all other cases, where the section does apply, it is best to merely notify the existence of the registration or application and ask for the acts complained of to cease, without going so far as threatening proceedings.

11.15 Dealings with registered trade marks

Under s 26, a registered trade mark and a pending trade mark application are statutorily recognised as being personal property rights. Jointly owned trademarks cannot be used independently by either of the joint proprietors and in effect the trade mark is treated as if it were registered in a single person's name (s 27).

Just like any other piece of personal property, a registered trade mark can be surrendered, revoked, assigned, charged, willed or transferred by operation of law and can be so dealt with independently of the goodwill of the business in which it is used or with the goodwill of that business (s 28 of the 1996 Act). Furthermore, an assignment can be in respect of only some of the goods or services specified in the registration or it can be limited so as to apply to the use of the mark in a particular manner or in a particular locality (s 28(2) of the 1996 Act).

It is very important to remember that any instrument transferring a registered trade mark, be it a deed of assignment or a vesting assent, must be signed in writing by the assignor to be effective (s 23 of the 1996 Act).

Once the registered trade mark has been transferred, application must be made to the Controller of Patents and Trade Marks to have the particulars of the transaction entered in the register. This requirement to record dealings in a trade mark also applies to:

(a) licences of registered trade marks or an assignment of a licence;
(b) security interests (whether fixed or floating) taken over a registered trade mark or any right in it or under it;
(c) vesting assents by a personal representative in relation to a trade mark or any right in it or under it; or
(d) an order of a court or other competent authority, transferring a registered trade mark or any right accruing to it (s 29 (1) and (2) of the 1996 Act).

The penalty for ignoring the requirement to record the dealing in the mark is that until the application for recordal of the transfer has been made at the Patents Office, the transfer is ineffective as against a third party acquiring a conflicting interest in or under the registered mark in ignorance of the transfer, and, the rights of a licensee under sections 34 or 35 are not operative (ss 29(a) and 29(b) of the 1996 Act).

Furthermore, if the application for recordal of the transfer at the Patents Office is not made within six months of the date of the transaction (unless it can be shown that it was not practicable to make the recordal), the person acquiring the registered trade mark will not be entitled to an award of damages or an account of profits in respect of any infringement of the registered trade mark, which occurs after the date of the transaction but before the date that application to record the transaction is actually made at the Patents Office (s 29(4) of the 1996 Act).

Under s 29(5), provision is made for altering (or deleting) the details of transactions already recorded in the Register.

11.16 Licensing

The provisions regarding the licensing of a registered trade mark are to be found in ss 32–36 of the 1996 Act.

Most importantly it should be noted that a licence may be general in respect of all of the rights accruing to the registered trade marks or limited, for example, as to some of the goods or services for which the trade mark is registered or limited as to use of the mark only in a particular manner or in a particular locality (ss 32(1) and (2) of the 1996 Act). This mirrors the equivalent provisions in respect of trade mark assignments.

Again, like assignments, the licence must be signed by the grantor of the licence to be effective. Furthermore, a licence of a registered trade mark may permit a sublicence to be granted (ss 32(3) and (5) of the 1996 Act). As already mentioned in **10.15** above, a licence must be recorded before the Patents Office. Failure to do so shall result in serious implications for a licensee.

11.17 Exclusive licences

Under ss 33 and 35 of the 1996 Act, rights are given to an exclusive licensee that effectively puts them in the place of the trade mark owner. Under s 33(1), such a licence excludes the registered proprietor himself from any use of the mark during the period of the licence, and under ss 35 and 36, an exclusive licensee may, if so entitled, bring infringement proceedings in his own name. However, the right to do this does not supersede or remove the right of the proprietor to sue for infringement, and so the rights of the exclusive licensee in this regard run concurrent with those of the proprietor.

Under s 36, in order to bring infringement proceedings in his sole name, an exclusive licensee must obtain the permission of the court. Otherwise, the exclusive licensee can bring the infringement proceedings, but must join the registered proprietor either as a plaintiff or a defendant, except where an injunction is sought. However, should the registered proprietor be so joined to the action by the exclusive licensee, he will not be liable for any of the costs of the action, unless he actually takes part in the proceedings (s 36(2) of the 1996 Act). In a case where the registered proprietor and exclusive licensee have concurrent rights, the court has a discretion in assessing damages to take account of the terms of the licence and any pecuniary remedy already awarded or available to either of them in respect of the infringement. Furthermore, the court will not grant an account of profits if an award of damages has already been made or an account of profits has been directed in favour of one or other of them in respect of the infringement, the subject of the action. If this is not the case, and the court orders an account of profits, the court has the discretion to apportion the profits between the proprietor and the exclusive licensee as it sees just, subject to any agreement between them on this issue (s 36(3) of the 1996 Act).

Where the registered proprietor and an exclusive licensee have concurrent rights of action, the proprietor must notify the exclusive licensee before applying for a delivery up order under s 20 (s 36(5) of the 1996 Act).

If only the exclusive licensee or the proprietor is a party to the action, then the court has discretion under s 36(4) to direct that part of any pecuniary award be held on behalf of the non-party.

Finally, s 36(6) provides that these provisions, which govern the exercise of the concurrent rights of a registered proprietor and an exclusive licensee, may be contracted out of by the terms of the exclusive licence.

11.18 Non-exclusive licensees

Section 34 of the 1996 Act sets out the rights of an ordinary general licensee in the case of an infringement. Such a licensee can call on the proprietor of the registered mark to take infringement proceedings and if the proprietor refuses to do so or does not do so within two months of the call, the licensee may bring the proceedings in his own name as if he were the proprietor. As in the case of an exclusive licensee, the general licensee cannot pursue the action in his sole name without the permission of the court. However, he can proceed with the action without the leave of the court, if he joins the proprietor either as plaintiff or defendant to the action except where an injunction is sought.

A registered proprietor joined to the action as a defendant by the licensee will not be liable for the costs of the action, unless he actually takes part in the action. Where an action for infringement is taken by the registered proprietor, the court has discretion to direct a portion of any pecuniary remedy ie, damages awarded to the plaintiff proprietor, to be held on behalf of a licensee whom the court considers has suffered loss or damage.

11.19 Surrender, revocation and invalidity

An important litigation tactic is the ability of the defendant to seek revocation of a registered trade mark or a declaration of invalidity should appropriate grounds for such an application exist.

11.19.1 Surrender

Section 50 of the 1996 Act provides that a trade mark may be surrendered (voluntarily) by the registered proprietor in respect of some or all of the goods or services for which it is registered.

11.19.2 Revocation

Section 51 of the 1996 Act provides that a trade mark must be put to genuine use by the proprietor or with his consent in the State within five years following the date of publication of the registration in relation to the goods or services for which it is registered, unless there are proper reasons for non-use.

Section 51(1) (a) provides that a trade mark may be revoked if no use of the trade mark has occurred. Section 51(1)(b) provides for revocation where use has been made of the mark, but such use has been suspended for an uninterrupted period of five years without proper reason for the suspension of the use.

Section 51(1)(c) provides for revocation of the mark in circumstances where it has become a common name (ie, generic) in the trade for a product or service for which it is registered (see my earlier discussion of generic trade marks).

Finally, s 51(1) (d) provides for revocation where a trade mark has, because of the use made of it, become liable to mislead the public in relation to the goods or services for which it is registered eg, in regard to the nature of those goods or services, their quality or geographical origin.

An example might be a dairy product entitled 'Devon's Best' registered for cream. If this is used in relation to a synthetic cream or if it is used for a cream which is produced in Wexford, the mark may be liable as deceptive as to (a) quality; and (b) geographical origin, because the public would expect the product to be clotted cream or at least genuine full cream and produced in Devon.

When revocation proceedings are instituted, pursuant to s 51(3), the period of three months before the application is filed is disregarded, unless preparations for the commencement or resumption of the use of the mark began before the proprietor became aware that the application might be made.

It should be noted that under the 1996 Act, revocation proceedings can be instituted by any person and the onus to prove 'use' lies with the trade mark proprietor (s 99 of the 1996 Act). An application for revocation can be made either to the Controller of Patents, Designs and Trade Marks in the Patents Office or to the court (namely the High Court), except where proceedings (eg, infringement proceedings) concerning the trade mark are already pending in the High Court, in which case the application must be made to the High Court rather than to the Controller. In practice, where there are valid grounds, an application for revocation is usually made as a counterclaim to an action for infringement and is a very useful strategy.

As in the circumstances of surrendering, revocation can be in respect of some of the goods or services for which the mark is registered. In the commercial world, trade marks do not remain stagnant and are amended and altered over time. This is recognised in s 51 (2), which states that use of the mark will include use in a form differing in elements which does not alter the distinctive character of the mark in the form in which it was registered. 'Use' for the purposes of the provision will be deemed to include affixing of the mark to the goods or to the packaging of goods in the State solely for export.

If revocation proceedings are successful before the Controller of the Patents Office, the registration in question will be revoked and the rights of the proprietor deemed to have ceased as and from the date of the application for revocation or if the controller is satisfied that the grounds for revocation existed at an earlier date, that date will be applied.

11.19.3 Invalidity

Another key line of defence in infringement proceedings is the ability to contest the registration on the basis that it is invalid. The grounds for invalidity are set out in s 52 of the 1996 Act. The invalidity may be claimed on the basis that the mark was registered in contravention of the 'absolute' grounds in s 8 for refusal for registration. However, the mark will not be held to be invalid if the claim is one where invalidity is asserted, because the mark is alleged to contravene s 8 (1)(b), (c) or (d) but where the owner can show that by virtue of use since registration, the mark has now become distinctive. The grounds in the subsections are that the mark at the time of registration should not have been registered, because it lacked distinctiveness, was a purely descriptive term or sign, or was a generic term in the trade in which the mark was to be used.

Furthermore, under s 52, invalidity may be claimed on the basis of contravention of the 'relative' grounds for refusal as conflicting with earlier rights, unless the proprietor of earlier trade marks consented to the registration.

Again, there is discretion as to whether the application for a declaration of invalidity be made to the Controller or to the court but again, the application must be made to the court where there are existing proceedings pending in relation to the same trade mark in the court.

A further ground for claiming invalidity is that the registration of the mark was made in bad faith.

As in the case of revocation, the mark may be declared invalid in respect of only some of the goods or services for which it is registered. Where a mark has been deemed to be invalid to any extent, the registration shall, to that extent, be deemed never to have been made, providing that the declaration of invalidity will not affect transactions past and closed (ss 52(4), (5) and (6) of the 1996 Act).

Invalidity may be built on conflict with earlier rights but if the proprietor of the earlier conflicting trade mark, being aware of the use of the registered trade mark in the State, has acquiesced to that use for a period of five years, that proprietor loses the right to apply for a declaration that the registration of the later trade mark is invalid or to oppose the use of the later registered trade mark unless the registration of the later registered trade mark was applied for in bad faith. However, equally, the proprietor of the later registered trade mark cannot oppose the use (or exploitation) of the earlier trade mark (s 53 of the 1996 Act).

Finally, on the subject of invalidity, pursuant to s 76, the registration of the trade mark is *prima facie* evidence of the validity of the original registration and of any transactions, such as assignments, concerning it. In other words, there is a presumption of validity in favour of the registered proprietor.

11.20 Certification marks and collective marks

The 1996 Act makes provision for the registration of two unusual genres of marks, namely:

(a) Under s 54, Collective Marks means trade marks distinguishing the goods or services of members of an association (such as trade associations, chartered institutions, hotel chains, educational institutes) which is the proprietor of the mark from those of other undertakings. The provisions dealing with collective marks are contained in Schedule 1 to the 1996 Act.

(b) Under s 55, Certification Marks means trade marks indicating the goods or services in connection with which they are used, the marks being certified by the owner in respect of the origin, material, mode or manufacture of goods or performance of services, quality, accuracy or other characteristics. The provisions dealing with Certification Marks are contained in Schedule 2 to the 1996 Act.

An example of a Certification Mark is 'STILTON' which is owned by Stilton Cheese Makers Association which denotes cheese originating from a particular region and with certain characteristics as to quality. It is quite common for a Certification Mark to be used alongside a 'normal' trade mark.

Both these categories of marks are governed by regulations, which in the case of Collective Marks must be approved by the Controller and in the case of Certification Marks must be approved by the Minister for Enterprise, Trade and Employment. Once approval has been granted, the normal steps for registration must be completed.

11.21 Famous marks

Under s 61 of the 1996 Act, a 'well known' trade mark is defined as one which is well known in this State as being the mark belonging to a national of a member country to the Paris Convention or domiciled or operating commercially in a Convention country.

Such a well known mark need not be in use in Ireland. In other words, this refers to marks which are well known in Ireland but which are not necessarily used in trade in Ireland. Two examples which spring to mind are 'Harrods' and 'Abercrombie and Fitch' which are not in commercial use here but which are almost household names. Under s 61(2), the proprietor of such a 'well known' mark is entitled to restrain by injunction the use of the famous mark in Ireland.

11.22 Offences

The 1996 Act introduced for the first time offences for the fraudulent application or use of a registered trade mark. Section 92(1) of the 1996 Act sets out a list of acts which, if done in relation to a registered trade mark, will constitute an offence, but s 92(3) adds the proviso that an offence will only be committed if the acts are committed with a 'view to gain' or 'with intent to cause a loss to another.'

This subsection also provides that there is a defence to the charge if the person charged can establish that he believed on reasonable grounds that he was entitled to use the trade mark in relation to the goods in question. The penalties for the commission of such an offence are:

(a) on summary conviction – up to six months imprisonment or a fine of up to €1,269.74 or both;

(b) on indictment – up to five years imprisonment or a fine of up to €126,973.80 or both.

Other offences are falsification of the Trade Marks Register (s 93 of the 1996 Act) or falsely representing a mark as registered (s 94 of the 1996 Act).

11.23 Jurisdiction

While in general, the High Court has jurisdiction in regard to matters arising under the Act, you should note that s 96 of the 1996 Act confers jurisdiction on the local Circuit Court to make an order for delivery up under s 20 and for destructive or forfeiture of infringing goods under s 23.

11.24 Community trade mark

Finally, the Community trade mark (CTM) and important provisions relating to it are set out below.

11.24.1 Application

Formerly, the CTM system had a set of complex nationality requirements in order to be eligible to become the proprietor of a CTM. However, since EU Regulations were introduced in 2004, the Community system is now entirely accessible to any natural or legal person, including authorities established under public law, seeking trade mark protection throughout Europe.

11.24.2 Duration

As mentioned above, the duration of a CTM is the same as a national registration and, like a national mark, can be licensed, assigned, revoked, surrendered or invalidated.

11.24.3 Infringement

A CTM registration gives the registered owner the exclusive right to prevent others from using, in the course of trade, a mark that is identical or confusingly similar to that registered.

The provisions of Art 9 of the Regulation are identical to the provisions of s 14 of the 1996 Act. Once the provisions of Art 9 are satisfied, infringement will be deemed to arise.

However, registration of a CTM does not entitle the proprietor to prohibit the use of that mark in relation to goods which are put on the market in the Community by the proprietor or with their consent. The principle of 'exhaustion of rights' will not apply in circumstances where there is a legitimate reason to oppose the further commercialisation of the goods.

11.24.4 Jurisdiction

If infringement has occurred, where should the proceedings be instituted? It should first be noted that the Regulation did not set up a special court to deal with CTM issues such as infringement, invalidity and revocation. Instead, each Member State was asked to designate a court in their own jurisdiction to handle such matters. The court nominated by the Irish Government is the High Court.

The jurisdiction selected by a litigant is governed by the following rules as sent down in Art 93:

(a) proceedings are brought in the courts of the Member State in which the defendant is domiciled;

(b) if the defendant is not domiciled in any Member State, the proceedings are brought in the Member State in which the defendant has an establishment;

(c) if the defendant is not domiciled nor established in any Member State, the proceedings are brought in the Member State in which the plaintiff is domiciled;

(d) if the plaintiff is not domiciled in any Member State, the proceedings are brought in the Member State in which the plaintiff has an establishment;

(e) if neither the defendant nor the plaintiff are domiciled or have an establishment in any Member State, proceedings are brought in the Spanish Courts.

It is assumed that 'establishment' means 'a real and effective establishment' in the territory of one of the countries of the European Union.

Despite the above stringent conditions, there are two other circumstances in which a CTM court can be given exclusive jurisdiction which are:

(a) where the parties agree that a different CTM court will hear the dispute;

(b) where the defendant enters an appearance before a different CTM court.

The final choice of jurisdiction permits actions to be brought before the CTM court of the Member State where the act of infringement was committed. However, the court's jurisdiction relates only to acts of infringement committed or threatened within that Member State or acts of infringement committed between the date of publication of the application and the date of publication of registration within that Member State.

11.24.5 Remedies

When infringement has been deemed by the court to have occurred, it shall issue an order prohibiting the defendant from continuing with the conduct and apply the laws of the Member State ranging from damages or on account of profits to delivery up and destruction of infringing goods. Interim relief such as provisional and protective measures can also be granted. Additional reliefs are available under the European Communities (Enforcement of Intellectual Property Rights) Regulations 2006 (the 2006 Regulations).

Under the 2006 Regulations a court order for disclosure of information regarding the origin and distribution networks of goods or services which infringe an intellectual property right from persons involved in the infringing acts can be granted. Such information orders can contain such details as the court sees fit and can include information relating to: producers, manufacturers, distributors, suppliers, intended wholesalers and retailers of the infringing goods or services and the quantities or amounts of goods or services and the price paid for them.

The 2006 Regulations also provide the ability of the claimant to seek a court order, at the defendant's expense, to have goods destroyed, recalled or definitively removed from channels of commerce. The court will take into consideration the seriousness of the infringement, the other remedies available and the interests of third parties. Finally, there is the possibility that the court may order the publication of the judgment of the infringement proceedings at the expense of the defendant.

11.24.6 Assignment and licensing

As stated a CTM may be both assigned and licensed. Assignment must relate to the entire community. Assignments will be void unless they are made in writing and signed by all parties to the assignment (except where it is as a result of a court judgment). The assignment may be entered on the register at the request of one of the parties.

The licence of a CTM may be exclusive or non-exclusive and may relate to all or some of the goods or services and for the whole or only part of the community. There are no formalities for the granting of a licence of a CTM and as with assignments, the license may be entered on the register at the request of one of the parties. It is advisable though to record all assignments/licences on the CTM register.

11.24.7 Revocation and invalidity

A CTM can be revoked. The grounds for revocation are identical to those set out in s 51 of the 1996 Act. A CTM may also be declared invalid because it conflicts with the earlier rights of a third party.

11.24.8 Acquiescence

As with an Irish Trade Mark, if the proprietor of a CTM acquiesces for five years to the use of a later CTM, they cannot apply for a declaration that the later mark is invalid and from opposing the use of that mark unless the registration of that mark was made in bad faith.

11.24.9 Seniority

Where a CTM proprietor is the owner of an earlier National Registration for identical mark and goods/services, a claim for seniority can be made. By doing so, it means that if the proprietor failed to renew the national registration, they will continue to have the same rights as they would have had if the earlier national registration had been retained.

CHAPTER 12

COPYRIGHT

Mark Hyland

Please note that parts of this chapter were originally written by Rosaleen Byrne of McCann FitzGerald for an earlier publication for the Law Society of Ireland.

12.1 Introduction and overview

The purpose of this chapter is to provide an introduction to and an overview of the Copyright and Related Rights Acts 2000–2007. The primary focus of this chapter will be the Copyright and Related Rights Act 2000 (the 2000 Act) which brought about significant changes to copyright law in Ireland but consideration will also be given to the Copyright and Related Rights (Amendment) Act 2007 (the 2007 Act) which establishes a Public Lending Remuneration Scheme in this jurisdiction. The author will set the 2000 Act in context in European and international law developments and by outlining the extent to which those developments have shaped the Act. In addition, this chapter aims to highlight in what respects the 2000 Act introduces new concepts into Irish law, which depart from the law relating to copyright as set out in the Copyright Act 1963. Further, this chapter will address some of the basic building blocks of copyright law, namely the concepts of authorship, ownership, the nature and scope of copyright and the duration of copyright as it applies to various different works. Lastly, the chapter will look at the enforcement provisions of the 2000 Act.

12.1.1 Setting the scene

Prior to the 2000 Act becoming effective on 1 January 2001, the law in Ireland relating to copyright was set out in the Copyright Act 1963 complemented by Irish case law relating to the application of the 1963 Act. Only four significant amendments to the 1963 Act were made prior to the adoption of the 2000 Act. These were as follows:

(a) a Statutory Instrument (SI 158/1995) implementing the Term Directive (Directive 93/98/EEC): the most important effect of this was to enhance the period of protection of copyright from the life of the author plus 50 years to the life of the author plus 70 years;

(b) the introduction by way of statutory instrument (SI 26/1993) of the Software Directive (Directive 91/250/EEC) providing copyright protection to computer programs as literary works in whatever form the program exists (including source code and object code);

(c) the provision of higher fines and terms of imprisonment in relation to offences committed under the 1963 Act, in the Intellectual Property (Miscellaneous Provisions) Act 1998 (in or around 1997 the US threatened to commence proceedings before the World Trade Organisation (WTO) if Ireland did not take steps to introduce more effective laws in relation to combating piracy in accordance with its obligations under the WTO Agreement on Trade Related

Aspects of Intellectual Property Rights (TRIPs) and the 1998 Act was introduced in response to this threat);

(d) the introduction of legislation to address the conundrum of copyright subsisting in drawings (as artistic works) relating to spare parts and the anti-competitive effects of same, by the Copyright (Amendment) Act 1987.

It is clear that these important developments, which took place between 1963 and the adoption of the 2000 Act, related to very specific issues. It is also true to say that, in relation to three of these four issues, Ireland was coming under pressure either from the European Union or from the US to introduce legislation to comply with various treaty obligations. Notwithstanding these amendments, however, copyright legislation in Ireland as it existed prior to the adoption of the 2000 Act required a major overhaul. One reason for the overhaul was to ensure that Ireland changed its copyright law to reflect other obligations arising from international treaties and European harmonisation measures as outlined in more detail below. Another reason was the general requirement to modernise Irish copyright law to facilitate its application to modern technologies.

12.1.2 European Community law obligations

The driving force behind initiatives taken by the European Commission relating to intellectual property was the achievement of the objective of harmonising laws in the Community with a view to completing the Internal Market. It was clear from an early stage that intellectual property rights, given the fact that they confer a form of exclusive or monopolistic right, often relating to a specific territory, could be used to divide the Internal Market contrary to the general objectives of the Treaty of Rome in relation in particular to EC competition law principles (Art 81 and Art 82 (formerly Arts 85 and 86)).

Directorate General XV, now known as the Internal Market and Services Directorate General, was responsible for draft legislation in the area of harmonising intellectual property rights at Community level. This process commenced in 1988 with the publication by the Commission of its Green Paper on Copyright and the Challenge of Technology—Copyright Issues Requiring Immediate Action. A number of specific legislative acts were introduced subsequent to this Green Paper.

These are as follows:

(a) Directive 91/250/EEC on the legal protection of computer software programs. This Directive, commonly known as the 'Software Directive', granted protection to computer programs as literary works, irrespective of the form in which the programs existed. Prior to the adoption of this Directive, there was a considerable amount of case law, particularly in common law jurisdictions, regarding whether or not computer programs (which in object code form consist merely of a number of electronic, non-human readable instructions to the processing unit of a computer) could be protected as a form of copyright. In many jurisdictions the courts struggled with trying to apply the traditional concepts of copyright to this form of work, while at the same time acknowledging that sufficient originality and effort went into creating computer programs to justify their protection. This Directive stated that computer programs are literary works and are to be protected as such under copyright law. This Directive was initially implemented in Irish law by way of statutory instrument in 1993 (SI 26/1993), which was subsequently replaced by Pt II of the 2000 Act.

(b) Directive 92/100/EEC on rental rights and lending rights and on certain rights relating to copyright in the field of intellectual property This Directive is commonly referred to as the 'Rental and Lending Directive.' This Directive granted authors of copyright protected works exclusive rights to authorise the rental and lending of those works. This provides authors of protected works with a new form of right (ie, a new restricted act which they can prevent others from carrying out in relation to their work). It should be noted that the Directive does not apply to all works; eg, it does not apply to buildings or industrial designs. The Directive as it relates to rental and lending rights is implemented by virtue of s 42 of the 2000 Act. This Directive also deals with matters relating to neighbouring rights with a view to harmonising legislation relating to neighbouring rights.

(c) Directive 93/83/EEC on the co-ordination of certain rules concerning copyright and rights relating to copyright applicable to satellite broadcasting and cable re-transmission This Directive provides authors with a right to communicate works to the public by satellite broadcast and it includes a number of provisions regulating this right. In addition, the Directive contains provisions ensuring that, where this act of communication to the public takes place in a third country (ie, a non-EU country), rules relating to the existence of these rights cannot be avoided within the Community. The Directive also deals with the issue of cable re-transmission. The provisions of this Directive relating to satellite broadcasting are implemented by s 6 of the 2000 Act and the provisions relating to cable re-transmission are implemented by s 174 of the 2000 Act.

(d) Directive 93/98/EEC harmonising the term of protection of copyright and certain related rights. This Directive, commonly referred to as the 'Term Directive', has been repealed by Directive 2006/116. Essentially, Directive 2006/116 codifies Directive 93/98 by incorporating into a single text all the provisions of the basic act and all subsequent amendments. It does not alter the substance of the text in any way. The aim is to simplify and clarify the legislation and the Directive forms part of the European Commission's 'Better Regulation' initiative. Given that the codification process does not bring about substantive changes, it is worthwhile briefly describing Directive 93/98. Directive 93/98 lengthened the period of protection available for certain works from the life of the author plus 50 years to the life of the author plus 70 years. This increased protection related to copyright in literary and artistic works. It also outlined the duration of neighbouring rights and the duration of rights in relation to other types of works, eg, films, sound recordings and computer generated works. Directive 93/98 was implemented by statutory instrument in Ireland in 1995, which was later replaced by ss 24–36 of the 2000 Act.

(e) Directive 96/9/EC on the legal protection of databases. This Directive is commonly referred to as the 'Database Directive' and while it recognises that copyright protection can be afforded to some databases/compilations (referred to as 'original databases'), where an originality test is satisfied, it also introduces a new right known as the *sui generis* database right. This *sui generis* right protects a database or compilation on the basis that the creation of these works requires the investment of resources (financial, human and otherwise) and as a result they should benefit from some form of protection. The *sui generis* right entitles the owner of the right to prevent the unauthorised extraction and/or re-utilisation of the contents of the database. This right is referred to in ss 320–61 of the 2000 Act.

(f) Directive 2001/29 on the harmonisation of certain aspects of copyright and related rights in the information Society. Sometimes termed the EU Copyright Directive or, the Information Society Directive, Directive 2001/29 had a twofold objective. First, it adapted legislation on copyright and related rights to reflect technological developments and, in this regard, it brought European copyright rules into the Digital Age. Secondly, it transposed into Community law the main international obligations arising from the WIPO internet treaties of 1996.

Directive 2001/29 harmonised the rights of reproduction, distribution, communication to the public, the legal protection of anti-copying devices and rights management systems. Some of the more important provisions of the Directive include a mandatory exception for 'transient or incidental' acts or reproduction carried out by ISPs so long as the reproductions have 'no independent economic significance' (Art 5(1)), an exhaustive optional list of exceptions to the reproduction and communication to the public rights (Article 5(2) and (3)), the introduction of the concept of fair compensation for rightholders (recitals (35) and (36)), the provision of adequate legal protection against the circumvention of technological measures (Article 6(1)) and the provision of adequate legal protection for electronic rights-management information (Article 7). Formal adoption of the Directive also enabled the Community and its Member States to ratify the so-called internet treaties adopted by WIPO in 1996, namely, the WIPO Copyright Treaty and the WIPO Phonograms and Performances Treaty. Transposition of Directive 2001/29 was effected in Ireland through the 2000 Act and the European Communities (Copyright and Related Rights) Regulations 2004 (SI 16/2004). The latter makes fairly minor amendments to the 2000 Act to include, for example, a new definition of the phrase 'protection-defeating device' and by substituting new sections (for ss 244 and 374 of the 2000 Act) which deal with temporary acts of reproduction. This SI has been in force since 19 January 2004.

(g) Directive 2001/84/EC on the resale rights of authors of original works of art. In short, the resale right entitles artists to a payment where their art works are resold through the art trade. Under the Directive, a tapering scale of rates is put in place which is used to calculate the percentage of the resale price actually remitted to the artist. Only resales with a value above €3000 are caught by the provisions of the Directive. The Directive was transposed late in Ireland and only after the well known artist, Robert Ballagh, brought High Court proceedings against the State for loss of earnings occasioned by late transposition. It was transposed by way of the European Communities (Artists Resale Right) Regulations (SI 312/2006) which came into effect on the 13th June, 2006. Under this piece of secondary legislation, the obligation is placed on the seller to pay the royalty (reg 7) and the duration of the resale right is set at the artist's lifetime (reg 10).

(h) Directive 2004/48/EC on the enforcement of intellectual property rights. While the scope of this Directive is far broader than just copyright, it is important to mention it as its central objective was to approximate legislative systems so as to ensure a high, equivalent and homogenous level of IPR protection and enforcement within the Internal Market. The Directive requires the Member States to provide the measures, procedures and remedies necessary to ensure the enforcement of IPR. Such measures, procedures and remedies must be fair and equitable and must not be unnecessarily complicated or costly, or entail unreasonable time limits or unwarranted delays. Under the Directive, the judicial authorities of the Member States are entitled to:

(i) take provisional and precautionary measures (interlocutory injunctions, order the seizure or delivery up of the suspected infringing goods and order the precautionary seizure of movable and immovable property, including the blocking of bank accounts/other assets);

(ii) take corrective measures (recall infringing goods from channels of commerce, definitive removal of infringing goods from the channels of commerce or, their destruction);

(iii) issue injunctions (non-compliance with same could result in a recurring penalty payment);

(iv) take alternative measures (eg, grant pecuniary compensation to the injured party, where this appears satisfactory and fair from the injured party's perspective), and;

(v) award damages (which are appropriate to the actual prejudice suffered by the rightholder as a result of the infringement).

Directive 2004/48/EC was transposed into Irish law by way of the European Communities (Enforcement of Intellectual Property Rights) Regulations 2006 (SI 360/2006).

While Directive 2004/48/EC is concerned with the civil enforcement of IPR, it is important to note that the European Commission proposed a Directive on the criminal enforcement of IPR in July 2005 (COM/2005/0276 final). The proposed Directive will supplement Directive 2004/48/EC and at Article 3 of the proposal, an obligation is placed on the Member States to consider all intentional IPR infringements on a commercial scale as criminal offences. The proposal also covers attempting, aiding or abetting and inciting such offences. The 'commercial scale' criterion is borrowed from Article 61 of the 1994 Trade-Related Aspects of Intellectual Property Rights (TRIPs) Agreement, which was signed by all WTO member countries.

12.1.3 International treaty obligations

Ireland is a signatory to the Berne Convention for the Protection of Literary and Artistic Works, the most recent version of which is the Paris Act 1971. In addition, Ireland has certain obligations as a result of the conclusion of the GATT/TRIPs Agreement of 1993. It was as a result of this agreement that Ireland was pressured into adopting the Intellectual Property (Miscellaneous Provisions) Act 1998 to provide greater protection against piracy.

In the early 1990s, the World International Property Organisation (WIPO) had commenced work on a protocol to the Berne Convention, Paris Act 1971. This work culminated in the adoption of two treaties known as the WIPO Copyright Treaty (WCT) and the WIPO Phonograms and Performers Treaty (WPPT) adopted in December 1996 by a WIPO conference. These Treaties go a considerable way to addressing technological advances in the area of copyright protection and rights management and, in advance of being required to do so under EU law, Ireland took the initiative of introducing provisions in the 2000 Act to give effect to these aspects of the Treaties. (In this regard, see ss 370–76 of the 2000 Act relating to rights protection measures and rights management information and also s 40 relating to the so-called 'making available' right). Since then, the Dáil has agreed Motions approving the ratification by Ireland of the WCT and WPPT While all relevant national procedures for ratification have been completed, the Irish instruments are being held by the Department of Foreign Affairs pending agreement on a date on which it is intended all EC Member States will simultaneously lodge their instruments of ratification with WIPO.

As a result of Ireland's membership of the Berne Union and its most recent version, the Paris Act 1971, Ireland is obliged to provide for moral rights. This was a long outstanding obligation which had not been addressed by Ireland; however, it is now dealt with principally in ss 107–119 of the 2000 Act.

12.1.4 Modernising the law

A number of provisions in the 2000 Act are aimed at modernising the law in relation to copyright, and by doing so the provisions recognise the technologically advanced environments within which copyright works are created and exploited. By way of example, the following provisions in particular should be noted:

(a) Section 39: this section outlines what is meant by the term 'copying' and it makes it clear that storing a work in 'any medium' and making copies of works which are 'transient' or 'incidental' to some other use of the work as in fact constitute copying (s 87 contained an exception to this but s 87 has itself since been replaced by reg 3 of SI 16/2004. Regulation 3 provides that temporary acts of reproduction which have no independent economic significance are not deemed to be an act of copying for the purposes of the 2000 Act).

(b) Section 40: this section relates to the so-called 'making available' right. This section gives the owner of a copyright work a right to make available to the public copies of the work by wire or wireless means in such a way that members of the public may access the work from a place and at a time chosen by them (including the making available of copies of works through the internet). This section is intended to introduce a new right, whereby rightholders can control the making available of their works over the internet. This section is also intended to cover 'on demand' services such as video on demand, music on demand, etc. Section 40(3) and subsequent subsections deal with the position of service providers acting as mere conduits for making available copies of a work to the public. In essence, these subsections are intended to ensure that intermediaries, such as internet service providers, are not liable for the making available of copyright works in an unauthorised manner (ie, infringement of copyright works) where they have only made provision for facilities to make the works available. This exception is subject to a requirement that, once a person who provides such facilities is notified by the owner of the copyright in a work concerned, that the facilities are being used to infringe the copyright, that person has an obligation to remove the infringing material as soon as practical or else be liable for infringement. These provisions mirror the 'notice and take down' procedure of the Digital Millennium Copyright Act 2000 in the US.

Sections 40(3)–(5) of the 2000 Act were bolstered by the European Communities (Directive 2000/31/EC) Regulations 2003 (SI 68/2003) which transposed the provisions of the E-Commerce Directive into Irish law. Under SI 68/2003, the general exemptions granted to ISPs under the E-Commerce Directive for 'mere conduit' (Article 12), caching (Article 13) and hosting (Article 14) were transposed into Irish law (see regs 16–18 of SI 68/2003).

(c) Sections 80–82: these sections, among others, relate to the legal protection of computer programs and replace the statutory instrument, which implemented the Software Directive into Irish law.

(d) Section 87: this section refers to transient or incidental copying and it is aimed at ensuring that the mere caching of copyright protected material on one's hard drive does not constitute an infringement of copyright. This section simply states that the making of a transient or incidental copy of a work, which is technically required for the viewing of or listening to the work by a member of the public to whom a copy of the work is made lawfully available, does not constitute an infringement of the work.

(e) Sections 370–74: these sections deal with devices which are designed to circumvent rights protection technologies, and find their origin in the WIPO Treaties of 1996 referred to above.

(f) Sections 375–76: these sections deal with rights management information and they introduce new offences regarding unlawful acts relating to the removal of or interference with rights management information. These sections also have their origins in the 1996 WIPO Treaties.

12.1.5 Summary

In summary, we can see that the main drivers behind the introduction of this legislation were Ireland's EC and international law obligations together with the general requirement to update the law to deal with technological advances as regards creating and exploiting copyright works.

If asked to identify the most significant changes introduced by the Act, it is suggested that the following are among the most important:

(a) the introduction of the database right for the first time in Ireland;
(b) the introduction of moral rights for the first time in Ireland; and
(c) the general updating of Irish copyright law to deal with the Information Society.

Now that we have looked at the background to the introduction of the Act and the factors which shaped the Act, we will move on to consider some basic concepts of copyright law.

12.2 Basic concepts of copyright law

12.2.1 Nature of copyright

Section 17 of the 2000 Act sets out in broad terms the meaning of copyright as a form of protection and this section also outlines the different types of work in which copyright can subsist. Section 17(1) states:

> 'Copyright is a property right whereby, subject to this Act, the owner of the copyright in any work may undertake or authorise other persons in relation to that work to undertake certain acts in the State, being acts which are designated by this Act, as acts, restricted by copyright in a work of that description.'

It is important to note that copyright is described as a property right. This is relevant as regards licensing and assigning copyright and it also has a bearing on stamp duty issues.

In addition, it can be seen from s 17(1) that the right which copyright confers is a right to undertake certain restricted acts. The acts restricted by copyright in a work or, in other words, the rights of a copyright owner are set out in ss 37–43 of the 2000 Act. If restricted acts are carried out by a third party who has not been authorised to carry out those acts by or on behalf of the copyright owner, then this will constitute an infringement of copyright. Sections 37–43 of the Act set out what constitutes an infringement of copyright. In addition, ss 44–48 of the Act set out what are known as secondary infringements. However, for present purposes, one should note that copyright confers on the owner of the copyright the exclusive right to carry out restricted acts subject to certain exceptions.

We will now turn to consider the different categories of works in which copyright can subsist.

12.2.2 Copyright works

Pursuant to s 17(2) of the 2000 Act, copyright can subsist in:

(a) original literary, dramatic, musical or artistic works;
(b) sound recordings, films, broadcasts or cable programmes;
(c) the typographical arrangement of published editions;
(d) original databases.

Copyright will only subsist in a work if the requirements for copyright protection specified in the Act with respect to qualification are complied with.

Sections 182–90 (Chapter 18) of the 2000 Act deal with qualification for copyright protection. Certain requirements must be satisfied in relation to the author, country, territory, state or area in which the work seeking copyright protection was first lawfully made available to the public before copyright can subsist in a work. Although s 17 of the Act sets out the instances where copyright would subsist in works, this is with the proviso (s 17(4) of the 2000 Act) that such a work complies with the qualification requirements set out in Chapter 18 of the 2000 Act. While these qualifications refer to the author and the geographical area where the work was made, it is not clear from s 18(2) whether or not the requirements are alternatives or are cumulative. The general view, having regard to the equivalent English legislation and the terms of the Berne Convention, is that the requirements are alternatives.

These qualification criteria effectively limit qualification for the rights in question under Irish law to materials protected by corresponding laws in countries with which Ireland shares obligations under international law, and, in this regard, the Berne Convention is of particular relevance.

It is critical to understand that copyright protection does not extend to ideas, which underlie a particular work. Rather, it is the expression of an idea which copyright protects. Stated differently, the material concretisation of an idea can benefit from copyright protection and an idea is materialised when it is perceptible to the senses. This is reflected in s 17(3) of the Act, which states:

> 'Copyright protection shall not extend to the ideas and principles which underlie any element of a work, procedures, methods of operation or mathematical concepts...'

The practical effect of this can be demonstrated with a simple example. If a computer programmer has a new idea for an innovative piece of software, but does not actually write the code for the software or express the idea in any written or recorded manner, then if another computer programmer comes up with the same idea, either independently or through having heard of the idea, and writes the software code to give expression to the idea, then the computer programmer who had the original idea cannot take any action on the basis of copyright against the second programmer. It should be noted that depending on the circumstances surrounding the facts, the person with the original idea may have an action for breach of confidence against the person who ultimately uses the idea. Any such action, however, is based on equitable principles and is not a statutory right.

The categories of work set out above, namely original, literary, dramatic, musical or artistic works, are amongst the most common works which are protected by copyright. Accordingly, it is proposed to take a closer look at this category of works. Before looking at each of these categories separately to see what they encompass, we should consider the meaning of the word 'original' in the context of copyright law. Depending on the facts, there may be an action for breach of confidence, but copyright will provide no assistance to the person with the original idea if it has not been expressed in some form.

It is important to bear this in mind in practice, as clients will often seek your advice on whether or not they can take action to prevent a third party from using their idea. Clients are often of the view that they can rely on copyright protection even where they have not committed their idea to some form of expression.

(a) Originality

It is by now well-settled law that the word 'original' in the context of copyright law does not mean that the work must be the expression of original or inventive thought. Rather, it means original in the sense of not copied. The essential issue in copyright law is whether the person who claims copyright has independently created the work or merely copied the efforts of others. The judgment of Peterson J in the case of *University of London Press Ltd v University Tutorial Press Ltd* [1916] 2 Ch 601, at 608–09, is instructive in this regard:

> 'The word 'original' does not in this connection mean that the work must be the expression of original or inventive thought. Copyright legislation is not concerned with the originality

of ideas, but with the expression of thought, and, in the case of 'literary work' with the expression of thought in print or writing. The originality which it requires relates to the expression of the thought. But the Act does not require that the expression must be in an original or novel form but that the work must not be copied from another work - that it should originate from the author.'

In the past, the issue of originality has most commonly arisen in the case of compilations (or compilation copyright). Compilations generally consist of a collection of existing works or facts, and the issue which arises is whether or not there has been sufficient exercise of labour, judgement or skill in the production of a compilation so as to satisfy the test of originality. Generally, even if a work is based on a pre-existing work, if there is skill involved in redrafting, rephrasing, organising or reformatting the work, this could involve sufficient skill or judgment to make the resulting work an original work.

The House of Lords ruling in *Ladbroke (Football) Ltd v William Hill (Football) Ltd* [1964] 1 WLR 273 is instructive in this regard. There, the question arose as to whether fixed odds football coupons (which listed matches to be played and offered a variety of bets arranged in sixteen categories) were original compilations. In ruling that they were, the Law Lords stated that in assessing the criterion of originality, it would be inappropriate to dissect the labour, skill and judgment into pre-expressive and expressive stages. In *Ladbroke*, the pre-expressive stage encompassed all work done *prior* to the actual production of the work (ie, the football coupons). The expressive stage comprised the actual production of the football coupons.

The Law Lords considered that it was appropriate to place the commercial decisions about which bets to offer (pre-expressive) together with the form and arrangement of the football pool coupons/tables (expressive) when making a determination as to originality.

In assessing the degree of originality of a work created from old material, it is a mistake to dissect it into fragments and then enquire whether any fragment is the subject of copyright and, if so, whether it has been misappropriated by the defendant: for that is to rob each fragment of its collocation. The correct approach is to determine whether the work as a whole is original and only then to decide whether any part taken by the defendant is substantial.

This approach was adopted by Lords Hoffmann and Scott in *Designer Guild Limited v Russell Williams (Textiles) Limited (t/a Washington Dc)* (House of Lords, 23 November, 2000). Lord Hoffman criticised the Court of Appeal's analysis which dealt with the copied features 'piece-meal' rather than considering their 'cumulative effect'. Lord Scott of Foscote also criticised the Court of Appeal's approach which isolated the constituent features of the rival designs from the whole and then compared individual constituent features, one with the other.

Compellingly, in *Designer Guild Ltd*, Lord Scott also endorsed a test proposed in Laddie, Prescott and Vitoria, *The Modern Law of Copyright and Designs* (2nd edn, Butterworths, 1995), at pp 92/93, para 2-108, to determine whether an altered copy constitutes an infringement:

> 'Has the infringer incorporated a substantial part of the independent skill, labour (taste or judgement) contributed by the original author in creating the copyright work...?'

In the following sections, the terms 'literary, dramatic, musical and artistic works' are considered. It is not possible within the scope of this chapter to consider each of the different categories of work in which copyright can subsist. However, literary, dramatic, musical and artistic works are the most common works we come across in practice and these are discussed briefly below. Readers are referred to the annotated version of the 2000 Act which is very helpful in outlining in detail the nature and categories of all of the works covered by the Act.

(i) Literary work

The 2000 Act states that 'literary work' means a work, including a computer program, but does not include a dramatic or musical work or an original database which is written, spoken or sung. This is the only guidance that the Act gives as regards the meaning of the words 'literary work'.

One of the leading statements in relation to the meaning of the words 'literary work' was made by Peterson J in the case of *University of London Press Ltd* [1916] 2 Ch 601 where he said:

> In my view, the words 'literary work' cover work which is expressed in print or writing, irrespective of the question whether the quality or style is high. The word 'literary' seems to be used in a sense somewhat similar to the use of the word literature in political or electioneering literature and refers to written or printed matter.'

We can see from the above that 'literary work' does not mean scholarly or learned works of literature, but rather it means a printed or written work. Section 18(1) of the Act reflects this as it states:

> Copyright shall not subsist in a literary, dramatic or musical work or in an original database until that work is recorded in writing or otherwise by a written consent of the author.

An issue, which has arisen in the past and which tests the scope of the expression 'literary work', is whether or not copyright subsists in the title of a book, a song or an advertising slogan. In some cases, it has been held that titles to songs are 'too insubstantial' to attract copyright in the title alone. The cases relating to this issue have looked at whether or not sufficient skill and judgement have been exercised to warrant something being held to be literary. In general, the selection of a title for a book or a song from common phrases or everyday words has been considered not to have involved exercising sufficient skill and judgement.

It is clear, therefore, that although the meaning of 'literary work' is very broad and is taken to mean written or printed material, rather than a scholarly work, some degree of skill or judgement must be exercised if a work is to be described as a literary work.

(ii) Dramatic work

The Act defines a dramatic work 'as including a choreographic work or a work of mime' (s 2 of the 2000 Act). In order to qualify for protection under the Act, dramatic works, like literary works, must be original. A dramatic work must be capable of being physically performed (*Norowzian v Arks Ltd* [1999] FSR 79) and action or movement by people appears to be a key element of a dramatic work. Therefore, words, music or props by themselves (while they may attract separate protection) are not sufficient to constitute a dramatic work. It should also be noted that performance of a dramatic work may give rise to separate rights under Pt III of the Act relating to performers' rights.

(iii) Musical works

A musical work is defined in s 2 of the 2000 Act as:

> ...a work consisting of music, but does not include any words, or action, intended to be sung, spoken or performed with the music.

Therefore, the music of a song will enjoy copyright protection as a musical work, and separate literary copyright or dramatic copyright may attach to the song as a whole.

(iv) Artistic works

Artistic works are defined in s 2 of the 2000 Act as including:

> ...a work of any of the following descriptions irrespective of their artistic quality:

(A) photographs, paintings, drawings, diagrams, maps, charts, plans, engravings, etchings, lithographs, wood cuts, prints or similar works, collages or sculptures (including any cast or model made for the purposes of a sculpture);

(B) works of architecture, being either buildings or models for buildings; and

(C) works of artistic craftsmanship.

This, however, is not an exhaustive definition and it should be viewed in this light. It is clear from this definition that artistic merit or aesthetic value is not necessary for qualification as an artistic work.

(b) Authorship

Authorship and ownership of copyright need to be considered as two separate concepts. Although these concepts are linked, due to the provision that the author of a work is the first owner of copyright in the work, it is often the case in relation to works of commercial value that the original author is generally not the party who ultimately owns and exploits the copyright.

Section 21 of the 2000 Act states that the 'author' means 'the person who creates a work'. Section 21 then goes on to give a list of certain persons who are included within the definition of author for specific classes of works. By way of example, s 21 states that the author, in the case of a sound recording, includes the producer and in the case of a film includes the producer and the principal director. Other categories of note are computer-generated works in which case the person by whom the arrangements necessary for the creation of the work are undertaken is an author, and, in the case of a photograph, the photographer is an author.

There has been some criticism of the drafting of this section of the legislation, in particular, as the wording of this section leaves it open for other people to be included as an author. For example, in the case of a film, the Act states that 'author' means the person who creates the work and includes the producer and the principal director. It might be possible, therefore, for another party who has had a significant input into the creation of the film to claim that they are also an author of the film. Clearly, from a commercial point of view, this could give rise to difficulties in ascertaining who the author of the work is and who is entitled to exploit the rights in a work. This is important because, as a general rule, the author of a work is the first owner of copyright in that work. Accordingly, it would seem prudent that where parties have an input or involvement in the creation of a work, they should be specifically requested to waive any claim to authorship in respect of the work if the absence of such a waiver could lead to complicating circumstances. Section 22 of the 2000 Act deals with works of joint authorship.

(c) Ownership

Section 23(1) of the 2000 Act sets out the general rule that the author of a work shall be the first owner of the copyright. This section goes on to set out four exceptions to this general principle. The exception which practitioners come across most often, in practice, is that when a work is made by an employee in the course of employment, the employer is the first owner of any copyright in the work, subject to any agreement to the contrary. This is the main exception set out to the general rules.

Section 23(2) of the 2000 Act contains a specific rule relating to authors of works who are employed by proprietors of newspapers or periodicals. This section states:

> Where a work, other than a computer program, is made by an author in the course of employment by a proprietor of a newspaper or periodical, the author may use the work for

any purpose, other than for the purpose of making available that work to newspapers or periodicals, without infringing the copyright in the work.

This section was the subject of intense debate at all stages of the Bill and it was argued by the National Newspapers of Ireland that these residual rights of employed journalists should be omitted on the grounds that they potentially allowed an employed journalist to undermine his employer in the market place by using his rights in other media such as television or radio. According to the relevant Minister at the time, the final text was intended to be a reasonable and honourable compromise between competing interests.

(d) Duration of a copyright

The duration of copyright depends on the type of work being considered. Sections 24–30 of the 2000 Act set out the duration of copyright in various different types of work. Set out below are the main categories of works and the duration of copyright relating to these.

(i) Literary, dramatic, musical and artistic works or original databases – copyright expires 70 years after the death of the author, irrespective of the date on which the work is first lawfully made available to the public. In the event of any of the above works being anonymous or pseudonymous, copyright will expire 70 years after the date on which the work was first lawfully made available to the public.

(ii) Copyright in a film will expire 70 years after the last of the following people dies:
  (A) the principal director of the film;
  (B) the author of the screenplay of the film;
  (C) the author of the dialogue of the film;
  (D) the author of music specifically composed for use in the film.

(iii) Copyright in sound recording expires 50 years after the sound recording is made or, if first lawfully made available to the public during this 50 years, after the date of such making available.

(iv) Copyright in a broadcast will expire 50 years after the broadcast was first lawfully transmitted.

(v) Copyright in a work which is computer generated will expire 70 years after the date on which the work is first lawfully made available to the public. There are a number of other miscellaneous provisions relating to the duration of copyright contained in Pt I, Chapter 3 of the 2000 Act and these should be considered in detail if advising on an issue regarding the duration of copyright.

12.2.3 The scope of copyright protection: restricted acts

Section 37(1) of the 2000 Act sets out the acts which are restricted by copyright in a work, ie, the acts which the right holder has the exclusive right to do or to authorise others to do. These acts are as follows:

(a) copying the work;
(b) making available to the public the work;
(c) making an adaptation of the work or to undertake any of the acts referred to in (a) or
(d) in relation to an adaptation.

These rights are addressed in further detail in the provisions which follow s 37 of the Act. In particular:

(i) s 39 deals with the reproduction right;
(ii) s 40 deals with the making available right;
(iii) s 41 deals with the distribution right;

(iv) s 42 deals with the rental and lending right; and

(v) s 43 deals with adaptations.

These rights are subject to the exceptions set out in Chapter 6 of the Act and are also subject to the licensing provisions (see generally s 38, Chapter 8 and Chapter 16 of the Act).

It is an infringement to undertake any of the foregoing acts restricted by copyright or to authorise another to undertake any of the foregoing without the permission of the copyright owner (s 37(2) of the 2000 Act). Infringement can occur with respect to a substantial part of the work as well as to the whole of the work (s 37(3) of the 2000 Act). What constitutes 'substantial' is a question of fact and will differ in each case. In the case of *Ladbroke v William Hill* [1964] 1 WLR 273, the Court of Appeal held that whether or not the amount copied is substantial is a matter of quality rather than quantity. Accordingly, a person who only copies a small portion of a work may, nonetheless, be found to have infringed copyright. In this case, the court also stated that the reproduction of part of a work that is not original will not normally constitute a substantial part of the work.

Furthermore, although innocent infringement is no defence (*Mansell v Valley Printing Co* [1908] 2 Ch 441), where a court is satisfied that at the time of the infringement the defendant 'did not know and had no reason to believe' copyright subsisted in the relevant work, then no damages will be awarded. In those circumstances, other remedies such as injunctions or delivery up of infringing materials are still available to the plaintiff.

It is important to bear in mind, in proving that there has been an infringement of the right of the copyright owner, a plaintiff will have to show that the defendant copied the plaintiff's work and that the work produced is similar or identical to the plaintiff's work. An infringement cannot occur if a work was independently created. In addition, an infringing act can be undertaken directly or indirectly; therefore, it is irrelevant whether the work was copied directly or some other medium was used.

In *Computer Associates v Altai* [1992] 23 IPR 385, the court set out a four-pronged test to be applied in determining whether an infringement has taken place. The elements of this test are as follows:

(a) Is the plaintiff's work protected by copyright?

(b) Are there similarities between the plaintiff's and the defendant's work?

(c) Are there similarities as a result of copying?

(d) If copying is found, does it constitute a substantial part of the plaintiff's work?

In practice, a further question may be added, which is:

(e) Does the Act come within any of the exemptions set out in Chapter 6 of the Act?

We will now move on to consider the more detailed provisions of the Act in relation to these restricted acts.

(a) Reproduction right

Section 39 of the 2000 Act sets out the scope of the 'reproduction right', which as we have seen is one of the restricted acts. Section 39(2) states:

> 'There shall be a right of the owner of copyright to copy a work or to authorise others to do so which shall be known and in this part referred to as the "Reproduction Right".'

Section 39(1) explains that copying shall be construed as including references, in relation to a literary work, as storing the work in any medium and making copies of the work which are transient or incidental to some other use of the work. This subsection also explains what copying means in relation to other types of works.

(b) 'Making available' right

Section 40 sets out what is covered by this right. Most significantly, this right includes the making available to the public of copies of the works, by wire or wireless means, in such a way that members of the public may access the work from a place and at a time chosen by them (including making available of copies of work through the internet). This right also includes performing, showing or playing a copy of the work in public, broadcasting a copy of the work, and renting and lending copies of the work to the public.

Section 40 provides that the copyright owner has the exclusive right to undertake or authorise others to make copies of a work available to the public. This section also deals with the liability of intermediaries such as service providers. This issue was addressed in **12.1.4.** of this chapter, where certain provisions of the Act which relate to technological advances were discussed. In addition, the making available right is based on Art 8 of the WIPO Copyright Treaty.

(c) Distribution right

Section 41 confers a distribution right on the right holder. The right to issue or publish works to the public is part of the 'making available' right under s 40 and is also covered by the distribution right in s 41. This right is described as the right of a copyright owner to issue copies of a work to the public or to authorise others to do so.

This section explains that the 'issue of copies of a work to the public' can be construed as including the act of putting into circulation in a Member State of the European Economic Area (EEA) copies not previously put into circulation in the EEA, by or with the licence of the copyright owner, or the act of putting into circulation, outside Member States of the EEA, copies not previously put into circulation in a Member State of the EEA or elsewhere.

The right to issue works is subject to the Community doctrine of exhaustion, which provides that, once a work has been made available in a Member State of the EEA, the right holder cannot prevent further distribution within the EEA. Distribution outside the EEA may, however, be prevented and the right holder can prevent the importation of works into the EEA from countries outside the EEA. This is reflected in s 41(2).

(d) Rental and lending rights

Section 42 specifically states that there shall be a right of the owner to rent copies of a work or to authorise others to do so, which shall be known as the 'rental right', and there shall also be a right of the owner of copyright to lend copies of a work or to authorise others to do so, which shall be known as the 'lending right'. The rights apply in relation to literary, dramatic, musical and artistic works (except building or models of buildings), original databases, sound recording and typographical arrangements.

The distinction between rental and lending is as follows:

(i) rental involves an economic or commercial advantage accruing to the right holder and it involves the work being returned after a period of time;
(ii) lending on the other hand does not involve an economic or commercial advantage accruing to the right holder and it can be done through a public establishment such as a library;
(iii) rental or lending under the Act is for private purposes and specifically excludes the performance, playing or showing in public of a work (which acts are covered by a making available right in s 40).

12.3 The enforcement of copyright

12.3.1 Introduction

This part of the chapter will focus on the enforcement of copyright and the potential remedies available to rightsowners under the 2000 Act. The relevant provisions in the 2000 Act are not neatly grouped together but tend to appear in the relevant chapter alongside the relevant right being discussed. So, for example, remedies in respect of an infringement of performers' moral rights are contained in s 319 of the 2000 Act, in contradistinction to general moral right remedies which occur much earlier in the Act, namely at s 137.

Some of the remedies available under the 2000 Act are inspired by international obligations. For instance, Ireland's obligations under the Trade Related Aspects of Intellectual Property Rights (TRIPs) legislation ensured that rights and remedies against parties who illegally interfere with rights management information were included in Part VII of the 2000 Act (see ss 375 and 376).

The range of remedies and the methods of enforcing these remedies under the 2000 Act can be somewhat complex, covering such potential remedies as the obvious one of damages, orders for delivery up, application to the District Court for seizure of infringing material, the right of the copyrightholder himself to seize infringing materials and even a provision which enables the copyright owner to prevent importation into the State of suspected infringing material. This last mentioned provision (s 147 of the 2000 Act) requires the intervention of the Revenue Commissioners following notification by the copyright holder. Remedies are also provided for breach of the copyright holder's moral rights (s 137) and, as mentioned above, for interference with rights management information.

It should prove useful at this juncture to briefly set out which provisions in the 2000 Act relate to which remedies/enforcement rights.

(a) The principal set of remedies (civil remedies) is contained at ss 127–134, inclusive, of the 2000 Act. Section 127(1) provides that copyright infringement in a work is actionable by the copyright owner. The same section provides that all relief by way of damages, injunction, account of profits or otherwise is available to the Plaintiff as it is available in respect of the infringement of any property right. The court may direct that evidence in relation to the ownership of copyright be given on affidavit. But, if there is a conflict of evidence between the affidavits, then the court may order that oral evidence be adduced. Interestingly, where ownership of the copyright is contested, hearsay evidence is also admitted (s 127(4)).

(b) The rights and remedies of an exclusive licensee are set out in s 135.

(c) Remedies for the infringement of moral rights (paternity right, integrity right, false attribution of work and right of privacy in photographs and films) are set out in s 137.

(d) The criminal enforcement provisions are contained at ss 140–145, inclusive.

(e) Remedies in relation to performers' rights/performances are contained in ss 255–264, inclusive;

(f) Remedies available to the owner of performers' property rights or his exclusive licensee are contained in ss 303–306, inclusive.

(g) Remedies for the infringement of performers' moral rights are contained in s 319.

(h) Remedies relevant to the illegal interference with rights management information are contained in ss 375 and 376.

12.3.2 Presumptions which apply in proceedings

Certain statutory presumptions apply in any proceedings, whether civil or criminal, for infringement of the copyright in any work. Copyright is presumed to subsist in a work until the contrary is proved and the plaintiff is presumed to be the owner/exclusive licensee of the copyright, until the contrary is proved (s 139 of the Act).

12.3.3 Distinguishing between primary and secondary infringements

Before highlighting some of the specific remedies available to a copyrightholder under the 2000 Act, it is important to distinguish between primary and secondary infringement of copyright. Primary infringement relates to the activities of those involved in infringing the copyright owner's exclusive rights. Stated differently, primary infringement is concerned with people who are directly involved in the unauthorised reproduction, performance etc of the copyrighted work. In contrast, secondary infringement is concerned with people in a commercial context who either deal with infringing copies, facilitate such copying or facilitate public performance. Secondary infringement involves accessories who become liable for assisting in the making or distribution of infringing copies or the giving of infringing performances. Another important difference between the two forms of infringement is the mental element that the defendant must possess before he can be found liable. As regards acts of primary infringement, the state of mind of the defendant is not formally taken into account when deciding whether an act of primary infringement has occurred. In the case of secondary infringement, however, liability is dependent on the defendant knowing or having reason to believe that the activities in question are wrongful.

The provisions in the 2000 Act which govern secondary infringement are ss 44–48, inclusive. Section 45 makes it illegal to deal with infringing copies. Under s 45, copyright is infringed when someone without the authority of the copyrightholder:

- sells, rents or lends, or offers or exposes for sale, rental or loan, a copy of the rightholder's work which he knows or has reason to believe is, an infringing copy of the work;
- imports into the State, otherwise than for his or her private and domestic use, a copy of the rightholder's work which he knows or has reason to believe is, an infringing copy of the work;
- in the course of business, trade or profession, has in his possession, custody or control, or makes available to the public, a copy of the rightholder's work which he knows or has reason to believe is an infringing copy of the work;
- otherwise than in the course of a business, trade or profession, makes available to the public to such an extent as to prejudice the copyrightowner's interests, a copy of the rightholder's work which he knows or has reason to believe is an infringing copy.

Section 46 is drafted in similar terms to s 45 but relates to an article specifically designed or adapted for making copies of the protected work, where the relevant person (maker, seller, importer etc) has the requisite knowledge/belief.

A person who gives permission for a place of public entertainment to be used for the performance of an infringing work will also be liable for the infringement unless he believed, when granting permission, that the performance would not infringe copyright (s 47).

Under s 48, the focus is on the apparatus used to facilitate an infringement of copyright by way of a public performance. The apparatus may be used for: (a) playing sound recordings; (b) showing films; or (c) receiving sounds or images or any combination of sounds or images, or the representations thereof. Those who can be held liable for such an infringement include:

(a) a person who supplied the apparatus or any substantial part thereof if he believed that the apparatus was likely to be used to infringe copyright;

(b) an owner or occupier of premises who gave permission for the apparatus to be brought onto the premises if, when he gave permission, he believed the apparatus was likely to be used to infringe copyright; and

(c) a person who supplied a copy of a sound recording or film used to infringe copyright if, when he supplied it, he believed that what was supplied, or a copy made directly or indirectly therefrom, was likely to infringe copyright.

12.3.4 Remedies available to the copyright owner

There are a number of remedies available to the copyrightowner under the 2000 Act and they can be divided into civil and criminal remedies. Section 127 of the 2000 Act states that an infringement of the copyright in a work is actionable by the copyright owner. Therefore, the author of a work or his assignee could invoke copyrightowner rights under the Act.

12.4 Civil remedies

12.4.1 Damages

In an action for copyright infringement, a court may award such damages as, having regard to all the circumstances of the case, it considers just (s 128). An exception exists where there is a case of innocent infringement, ie the defendant did not know and had no reason to believe that copyright subsisted in the work to which the action relates (s 128(2)). The court is entitled to award aggravated or exemplary damages or both aggravated and exemplary damages (s 128(3)).

The 2007 ruling in *Retail Systems Technology Ltd v McGuire* [2007] IEHC 13, 2 February 2007 HC (Commercial), Kelly J is worth examining as it reconsidered the law in relation to assessment and quantification of damages for copyright infringement. In that case, Kelly J measured copyright damages by applying the principles used for evaluating damages in patent infringement cases.

The case revolved around an electronic point of sale (EPOS) system called iTouch developed by the plaintiffs at a cost of Stg£300,000 and released on the market in September 2003. After experiencing significant difficulties in obtaining appropriate discovery of the defendants' documents, the plaintiff finally obtained adequate discovery of the other side's documentation. The results of the discovery lead to the conclusion that 59 infringing items of software had been supplied by the defendants. Some of the infringements related to both software and hardware (as iTouch software was normally sold as part of a package, to include the related hardware).

In calculating damages, Kelly J relied on guidelines laid down by Lord Wilberforce in *General Tire and Rubber Co v Firestone Tyre and Rubber Co* [1975] 2 All ER 173. While *General Tire* was a decision in a patent infringement case, Kelly J relied on the Court of Appeal decision in *Blayney v Clogau St David's Goldmines Ltd* [2003] FSR 361 to rule that the *General Tire* principles were equally applicable to copyright cases. Mr Justice Kelly also found the *Blayney* judgment compelling because it found the entitlement of a claimant to damages computed both by reference to profits foregone in respect of lost sales and by way of royalty for other infringing sales, to be appropriate to cases of copyright infringement (having previously been well established in patent infringement cases).

Applying the principles laid down in *General Tire* and *Blayney*, Kelly J adopted the following approach in assessing damages:

(1) Every infringing sale by the defendants is a separate infringement of the plaintiff's rights. In respect of those sales which resulted in sales lost to the plaintiff, the measure of damages is the profit on those sales lost by the plaintiff.

(2) As regards those sales which do not directly represent lost sales to the plaintiff, there is still an infringement of the plaintiff's copyright and it is necessary to determine an appropriate measure of damages in respect of those sales. Such damages should be assessed by reference to a notional licence.

Kelly J then had to consider the issue of the plaintiff's financial losses arising from illegal sales of the hardware (normally sold together with the software) and whether they should be compensated for such losses? Ruling in the affirmative, Mr Justice Kelly once again relied on a patent ruling, namely, *Gerber Garment Technology Inc v Lectra Systems Ltd* [1997] RPC 443, The Court of Appeal to apply the 'convoyed goods' principle to the copyright arena. In short, the aforementioned principle holds that damages in respect of infringement under the UK Patents Act do not distinguish between profit on the sale of patented articles and profit on the sale of other goods commonly sold together with them.

In *Gerber Garment*, the court held that the relevant provision of the UK Patents Act 1977 (ie s 61(1)(c)) did not distinguish between profit on the sale of patented articles and profit on the sale of other goods commonly sold together with them (the 'convoyed goods' principle). No rule of law could be found which restricted the scope of recovery by way of loss of profits to activities which themselves constituted infringements of the patent. Kelly J stated that such an approach could also apply to cases involving copyright infringement. He referred to how the wording of s 128 of the 2000 Act was broader than the relevant provision of the 1977 UK Patents Act and how the former does not restrict the assessment of damages only to loss of profits on the sale of the copyrighted material, but instead includes loss of profits on the sale of goods commonly sold together with the protected goods. For the foregoing reasons, Kelly J ruled that the 'convoyed goods'" principle was appropriate for application in this case.

The plaintiff also contended that it should be awarded damages in respect of damage to its business generally. Of the 75 infringing EPOS units sold by the defendants, Kelly J believed that the plaintiffs would have captured 50% of the sales registered by the defendants. That meant that the plaintiffs would be entitled to recover damages calculated on the profit lost by 37 units. Factoring in the convoyed goods principle, Mr Justice Kelly found on the evidence that the likely loss of profits in respect of them was €4000 per unit, thus totalling €148,000.

The balance of 38 infringing units could still attract damages on the basis of a notional royalty. This exercise required the presiding judge to set a notional fee equal to the sums which the defendants would have had to pay by way of royalty, had they acted legally and sought a software licence from the plaintiff. Kelly J reasoned that if the defendants had sought a licence from the plaintiff, the latter would have charged a higher licence fee than the standard list price of the software because it would not have stood to make any profit in the sale of hardware. Using the plaintiff's June 2005 trade pricelist as a benchmark/reference point, Mr Justice Kelly awarded €21,000 damages in total (calculated using a specific sum in damages for point of sale modules and back office modules).

Kelly J also awarded a distinct sum in damages under the head of 'damage to the plaintiff's business' but encompassing the elements of non-achievement of sales projections by the plaintiff and destruction of some of the plaintiff's goodwill (through rebranding of the plaintiff's software in the defendant's name). Mr Justice Kelly makes no secret of the difficulties facing a judge in assessing damages in such circumstances and he took some solace in quoting Lord Shaw of Dunfermline in *Watson, Laidlaw & Co Limited v Pott, Cassels and Williamson* [1914] 31 RPC 104 at 118 where that judge said that compensation should be assessed using the rather unscientific and imprecise basis of 'inference, conjecture and the like, by the exercise of sound imagination and the practice of the broad axe'! Kelly J awarded a further sum of €35,000 damages under this head.

Aggravated damages in the sum of €10,000 were awarded by Mr Justice Kelly to demonstrate the court's disapproval of the defendants' behaviour throughout the litigation and the general way in which they conducted themselves. The defendants' unsatisfactory behaviour took the form of procrastination and delay on many occasions. While information was obtained by the plaintiff both by discovery and particulars, it was only achieved after numerous applications to court.

In total, €214,000 in damages was awarded to the plaintiff against the first and second defendants.

12.4.2 Order for delivery up

Section 131 of the 2000 Act governs the remedy of delivery up. Under this provision, a copyright owner may apply to court for an order that an infringing copy of a work (held in the course of business, trade or profession), an article specifically designed/adapted for making copies of a copyright work, or a protection-defeating device be delivered up to him or to such other person as the court may direct. Generally speaking, the application for delivery up cannot be made after the expiration of six years from the date on which the infringing copy, article or device was made. Exceptions to the six-year rule are made where the copyright owner was under a disability, or was prevented by fraud or concealment from discovering the facts entitling him to apply for an order. Where a third party is directed by the court to take delivery of the infringing copy/article or device, he must retain it until the court orders that it be forfeited to the copyright owner, destroyed or otherwise dealt with as the court directs (under s 145 of the Act).

12.4.3 Application to district court for seizure of infringing material

Under s 132 of the 2000 Act, the copyright owner may apply to the District Court and where it is satisfied that there are reasonable grounds for believing that infringing copies of a protected work, articles specifically designed or adapted to create infringing copies, or protection-defeating devices are being hawked, carried about or marketed, then it may authorise the Garda Síochána to seize without warrant the copies, articles or devices and to bring them before the District Court.

The District Court may then order the copy, article or device to be destroyed or to be delivered up to the copyright owner or otherwise dealt with as the court thinks fit. Hearsay evidence adduced by a witness or deponent as to the possible location of infringing material is permitted under s 132(3). In addition, the witness or deponent is not obliged to divulge the source of the information upon which they formed a belief about the infringing material's possible location.

These statutory provisions are clearly weighted in the copyright holder's favour. They are somewhat balanced by a provision permitting an award of damages to a person aggrieved by a malicious action (s 132(5)). There, the awarding court must be satisfied that no copyright infringement was actually established and the information on which the copyright owner applied for the order was given maliciously.

12.4.4 Right of copyright owner to seize infringing materials

A rather bizarre provision entitling the copyright holder to seize infringing material himself is also contained in the 2000 Act. It is s 133 and the rationale behind the provision is ostensibly to safeguard the copyright holder's rights in a situation where application to the District Court under s 132 would be impracticable. In short, s 133 entitles the copyright holder (or his designated representative) to seize/detain any copy, article or device (referred to in s 131) where it is found being hawked, carried about or marketed. In essence, it is a form of self-enforcement but it entails the legal obligation to forewarn the Garda Síochána of the time and place of the proposed seizure! Where infringing materials are seized, the person who seized the infringing materials must apply to the District Court for an order to dispose of those materials within 30 days of the seizure. It would seem that the scope of application of s 133 is limited to street vending/hawking as subsection (6) precludes seizures at a 'permanent or regular place of business, trade or profession'. The same subsection also precludes the use of force.

Where there has been an exercise of the right to seize and detain, the court may, on the application of a person aggrieved by it, award damages against a person who exercised that right, where the court is satisfied that no infringement of copyright was established and the person had no reasonable grounds for such seizure.

12.4.5 Remedies: moral rights

Under s 137 of the 2000 Act, an infringement of one or more of the moral rights contained in ss 107, 109, 113 or 114 (paternity right, integrity right, false attribution of work and right to privacy in photographs and film, respectively) is actionable as a breach of statutory duty owed to the copyright holder. Where infringement of one of the categories of moral rights occurs, the copyright holder may apply to the appropriate court for damages or other relief. As regards the breach of the integrity right (safeguarded under s 109), the appropriate court may grant an injunction prohibiting any act unless a sufficient disclaimer is made, on such terms and in such a manner as is approved by the court, dissociating the person entitled to the right from the treatment of the work.

12.5 Criminal remedies

12.5.1 The criminal prosecution of copyright infringement

As copyright infringement can be prosecuted both civilly and criminally, a number of provisions on the criminal aspects of copyright infringement are contained in the 2000 Act. The relevant sections are ss 140–145. Section 140 makes it an offence for a person, without the consent of the copyright owner, to:

- make for sale, rental or loan;
- sell, rent or lend, or offer or expose for sale, rental or loan;
- import into the State, otherwise than for private and domestic use;
- in the course of a business, trade or profession, to have in one's possession, custody or control, or make available to the public; or
- otherwise than in the course of a business, trade or profession, make available to the public, thereby prejudicing the interests of the copyright owner;

a copy of a work which that person knows or has reason to believe is, an infringing copy of the work.

The section clarifies that the term 'loan' means a loan for reward and excludes loans to family members, friends or for private and domestic use. The term 'lends' is also to be construed along those lines.

Section 140(3) makes it a criminal offence to make, sell, rent or lend, import into the State or have in one's possession an article specifically designed or adapted for making copies of a work, knowing or having reason to believe that it has been used or is to be used to make infringing copies. Similarly, the creation, sale or rent, importation or possession of a protection-defeating device used to circumvent rights protection measures is also made a criminal offence (s 140(4)). Certain acts of public performance and broadcasting are brought within the criminal ambit of the 2000 Act. Thus, where copyright is infringed by:

(a) the public performance of a literary, dramatic or musical work;

(b) the playing or showing in public of a sound recording, artistic work, original database or film; or

(c) broadcasting a work or including a work in a cable programme service;

the person who caused the work to be so performed, played, broadcast, included in a cable programme service or shown shall be guilty of a criminal offence. The penalties imposable under s 140(7) and (8) are relatively heavy with summary conviction attracting a maximum fine of €1,875 (£1500) in respect of each infringing copy, article or device or a term of imprisonment not exceeding 12 months, or both. Conviction on indictment carries a maximum fine of €130,000 (£100,000) or a term of imprisonment not exceeding five years or both.

Similar to the remedies available under the civil prosecution of copyright, s 142 of the Act enables the court to make an order for delivery up to the copyright owner of an infringing copy, an article specifically designed or adapted for making infringing copies, or a protection-defeating device. The person to whom an infringing copy/article or device is delivered up, is obliged to retain it pending the making of a final order. The criminal regime of the 2000 Act also makes provision for the issuance of search warrants and seizure of works/articles or devices suspected of having a link to offences committed under s 140. Under s 143, the search warrant remains valid for 28 days and the garda who execute the warrant may seize anything on the premises which s/he 'believes on reasonable grounds may be required to be used in evidence in any proceedings brought in respect of an offence under this Act. The executing garda are also empowered to make an inventory of incriminating evidence and may be assisted by the copyright owner (or designated representative thereof) in this task. Anyone who obstructs or interferes with a person acting under the authority of a search warrant is guilty of an offence and may be liable on summary conviction to a maximum fine of €1,875 (£1500), or to imprisonment for a term not exceeding 12 months, or both.

12.5.2 Order as to disposal of infringing copy, article or device

Under s 145, a copyright owner may apply to the appropriate court for the forfeiture to him of seized or detained copies, articles or devices. Application can also be made for their destruction. The court has considerable discretion when adjudicating this matter and may decide that 'other remedies available in an action for infringement ... would be adequate to compensate the copyright owner and to protect his interests' (s 145(2)). If the court decides that no order is to be made under this section, then the person who had the copy/article or device in his possession or control immediately before it was delivered up or seized, will be entitled to its return.

12.5.3 Provision for preventing importation

Where the copyright owner suspects that infringing copies, articles or devices will arrive in the State, he may give notice in writing to the Revenue Commissioners under s 147 of the 2000 Act requesting them to treat such copies, articles or devices as prohibited goods for a specified period. Such period may not exceed five years and cannot extend beyond the period for which copyright is to subsist. In his notice to the Revenue Commissioners, the copyright owner should specify the time and place of expected importation. When such notice is in force, the importation of goods to which the notice relates, other than copies of a work imported by a person for his private and domestic use, is prohibited (s 147(4)).

12.5.4 Power of Revenue Commissioners to make regulations

These powers are set out in s 148 of the 2000 Act. The Revenue Commissioners may prescribe the form in which notice is to be given and require a person giving notice to furnish them with such evidence as may be prescribed. In addition, the copyright owner may be required to give security to the Revenue Commissioners for any liability or expense that they might incur by reason of the detention of any infringing copy, article or device or anything done to such thing whilst being detained. In addition, the copyright owner may be required to indemnify the Revenue Commissioners against any possible liability or expense, whether or not security has been given.

12.6 Copyright and Related Rights (Amendment) Act 2007

Before setting out some general conclusions, the author will deal with the Copyright and Related Rights (Amendment) Act, 2007 which created the legislative framework for the establishment of a Public Lending Remuneration Scheme. The 2007 Act which was brought into force on 4 December, 2007, makes provision for the aforementioned scheme, in conformity with Directive No 92/100/EC (Council Directive 92/100/EEC of 19 November 1992 on rental rights and lending rights and on certain rights related to copyright in the field of intellectual property).

In establishing the legislative framework for a future Public Lending Remuneration Scheme, the 2007 Act amends the 2000 Act and the Local Government Act, 2001.

Section 7 is the all-important provision in the 2007 Act. It inserts a new section (ie s 42A) in the 2000 Act which empowers the Minister for the Environment, Heritage and Local Government, by regulation, to establish a scheme to be known as the Public Lending Remuneration Scheme, to remunerate authors for the lending by public libraries of their works (termed 'qualifying works' under the Act). The remuneration would be paid out of moneys voted by the Oireachtas for this specific purpose (s 42A(1)).

Under s 42A(2), important clarifications are made. A work will be deemed a 'qualifying work' in relation to a particular period if: 'in relation to that period, it is a work included in a class of works declared by regulations made for the purposes of that subsection (ie subsection (1)) to be a class of works to which the scheme applies.' The authors to be covered by any future scheme would be authors/joint authors who are citizens/subjects of, or, domiciled/ordinarily resident in an EEA Member State.

Section 42A(3) provides that regulations made under subsection (1) shall make comprehensive provision for the operation of the Public Lending Remuneration Scheme, and *may* include, in particular, provisions relating to:

(a) the manner of participation in the scheme by individual authors;
(b) where requirements for the registration of authors are established, the manner of maintaining the register, and, the form and particulars of entries in it;
(c) the manner of calculating the entitlements of participating authors;
(d) the manner in which payments under the scheme are to be made;
(e) the establishment or designation of one or more persons or bodies to exercise powers and perform duties in respect of the administration of the scheme or any part if it; and
(f) the making of arrangements with authorities in other countries for –
   (i) reciprocal registration of authors and works, and
   (ii) the sharing and exchange of data relating to the operation of the scheme and similar schemes in those countries.

The potential penalty for the contravention of provisions of regulations made by the Minister under s 42A(1) is quite heavy. A fine of up to €5000 may be imposed on those found guilty of an offence punishable on summary conviction (s 42A(4)).

Section 42A(5) clarifies the scope of the term 'author'. It includes, in relation to a recording of a performance, the performer.

Finally, ss 8 and 12 of the 2007 Act are important in that they confirm that neither copyright (s 8) nor performers' rights (s 12) is/are infringed by the lending by educational establishments of a copy of the copyrighted work/a copy of a recording of a performance.

12.7 Conclusions

The provisions of Directive 2001/29 go a considerable way in adapting copyright law to the challenges of the digital world. Not only does the Directive take a technologically realistic approach to twenty-first century reproduction (with its provision on transient or incidental acts), but it also adopts a proactive approach to potential digital infringement by providing for adequate protection of electronic rights management information and requiring protection against the risk of circumvention of technological measures.

Copyrightholders' rights are further bolstered by Directive 2004/48, the aim of which is to achieve a high level of intellectual property rights protection and enforcement within the internal market. Pointedly, this Directive aims to make IP protection straightforward, attainable (in terms of cost) and speedy from the perspective of the IP owner, thereby emphasising that IP protection should be just as available to the ordinary citizen as it is the large corporation.

Copyright in sound recordings gained a higher public profile in this jurisdiction over the last few years as litigation was commenced by the large record companies against internet service providers in a bid to force the latter into disclosing personal details of subscribers suspected of illegal music downloading activities. The principal ruling is *EMI Records and Ors v Eircom Ltd and Ors* [2005] IEHC 233, [2005] 4 IR 148 where Mr Justice Kelly, relying on the Norwich Pharmacal jurisdiction, ordered the defendants to disclose to the plaintiffs, the personal details of 17 individuals who were identified (through internet protocol addresses) as being involved in the making available to the public of significant volumes of copyrighted sound recordings. Importantly, Kelly J's order was made conditional on the Plaintiffs giving an undertaking not to disclose to the general public any of the subscriber information disclosed by the defendants on foot of the court order. Essentially, this was a safeguard built into the order to protect the rights and entitlements of the subscribers as there was always the possibility that some of them may not have actually operated the relevant computers and therefore were not guilty of any wrongdoing. Two further applications were made to the High Court in 2006 and 2007, identifying some 99 users in all. All this points to the Irish music industry shifting its focus away from the end user and towards the ISP, with increasing pressure being brought to bear on the latter to police the activities of the former.

CHAPTER 13

THE LAW OF PASSING OFF

James Murray

This chapter seeks to provide a practical introduction to the law of passing off. Many of those reading this will have studied intellectual property law as part of their legal studies, and will be familiar with passing off as one of the core 'areas' of intellectual property law. That said, it is often the case that passing off constitutes an area tucked away at the end of the text books or series of lectures, after one has dealt with what are seen as the key areas of patents, copyright and trademarks. Indeed, in intellectual property litigation, passing off is often somewhat of an afterthought, shoved into a plenary summons to ensure that absolutely everything is covered and often not pursued in subsequent proceedings. This chapter, in addition to restating the core elements of a passing off action, also seeks to outline the practical uses of this common law remedy, and to suggest how, in practice, one might both recognise and deal with such a claim.

What is passing off? Passing off is part of the law of tort and therefore founded in common law, based purely on case law and therefore has no statutory basis (in either primary or secondary legislation). Effectively, it seeks to protect the rights of an individual or business, by protecting the goodwill of that business from unfair trading by other parties. This is achieved by preventing other parties from carrying on business or from selling their products under a name, mark, description or in any other manner which could mislead the public (in the sense of the likely market for that business or product) by confusing them to believe that the business or goods in question are those of the plaintiff. In this way, businesses who have invested considerable time, effort and resources in creating a reputation in a particular product or service (but who cannot or have not, for whatever reason, any protection from the law of trademarks) are allowed to protect their investment. Some see passing off as the poor relation of trademark law, and something to be used only when one does not enjoy trademark rights. Certainly, trademark rights constitute a monopoly right which can often be easier to assert by reliance on the trademark register, but passing off has its own advantages and variations and has evolved in recent years to offer protection in a wider range of areas than might ever have been envisaged some decades back. These include the twin areas of character merchandising and personality rights, and some have even touted it as forming the basis of a new tort of unfair competition.

Being a tort, one is forced to trawl through a considerable body of case law, primarily English, but also some more recent Irish case law, to extract a working definition of the tort, which allows one to understand and examine the various concepts which go to make up passing off. Each practitioner has his own preferred case which sets out the elements of passing off, and this author will use the case of *Ervin Warnink BV v J Townsend & Sons (Hull) Ltd* [1979] AC 731 – a case commonly called the Advocaat case. Lord Diplock in that case set out the five elements which must be present in a given set of circumstances to create a successful cause of action for passing off:

There must be a:

1. misrepresentation
2. made by a trader in the course of trade

3. to prospective customers of his (or ultimate consumers of goods or services supplied by him)
4. which is calculated to injure the business or goodwill of another trader
5. which causes actual damage to a business or goodwill of the trader by whom the action is brought, (or will probably do so).

The only way to properly understand how to assess whether or not a case of passing off exists, is to examine each of these five elements in turn, and discuss briefly the case law pertaining to each of these elements. Such a step by step approach should be used also by practitioners to assess, when approached by a client, whether or not passing off constitutes a reasonable plea. What then of the individual five elements?

13.1 Misrepresentation

Misrepresentation in itself constitutes a core action in tort law, and all practising lawyers come across misrepresentation in a wide variety of situations in their litigation case load. There is no great novelty to the definition of misrepresentation in the context of passing off. The vital thing to bear in mind is that any false representation made by the defendant seeking to create, in the mind of the public/consumers, an unwarranted association with another person (the plaintiff), can be actionable in passing off *if* there is a real risk of damage occurring to the plaintiff. A useful example of this is the case of *An Post & Others v Irish Permanent* [1995] IR140, where the defendant, in July 1994, launched a new product known as 'Savings Certificates', in circumstances where the plaintiffs had been involved for 65 years in the promotion and sale of a financial savings product under the name 'Savings Certificates' (and where evidence was produced that some IR£3 billion of savings certificates had been sold by An Post in the previous three years). The plaintiffs in that case successfully obtained an interlocutory injunction, despite the defendants' argument that the words 'Savings Certificates' were a generic or descriptive name in which the plaintiffs enjoyed no rights. The High Court ruled that there was a case to answer in relation to the allegation that the defendants were seeking to unfairly take advantage of the considerable reputation built up over many decades by the plaintiffs. The misrepresentation in question was found to be material as the court found it could have a direct effect on sales of the plaintiffs' 'Savings Certificates' products.

There are numerous examples, even in Irish case law, illustrating the issue of misrepresentation in so called 'copycat' or 'lookalike' cases. One such case is that of *Gabicci plc v Dunnes Stores* (1991, unreported, HC, Ms Justice Carroll), where the plaintiff successfully obtained an injunction against Dunnes Stores preventing the sale of jumpers, which, it was alleged, were a direct imitation of designs from the 'M range' made popular by the plaintiffs, but sold by Dunnes Stores at half the price. Ms Justice Carroll herself stated that it was extremely difficult to tell the two jumpers apart, and matters were further complicated by the fact that Dunnes Stores' jumpers were made by the Italian factory, which also manufactured the Gabicci product. She said '[t]his is not a case of Dunnes following a fashion trend and giving good value. It concerns the sale of sweaters which, to all intents and purposes, are 'the plaintiff's sweaters' and which it is alleged has created confusion to the public, with resultant damage to the plaintiff's goodwill.'

The 1995 case of *B & S Ltd v Irish Autotrader Ltd* [1995] IR 142 is an example, however, of refusal of an interlocutory injunction. The plaintiffs were publishers of the well known magazine 'Buy and Sell.' That magazine, circulating mainly in the Republic of Ireland, included advertisements for motor vehicles and accessories and, since February 1994, had carried the words 'including Autotrader' on the cover page of the magazine, with the heading 'Autotrader' also appearing over the motor section. The defendants had, for the previous ten years, published in the United Kingdom, a magazine under the name

'Auto Trader' devoted purely to advertising motor vehicles and accessories, and in February 1995 it launched a magazine, intended to have an all-Ireland readership, dedicated to advertisements for motor vehicles and accessories, called 'Irish Auto Trader'. However, Mr Justice McCracken refused to grant the interlocutory application on the basis of the balance of convenience, finding that the possible loss to the defendant, by either preventing distribution of the magazine in Ireland or forcing them to change the name, would considerably exceed the possible loss to the plaintiffs. He was clearly influenced by the fact that the bulk of advertising in both magazines (and upon which both publications heavily relied) came from traders, whom the court felt would not be easily confused between the two magazines when choosing where to advertise.

In the 1996 case of *R Griggs Group Ltd & Others v Dunnes Stores* (1996, unreported, HC, Mr Justice McCracken), the court also refused to grant the plaintiffs an interlocutory injunction. The plaintiffs were the manufacturers of the famous Doc Martens footwear, whilst Dunnes Stores was selling children's boots which were practically identical (although, again, cheaper) to the plaintiffs' products. Dunnes Stores had also labelled the boots as 'Docs', the name by which the authentic footwear had been colloquially known for many years. Despite the facts, the court refused to grant the interlocutory injunction on the basis that the plaintiffs were a worldwide company which would suffer minimal damage between the hearing of the interlocutory injunction and the plenary hearing, whereas the likely loss to Dunnes Stores arising from an injunction would be much greater. It was on this basis, that of the balance of convenience, that the court refused to grant the injunction. This decision was criticised by some commentators as taking an unduly generous approach towards lookalike products, but the court may have been influenced in those circumstances by certain undertakings provided to the court by the defendant which lessened the likelihood of damage being suffered by the plaintiff prior to plenary hearing.

A rare Supreme Court decision in relation to passing off, some years earlier, was the case of *Adidas v Charles O'Neill & Co Ltd* [1983] ILRM 112. That case concerned the distinctiveness of a three stripe design on sportswear. The evidence was that in 1967 the world famous Adidas company commenced manufacture of sportswear, such as tracksuits, which had a distinctive three stripe design down the sides of the arms and legs of the tracksuits and jerseys. In 1976, Adidas commenced manufacturing their sportsgear in Ireland, thereby coming into direct competition with O'Neill & Co., who were by then long established in the Irish sports market. The evidence was that in 1965 O'Neill's started putting stripes on their products, initially varying between one and three stripes, but within a few years concentrating on a three stripe design. Evidence at the trial alleged that the three stripe design had been used by manufacturers of sportswear in many countries, but that Adidas were the only manufacturer which exclusively used the particular arrangement of light coloured stripes of equal width, set against a differently coloured background. The implication was that O'Neill's, by using a three stripe design, were passing off their products as those of Adidas. The defendants claimed that the Adidas three stripe design was not part of Adidas goodwill and that the plaintiffs could not prove that they had an exclusive association with that design on products in Ireland. The High Court refused to grant relief, and this was upheld by the Supreme Court, which stated that the use of the stripes of varying colours and numbers on sports garments was a fashion in the trade and that O'Neill's, in resorting to fashionable demands, had not attempted to deceive or pass off, and in fact had not done so. The court stated that '[t]he mere copying of a design or the anticipation of a fashion, or the taking advantage of a market or demand created by another's advertising, is not of itself sufficient to support an action for passing off if the trader against whom the complaint is made has sufficiently distinguished his goods so that confusion is not created.'

There is much case law on this point but, unfortunately for the purposes of elucidating legal principles, the majority of it concludes at the interlocutory injunction phase (following which most parties appear to either reach settlement or simply decline to proceed with the action to plenary hearing). The position in relation to the Irish law of passing off at interlocutory stage was effectively endorsed by Ms Justice Finlay Geoghegan in 2006, in the case of *Contech Building Products Ltd v Walsh and others* [2006] IEHC 45, which endorsed the earlier approach of Miss Justice Laffoy in the *Miss World Ltd case* [2004] IR 394. The key elements in an interlocutory injunction in IP matters were well set out in Contech, when the court granted an injunction on the basis that the plaintiff had moved without delay. However, the above case law provides a useful snapshot of the types of misrepresentations which are potentially actionable under the law of passing off. It is worth stating at this point that it is not absolutely essential that the defendant and plaintiff operate in precisely the same field, so long as it can be demonstrated that the plaintiff has a reputation which could potentially be affected by the defendant taking business advantage of that reputation.

13.2 Made by a trader in the course of trade

This requirement is relatively self-explanatory and, indeed to a large extent is superfluous, as a plaintiff who is not trading will presumably not be able to demonstrate damage to his business or goodwill (and thereby not meet part 5 of the requirements). There is little to note in the case law regarding this requirement, and certainly Irish courts do not appear to have made an issue of it at any time. It appears that anyone who makes an income from the provision of goods or services can qualify as a trader, and the range of organisations which have been able to pursue actions in passing off include the British Medical Association, the BBC and Dr. Barnardo's, although it has also been found by UK courts that a political party could not qualify as a trader on the basis that its involvement was not in commercial activity. In the majority of cases, however, this will not be a real concern for the legal practitioner.

13.3 To prospective customers

In many cases, the plaintiffs will seek to adduce evidence from actual or potential customers regarding actual confusion allegedly arising from the representation made by the defendant. This can take the form of personal evidence or survey evidence. The purpose of introducing such evidence is to forcefully demonstrate to the court the impact of the misrepresentation on the business or goodwill of the plaintiff. It can be useful, from a practical point of view, if the plaintiff can show real life examples of either confusion or deception on the part of a customer when faced with the defendant's product or service. That said, it is ultimately a matter for the judge hearing the case as to whether or not he or she is convinced that a reasonable man or, indeed, a reasonable purchaser, could be confused by the existence of the defendant's product or business.

A good illustration of this is the case of *Symonds Cider & Other v Showerings (Ireland) Ltd* [1997] 1ILRM 482. That case concerned 'Scrumpy Jack' cider imported into Ireland and a rival product known as 'Golden Scrumpy'. In refusing to grant the injunction sought in those proceedings, Ms Justice Carroll also made clear that she was not having any regard to the market research evidence submitted by the parties in relation to the likelihood of confusion. She said, 'I believe that my experience as an ordinary shopper or consumer enables me, just as well as any other, to assess the likelihood of confusion.' Indeed, she clearly felt that it was more appropriate for the court to make this decision without, perhaps, being manipulated by the evidence of either party on this point. In an Irish court, the reasonable man, or the prospective customer of the plaintiff, is a test which ultimately falls to be considered by the judge hearing the case.

13.4 Business or goodwill

This element would again seem to be self-explanatory, and all lawyers will know what is meant by business or goodwill in the normal sense of those words. However, the meaning of goodwill in the context of passing off actions has shifted somewhat in recent years. It remains clear that the plaintiff must satisfy the court that the business affected by the alleged passing off has been trading for some time, and has built up goodwill within the jurisdiction in that product or business. An important Irish case is *C&A Modes Ltd v C&A Waterford Ltd* [1978] SSR 126. In that case, the court accepted that even though the plaintiff, a group of chain stores with branches throughout Europe, had no store in the Republic of Ireland, there was regular custom from this jurisdiction to the C&A store in Belfast, and exposure in the Republic of Ireland to C&A Modes' advertising in various British publications and British television circulating within this jurisdiction. Therefore, although not actually trading within the jurisdiction, foreign trading in a context which created considerable public exposure in the jurisdiction was sufficient to fulfil this element of passing off.

Another Irish case worth noting is *O'Neill's Irish International Sports Co Ltd & Other v O'Neill's Footwear Dryer Company Ltd* (30 April 1997, unreported, HC, Barron J). The defendant company, owned by a Mr John O'Neill, had succeeded in obtaining a patent for an electronically operated shoe dryer, but he could not find any financial support from sports manufacturers (including the plaintiffs) to enable him to manufacture it himself. He therefore imported a similar product from the Far East and sold it in a box similar to a shoe box, with the box label referring variously to an O'Neill's footwear dryer, Celbridge, Ireland, and 'Made in China'. The plaintiffs (the company which was defendant in the Adidas case discussed above) sought an injunction on the basis of passing off, claiming that the defendant was trading on the reputation which they had built up in the name O'Neill's, and despite the plaintiffs own surname, the court agreed with this,. Having reviewed the authorities, the court was satisfied 'that the Defendant had presented its goods to the public in such a manner as to be able to take advantage of the reputation and goodwill generated by the Plaintiffs.' The court clearly felt that the manner in which the product was marketed, together using the word 'O'Neill's', constituted an effort to obtain deliberate advantage – due simply to the pre-existing reputation of the O'Neill's brand in a parallel market.

Another case is *Guinness Ireland and other v Kilkenny Brewing Co Ltd* [1999] ILRM 531. The world famous plaintiff company marketed, *inter alia*, Kilkenny Irish Beer, while the defendant company was incorporated in 1995 with a view to carrying on the business of brewing and marketing beers. The plaintiffs claimed an exclusive reputation in the use of the name 'Kilkenny' in connection with beer, alleging that consumers could be confused/deceived into perceiving an association between the defendant and Guinness. Miss Justice Laffoy granted an injunction stating that:

(a) Passing off included the incorporation of a company with a name likely to give an impression to the public that it is associated or connected with another company – whether the impugned name was intentionally or innocently chosen was irrelevant.

(b) By December 1995 (the date of incorporation of the defendant), the plaintiff had an established goodwill in the name Kilkenny when used with beer (mainly through the product known as 'Kilkenny'). There was a real likelihood that the public would get an impression of a connection between the two businesses.

(c) The fact that the defendant intended to act as a land holding company, not as a trading company, did not immure its choice of name from public perception.

A further point to be made, which will perhaps have become clear from the case law mentioned, is that the conduct need not be 'calculated' in the sense that one might ordinarily use that word. It is enough that the effect of the conduct is to create a situation of passing off, and the question of whether or not the conduct was deliberate is not crucial either way. What is crucial is that confusion has arisen with resulting damage to the plaintiff.

13.5 Damage

Obviously, a key element in any successful tort action is demonstrating that the defendant's actions caused or are likely to cause damage to the plaintiff. Where the plaintiff has already suffered damage, in the sense that it can be shown that the public are confused as to ownership of products or services, with resultant damage to the plaintiff's goodwill and/or reputation, this is not a difficult element to prove. However, the vast majority of passing off actions which come to court arise at the interlocutory injunction stage, where it is likely that the plaintiff is attempting to pre-empt the establishment of a reputation by the defendant and therefore the defendant will (hopefully) have had little opportunity to cause damage. However, in practice, once goodwill and reputation are shown, it is generally not difficult to demonstrate that damage is likely to occur.

The leading Irish case to examine the question of damage is *Falcon Travel Ltd v Falcon Leisure Group* [1991] IR 175. In that case, the plaintiff was a travel agency operating in Dublin and Wicklow since 1970, with a significant reputation in the retail travel agent business. The defendant was a major tour operator in the UK since the early 1980s, primarily operating as a wholesaler selling its products to travel agents, such as the plaintiff. However, in 1988, it launched a brochure directed exclusively to the Irish market, and opened an office in Ireland. The evidence was that, whilst aware of the existence of the plaintiff, it did not anticipate any confusion between them because of the differences in their area of operation. Whilst there had been some initial confusion following the direct entry of Falcon Leisure into the Irish market, those instances of confusion had diminished significantly to the date of the action in 1990. The judge accepted that there was no fraud or deceit involved, and that the defendant did not intend or expect to expropriate the reputation of the plaintiff or any part of the business of the plaintiff. The plaintiff had not lost any customers to the defendant, but its main complaint was the fear that people would think it was the defendant. The defendant asserted that as a matter of law, the plaintiff could not succeed in an action for passing off, *unless* it established that the action complained of not merely gave rise to confusion, but confusion which caused damage, or at least the real likelihood of damage. However, Mr Justice Murphy granted the plaintiff damages, whilst stating the following:

(a) That it is possible to establish measurable and observable damage in many actions of passing off which was a consequence of a defendant's wrongful appropriation of the plaintiff's goodwill.

(b) That in a passing off action, *it was the appropriation of the goodwill in itself which constituted the damage required and not the consequences of appropriation, such as loss of business* (emphasis added). The tort was complete when the reputation was appropriated.

(c) The plaintiff was entitled to succeed because its goodwill had become submerged in that of the defendant, as a direct result of the defendant's actions.

The court then took the unusual step of not granting an injunction to the plaintiff, but instead awarded damages, thereby enabling the plaintiff to launch an advertising campaign, which would ensure that the public was aware of the differences between the plaintiff and the defendant.

This case is an unusual example of the fifth element of the passing off action. Generally, it will be clear whether or not the plaintiff is likely to suffer damage resulting from the action of the defendant and, more likely than not, that damage will be financial resulting from lost sales or potential loss of goodwill or reputation. The court, when requested, and on finding that there is a case of passing off, is likely to grant interlocutory relief. Many cases will concern start-up or relatively new businesses as defendants, and the granting of such relief is seen as the surest way to protect the reputation of plaintiffs from such attack.

That is a brief summary of the five crucial elements required to found an action for passing off. Some of the case law uses a three pronged test, while other case law uses a five pronged test (as this author has done), but all of the elements mentioned above will have to be satisfied at the end of the day. Hopefully, the gist of the action of passing off will now be clear and the reader will be in a position to recognise when it might be an appropriate plea to raise (whether that be in plenary proceedings or as part of an interlocutory application). It goes without saying that there is often a high level of subjectivity in assessing whether or not a plaintiff has a good case in passing off. It can often be extremely difficult to ascertain whether or not passing off is present, and many situations where this tort is alleged are borderline. Lawyers practising in the area of passing off realise that passing off can be alleged in relation to absolutely any good or service which is being traded. One must consider all the circumstances of the case, and bear in mind that the ultimate test is that of the reasonable purchaser who might wish to purchase the plaintiff's product.

That purchaser may know much more about the nature and qualities of the product in question than Joe Bloggs on the number 10 bus, a point illustrated by the decision in the Buy and Sell case. That purchaser must be confused into thinking that he is buying either the plaintiffs products/services or products/services associated with the Plaintiff. It is not enough in most cases to show that the consumer thinks this is a good enough imitation, at a cheaper price, to satisfy his needs.

This, to an extent, is illustrated by the attitude of Ms Justice Carroll in *Symonds*, which illustrates that the court will make the decision whether or not the reasonable consumer would be confused by the parallel goods or services in question. Confusion, or even deceit, is inherently subjective, and what might confuse one individual on a given day in a particular set of circumstances might not confuse another individual. In addition, it must be borne in mind that the context in which the tort of passing off is set is an ever changing one. Consumer awareness and brand awareness shifts on a regular basis and, for example, many would submit that anyone buying a Manchester United shirt on Talbot Street for €5 is certainly not under the illusion that he is buying the real thing, and therefore a crucial element is missing in order to satisfy a passing off action. Such circumstances may of course give rise to alternative legal remedies. In relation to counterfeit goods and the particular statutory regime governing the area, one should bear in mind the potential overlap with the law of passing off in such cases.

13.6 The evolution of passing off – character merchandising

To an extent, the tort of passing off has taken a new lease of life within the past decade or so, due to the ever changing nature of merchandising goods and the ever growing acknowledgement of the value of brand awareness in today's marketplace. Passing off has been used to underpin the protection of so-called 'character merchandising', and the law in this area is generally taken to derive from the New South Wales case of *Children's*

Television Workshop Inc v Woolworths (New South Wales) Ltd [1981]. Woolworths were selling unlicensed products of Muppet characters from Sesame Street, whose popularity in Australia at the time was demonstrated by the fact that many millions of Australian dollars *per annum* were being spent on licensed Sesame Street merchandise. The plaintiffs did not actually produce the Sesame Street merchandise themselves, but rather licensed their rights to third parties, but the court felt that the public of 1981 would be aware of the practice of character merchandising, and that their reputation and goodwill would thereby suffer by the fact that the Woolworths' toys were cheaper and of inferior quality to the licensed products. Since then, courts in Australia, and also in the US, have used the tort of passing off to protect the licensing practices of parties, such as the plaintiffs in the Muppets' case, to cover Teenage Mutant Ninja Turtles, Crocodile Dundee imitations in television ads and other products of character merchandising.

13.6.1 Personality rights

The courts in England have been less ready to protect such rights, and the Spice Girls famously failed to obtain an injunction against an Italian company which used photographs of them as collectable stickers on their products. As yet, the Irish courts have failed to protect character merchandising using passing off, but nevertheless an Irish court might well be prepared to grant an injunction in such circumstances. The only reported case, and that was only a newspaper report, was an action taken in 2001 by Olympic gold medallist Mary Peters against Ark Life Assurance Company. She alleged that by using her image in an advertising campaign which recalled key events of various years (including 1972, the year in which Ms Peters won Olympic gold), they were creating the impression that she had agreed to do this. Crucially, she also claimed that inclusion in the Ark Life ads precluded her from doing business with other Irish financial institutions, and she claimed that she had intended to exploit her image in the future. The case was settled out of court, supposedly for a 'substantial five figure sum.'

An important development was the 2001 English case of *Irvine v Talksport Ltd*, a case involving the well known racing driver, Eddie Irvine. The defendant radio station had acquired, from an agency, a photograph of Irvine using a mobile telephone and had manipulated that photograph to give the appearance that he was in fact listening to a radio. The photograph was subsequently circulated on brochures for the defendant radio station (which specialised in coverage of sporting events), and Irvine claimed that the use of his photograph in such circumstances amounted to a misrepresentation that he endorsed the defendant's programme. The question therefore was whether a false representation of endorsement could amount to a passing off, and Mr Justice Laddie of the English High Court found that it could. He stated 'large sums are paid for endorsement ... because ... those in business have reason to believe that the lustre of a famous personality, if attached to their goods or services, will enhance the attractiveness of those goods or services to their target market.' The court explicitly found that exploitation of a famous personality's goodwill can be distinguished from mere merchandising, and therefore that passing off can be used to prevent unlicensed use of goodwill, which could reduce, blur or diminish its exclusivity. Importantly, the court said that an underlying principle of the tort of passing off was the 'maintenance of what is currently regarded as fair trading,' and approved the evolution of the passing off action from very narrow parameters, to the extent of what is envisaged by the Irvine case. The court ruled that such a case could succeed where the plaintiff could first show that he or she has a significant reputation or goodwill to protect and, secondly, that the actions of the defendant communicated a 'false message' that the plaintiff endorsed or approved the goods or services provided by the defendant.

It is submitted that this decision by the most eminent intellectual property lawyer on the English Bench is likely to be influential in the event that a similar case comes before an Irish court. There is the potential additional factor in Ireland, mentioned in some of the intellectual property commentaries, that the State is constitutionally obliged to protect the property rights of all its citizens, although this protection in itself has not been explored to the fullest. Character merchandising is not confined, of course, to cartoon characters, such as Barbie or Barney, or whatever children's favourite at the time might be. There is also the question of whether or not, for example, famous footballers, could utilise the tort of passing off to assert so-called 'personality rights' to prevent a third party unfairly taking advantage of their reputation. Some decades back, the argument might have been that a footballer was a public figure and, particularly when the game was amateur, that there was no reason not to use the names of prominent individuals when promoting your product. With the evolution of the market in recent years, many footballers, musicians and others derive a considerable part of their income from exploitation of the value apparently to be gained by endorsement of specific products. More importantly, consumers are more aware of this practice and seem to attach far more importance to whether something is for example an 'authorised' product or 'recommended' by a particular personality. Whilst originally individuals were only able to protect their rights in this regard by use of the breach of confidence action, together with some kind of muddled (though never explicitly stated) right to privacy, there appears to be no specific reason why such individuals cannot now satisfy all the elements of the passing off action where a third party seeks to use their image or name to protect a particular product. It may not be long before an Irish court is asked to adjudicate on this area and the role of the tort of passing off in protecting such putative rights.

13.6.2 Practical steps in dealing with passing off

The author will conclude this chapter with some practical advice for those who find that they have successfully identified that there is indeed a passing off element arising in their client's case, whether it be as plaintiff or defendant. What should they do? What must they avoid? A key point to remember is that the vast majority of passing off actions which come to court are decided at the interlocutory injunction stage. Following an injunction ruling, parties almost invariably work things out between themselves rather than face a long and expensive road to plenary hearing. The success or failure of an attempt to obtain interlocutory relief is crucial in determining whether or not the goods or services alleged to have been passed off, will have anything other than a very short lifespan. Therefore, when confronted with facts which alert one to the existence of a passing off action, think in terms of the proofs required to satisfy the granting of an interim or interlocutory injunction, as well as the five elements set out in this chapter to succeed in a passing off action.

As a plaintiff, one needs to move quickly as any delay in taking action against the alleged offender will be viewed harshly by the court. Delay is the death knell for many would-be interlocutory applications. Remember that failure to succeed in progressing the matter to an interlocutory hearing within a short period of time could, in some circumstances, give rise to the prospect of a defendant who, two years down the line, has built up his own reputation in a particular product and will not be found by a court to have fed off another person's reputation. The Contech case mentioned earlier is just one example of a constant refrain from the courts – one must move quickly to protect the status quo. It should be added here that the advent of the Commercial Court has made it significantly easier for plaintiffs to move quickly in IP cases, and that that court's willingness to accept IP cases onto its list has considerably increased the practical options open to plaintiffs in respect of passing off and other areas of intellectual property.

Once one is made aware that there is a case which sounds like it might fall within the parameters of passing off, comprehensive instructions should be taken in order to draft a 'cease and desist' letter. That letter should contain as much information as possible about what your client knows of the nature of the potential infringement, when and where it has taken place and should issue an ultimatum to the potential defendant to cease the offending action. Remember that this letter could be the foundation of an interim or interlocutory application, and it should seek to deal with all of the defendant's activities (including marketing activities which could offend a client's rights). One caveat here is that such a letter should not fall foul of the provisions in trademark law (see Chapter 11) which deal with groundless threats of trademark infringement. Failing a response from the defendant, or at least failing a response which adequately meets a plaintiff's demands, counsel should be briefed immediately (having considered the existence or otherwise of the five elements named above), with a view to instituting proceedings. One cannot emphasise enough that the approach to a passing off case must display a level of urgency that, for example, would not be present in a typical personal injuries case. Once counsel has been briefed he or she can advise on the necessary proofs in order to proceed to enforce a client's rights. Crucial to this, as we have already seen, will be evidence of existing reputation and goodwill, and evidence of confusion on the part of existing or potential customers. For example, one may need to assemble all evidence of a client's marketing activities over previous years, together with evidence regarding volume of sales and any other impact in the market place. The key thing to remember in passing off is to move quickly as delay may be fatal to protection of valuable intellectual property rights.

CHAPTER 14

DESIGNS

Andrew Parkes

14.1 Introduction

Design law is concerned with the appearance of things. In many respects it is closely related to copyright but it takes features from the patent system also. Until recently, it was a form of protection that could only be obtained by registration. EU law now allows a short period of protection against copying even if the design is not registered. This is becoming of considerable commercial importance, particularly in the fashion clothing business.

14.2 Legislation

A system for registration of designs existed in Ireland under the old UK laws. This was carried over by the Industrial and Commercial Property (Protection) Acts 1927 to 1958, which governed design law in the State until 2002. Designs registered under the old Act continue to be governed by that Act. They can be kept in force for 15 years from the date of registration.

Following changes at EU level, the design law has changed fundamentally. The Industrial Designs Act 2001 (IDA 2001), which commenced on 1 July 2002, gave effect to Directive 98/71/EC of 13 October 1998 on the legal protection of designs (the Harmonization Directive). IDA 2001 is implemented by the Industrial Designs Regulations 2002 (SI 280/2002, called IDR 2002 in this text). A design right is obtained by registration at the Patents Office in Kilkenny but with a filing office in Dublin.

At much the same time, the EU adopted Council Regulation (EC) No. 6/2002 of 12 December 2001 on Community designs. The Community Design Regulation (CDR) introduced two forms of protection: the Registered Community Design available since 1 April 2003 and the Unregistered Community Design right effective since 6 March 2002.

As a result of the Community Design, the use of the national design registration system has fallen to a low level. In 2005, there were only 60 Irish applications covering 134 designs, whereas there were 16,741 Community design applications for a total of 63,255 designs. In practice, therefore, the most important forms of design protection in Ireland in the future are likely to be under the Community Design Regulation.

14.2.1 Registered Community Design (CDR, Art 12)

The Community Design registration system is administered by the Office for Harmonisation in the Internal Market (OHIM), in Alicante, Spain. It grants a unitary right covering all EU countries (similar to the Community Trade Mark). A Registered Community Design has a five year term from the date of registration, renewable up to a maximum of 25 years. The system allows for registration of multiple designs in a single application. A Registered Community Design is an exclusive right similar to a patent – there is no need to prove copying by the infringer.

14.2.2 Unregistered Community Design (CDR, Arts 11 and 19(2))

The Community Design Regulation also introduced a three year period of protection against copying of a design even if the design is not registered. The protection runs for three years from the date on which the design was first made available to the public within the Community. An unregistered design must meet same requirements (eg, novelty, individual character) as for a registered design. The holder has the right to prevent any third party from using the design if the contested use results from copying the protected design.

In general, the law laid down in the Community Design Regulation is self-sufficient. Only minor matters required implementation under national law. The European Communities (Community Designs) Regulations 2003 (SI 27/2003) made provision for the filing of applications for registration of Community designs *via* the Irish Patents Office, and designated the High Court as a Community design court of first instance, with the Supreme Court being designated as a Community design court of second instance. The European Communities (Enforcement of Community Judgments on Trade Marks and Designs) Regulations 2006 (SI 646/2006) nominated the High Court as the competent authority for enforcement of decisions of the OHIM concerning costs.

Some aspects of the enforcement of design rights also come within the European Communities (Enforcement of Intellectual Property Rights) Regulations 2006 (SI 360/2006).

14.2.3 Hague Agreement concerning the International Registration of Industrial Designs (Geneva Act 1999)

The World Intellectual Property Organization (WIPO) operates an international design registration system. The European Community acceded to the Geneva Act on 18 December 2006, in order to establish a link between the Community design system and the WIPO system (Council Regulation (EC) No 1891/2006). Section 79 of IDA 2001 authorises the Minister for Enterprise, Trade and Employment to prescribe such matters as he or she considers appropriate for giving effect in the State to the Hague Agreement.

14.2.4 Interpretation

Section 2(5) of IDA 2001 makes clear that in construing a provision of the Irish Act, a court must give effect to the Harmonization Directive, having regard not only to the provisions of the Directive but also to the preambles. In this chapter, the law is quoted from the Directive, unless otherwise noted. The substantive law in the Community Design Regulation corresponds to that in the Directive, with only minor changes in wording to take account of the different applicability and the fact that the Directive does not cover unregistered designs.

14.3 Protectable designs

14.3.1 Definition of Design (IDA 2001, s 2(1); Harmonization Directive, Art 1(a); CDR, Art 3(a))

The definition of a design is essentially the same in the Irish Act, the Harmonization Directive and the Community Regulation applicable to both registered and unregistered Community Designs:

- '"design" means the appearance of the whole or a part of a product resulting from the features of, in particular, the lines, contours, colours, shape, texture and/or materials of the product itself and/or its ornamentation.'

Although the Irish Act uses 'or' rather than 'and/or', the wording must be interpreted to be consistent with the Harmonization Directive.

14.3.2 Definition of Product (IDA 2001, s 2(1); Harmonization Directive, Art 1(b) and (c); CDR, Art 3(b) and (c))

The definition of a product (whose appearance is protected as a whole or in part) is identical in the three texts:

- 'Product' means any industrial or handicraft item, including *inter alia* parts intended to be assembled into a complex product, packaging, get-up, graphic symbols and typographic typefaces, but excluding computer programs.

- 'Complex product' means a product which is composed of multiple components which can be replaced permitting disassembly and reassembly of the product.

Taken together, the definitions of 'design' and 'product' are broader in several respects than their counterparts in the Irish Act of 1927, which were:

- the word 'design' means only the features of shape, configuration, pattern or ornament applied to any article by any industrial process or means ...which in the finished article appeal to and are judged solely by the eye ...

- the word 'article' means ... any article of manufacture and any substance artificial or natural or partly artificial and partly natural.

Design law now applies to handicraft items as well as industrial products and therefore the title 'Industrial Designs Act' is slightly misleading. The design may relate to only a part of the product. Any element of appearance is potentially protectable, not merely 'shape, configuration, pattern or ornament'; eg colours, texture or materials of the product can be the subject of design right. A product need not be an article of manufacture but may be get-up or even graphic symbols such as logos. The scope for protecting designs has therefore been enlarged significantly.

There is no specific requirement of appeal to the eye or of aesthetic quality. However, wholly functional designs are still excluded.

14.3.3 Designs dictated by their technical function and designs of interconnection (IDA 2001, s 16; Harmonization Directive, Art 7; CDR, Art 8)

- A design right shall not subsist in features of appearance of a product:
    1. which are solely dictated by its technical function, or
    2. which must necessarily be reproduced ... to permit the product ... to be mechanically connected to, or placed in, around or against another product so that either product may perform its function.

These exclusions are explained in Preamble 14 Harmonization Directive and Preamble 10 CDR:

- Whereas technological innovation should not be hampered by granting design protection to features dictated solely by a technical function; whereas it is understood that this does not entail that a design must have an aesthetic quality; whereas, likewise, the interoperability of products of different makes should not be hindered by extending protection to the design of mechanical fittings; whereas features of a design which are excluded from protection for these reasons should not be taken into consideration for the purpose of assessing whether other features of the design fulfil the requirements for protection.

The English Court of Appeal has held that the exclusion only applies where the part of the design in question was the *only* way to achieve the particular function (*Landor & Hawa International Ltd v Azure Designs Ltd* [2006] EWCA Civ 1285).

In addition, the exclusion does not apply to the mechanical fittings of modular products (s 16(3) of IDA 2001; Art 7(3) Harmonization Directive; Art 8(3) CDR).

14.3.4 Requirements for Protection (IDA 2001, Harmonization Directive, ss 11–14; CDR, Arts 3(2)–5; Arts 4–6)

- 'A design shall be protected by a design right to the extent that it is new and has individual character.'

In the case of a component part of a complex product, such as a motor vehicle, the part must remain visible during normal use, which is defined as 'use by the end user, excluding maintenance, servicing or repair work'.

14.3.5 Novelty

- 'A design shall be considered new if no identical design has been made available to the public.'

'The date for assessing novelty in the case of a registered design (either national or Community) is the filing date/priority date of the application for registration, whereas in the case of an Unregistered Community Design, it is the date on which the design for which protection is claimed has first been made been made available to the public.

Designs are regarded as 'identical' if their features differ only in immaterial details. There is however an additional requirement that the design to be protected has 'individual character'. This is different from the copyright concept of originality.

Individual character:

- A design has individual character if the overall impression it produces on the informed user differs from the overall impression produced on such a user by any design which has already been made available to the public.
- In assessing individual character, the degree of freedom of the designer in developing the design shall be taken into account.

Preamble 13 Harmonization Directive and Preamble 14 CDR say that the overall impression is judged against 'the existing design corpus, taking into consideration the nature of the product to which the design is applied or in which it is incorporated, and in particular the industrial sector to which it belongs...'

There is scope for considerable debate about the extent to which the overall impression must differ, about the identity of the 'informed user', about the extent of the 'design corpus' and about the 'degree of freedom of the designer.' These questions have been analysed by Mr Justice Lewison of the English Patents Court in *The Procter & Gamble Company v Reckitt Benckiser (UK) Ltd* [2006] EWHC Ch 3154, referring to *Woodhouse UK v Architectural Lighting Systems* [2006] RPC 1 and to decisions of the OHIM Invalidity Division including in particular *Eredu v Armet* (OHIM ref: ICD000000024; 27 April 2004).

14.3.6 Prior Disclosure (IDA 2001, s 2(1); Harmonization Directive, Art 6(1); CDR, Art 7(1))

- A design is deemed to have been made available to the public if it has been published ... exhibited, used in trade or otherwise disclosed ... except where these events could not reasonably have become known in the normal course of business to the circles specialised in the sector concerned, operating within the Community (or the EEA).

This definition, which is crucial to the decision as to whether a design is 'new', differs from the 'universal novelty' test of European patent law, where the state of the art includes everything made available to the public anywhere in the world, and also from the 'local novelty' test of the Irish Act of 1927, where only publication in the State was relevant. There are many questions to be answered about what 'could reasonably have become known' and who are the 'circles specialised in the sector concerned.' Similar unclear wording is used to define the commencement and term of an Unregistered Community Design – Article 11(2) CDR.

A design disclosed to a third person under conditions of confidentiality is not deemed to have been made available to the public.

14.3.7 Grace Period for Own Disclosure (IDA 2001, s 2(7); Harmonization Directive, Art 6(2); CDR, Art 7(2))

When considering the novelty and individual character of a Registered Design (either Community or national), there is a grace period of 12 months for disclosures made:

- by the designer,
- his/her successor in title, or
- a third person as a result of information provided or action taken by the designer or his/her successor in title.

Such a disclosure is not taken into consideration if the design has been made available to the public during the twelve month period before the date of the application for registration or, if priority is claimed, the date of priority. This means that the designer can test the market, relying on the Unregistered Community Design right, for a year before applying for registration. However, there is a risk that a second party will create a similar design independently during the grace period, and this independent design will form part of the 'existing design corpus' against which the novelty and individual character of the first party's design will be judged.

The twelve month grace period also applies if the design has been made available to the public as a consequence of an abuse in relation to the designer or his/her successor in title.

14.4 Infringement

14.4.1 Scope of Protection (IDA 2001, s 45(3); Harmonization Directive, Art 9; CDR, Art 10)

- The scope of protection conferred by a design right shall include any design which does not produce on the informed user a different overall impression.
- In assessing the scope of protection, the degree of freedom of the designer in developing his design shall be taken into consideration.

The language corresponds to that used in defining novelty for a design, as discussed above, and gives rise to similar difficulties in interpretation. For a Community Registered Design, the scope is not limited to the product in which protected design is incorporated or to which it is applied (Art 36(6) CDR).

For an analysis of the scope of protection, see the judgement of Mr Justice Lewison of the English Patents Court in *The Procter & Gamble Company v Reckitt Benckiser (UK) Ltd* [2006] EWHC Ch 3154.

14.4.2 Rights Conferred (IDA 2001, s 42(4); Harmonization Directive, Art 12; CDR, Art 19)

- The registration of a design (either Community or national) confers on its holder the exclusive right to use it and to prevent any third party not having the holder's consent from using it. This includes, in particular, the acts of making, offering, putting on the market, importing, exporting, or using a product in which the design is incorporated or to which it is applied, or stocking such a product for those purposes.

An exclusive right of this kind is well known in patent law. It can be enforced even if the third party has developed its design independently.

However, the position is different for an Unregistered Community Design. In this case, the holder has the right to prevent these acts if the contested use results from copying the protected design. A contested use is not deemed to be copying if it results from an independent work of creation by a designer who may reasonably be thought not to be familiar with the design made available to the public by the holder.

14.4.3 Action for Infringement (IDA 2001, s 51–62; CDR, Arts 80–92)

An action for infringement of a design right is brought in the High Court, which in the case of a Community Design is acting as a Community design court. The proceedings may be entered into the Commercial Court list – see *Coast Stores v Dunnes Stores* [2007] 00017 P; The Irish Times news report, 06.02.2007.

An Irish design right is infringed by a person who (without the licence of the proprietor) undertakes or authorises another to undertake an act which is the exclusive right of the proprietor. In addition, IDA 2001, ss 52–54 contain provisions about secondary infringement regarding trade in infringing products and providing means for infringement such as articles specifically designed for applying the design to a product. CDR, Art 89 authorises seizure of infringing products and of materials and implements predominantly used in order to manufacture the infringing goods.

Otherwise, the usual remedies for infringement under national law are applicable. IDA 2001, ss 71–72 contain some special provisions relating to delivery up and disposal.

14.4.4 Groundless threats (IDA 2001, s 56)

Care must be taken when threatening a person with infringement of a design right. A person aggrieved by the threats can bring court proceedings for an injunction and damages if the threats are groundless. However, a notification of the existence of a registered design does not constitute a threat, and a person making or importing any object cannot claim to be a 'person aggrieved'.

14.5 Defences to infringement

The main defences to infringement are that the defendant's acts do not fall within the scope of protection of the design right and/or that the design right is invalid (see below).

Apart from the general issue as to whether the defendant's design produces a 'different overall impression' as mentioned above, there are specific defences to infringement provided in the legislation.

14.5.1 Limitation of the rights conferred (IDA 2001, s 48; Harmonization Directive, Art 13; CDR, Art 20)

The Harmonization Directive defines a number of exceptions to design right protection. Most of these are parallel to exceptions recognised under patent law, whereas item (c) is derived from copyright law:

- The rights conferred by a design right ... shall not be exercised in respect of:
  a. acts done privately and for non-commercial purposes;
  b. acts done for experimental purposes;
  c. acts of reproduction for the purposes of making citations or of teaching, provided that such acts are compatible with fair trade practice and do not unduly prejudice the normal exploitation of the design, and that mention is made of the source;
  d. the equipment on ships and aircraft registered in another country when these temporarily enter the territory of the Member State concerned;
  e. the importation in the Member State concerned of spare parts and accessories for the purpose of repairing such craft;
  f. the execution of repairs on such craft.

In the parallel provision in the Irish Act, the words 'the Member State concerned' are replaced by 'the State' while in the Community Design Regulation they are replaced by 'the Community'.

14.5.2 Spare parts for repair of complex products (IDA 2001, s 42(5); CDR, Art 110)

Although not obligatory under the Harmonization Directive, the Irish Act did include a special exclusion for spare parts used in the repair of complex products such as motor vehicles, corresponding to an exclusion in the CRD:

- The design right shall not apply to the use of a component part of a complex product for the purpose of repair of that product to restore its original appearance.

The European Commission is seeking agreement on a proposal [COM(2004)582] to change the Harmonization Directive in order to complete the internal market in spare parts, as required under Art 18 of the Harmonization Directive.

14.5.3 Prior user's right (IDA 2001, s 50; CDR, Art 22)

There is a limited right of continued use for a third party who commenced use in good faith or made serious and effective preparations to that end before the date of the registered design, if the prior user's design was not copied from the registered design. To avoid infringement of a Registered Community Design, the prior use must have been in the Community, whereas for a national registered design the prior use must have been in the State.

14.6 Invalidity

14.6.1 Grounds for invalidity (IDA 2001, s 47; Harmonization Directive, Art 11; CDR, Art 25)

A design right can be declared invalid on various grounds, the most important of which are:

- that the subject matter does not come within the definition of a design;
- that it is not new or lacks individual character;

- that it is dictated by its technical function;
- that it is contrary to public policy or to accepted principles of morality;
- that the holder of the design right is not entitled to it;
- in the case of a registered design, that it conflicts with an unpublished design of earlier filing/priority date.

14.6.2 Counterclaim for invalidity/declaration of invalidity (IDA 2001, s 47; Harmonization Directive, Art 11; CDR, Arts 24, 84–87)

A counterclaim that the design right is invalid may be made in infringement proceedings. In addition, an application to invalidate an Irish Registered Design may be made to the Controller of the Patents Office and an application to invalidate a Community Registered Design may be made to the OHIM. An Unregistered Community Design can only be declared invalid by a Community design court such as the Irish High Court.

14.7 Criminal cases

14.7.1 Offences (IDA 2001, ss 66 and 69–70)

IDA 2001, s 66 lays down that a person carrying on certain dealings in infringing products is guilty of an offence and is liable to a fine or imprisonment. Section 69 provides for delivery up in criminal proceedings and section 70 allows a judge of the District Court to authorise search and seizure where there is reasonable ground to suspect that an offence has been committed.

14.8 Authorship and ownership of designs

14.8.1 Authorship (IDA 2001, ss 17–18)

The Irish Act uses the term 'author' but defines this as meaning 'the person who creates the design' and therefore it seems to be the same as 'designer' used in the CDR. If the design is computer-generated, the author is the person by whom the arrangements necessary for the creation of the design are undertaken. There may be joint authorship if the contribution of each author is not distinct from that of the other author(s).

14.8.2 Ownership (IDA 2001, s 19; CDR, Art 14)

The right to a design is vested in the author/designer, unless the design is created by an employee in the course of employment, in which case it is vested in the employer, subject to any agreement to the contrary. A design may be assigned to another person who becomes the proprietor or joint proprietor. Note that, unlike the UK, there is no provision dealing with a commissioned design in either the Irish Act or the CDR. A clause clarifying ownership should therefore be included in any contract for a design commission.

14.8.3 Right of the designer to be cited (IDA 2001, s 19(3); CDR, Art 18)

Where the author/designer is not the proprietor of the design, he/she has the right to be cited as such in an application for registration or in the Register.

14.9 Registration

14.9.1 Application for registration (IDA 2001, s 20–29; CDR, Arts 35–48)

Applications are filed at the Irish Patents Office for national protection or at the OHIM for Community-wide protection. A representation of the design suitable for reproduction must be submitted, although in certain circumstances at the OHIM a representation of a 2-dimensional design (such as a fabric) may be replaced by a specimen. Examination is generally restricted to formal matters.

14.9.2 Filing date and priority right (IDA 2001, ss 25–26; CDR, Arts 38 and 41–43)

A satisfactory application is accorded a filing date which is the basic date for calculating the term of protection. A claim may also be made for the benefit of the date of an application for the same design made within the preceding six months in another country (with a few exceptions). This earlier date is called the priority date because it gives the applicant a right of priority over another party who may have applied for or disclosed a similar design during the six month period.

14.9.3 Classification of products (IDA 2001, s 24; CDR, Art 36)

An application for registration must include an indication of the products in which the design is intended to be incorporated or to which it is intended to be applied.

Products are classified under the International (Locarno) Classification for Industrial Designs.

14.9.4 Multiple designs in one application (IDR 2002, r 19; CDR, Art 37)

A large number of designs can be covered in a single application if the products are all in a single Class of the Locarno Classification or if the design is for ornamentation. For an Irish application the maximum number is 100 while at the OHIM there is no limit. Fees are payable in accordance with the number of designs.

14.9.5 Deferment of publication (IDA 2001, s 32; CDR, Art 50)

A design will normally be published upon registration. However, a request can be made for thirty month deferment of publication of the registration or (if multiple designs are included in one application) for selected designs within the registration. When a Community Registered Design is subject to deferment of publication, the rights conferred are similar to those for an Unregistered Community Design ie, the right to prevent copying of the protected design.

14.9.6 Term of protection (IDA 2001, s 43; Harmonization Directive, Art 10; CDR, Arts 11 and 12)

A registered design (either Community or Irish) is protected for a period of five years from the filing date of the application for registration. The term can be renewed for one or more periods of five years, up to a total of 25 years.

A Community Unregistered Design is protected for a period of three years as from the date on which the design was first made available to the public within the Community. It was apparently the intention of the legislators that the unregistered design right would apply only to designs first disclosed in the Community (as opposed to designs published in, say, the USA in such a way as to make them known in Europe) but it is not entirely clear that the intention was achieved by the language used.

14.9.7 Relationship to other forms of IP protection (Harmonization Directive, Art 16; CDR, Art 96(1))

The Harmonization Directive and Community Design Regulation do not exclude the application to designs of national or Community legislation relating to:

- National Unregistered Design Right (as found in the UK);
- Trade Marks;
- Patents/Utility Models;
- Unfair Competition or Civil Liability.

14.9.8 Relationship to copyright (IDA 2001, s 89; Harmonization Directive, Art 17; CDR, Art 96(2))

A design protected by a design right is also eligible for protection under the law of copyright. This 'principle of cumulation of protection' represents a substantial change from the previous Irish law. In the absence of complete harmonisation of copyright law in the Community, Member States are free to establish the extent of copyright protection and the conditions under which such protection is conferred. This has been done by IDA 2001, s 89 which amends certain provisions of the Copyright and Related Rights Act 2000.

14.9.9 Extent of copyright protection for designs in Ireland (IDA 2001, s 89)

The copyright in a design registered under the IDA 2001 expires 25 years after the filing date of the design application ie, the copyright cannot run longer than the maximum term of the registration.

Where the design is for anything other than an artistic work or a typeface, and the design is for any aspect of shape or contours, other than surface decoration, the copyright in a design document or model recording or embodying the design is not infringed by the making of a product to the design or the copying of a product made to the design.

14.10 Effect of exploitation of artistic works

Where an artistic work has been exploited by (or with the authorisation of) the copyright owner:

- by making copies by an industrial process; and
- marketing the products,

copyright in the work becomes unenforceable against others making such products after 25 years from the year of first marketing.

14.11 Overlap with trade marks

There is also potential overlap between design rights and trade marks protectable under the Trade Marks Act 1996 (TMA 1996) or the Community Trade Mark Regulation (CTMR). The definition of a trade mark includes both 'designs' and ' the shape of goods or their packaging' (TMA 1996, s 6(2); CTMR, Art 4). On the other hand, the definition of 'product' in the design laws includes packaging, get-up and graphic symbols such as logos, which were previously regarded as only having trade mark character (TMA 1996, s 2; CDR, Art 3). The nature of the protection obtainable under the respective laws differs substantially but there is scope for competition between the two systems.

14.12 Conclusion

Protection of designs has become much more accessible for designers under the new national and Community laws. The Unregistered Community Design, in particular, will give rise to significant contentious issues until the scope of the law is better known and understood.

CHAPTER 15

CONFIDENTIAL INFORMATION

Carol Plunkett

15.1 Introduction

In certain instances where the laws relating to copyright and design, patents, trademarks and contractual obligations do not protect against the unauthorised use of information or of a concept, the courts have held that a duty to preserve such a confidence may be imposed. This is a difficult area of the law, in that, because it is entirely 'judge-made' and very much based on equitable principles, there are a number of uncertainties and some of the cases indeed contradict each other. However, most of the case law agrees that there are three essential requirements to satisfy a claim for breach of confidence.

15.2 What are the essential requirements?

The first essential requirement is that the owner of the confidential information must establish that the information which he seeks to protect is in fact confidential, that is, that it has the necessary quality of confidence about it. The information must be inaccessible to the public, although as we shall see later it need not be something which a third party or a member of the public could not compile themselves.

The second essential element is that the confidential information must have been imparted in circumstances which imposed an obligation of confidence on the person receiving it.

Thirdly, the person alleging that a breach of confidence has occurred must be able to show that the person whom he complains has breached that obligation has used the information in a manner that is not intended by its owner and is not authorised by him.

15.3 Why should confidential information be protected?

Paul Lavery in his book, *Commercial Secrets*, includes a very good quotation from Robert A Spanner's treatise – 'Who owns innovation' (Dow Jones-Irwin, 1984) – as follows:

> 'The old adage 'knowledge is power' is coming to have its commercial counterpart in the more sordid but equally valid aphorism 'information is money.' In a nation that is entering the so-called post-industrial information society, 'information has quite literally become Capital.'

This quote really sums up the reasons why this body of the law is evolving. The dependence of economies on possession of land or machinery and the importance of that dependence is now outweighed by the importance of dependence upon what might be called Intellectual Capital. Economies which have the knowledge to produce things more efficiently, to develop new technology to do this and to improve efficiency overall, gain the competitive edge. Intellectual Capital or, quite simply, ideas, are paramount in this. As soon as an idea is shared with a third party, it is open to attack. It is essential that commercial secrets can be protected against disclosure and that the courts impose this obligation to hold information confidential.

Obviously, if this prohibition on releasing information had no exceptions, then economies would stagnate and so the courts have balanced these two opposite ends of the spectrum. In general, the court will not allow the use of information which has been disclosed in confidence in a way that is inconsistent with the purpose for which the information was imparted. Nor will the courts allow use of information which was stolen from its owner.

On the other hand, no one will be prevented from using information which is already in the public domain. If someone can prove that they have independently carried out their own research in developing a product, the courts will not grant an injunction stopping them from using that product even if it has already been developed by another company. No one can be stopped from '*reverse engineering*' a product; that is, no one can be stopped from purchasing at market value any product in the market place and working backwards to find out how it is manufactured. Obviously, if patent protection exists in respect of the product this is a different matter, since it cannot be made without licence of the owner of the patent, but in all other cases reverse engineering is permitted. Furthermore, the courts have always allowed an employee to use his skill and experience which he has gained while employed. This is different from using the secrets of his former employer.

15.4 History

The protection of commercial secrets is not a new phenomenon. The world's oldest written code of laws, the Hammurabic code of 2100 BC, apparently ordered the loss of an eye for those who were caught with forbidden secrets.

In Roman law, an action existed in relation to the corruption of a slave. This arose most often where a Roman citizen had persuaded the slave of a competitor to give him his master's commercial secrets. Prior to the 18th century, the government in England took a very paternalistic attitude and the economy was strictly regulated. Guilds were set up to govern various trades and had strict rules setting out who could receive certain information or trade secrets. During the 18th and 19th centuries, however, economic policy became permissive and *laissez faire* was the order of the day. The City and Guilds groups became less powerful and the restrictive legislation was repealed.

As a result, trades people and manufacturers had to seek new remedies to protect their knowledge, and the courts gradually introduced the action for breach of confidence.

Cases are reported as far back as the 1730s and the 1750s. In *Webb v Rose* 98 ER 924 an injunction was granted to stop the defendant from printing the plaintiff's father's drafts. In *Pope v Curl* 26 ER 608 Mr Pope obtained an injunction restraining Mr Curl, a book seller, from selling a book called 'Letters from Swift, Pope and Others' as long as the book contained letters in Mr Pope's name.

Although initially the action for breach of confidence related to information in written form, over the years the law advanced and protected not just matters of copyright, but specifically, the underlying confidence of the information which was imparted. In the case of *Prince Albert v Strange*, the defendants were stopped from publishing etchings owned by the Royal Family which had been left with a printer to have copies made.

Over the years, the courts have fixed certain principles in relation to confidential information. They are:

1. You cannot use information in a manner which is inconsistent with the manner of its disclosure to you.
2. You cannot use secrets.
3. You can use information in the public domain.

The cases have required the courts to strike a fair balance between the right to confidentiality alleged by the plaintiff as against, in Ireland, our constitutional right to convey information to the public.

Over the years, two main circumstances, that of an 'unemployment' situation and an employment relationship, have evolved in which confidential information arises.

One manner of describing confidential information is to use the term 'know-how'. 'Know-how' can be secret formulae, it can be processes in manufacturing or it could also be simple things like lists of names of customers and sales information. It is this category to which the author was referring when earlier she said that the information need not necessarily be secret. It can be information which has been gathered and is preserved in a particular manner by its owner.

Over the years, the court has divided information into three categories. The first of these is trivia or public information. This information is not protected and there can be no duty to hold it confidential.

The second category of information is skill and experience. This is not protected in ordinary circumstances, but it can be restricted in, for example, a contract of employment by a restriction of trade clause. Clearly, restriction of trade clauses are a difficult area, since an employee has a constitutional right to be able to leave one employment and commence another and to use certain aspects of the skill and experience which he has gained in one employment in furtherance of his career. Having said that, the courts will impose an obligation on an employee to comply with a reasonable restriction of trade clause. So, cases which prohibit trading in a certain area for a particular length of time, can be regarded as reasonable.

The third type of information is that of trade secrets and the courts have found that irrespective of any written obligation, an employee has an obligation to hold trade secrets safe even after they have left a particular employer.

Because this area of the law is judge and case driven, the best way of explaining how the law of confidential information has evolved is to discuss several of the more interesting cases and for this purpose they have in this chapter been divided into three categories. The first category is where an employee has been sued for setting up in business in competition with a former employer, allegedly using trade secrets owned by that former employer; the second is of non-employment cases; and the third is a growing body of law where so-called celebrities seek to preserve their privacy by various different means.

15.5 The employment cases

The first of these cases is *Meadox Medicals v VPI Ltd and Denis Cummings and George Goicoechea* (1981, unreported) HC. This is a case heard before Mr Justice Hamilton in 1981. Mr Cummings and Mr Goicoechea had worked for Meadox Medicals in the US and during that employment had access to know-how and trade secrets relating to the development of what was called a woven double velour graft which was used as a replacement artery.

These gentlemen resigned from Meadox Medicals, became employees of a French company, left that company and within a year of having left Meadox Medicals, had set up their own company in Shannon, manufacturing arterial prostheses. The court gave a lengthy judgment and was satisfied that it was highly improbable, if not inconceivable, that the product could have been conceived within the time without the benefit and knowledge and confidential data required by Dr. Goicoechea and Denis Cummings in the course of their employment by the plaintiff. Both gentlemen had signed confidentiality agreements with Meadox and the court was satisfied that they were in breach of those agreements.

In *Faccenda Chicken v Fowler* [1986] 1 All ER 617, the plaintiff sold fresh chickens and in 1973 employed Mr Fowler as a Sales Manager. At his suggestion, the company adopted a method of selling fresh chickens from refrigerated vans. Over the years, sales information, customers' names and addresses, routes and prices charged and so on was gathered. In 1980, Mr Fowler left and set up his own business in exactly the same area doing exactly the same thing, together with five of the salesmen from Faccenda Chicken. None of the employees had a restrictive covenant in their employment contract. Judge Goulding, who heard the case said that there were three categories of information, those which we have already discussed, trivia, public information which isn't protected, skill and experience which is not protected but can be restricted by contract, and trade secrets which are protected. He found that Fowler and the others had acquired skill and experience, not secret information, and he refused to grant an injunction.

The penultimate case in this category is *Lawrence David Ltd v Ashton* [1991] 1 All ER 385. In this case, the plaintiff's manufactured vehicle bodies and employed Mr Ashton as a Sales Director. His contract of employment said that he would not during or after employment, disclose to anyone any information relating to the plaintiffs or their customers or divulge any trade secrets and that he would not be involved for two years after his employment in the design, development, manufacture or supply of similar products. Mr Ashton was fired and he went to work for a competitor. The plaintiffs sought damages for breach of contract and an injunction to stop Mr Ashton's use of confidential information and to enforce the restraint of trade clause.

The English Court of Appeal refused the injunction against disclosing confidential information because it was not possible to define the confidential information or the trade secrets which the plaintiff sought to protect.

This case makes it clear that it is very important that the employee knows precisely what it is he may and may not do, and emphasises the importance of clarity in the drafting of such contracts.

The last case, which is possibly the most important case in Ireland on this topic, is *House of Spring Gardens v Point Blank* [1985] FSR 327. This case involves the development of a bullet-proof vest by an inventor who entered into agreements with Point Blank Limited to manufacture the vests for him. Relationships broke down. It was agreed that the inventor would get royalties from any further contract of the supply of vests by Point Blank Limited, particularly to the Libyan authorities. The defendants did not pay any royalties. The inventor claimed for breach of contract and copyright but also claimed an injunction for breach of know-how and abuse of confidential information. Judge Costello granted the injunction and the Supreme Court upheld his decision. Judge Costello's judgment gives a very good analysis of the UK cases and points out that he is enunciating the law in Ireland in relation to confidential information for the first time. Judge Costello's rules are: first, decide if there is a relationship between the parties which imports confidence; and secondly, decide whether the information can properly be recorded as confidential.

15.6 The non-employment cases

Turning to the second category, the first case is that of *Saltman Engineering against Campbell Engineering* (1948) 65 RPC 203, a case decided in 1948. Lord Greene gave judgment in this case and is often cited in later cases. The facts of this case were that Campbell Engineering made tools for leather punching for Saltman Engineering, based on drawings which were provided by Saltman. The relationship broke down and after Saltman and Campbell parted company, the defendants continued to manufacture and market leather punches. The plaintiff claimed that this was an abuse of the confidential information contained in the drawings, which had been provided to Campbell Engineering.

The court agreed. The defendants claimed that there was no secret in the drawings. They could after all have gone out and bought any of the Saltman punches; dismantled them, drawn specifications and reverse engineered them. Whilst the judge did not disagree with this, his concern was that by using the drawings, the defendant had saved himself a substantial amount of time, rather than investing the time and effort which should have been necessary to produce their own punches.

Lord Greene said:

> 'The information to be protected must have the necessary quality of confidence about it. That is it must not be something which is public property or public knowledge, but it is perfectly possible to have a confidential document which is the result of work done by its maker on materials which are available to anyone. What makes the document secret is that its maker used his brain to come up with the results which it contains and this produced a result which could only have been produced by someone going though the same process.'

In *Terrapin v Builders Supply (Hayes)* [1960] RPC 128, which was decided in 1960, the plaintiff had been using the defendant company to market portable buildings for them and during negotiations, had disclosed details or an updated version that they were designing. The relationship broke down. The defendants began to make their own portable buildings including some of the updating features which had been discussed with them by the plaintiff. The plaintiff sought an injunction for abuse of confidential information and Judge Roxburgh granted it. He said that:

> 'I understand the essence of this branch of the law, whatever the origin of it may be is that a person which has obtained information in confidence is not allowed to use it as a spring board for activities detrimental to the person who made the confidential communication and springboard it remains even when all the features have been published or can be ascertained by actual inspection by members of the public. The dismantling of a unit might enable a person to proceed without plans or specifications or other technical information but not I think without some of the know-how and certainly not without taking the trouble to dismantle.'

He goes on to say that it is his view that the possessor of such information must be placed under a special disability in the field of competition in order to ensure that he doesn't get an unfair start.

There were two *Seager v Copydex cases*. These cases involved the manufacture of carpet grips by Seager, and Copydex marketed them. At one meeting, Mr Seager disclosed details of another idea which he had for a corner grip. Mr Seager explained the design, showed drawings and specifications and explained its advantage over existing carpet grips on the market. Relations broke down. Copydex brought a grip onto the market. Although Mr Seager had a patent, it was found that Copydex were not infringing it. However, Lord Denning said that although he believed Copydex when they said they did not consciously abuse Seager's secrets, the court found that the two products were so strikingly similar that Copydex must unconsciously have used the information which Seager had disclosed at the meetings. Lord Denning applied the 'springboard principle', that a person who has obtained information in confidence is not to use it as a springboard for activities detrimental to the person who made the confidential information, and springboard it remained even when all the knowledge has become public. The second *Seager v Copydex* case dealt with the principles on which damages were to be assessed and held that they should be assessed on the market value of the information as between a willing buyer and willing seller. The case further said that when damages were assessed and paid, the property and the confidential information vested in the defendant company, and they had a right to make use of it.

Coco v Clarke [1969] RPC 41 set out the essentials of the doctrine of confidential information, those which are mentioned at the beginning of this chapter:

1. the information itself must have the necessary quality of confidence about it;
2. the circumstances in which the information was imparted must have imparted confidentiality; and
3. there must have been unauthorised use of information to the detriment of the imparting party.

That case is where Coco invented a Moped and he approached the defendant to make it. He showed them a prototype, specifications and drawings. The relationship broke down. Clarke said they were going to use their own design because there were too many problems with Coco's. When the Clarke Moped came on the market, Coco believed it wasn't a new invention but had been manufactured by use of the know-how he had disclosed. The defendants agreed to keep an account and pay a royalty of 5 shillings per engine up to the trial so that no injunction was granted.

Then there are two Irish cases worth mentioning: the first is *Oblique Financial Services v Promise Production Co Ltd and those involved in the Phoenix magazine* [1994] ILRM 75. The plaintiff was a company partly owned by Mary Breen-Farrelly. It organised financial support for film production and entered into a contract with the Promise Production Company Limited to finance a film. The name of the investor was to be kept secret but unfortunately the Phoenix published an article to the effect that the Roman Catholic Church was the investor, commenting that this was a rather unusual investment for such a body. This case came before the Irish court as an application under s 11 of the Jurisdiction of Courts and Enforcement of Judgments Act, for 'an order in aid' of proceedings, which had taken place in the UK. The court held that the obligation of confidentiality, which is enforced by the courts, is not merely applicable to parties to a contract, but also in relation to the third parties who may also come into possession of that information.

The court enforced the obligation of confidentiality of the company against Phoenix Magazine. This was in spite of the fact that the defendants argued that granting an injunction would infringe the constitutional rights of the Phoenix Magazine as an organ of opinion under Article 40 of the Constitution. However, the court said that this is not an absolute right, but one which is qualified having regard to other legal constraints. It should be remembered that this was an interlocutory injunction and the matter was settled afterwards.

The last case in this category is *National Irish Bank v RTÉ* [1998] 2 IR 465. This involved the proposed disclosure by RTE of a certain tax structure, which apparently allowed investors in a particular scheme to evade their tax liabilities. The bank argued that publication of details in relation to this would irreparably damage the relationship of trust and confidence between the bank and their customers and would result in a loss of customers. They denied that there was any wrong doing in relation to the operation of the scheme. It was common case that the information was confidential and so the court had to decide the balance of the public interest in preserving confidences as against the public interest in favour of disclosure of serious wrongdoing. At the interlocutory stage, Judge Shanley discharged the *ex parte* injunction which had been granted, and this was upheld by the Supreme Court, which said that information concerning allegations of tax evasion was a matter of genuine interest and importance to the general public. Therefore, it was in the public interest that the general public be given the information.

15.7 Celebrities

Over the past few years, celebrities have begun to sue in situations where they believe that their privacy and/or human rights have been infringed. Prior to those cases, the usual course of action had been to seek damages in defamation: see *Tolley v JS Fry and Sons Ltd* [1931] AC 333, where a well known golfer whose image had been used in a chocolate advertisement succeeded in a claim; or, in passing off: see *Edmund Irvine & Tidswell Ltd v Talksport Ltd* [2002] 2 All ER, where Eddie Irvine's personam had been used in such a manner as to appear that he had endorsed the defendant's radio station. Those are topics for another chapter, but allied to those claims, in several instances, has been a claim for breach of confidential information. This has widened the tort somewhat, and it no longer now appears to be limited, as it was in the cases just described above, to a commercial relationship. It is again including the principle enunciated in the old cases of *Pope v Curl* (1741) 2 Atk 342 and *Prince Albert v Strange* (1849) 2 Dr G & Sm 293, 1 MAc & G 25, that an obligation of confidence may be imposed even where there is no commercial relationship at all.

There are a number cases in this category – *Campbell v MGN Ltd* UKHL/2004/22 – where Naomi Campbell fought all the way to the House of Lords and got judgment on 6 May 2004. The court reinstated an initial award of Stg£3,500 and reversed a large costs order. In that case, photographs were published of Ms Campbell leaving a Narcotics Anonymous meeting. The court held that a duty of confidentiality could be imposed where information could reasonably be regarded as private and that this duty must be balanced against the public interest and freedom of expression.

Ewan McGregor won an action against a French based picture agency, Eliot Press, to prevent further publication of pictures of his children which were secretly taken while the family was on holiday in Mauritius.

The former athlete Sebastian Coe brought a case in May 2004 in which he sought an injunction against the Mail on Sunday and the Sunday Mirror to stop publication of details of his ten year extramarital affair with fashion designer Vanessa Lander for whom he had financed an abortion. The court held against him on the basis that Ms Lander's right to freedom of speech outweighed Lord Coe's right to privacy in relation to the affair. Details of the affair were apparently already in the public domain, having been published in 1995 by another newspaper.

There are two other cases worthy of mention. The first is that of the case of *Hannover v Germany* where Princess Caroline (Appl no 59320/00), won a ruling on 24 June 2004 from the European Court of Human Rights that photos taken of her in a public place was a violation of her right to privacy. Then, in January 2005, the heir to the Versace empire won a complaint to the Press Complaints Commission in the UK against Now magazine to the effect that that magazine had infringed her right to privacy by publishing photos of her shopping in London.

In *Douglas and others v Hello and others* [2007] UKHL 21, a case which took seven years to wend its way through the court system, the House of Lords gave judgment on 2 May 2007 confirming that Hello magazine had breached rights of commercial confidence when they published 'spoiler' photographs of Catherine Zeta-Jones and Michael Douglas' wedding in the Plaza Hotel in New York. The couple had received £1 million from OK! Magazine to publish exclusively photographs of their wedding. The High Court found that Hello had breached confidence by publishing the photographs against the Douglases and OK!'s wishes. The decision was reversed by the Court of Appeal, which decided that while the Douglases privacy had been infringed, this right did not extend to a commercial entity such as OK!. The House of Lords overturned this finding. OK! had entered into a formal agreement with the Douglases and the fact of the agreement was publically known. Security was tight at the wedding. The Lords found that Hello knew of the attempts to preserve the confidentiality and exclusivity and were therefore subject to those aspects even if not strictly a party to the agreement. The case confirms that the obligation of confidence can be extended to commercial third parties outside an agreement which has commercial value. Nor is the tort just referable to private individuals. In this case, OK! was found to be entitled to seek the protection of the tort. The case is important for this reason.

Even more recently, in June 2007, in *His Royal Highness the Prince of Wales v Associated Newspapers Limited*, the High Court in London granted summary judgment and an injunction prohibiting publication of eight of the Prince's private journals which contained his personal views and memories of his visits abroad. The Mail on Sunday had published extracts describing the Prince's thoughts on his trip to Hong Kong. The court found that the public interest in such matters did not outweigh the confidential aspect of the journals.

These areas of the law, privacy, confidential information combined with rights under data protection laws and human rights are all being cited in the cases being brought by 'celebrities' to protect their rights. The Douglas case and the Naomi Campbell case both cited some if not all of these areas in their claims, as did Ewan McGregor, Lord Coe and the Prince of Wales.

So the laws of breach of confidence and privacy are being closely entwined and allied with claims for breaches of Data Protection Law and Human Rights Law.

15.8 Remedies

A brief note in relation to remedies. Clearly because this is an equitable solution to an equitable problem, the first thing to consider is an application for an injunction. In all applications for injunctions but particularly in this area, speed is of the essence. If a client comes to you some months after the employee has left, then in all likelihood you will not be granted an injunction and shouldn't waste money seeking one. Obviously, if you have clear evidence that either documentation or computer files have been stolen then your case may be strengthened. Do not forget that you will still have to prove that the balance of probability lies with the plaintiff, that there is a stateable case and that damages do not constitute an adequate remedy.

Consider the seeking of a *Mareva* injunction, that is one to freeze all bank accounts etc. and perhaps an *Anton Piller* where you are permitted to go and remove any documentation which may be relevant to the issues in order to preserve it until the trial.

In relation to damages, at the plaintiff's option these can be either straight damages or an account of profits made by the defendant. The case law, at least in the employment cases and after a great deal of discussion, appears to be in favour of awarding the plaintiff the amount of money the defendant would have spent in gathering the information, together with the profit the defendant has made as a result of the spring board advantage they had. In the non-employment cases, the position is less clear, but so far, awards have been for relatively small amounts.

CHAPTER 16

PROTECTION OF COMPUTER PROGRAMS AND DATABASES

Carol Plunkett

This chapter is designed to explain the provisions of copyright law and in particular those set out in the Copyright and Related Rights Act 2000 relating to computer programs and databases. It will also refer briefly to the historical context against which these legislative provisions have been set, so as to explain the rationale behind the legislation.

16.1 Protection of computer programs

16.1.1 Background

When legal protection of computer programs first arose, there was doubt as to whether copyright subsisted in them or whether they were protected by some other legal right or simply by contract.

To understand why ultimately copyright has been chosen to protect computer programs, it is necessary to look at the nature of a computer program, because it is the understanding of what exactly a computer program is that has caused difficulties in relation to its legal protection.

The following is a layperson's description: a computer program consists of a set of instructions, in electronic form, given to the central processing unit (CPU) of a computer to ensure that the computer performs certain functions. These instructions are not in human readable form.

When developers are writing a computer program, they set out the instructions that need to be given to the computer in language intelligible to a computer programmer. This language, supplemented by texts and drawings, and known as source code, is the result of skill and labour in creating the technical means by which instructions will be given to the CPU of a computer in the form of a program.

In this form, the computer program communicates information to human persons (albeit to reasonably skilled programmers only). Furthermore, in this form, there is a written expression of the computer program.

When these instructions are given to a computer, the instructions take the form of languages, known as machine code or object code, which the computer will understand. Object code is a set of electronic pulses, which communicate with the computer, and is not expressed in a written form.

The background to the difficulty in relation to protecting computer programs is that while the source code can be considered to be a literary or artistic work and can therefore be protected by copyright, there is no obvious category of copyright works into which the electronic pulses, the object code, would fit

The difficulty was the fact that although there was no obvious method for protecting the object code, if the object code was copied or reverse engineered, the person who carried out the copying could have the benefit of the computer program, even though they obtained that benefit as a result of the skill and labour of the author of the original source code underlying the object code in question. In the absence of any protection for source code and object code, the skill and labour of the computer programmer could be exploited without any infringement having taken place. It was this conundrum which legislators had to resolve in protecting computer programs.

The World Intellectual Property Organization (WIPO) suggested that computer programs should be protected by way of a new separate category or a *sui generis* right. Subsequently, however, mainly as a result of developments in the United States (the Computer Software Copyright Act 1980), the international community, including the European Commission, decided to protect computer programs by categorising them as literary works so that they could avail of copyright protection.

16.2 International treaty law

Article 10(1) of the TRIPs Agreement obliges Member States of the World Trade Organization to protect computer programs as literary works under the Berne Convention.

Furthermore, the WIPO Copyright Treaty (agreed in Geneva in December 1996) states that computer programs should be protected as literary works. Article 4 of the Treaty states as follows:

> 'Computer programs are protected as literary works within the meaning of Article 2 of the Berne Convention. Such protection applies to computer programs whatever may be the mode or form of their expression.'

16.2.1 Developments at EU level

After intense debate, the Software Directive (Council Directive No. 91/250/EEC of 14 May 1991 on the legal protection of computer programs) was adopted.

16.2.2 Implementation of the Software Directive in Ireland

The Software Directive was initially implemented in Ireland by way of statutory instrument (SI 26/1993). This statutory instrument has been restated in the Copyright and Related Rights Act 2000.

As computer programs fall within the definition of 'literary works' a number of the provisions of the Copyright Act relate to computer programs, but ss 80–82 relate specifically to computer programs. These sections are included in chapter 6 of the Act, under the heading 'Acts permitted in relation to works protected by copyright.' In addition to the general provisions relating to the protection of literary works, there are specific provisions regarding computer programs set out in this section of the Act dealing with exceptions to copyright protection.

16.3 Definition of computer program

Section 2(1) of the Copyright and Related Rights Act provides that 'computer program' means a program which is original in the sense that it is the author's own intellectual creation and includes any design materials used for the preparation of the program. The Directive did not, in fact, contain any definition of a computer program. It simply outlined some material regarded as being within the definition and it also made reference to the relevant originality standard.

In addition, literary work is defined in Section 2 of the Act as including a computer program.

16.4 Protection

Section 17(2) of the Act states that copyright subsists in original literary works. It is this section which confers copyright protection on computer programs.

Given the definition of computer program in s 2(1) of the Act as an *original* program which is the *author's own intellectual creation*, it is arguable that the originality test for literary works which is generally considered to be a very low test (it simply means the work must not be copied) is somewhat raised in relation to computer programs. This is something which was required by Article 1(3) of the Software Directive, which states that the work must be the author's own intellectual creation. The requirement to have a uniform level of originality for the granting of copyright protection throughout the European Union caused considerable difficulty when the Software Directive was being considered.

Section 17(3) of the Act, which states that copyright protection shall not extend to the ideas and principles which underlie any element of a work, is particularly important in the context of computer programs. Although the idea/expression dichotomy is a general principle of copyright law, this distinction was specifically required by Article 1(2) of the Directive.

16.5 Authorship and ownership

The provisions of ss 21–23 of the Copyright and Related Rights Act 2000 deal with authorship and ownership. These provisions also apply to computer programs.

In practice, one issue which always arises is the ownership of software which has been developed by a software developer or a specialised firm of software developers on behalf of a business. The general rule is that the author of the work is the first owner of the copyright. Where software is developed by employees of the software development firm, then the rule is that the employer owns the copyright in the software. However, it is very important to note that this will not change the position vis-à-vis the party who has commissioned the software to be developed as in either case the party who has commissioned the work will not be the owner of the copyright in the software. If the business wishes to take ownership of the software, then this **must** be agreed in writing.

It is also very common in the software industry for developers to work on a contract basis for software firms. In such cases, it is critical to know that the rule relating to employees and employers will not apply and a specific clause in the contract of the independent contractor relating to ownership of intellectual property rights will be necessary. In most cases, a contract between the person hiring the contractor and the contractor will state that any intellectual property created by the contractor in the course of his work under the contract in question will be owned by the person who has contracted his services.

Whether acting for a software company in entering into a licence agreement (in the context of reviewing what warranties can be given in relation to ownership) or whether carrying out a due diligence on behalf of a client intending to purchase a company whose main assets are intellectual property based, it is essential to enquire as to which parties were involved in the creation of the intellectual property work(s) in question. This applies to all classes of intellectual property work but is particularly relevant in the case of software, as one regularly finds that a number of parties of varying status might have worked together on a software development project and this could create complications in respect of authorship and, as a result, ownership of the software in question.

On a related note regarding employees, the 2000 Act states that if a work is created by an employee in the course of his employment by his employer, then copyright in the work will be owned by the employer unless there is an agreement in writing to the contrary. It is important therefore to check all employment contracts and other agreements which may exist between employee and employer to see whether anything has been agreed to the contrary in writing.

In practice, companies regularly pay software developers to develop software on their behalf without first having agreed that the company which has commissioned the work should own the copyright in the work. Situations where this happens range from the development of websites to the development of a company's core software. Generally people assume that once they have paid for something, they own it. This is not the case in relation to copyright unless specifically agreed in writing.

In practice, it is common for a software developer to retain ownership of the copyright in the core computer program which they develop, and then to license this on a non-exclusive basis. This leaves the software developer free to license its core software to other parties. In the event that a party has contracted a software developer to develop bespoke software for their specific needs, then the copyright in this bespoke software would usually be assigned to the client or the client would be given a sole or exclusive licence, or a licence in perpetuity in respect of it. In certain cases where the software to be developed is of such a specialised and specific nature, the software developer might have no difficulty in assigning the copyright in it to the third party who has commissioned it, as it may have no commercial value in terms of being licensed to other parties.

In cases where parties to a software development contract fail to address the issue of copyright ownership in advance of the completion of the project and the party who has commissioned the work pays a fee for the development work, it may be possible, if acting for this party, to rely on equitable concepts such as implied contract and constructive trusts in relation to the ownership of copyright in any resulting computer program. Essentially, the person who commissioned the computer program could argue that although based on s 23 of the Act, the author is the legal owner of the copyright, the party who commissioned and paid for the work at the very least would have an implied licence to use the work and may in fact be the beneficial owner of same. (*Robin Ray v Classic FM* [1998] FSR 622 and contrast *Clearsprings Management Ltd v Businesslinx Ltd* [2006] FSR 3. See also Laurence *Wrenn, Integrated Multi-Media Solution Ltd v Stephen Landamore* [2007] EWHC 1833 (Ch), 23 July 2007).

16.6 Restricted acts

Section 37(1) of the Copyright and Related Rights Act sets out the acts which are restricted by copyright in a work ie, the acts which the right holder has the exclusive right to do or to authorise others to do. These acts are as follows:

(a) to copy the work;

(b) to make available to the public the work;

(c) to make an adaptation of the work or to undertake any of the acts referred to in (a) or (b) in relation to an adaptation.

These rights are addressed in further detail in:

- s 39 – the reproduction right;
- s 40 – the making available right;
- s 41 – the distribution right; and
- s 42 – the rental and lending right;
- s 43 – adaptations.

Section 37(2) makes it clear that a person who, without the licence of the copyright owner, undertakes or authorises another to undertake any of the restricted acts, infringes copyright in a work.

16.6.1 The reproduction right

Section 39(1)(a) of the Act says that copying includes storing the work in *any medium* and making copies of the work, which are *transient* or *incidental* to some other use of the work.

Given this very broad definition of the term 'copying', almost any use of a computer program will constitute copying. Therefore even if a backup copy of a computer program is made or a computer program is incidentally cached on the hard drive of a computer without the knowledge of the computer user, this will constitute copying. In the event that this is done without the licence or authorisation of the copyright owner this will constitute an infringement. However, there are exceptions to this very broad definition (see ss 80, 82 and 87).

16.6.2 Distribution of computer programs

The right to make available to the public copies of a work is commonly known as the 'making available right.' This right is set out in s 40 of the Act and it applies *inter alia* to literary works. This section would apply where the copyright owner of a computer program distributes the program over the internet.

The distribution of tangible copies of computer programs is covered by the distribution right in s 41 of the Act.

16.6.3 Making an adaptation

The making of an adaptation of a work is also a restricted act. Section 43(2) of the Act states that in relation to a computer program, adaptation includes the translation, arrangement or other alteration of the computer program and in particular it includes the making of a version of the computer program in which it is converted into or out of a computer language or code or into a different computer language or code.

16.7 Exceptions to restricted acts

Since practically any use of a computer program could amount to a restricted act, there are numerous exceptions, as follows:

16.7.1 Backup copies

Section 80 of the 2000 Act states that it is not an infringement of the copyright in a computer program for a lawful (ie a party who is licensed by or on behalf of the copyright owner) user of a computer program to make a backup copy of it, which is necessary for him or her to have for the purpose of his or her lawful use.

Section 80(2) states that the person is a 'lawful user' of a computer program where he or she has a right to use the program to undertake any act restricted by copyright.

16.7.2 Decompilation right

Section 81(1) of the Act states that it is not an infringement of the copyright in the computer program for a lawful user to make a copy, translation, adaptation, arrangement or any other alteration to the computer program in order to achieve interoperability with that program of an independently created computer program. This provision, which is based on Article 6 of the Software Directive, is intended to allow reverse engineering of a computer program created/written by a rightholder in order to produce an interoperable program. This exception is subject to three conditions being complied with. These are as follows:

(a) the acts are performed by the lawful user or on his or her behalf by a person authorised to do so;

(b) the information necessary to achieve interoperability has not previously been available to the person who carries out the acts; and

(c) the permitted acts are confined to the parts of the original program which are necessary to achieve interoperability.

Section 81(2) goes on to say that s 81(1) of that section does not permit the information obtained through its application to be used other than to achieve interoperability of an independently created computer program, and it also expressly states that it does not permit the information obtained to be used for the development, production or marketing of a computer program substantially similar in its expression, or for any other act which infringes copyright.

The reason this exception is necessary is that computer programs do not work in isolation. They function with other hardware and software. If programs could not interact with other programs and hardware, their usefulness would be greatly hampered.

16.7.3 Incidental acts

Section 82 of the Act states that it is not an infringement of the copyright in a computer program for a lawful user to make a copy of a whole or part of the program or to translate, adapt or arrange the program where such actions are necessary for the use of the program by the lawful user in accordance with its intended use.

The purpose of this section is to ensure that the lawful user is entitled to carry out certain activities related to the work and in particular that the technical copying, translation and adaptation which may occur incidentally in the use of the computer program do not constitute an infringement.

Section 82(2) states that it is not an infringement of the copyright in the computer program for a lawful user to observe, test or study the functioning of the program in order to determine the ideas and principles which lie behind any element of the program provided that he or she does so while performing the acts of loading, displaying, running, transmitting or storing the program which he or she is authorised to do.

Section 87 of the Act limits the very broad definition of copying set out in s 39 of the Act. Section 87 is directed at ensuring that transient and incidental copies which are technically required for the viewing of or listening to the work by persons to whom the work has been made lawfully available (ie a lawful user) does not constitute an infringement. This is directed at ensuring, for example, that the caching of a computer program or the caching of a literary work in electronic form on the hard drive of a computer does not constitute an infringement of copyright

16.8 Databases

In considering the legal issues arising in the context of the protection of databases it is necessary to distinguish between original databases, which can avail of copyright protection, and databases which represent the creation of a mechanical collection or arrangement of facts or information and in which there has been no exercise of skill or judgment. The latter form of database, while not qualifying for copyright protection, can be protected by a new right, which was introduced in the 2000 Act, known as the Database Right.

The database right is a *sui generis*, that is, a separate and distinct right relating specifically to databases. Part V of the Act, which deals with the database right implements this *sui generis* right, first introduced by Council Directive 96/9 on the legal protection of databases. The purpose of that Directive was to ensure uniform protection for databases throughout Member States.

16.8.1 Original database

'Original database' is defined in s 2 of the Copyright and Related Rights Act 2000 as:

> 'a database in any form which by reason of the selection or arrangement of its contents constitutes the original intellectual creation of author.'

Whether or not copyright subsists in the contents of the database is irrelevant. Section 17(3) of the Act states that copyright protection shall not, in respect of original databases, extend to their contents and is without prejudice to any rights subsisting in those contents.

Databases which usually qualify for copyright protection are databases which are in the nature of compilations. By way of example, in the case of *Football League Ltd v Littlewood Pools Ltd* [1950] CH 637 Upjohn J considered that considerable skill and judgement was applied. In this case the issue was whether or not a compilation, which consisted of a list of football fixtures, constituted a literary work.

Many of the cases relating to compilations of works and whether or not they constitute literary works deal with issues that are relevant to ascertaining whether a database constitutes an original database and therefore qualifies for copyright protection.

If a database can satisfy the test of the author's original intellectual creation, then it can benefit from copyright protection and it is protected for a period of the life of the author plus 70 years.

16.8.2 'Non-original' databases

Part V of the Act deals with database rights. Where a database does not qualify as an original database, then a lesser form of protection is provided for such 'non original' databases, referred to in the Act simply as 'databases'.

A database is defined in s 2 of the Act as being:

> 'a collection of independent works, data or other materials, arranged in a systematic or methodical way and individually accessible by any means but excludes computer programs used in the making or operation of a database.'

The Database Directive contains a similar definition and in commenting on this part of the Directive, Laddie J has stated:

> 'to be independent, the works, data, or other materials should be capable of being, or intended to be appreciated or useful in isolation. This would not include individual chapters in a literary work or scenes in a dramatic work.'

16.8.3 Qualifying for protection

The database right covers electronic and non-electronic arrangements, and in order to qualify for database protection the works must be systematically or methodically organised. By way of example, arrangement of the works in an alphabetic or chronological manner would be sufficient to satisfy this requirement.

In addition to the requirement that the work must be systematically or methodically organised, in order to qualify for protection, substantial investment must have been made in the creation of the database. Section 321 provides that where substantial investment has been incurred in obtaining, verifying, or presenting the contents of the database then the *sui generis* right shall exist. Investment of resources as referred to in the Act means *'financial, human or technical resources'* and the reference to substantial means *'quantity or quality or a combination of both.'*

Where a copyright work is included in a database, copyright shall continue to subsist in that work as well as a separate database right subsisting in the database. It is not material whether the database or its contents are capable of being protected by copyright, as the purpose of the database right is to protect the investment and the effort which has been undertaken to create the database.

16.8.4 Acts restricted by the database rights

The owner of a database right has the right to undertake or to authorise others to undertake the following acts in relation to all or a substantial part of the contents of the database:

(a) extraction,
(b) re-utilisation.

The database right is infringed by a person who without the licence of the owner of the Database Right undertakes or authorises another to undertake either of these restricted acts.

Extraction is defined in s 320(1) of the Act in the same terms as in the Database Directive as:

'the permanent or temporary transfer of all or a substantial part of the contents to another medium by any means or any form.'

Re-utilisation is defined in s 320(1) of the Act as:

'in relation to the contents of a database making those contents available to the public by any means.'

There is no definition of 'substantial' in the Act. However, s 324(3) states that for the purposes of this part of the Act, the repeated and systematic extraction or re-utilisation of insubstantial parts of the contents of a database which conflicts with the normal exploitation of a database or which prejudices the interests of the maker of the database shall be deemed to be extraction or re-utilisation of a substantial part of the contents.

In other words a one off action by itself in relation to an insubstantial part of the database will not constitute an infringement of the Database Right, however, if carried out repeatedly, it will be contrary to s 324 and will constitute an infringement.

16.8.5 Term of protection of database right

The Database Right expires 15 years from the end of the calendar year in which the making of the Database was completed.

However, any substantial change to the contents of the database including a substantial change resulting from the accumulation of successive additions, deletions or alterations, which would result in the database being considered to be a substantial new investment, shall qualify the database resulting from that investment for its own terms of protection. Accordingly, a database which is continually updated could have the benefit of protection under this new Database Right indefinitely.

To date, there has only been one significant case relating to the interpretation of the Database Directive. This case is the *British Horseracing Board Ltd and others v William Hill Organisation Ltd*. Mr Justice Laddie gave the first judgment in this matter on 9 February 2001. The final Court of Appeal decision was handed down on 13 July 2005. The case was concerned with the extent to which the plaintiffs could prevent the defendant from using, without their licence, certain data (the Jockey Club racing fixtures list, details of registered horses, owners and colours, handicap ratings etc) which, according to the plaintiff, had been derived indirectly from them.

Initially, the plaintiff partly succeeded. William Hill argued that the indirect capture of data (ie, through a third party) from a database was not an extraction as it merely replicated the data. This argument was rejected. It was also argued that in the case of the database that was consistently updated, repeated and systematic taking of minor data could not be considered to be cumulative and therefore could not be considered to be an infringement, as the data was taken from different databases. This argument was also rejected.

The case was appealed and the Court of Appeal referred a number of questions to the European Court of Justice (ECJ). The ECJ answered the questions posed to it and the matter returned to the Court of Appeal which changed its initial view of the interpretation of the Database Right as a result.

The Court found that the expression 'investment in ... the obtaining ... of the contents' of a database must, as William Hill had argued, be understood to refer to the resources used to seek out existing independent materials and collect them in the database. It did not refer to the resources used for the creation of independent materials.

The purpose of the protection of the *sui generis* right provided for by the directive is to promote the establishment of storage and processing systems for existing information and not the creation of materials capable of being collected subsequently in a database.

The Court of Appeal found that resources used for creating, which includes checking, the lists of entries, were not used in obtaining or verifying the contents of the data base within the meaning of Article 7.

On that approach, 'the resources used to draw up a list of horses in a race and to carry out checks in that connection do not represent investment in the obtaining and verification of the contents of the database in which that list appears.'

Thus the database right had not been infringed by William Hill.

There is widespread concern that the database right is not functioning as intended. It is complicated and confusing and it is anticipated that the area will be revised in reasonably early course.

16.9 Conclusion

In considering any issues from a practical perspective which arise in relation to computer programs or databases, the most important points to address are the following:

- What form of protection is available for the work in question?
- What is the duration of the protection afforded?
- Are all aspects of the work protected?
- Who created the work?
- Who owns the rights in the work?
- Apart from copyright or database right protection, could any other forms of IP protect the work?
- How best should the work be exploited?
- In considering whether an infringement has taken place, consider what are the restricted acts which are applicable to each type of work.
- In the case of infringement do any of the exemptions apply?

Armed with these questions, and now with the information and knowledge to answer them, hopefully a practitioner can avoid any of the pitfalls which await when one is advising clients in relation to computer programs and databases, often the most important asset the client has in its business.

CHAPTER 17

LIFE SCIENCES

Colin Sainsbury

17.1 Introduction

17.1.1 Importance of life sciences sector

The importance of the life sciences sector to the Irish economy cannot be over estimated. Ireland has in excess of 170 life sciences companies employing 35,000 people in the life sciences sector. In 2005, the Irish pharmaceutical sector exported products valued at over €40 billion. Sixteen of the world's top twenty pharmaceutical companies have substantial operations in Ireland with many of these companies increasingly conducting significant research and development in Ireland. The last number of years has also seen a significant increase in the activities of indigenous Irish life sciences companies and an expansion in the technology transfer activities of Irish universities.

The life sciences umbrella covers the pharmaceutical, chemical, biopharmaceuticals, medical device and diagnostic sectors. Although the application of biotechnology extends beyond the life sciences sector, for example in the food and plant sectors, this chapter focuses on the life sciences sector.

The importance of intellectual property rights in the life sciences sector also gives rise to significant policy issues such as the interplay between the enforcement of intellectual property rights and competition law and the export of generic medicines to poorer countries.

The life sciences sector depends heavily on patent protection. Developing a new chemical entity may take a number of years and cost several hundred millions of euro. The purpose of this chapter is to identify those provisions of intellectual property law which have particular application to the life sciences sector such as compulsory licensing, supplementary protection certificates and the use of human tissue in medical research and treatment. This chapter also analyses the interplay between intellectual property with both regulatory law and competition law.

17.2 Patents

17.2.1 Irish patent legislation

This section identifies those provisions of Irish patent law which have particular application to the life sciences sector.

17.2.1.1 *Medical treatment*

Under the Patents Act 1992 (PA 1992), the patentability of methods for the treatment of the human or animal body by surgery or therapy and a diagnostic method practised on the human or animal body was regulated by PA 1992, s 9(4) (Patentable Inventions). Pursuant to amendments made by the Patents (Amendment) Act 2006 (the 2006 Act), patentability or otherwise is to be regulated by PA 1992, s 10 as amended by the 2006 Act (Exceptions to Patentability).[1] Under PA 1992, s 10(1) (as amended by the 2006 Act) 'a patent shall not be granted in respect of...... (c) a method for treatment of the human or animal body by surgery or therapy and a diagnostic method practised on the human or animal body.'

The second sentence of PA 1992, s 9(4) is to be rewritten by the 2006 Act as PA 1992, s 10(2) which provides as follows:

> 'Sub-section (1) (c) shall not apply to products, in particular substances or compositions, for use in any such method.'

Section 10(1)(c), like its predecessor PA 1992, s 9(4) is based on Article 52(4) of the European Patent Convention (EPC) to which Ireland has been a party since August 1992. The reason for the exclusion of patenting claims in relation to the medical treatment of a human or animal is that a medical practitioner should not be restricted by patent law from treating a patient, that is, to prevent the practice of medicine from being hampered by the existence of a patent.

Under PA 1992, s 11(4),[2] the use of a known substance or composition in such a 'method for treatment' is deemed to meet the novelty requirements for patentability, provided that its use in any such method is novel. This means that the development of medicine for a therapeutic treatment may be patentable, even though the treatment itself is not patentable. Consequently, a patent may be obtained for a substance or composition which is already known but has no known pharmacological activity. This type of patent (also described as a 'first medical use' patent) makes a claim to the effect that the substance or composition is for use as a medicament.

In addition, it is also possible to make what are called second medical use claims (also known as 'Swiss form' claims) where a claim is made for a previously known substance or composition for the manufacture of a medicament for a new and inventive therapeutic application, where the novelty might only lie in a new indication and/or in the dose to be used or in the manner of its application. A Swiss form claim is normally in the following format 'use of substance X for the manufacture of a medicament for the treatment of disease Y.'

The non-statutory basis for 'Swiss form claims' had long troubled many in the pharmaceutical industry and had been criticised by a number of national courts including those in the United Kingdom. The Swiss form claim has been the subject of a number of cases before the Board of Appeal of the European Patent Office (EPO). The Board of Appeal has made determinations which are inconsistent with court decisions of certain member countries, including the English Court of Appeal. In addition, there are certain inherent weaknesses associated with Swiss form claims, for example, 'off-label' prescribing where a medical practitioner prescribes a competitor's pharmaceutical product for the patented use, even though the competitor's product is not approved for that use.

The European Patent Convention 2000 (EPC 2000) is due to come into force in December 2007. Article 54(5) of the EPC 2000 will permit 'further medical use' patents of a known substance or composition using a straightforward claim, rather than the Swiss-claim format in current usage. This is to be implemented in Ireland by new PA 1992, s 11(5) inserted by the 2006 Act which recognises the novelty of a substance or composition 'for any specific use' in a method of treatment or diagnosis provided that such specific use is not already known. However, the Swiss-type claim will still be allowable.

[1.] At the time of writing, this amendment has not yet come into operation.
[2.] To be rewritten by the 2006 Act without apparent change in substance.

17.2.1.2 *Exceptions to patentability*

Section 10(1)(a) of PA 1992 (as slightly amended by the 2006 Act[3] to comply with Article 27.2 of the TRIPs Agreement and Article 53(a) of the EPC 2000) provides that a patent shall not be granted in respect of '(a) an invention the commercial exploitation of which would be contrary to public order or morality, provided that the exploitation shall not be deemed to be so contrary only because it is prohibited by law.' The other two categories of exemptions relate to (b) a plant or animal variety or an essentially biological process for the production of plants or animals other than a micro-biological process or the products thereof; and (c) medical or diagnostic methods as referred at para **17.2.1.1** above.

Biotechnological Inventions

In 1998, EU Directive 98/44/EC (the 1998 Directive) on the legal protection of biotechnological inventions was adopted. The 1998 Directive was implemented into Irish Law by European Communities (Legal Protection of Biotechnological Inventions) Regulations, 2000 (SI 247/2000). The Regulations set out a non-exclusive list of biotechnological inventions which are considered patentable and non-patentable. Under Reg 5(1), the human body and the simple discovery of one of its elements, including the sequence or partial sequence of a gene, is not patentable. However, an element isolated from the human body, or otherwise produced by means of a technical process, including the sequence or partial sequence of a gene, may constitute a patentable invention, even if the structure of that element is identical to that of a natural element.

Regulation 6(1) states that:

> 'A patent shall not be granted in respect of a biotechnological invention the commercial exploitation of which would be contrary to public order or morality, provided that the exploitation shall not be deemed to be so contrary only because it is prohibited by law.'

Regulation 6(2) states that the following shall not be regarded as a patentable invention on the basis of reg 6(1) (ie as being contrary to public order or morality):

'(a) a process for cloning human beings,

(b) a process for modifying the germ line genetic identity of human beings,

(c) the use of human embryos for industrial or commercial purposes,

(d) a process for modifying the genetic identity of animals which is likely to cause them suffering without any substantial medical benefit to man or animal, and animals resulting from such a process.'

Human tissue and stem cells

There is also an issue in relation to the patenting of an article or material of human origin and the necessity of obtaining consent from a person from whom body material has been taken. If consent is not obtained then there are likely to be question marks over the ownership of the results of the use made of donated human body material such as human tissue.

Recital 42 of the 1998 Directive provides an exception to the exclusion of patenting uses of human embryos for industrial or commercial purposes but this does not prevent the grant of patents for 'inventions for therapeutic or diagnostic purposes which are applied to the human embryo and are useful to it.'

In 2006, the Board of Appeal of the European Patent Office reviewed that patentability of inventions involving human embryonic stem cells. In Case G2/06 the President of the European Patent Office made comments in a case relating to the patentability of stem cells

---

[3.] Not yet in operation at the time of writing.

and other research that used human embryos. The President noted that the legislative intent of the EPC is to limit uses of human embryos to inventions which could at some point benefit the used embryo itself, thereby excluding anything in which the practice of the invention necessarily resulted in the death of the embryo. The interests of humans who might benefit from such an invention are not taken into account.

There appears to be a continuing reluctance by the EPO to grant patents in relation to human embryonic stem cell culture technology. As such, those engaging in stem cell research may consider the fact that patent protection may be unlikely. In the light of advances in biotechnology concerning the uses of human tissue, there are likely to be further changes in Irish and EU law. Indeed in April 2007 the European Parliament approved a new regulatory regime to permit the approval of medicines based on genes, stem cells and tissue engineering with the proviso for opt out by member countries on moral grounds.

17.2.1.3 *Compulsory licences*

The 2006 Act has made a number of amendments to the provisions of ss 70–75 of PA 1992 which regulated compulsory licences. The purpose of these amendments is to comply with Articles 27.1 and 31 of the WTO Agreement on Trade-Related Intellectual Property Rights (TRIPs) of December 1994.

Section 70(3)(f) of PA 1992 contained specific provision regarding inventions relating to food or medicine. In the context of settling the terms of any licence granted in respect of a patent which relates to food or medicine, the Controller was obliged to endeavour to secure that food and medicine should be made available to the public at the lowest prices consistent with the proprietor of a patent deriving reasonable remuneration having regard to the nature of the invention. This provision was considered to be inconsistent with Article 27.1 of the TRIPs Agreement (which provides that patents shall be available and patent rights enjoyable without discrimination as to the field of technology).

A compulsory licence may not be granted under s 70(1) (as amended by PA 2006) if the demand for a product covered by the patent is met by importation from a World Trade Organisation (WTO) member country. The amended provision also provides that the grant of a compulsory licence should be 'predominantly for the supply of the domestic market' (PA 1992, s 70 (3)(ii)).

Regulation (EC) 816/2006 was adopted on 17 May 2006 and provides for the compulsory licensing of patents in relation to the manufacture of pharmaceutical products for export to countries with public health problems. The Regulation came into force on 29 June 2006 and applies to any pharmaceutical products (including medicinal products for human use, active ingredients and certain diagnostic kits). The Regulation contains provisions which must be complied with by applicants for compulsory licences and determines the nature and extent of a compulsory licence which may be granted. Such a compulsory licence must be limited to the manufacture and export of specified quantities of the named product to meet the needs of the importing country. There are also detailed provisions with regard to the marking of such products. The Regulation prohibits the re-importation of such products into the EU.

The Regulation (which is based upon a WTO decision of August 2003) goes further than the previous compulsory licence provisions referenced above which sanctioned the use of compulsory licences in order to encourage supply on the domestic market. The purpose of the Regulation is to provide access to essential medicines for those countries most in need.

17.2.1.4 *Supplementary Protection Certificates*

With effect from January 1993, Supplementary Protection Certificates (SPCs) were introduced on an EU wide basis for medicinal products for both human and veterinary use. Council Regulation 1768/92 EEC (the 1992 Regulation) was designed to ensure harmonisation of the rules for patent term extensions across Europe and to encourage research and development in Europe for the development of pharmaceuticals. Given the time taken to develop many pharmaceutical products, it was considered that the 20 year protection period provided by patent law was not sufficient to provide a return to a patentee who had conducted extensive research, including extensive clinical trials. The 1992 Regulation constituted a compromise between the objectives of the EU innovative pharmaceutical industry and the European generics industry.

An SPC does not extend the term of a patent as such but rather provides an extra period of protection for the active ingredient(s) of a medicinal product which is covered by a patent and is also the subject of a marketing authorisation.

17.2.1.4.1 *Medicinal product*

In order to obtain an SPC, the product must be covered by a 'basic patent' which protects the product itself, a process to manufacture the product, or a particular application of the product. The product in question must constitute a 'medicinal product' which contains 'the active ingredient' or a 'combination of active ingredients of a medicinal product.'

There has been a significant amount of case law before the European Court of Justice (ECJ) with regard to what is meant by an active ingredient or a combination of active ingredients of medicinal products. The phrase 'combination of active ingredients of a medicinal product' was narrowly interpreted by the European Court of Justice in a 2006 ruling in the case of Massachusetts Institute of Technology (MIT) (Case C-431/04). In the MIT case the inactive excipient assisted in the overall activity of the medicinal product by ensuring the controlled release of the active ingredient. The ECJ refused the grant of an SPC for the combination of an active ingredient with a pharmaceutically non-active ingredient. Commentators have concluded that this judgment virtually rules out the possibility of obtaining SPCs for new formulations of active and non-active ingredients and may discourage pharmaceutical companies from conducting researching into combination products. Regulatory exclusivity for such a product may still be possible.

17.2.1.4.2 *Requirements to obtain an SPC*

Whether or not a product is protected by a basic patent is to be determined by the applicable national rules which govern the scope of the protection of the relevant patent. In addition, the product must have been granted a valid marketing authorisation in the applicable member state and the product must not already have been the subject of an SPC in that member state. An SPC does not extend the duration of a patent itself, but only the protection for the specific part which is subject to a market authorisation. If two or more patents protect a product and these are held by different owners, then it may be possible to obtain an SPC for each patent for the same product.

Complex rules apply where a number of patents cover the same medicinal product at the time of the application. The application for an SPC must be filed in each member state within six months from the later of (a) the granting of the first marketing authorisation in that member state and (b) the grant of the relevant basic patent in that member state. The patent offices of certain member states may exercise a discretion to accept late filed applications under certain circumstances.[4] The provisions regulating the application for an

---

[4]. See the decision of the UK Patent Office in *Abbott Laboratories' SPC Application* [2004] RPC 20 which allowed an extension where the deadline for lodging the application had been missed owing to unforeseen circumstances. Other jurisdictions where extensions have been allowed were identified in the decision.

SPC in Ireland are contained in European Communities (Supplementary Protection Certificate) Regulations, 1993 (SI 125/1993).

17.2.1.4.3 *Duration of an SPC*

The duration of an SPC depends on the time that has elapsed between the filing of the patent application and the granting of the first marketing authorisation in the European Economic Area. At a maximum, an SPC can last for the lesser of (a) up to 15 years from the date the marketing authorisation was first granted, or (b) five years from the date the applicable patent expires. There is provision for a six month extension of an SPC for paediatric products (see para **17.4.2.5**).

If the basic patent does not cover derivatives of an active ingredient (such as salts and esters), then the SPC grant for the patent also excludes the derivatives. This is a complex issue that requires careful consideration on a case by case basis.

17.2.1.4.4 *EU competition law*

The significant intersection between the enforcement of intellectual property rights and European Competition Law can be seen from a decision of the European Commission in June 2005 when it fined Astro Zeneca €60 million for breaching Article 82 of the EC Treaty for allegedly providing misleading information to national patent offices with regard to the incorrect date of a first marketing authorisation in relation to Losec®. An appeal against this decision is currently pending before the Court of First Instance.

17.2.1.4.5 *Generic medicines*

The amendment to PA 1992, s 42 (Research exemption) by the 2006 Act is considered under para **17.4** (Regulatory procedures).

17.3 Trade marks

17.3.1 Selection of trade mark

The selection of a trade mark for pharmaceutical products is the subject of a considerable regulatory procedures and legislation. For products which are approved through the centralised procedure (as described at para **17.4.1** below) a single name is generally required throughout the European Union. The proposed trade mark is considered by a name review group within the EMEA which reviews applications from the perspective of safety and public health.

The Guidelines, on the acceptability of names for human medicinal products processed through the centralised procedure were adopted in April 2005 and were most recently updated in February 2007 (www.emea.europa.eu). The Guidelines contain detailed provisions with regard to whether the invented name proposed for a medicinal product could create a public health concern or potential safety risk. However, the Guidelines expressly state that the EMEA will not take into account whether or not the proposed invented name will or may constitute an infringement of another entity's intellectual property rights.

17.3.2 Free movement and parallel trade

The Trade Marks Act 1996 implemented Council Directive 89/104/EC (also known as the Trade Mark Harmonisation Directive). There has been a significant volume of case law regarding the balance to be struck between the legitimate interests of (a) the trade mark owner in protecting the reputation of its trade mark and (b) a reseller being able to resell goods which have been lawfully placed on the market in an EU country. The conflicting objectives of EU Treaty principles of Article 28 (Freedom of Movement of Goods) and Article 30 (the exercise of intellectual property rights) have been clearly demonstrated in the case law concerning parallel trade in pharmaceuticals and the compatibility of imposing limitations on parallel trade with EC competition law with regard to supply quota systems and dual pricing. A detailed analysis of the various ECJ and national court decisions with regard to repackaging and relabelling is outside the scope of this chapter.

Although parallel trade applies across a broad range of sectors, the pharmaceutical market is unique in that the pricing for medicinal products is to a very significant degree controlled and established by national authorities. As such, the price at which pharmaceutical products are sold in a member state will generally not be set by the pharmaceutical company thereby creating the opportunity for parallel importers to obtain and export products from lower price countries (such as Greece and Portugal) to higher price countries (such as Ireland).

Pharmaceutical companies have adopted a range of strategies to deal with the issue of parallel trade including supply quota systems and dual pricing structures. An evaluation of the permissibility of such strategies has been the subject of a number of decisions of the ECJ. The decisions by the ECJ highlight the significant overlap as between the enforcement of intellectual property rights and EC Competition Law (a detailed analysis of which is outside the scope of this chapter).

17.3.2.1 *Case law*

In addition, there has also been extensive litigation in various member states and before the ECJ with regard to the relabelling and repackaging of medicinal products. Repackaging is particularly a phenomenon in the pharmaceutical industry given the fact that the member states may have different requirements with regard to product information leaflets and package sizes.

The general principle is that a trade mark owner cannot stop an imported product, even where it has been repackaged, if stopping import would contribute to the artificial partitioning of the market between member states.

In certain circumstances, the parallel importer may be entitled to modify the original packaging if the product could not be otherwise imported. The ECJ has provided guidelines in a number of cases including the 1996 case of *Bristol Myers Squibb v Paranova* (Case C-427/93) which gave rise to what are known as the 'BMS conditions' or the 'Paranova Conditions'. The parallel importer must establish (i) that it is necessary to repackage the product in order to market in the applicable country, (ii) that the new packaging does not adversely affect the original condition of the product, (iii) that the new packaging states by whom the product has been repackaged, (iv) the new packaging must not damage the reputation of the trade mark or the owner of the trade mark, and (v) the trade mark owner must receive prior notice before the repackaged product is put on sale. The importer is not entitled to repackage where the importer is simply endeavouring to secure a commercial advantage.

In April 2007, the ECJ issued the decision in the case of *Boehringer Ingelheim v Swingward* (Case C-348/04) in relation to the repackaging of pharmaceuticals products by parallel importers. An opinion had been given by the advocate-general, Eleanor Sharpston in April 2006. This opinion has been considered by commentators to be in favour of the parallel importer rather than the pharmaceutical trade mark owner. Essentially, the advocate-general came to the conclusion that the previous case law of the European Court of Justice in relation to repackaging did not apply to 'overstickered' packs.

In this decision, the ECJ provides for more detailed guidance as to what forms of 'repackaging' or 'overstickering' are acceptable. The recent decision of the ECJ has clarified the application of the 'BMS Conditions'. It is now clear that the BMS Conditions apply not only where there has been repackaging but also where there has been the attachment of a label to the original packaging ('over stickering'). The precise interpretation of the BMS Conditions will be a matter for national courts to determine. The ECJ held that in the main the burden of proof in relation to compliance or otherwise with the BMS Conditions rest with the parallel importers.

17.3.3 Counterfeiting

According to statistics published by the World Health Organisation (WHO), in excess of 10% of the global market for medicines is made up of counterfeit product. Directive 2004/48/EC currently regulates the measures, procedures and remedies which can be ordered by the courts of member states in case of intellectual property infringements. This Directive was implemented into Irish law by European Communities (Enforcement of Intellectual Property Rights) Regulations 2006 (SI 360/2006). A number of remedies are available to a court including injunctive relief and orders for recall, removal or destruction.

The European Commission has recently published a draft directive which, if implemented, would provide for criminal law penalties in connection with counterfeit products, with particular reference to circumstances in which there is a risk to personal health or safety. The European Communities will decide in 2008 whether to adopt more stringent regulations to tackle the sale of counterfeit medicines.

Pharmaceutical companies pursue many innovative mechanisms to trace and protect against counterfeiting including the incorporation of anti-counterfeiting procedures into pharmaceutical products.

17.4 EU regulatory law

17.4.1 Introduction

The interaction between the exercise of intellectual property rights and EU regulatory procedures has already been examined in relation to the limitations upon the applicant for a trade mark for a pharmaceutical product (para **17.3.1**). In considering the nature and extent of the relationship between Intellectual Property Rights in the life sciences sector and EU Medicines law, it is necessary to understand the landscape for the regulation of medicinal products. The approval and marketing of pharmaceuticals has been regulated at EU level since 1965. Medicinal products may be approved under the mutual recognition procedure or the centralised procedure. The centralised procedure is compulsory for certain categories of products, including biotechnology products and products containing new chemical entities for certain indications.

On 30 April 2004, new EU legislation was published which established a new legal framework for the approval of medicinal products as follows:

1. Regulation 726/2004 (which replaced a 1993 Regulation). This Regulation, which came into force in November 2005, sets out the centralised procedures for the authorisation and supervision of medicinal products for human and veterinary use and also established the European Medicines Agency (EMEA).
2. Directive 2004/27/EC (the 2004 Directive) which amended Directive 2001/83/EC (together the Directive) is also known as the Code for Human Medicines Directive. The Directive regulates the procedures by which medicinal products are authorised by national procedures (also known as the mutual recognition procedure).

The deadline for implementation of the 2004 Directive was 30 October 2005. The requisite regulations required to transpose the 2004 Directive into Irish law have been delayed.

Transitional arrangements were agreed between the Department of Health and Children and the Irish Medicines Board (IMB) in relation to the new requirements of the 2004 Directive. A guidance publication by the Irish Medicines Board in November 2005 sets out those provisions which were implemented as and from 30 October 2005 with other provisions being applied by current practice of the Irish Medicines Board. This guidance is available on the Human Medicines Section of the Irish Medicines Board website (www.imb.ie).

As stated on the IMB website, the Irish Government has sent the draft Irish regulations to implement the new medicines legislation to the EU Commission. The four draft regulations are subject to examination and comment by the EU Commission and other Member States until 6 June 2007.

While a detailed analysis of EU Medicines law is beyond the scope of this chapter, there are certain provisions which impact the nature and extent of Intellectual Property Rights from the perspective of the innovator company and also an applicant for generic approval of a medicinal product.

The relationship between regulatory procedures and intellectual property rights impacts a number of areas including the following:

- data exclusivity;
- market exclusivity for orphan medicines;
- additional data exclusivity for certain products for paediatric use;
- the regime for the approval of generic products (including biological and medicinal products) including the so called 'Bolar' exemption relating to the approval of generic products.

17.4.2 Data exclusivity

Data exclusivity may be contrasted with intellectual property protection (for example a composition of matter patent which provides patent protection in relation to an active ingredient). In order to market a pharmaceutical product, a company must seek approval for a marketing authorisation under the centralised procedure pursuant to reg 726/2004 (as referenced at para **17.1.4.1** above) or under the mutual recognition procedure (which will be fully implemented by the Medicinal Products (Control of Placing on the Market) Regulations (SI 540/2007) which came into force on 23 July 2007.

An applicant for a marketing authorisation is required to make a significant investment over a number of years by supplying significant data, including data arising from pre-clinical studies, clinical trials and information relating to the manufacture of the applicable product. In recognition of this investment, the applicant is granted a period of exclusivity during which other companies seeking to have the same product approved must generate their own data. The conduct of such activity is also subject to the nature and extent of the intellectual property rights of the innovator company.

Given the investment required to have a medicinal product approved, a generic company would not normally elect to generate its own scientific data but rather would 'piggy back' upon the data generated by the innovator pharmaceutical company which had sought and obtained the original marketing authorisation. Until October 2005, the data exclusivity period varied on a country by country basis throughout the EU from six to ten years for a product approved under the decentralised procedure; a medicinal product authorised under the centralised procedure benefited from a ten year period of exclusivity. The data protection periods provided for by the Directive do not apply to reference products for which an application for a marketing authorisation was submitted prior to 30 October 2005. As such, the new regime will not come fully into force until 2014. Under the new regime and once the transitional provisions have 'washed through', a harmonised data exclusivity period will apply regardless of whether the innovator product was the subject of the centralised procedure or the mutual recognition procedure.

Essentially, the EU Medicines legislation constitutes a compromise between the conflicting demands of the innovative pharmaceutical companies and the generics industry.

17.4.2.1 *8+2+1*

Under the new rules which came into force in October 2005, an application may now be made for the approval of a generic product after eight years following the approval of the reference product. However as a general rule, the generic product can only be marketed after ten years. Essentially after the eighth anniversary, the generic company can use the two year period to take the regulatory and commercial steps required to be in a position to launch a generic product on the tenth anniversary.

The two year period of market exclusivity may be further extended for a further one year period under certain circumstances, for example where a new therapeutic indication is approved, or where there has been a switch in the innovator's product from prescription to OTC (over the counter).

Under the new regime for both the centralised procedure and the mutual recognition procedure, the general rule is that an innovative company will have ten year protection against generic competition. For the first eight years of the ten year period the data (both non-clinical and clinical) that is contained in the dossier supporting the marketing authorisation cannot be referred to by other companies to obtain a marketing authorisation for another product (data exclusivity). For a further two year period, there is a prohibition on marketing of the product (marketing protection). In other words, a generic product cannot be placed on the market until ten years have elapsed from the initial authorisation of the referenced product (Article 10 of the Directive). The equivalent provision with regard to centralised products is contained in Article 14(11) of Regulation 726/2004.

17.4.2.2 *Additional 1 year new indication*

Article 10(1) of Directive 2004/27 provides for an additional one year's marketing protection if during the first eight years of protection the marketing authorisation holder obtains an authorisation for one or more new therapeutic indications which, during the scientific evaluation prior to their authorisation, are held to bring a significant clinical benefit in comparison with existing therapies. Regulation 726/2004 contains a similar provision with regard to products approved pursuant to the centralised procedure.

The EMEA has published draft guidelines with regard to what is meant by 'new therapeutic indication', 'significant clinical benefit' and 'existing therapies' (Draft Guideline of 16 December 2005 on the elements required to support the significant clinical benefit in comparison to existing therapies of a new therapeutic indication in order to benefit from an extended eleven year's marketing protection).

17.4.2.3 *Additional year – well established substances*

Article 10(5) of the Directive provides for an additional one year's period of data exclusivity for a new indication for a medicinal product where an application is made for a new indication for a well-established substance, provided that significant pre-clinical or clinical studies were carried out in relation to the new indication. The EMEA has published draft guidelines regarding what constitutes a new therapeutic indication and significant pre-clinical and clinical studies (Draft Guideline of 16 December 2005 on a new therapeutic indication for a well-established substance).

17.4.2.4 *Orphan medicines*

A ten year period of regulatory data exclusivity for 'orphan' medicines is provided for by Regulation No 141/2000. In order to obtain orphan designation, an applicant is required to establish that the medicine is intended for the diagnosis, prevention or treatment of a life-threatening, chronically or seriously debilitating condition and either affects no more than 5 in 10,000 persons in the EU when the application is made, or is unlikely without incentives to generate sufficient return if marketed in the EU.

In addition, the applicant must establish that there is no satisfactory method of diagnosis, prevention or treatment of the condition concerned that has been authorised in the EU or if such method exists, the medicine will be of significant benefit to those affected by that condition.

The period of ten year marketing exclusivity may under certain circumstances be reduced to six years.

17.4.2.5 *Paediatric use*

In 2006, the Council of Ministers and the European Parliament reached agreement on a proposed regulation on children's medicine which requires specific paediatric testing for drugs which are to be given to children in return for a potential six month extension of patent protection or additional market exclusivity, as well as a new type of marketing authorisation (Regulation 1901/2006 on medicinal products for paediatric use, as amended by Regulation 1902/2006) (the Paediatric Regulations). For products subject to a patent there is a potential six month extension of a supplementary patent certificate (SPC), and for non-patent medicines an additional six month data exclusivity period of protection for the paediatric non-clinical and clinical data contained in the applicable regulatory dossier. The Paediatric Regulations, which came into force on 26 January 2007 contain detailed provisions in relation to the commencement of their application to new and existing products. In addition an applicant cannot benefit from both the paediatric extension and the 11th year of data/market exclusivity as referenced at para **17.4.2.2**.

17.5 Generic products

Both applicants seeking to have generic products approved and the innovator pharmaceutical companies concerned must have regard both to intellectual property law and to the EU regulatory regime in order to determine the constraints imposed upon an applicant seeking to have a generic approved.

17.5.1 Generic medicinal product

Article 10(1) of the Directive provides as follows: 'By way of derogation from Article 8(3)(i), and without prejudice to the law relating to the protection of industrial and commercial property, the applicant shall not be required to provide the results of pre-clinical tests and of clinical trials if he can demonstrate that the medicinal product is a generic of a reference medicinal product which is or has been authorised under Article 6 for not less than eight years in a Member State or in the Community.'

As a consequence of the amendments to the data exclusivity periods referenced at para **17.1.4.2**, generic companies effectively have two or three years to prepare the marketing authorisation dossier, to file the abridged application and to obtain a marketing authorisation. The marketing authorisation can be obtained prior to expiry of the applicable patent/supplementary patent certificate protection and also prior to the expiry of the marketing protection.

The foregoing provision also applies to medicinal products approved under the centralised procedure.

17.5.2 Definition of a generic medicinal product

For the first time what is meant by a 'generic medicinal product' is defined in the Directive. The defined term replaces the previous concept of 'essential similarity'. Article 10(2)(b) of the Directive defines a generic medicinal product as having the same qualitative and quantative composition in active substances and the same pharmaceutical form as the reference medicinal product, whose bioequivalence with the reference medicinal product has been demonstrated, by appropriate bioavailability studies.

The legislation has taken into account definitions commonly accepted by member states with regard to generic applications and the case law of the ECJ. The definition of 'generic medicinal product' further provides that the different salts, esters, ethers, isomers, mixtures of isomers, complexes or derivatives of an active substance shall be considered to be the same active substance, unless these differ significantly in properties with regard to safety and/or efficacy. In such cases, additional data must be supplied.

Article 10(2)(b) also provides that the various immediate-release oral pharmaceutical forms shall be considered to be one and the same pharmaceutical form.

Article 10(1) provides that it is possible to seek approval of a generic product even where the applicable reference product has not been authorised in the applicable member state. In such a case, the applicant is to indicate in the application form the member state in which the reference medicinal product is or has been authorised.

17.5.3 Line extensions

Article 6(1) of the Directive provides that additional strengths, pharmaceutical forms, routes of administration and presentations should be considered as belonging to the same global marketing authorisation for the purpose of the application of Article 10(1). As such it would seem that a period of additional data exclusivity for line extensions of the referenced medicinal product is excluded from the ambit of the Directive.

The Directive essentially draws on the outcome of a number of decisions of the ECJ such as (a) whether line extensions could attract new data exclusivity and (b) whether a capsule or tablet could be considered to be the same pharmaceutical form.

17.5.4 Biological medicinal products (Biosimilars)

Article 10(4) of the Directive sets out the regulatory framework for approving generics of biological medicinal products (biotechnology products, blood and plasma products and immunological products). Article 10(4), which recognises the complexities associated with biological medicinal products, provides that where a biological medicinal product which is similar to a referenced biological product does not meet the conditions in the definition of generic medicinal products, owing to, in particular, differences relating to raw materials or differences in manufacturing process between the biological medicinal product and the reference biological medicinal product, the results of appropriate pre-clinical tests or clinical trials relating to these conditions must be provided.

Annexed to the Directive are the relevant criteria and references to related detailed guidelines. Additional guidelines have been released by the EMEA. These guidelines are published by the EMEA on its website (www.emea.eu.int).

17.6 The Bolar exemption

17.6.1 Background

The cross over between intellectual rights and EU regulatory law is perhaps no better demonstrated than the manner in which the research exemption contained in PA 1992, s 42 was amended in 2006.

Until the implementation of the Directive there was no harmonised community legislation with regard to what studies and regulatory steps could be undertaken without infringing underlying patent rights or supplementary protection certificates in member states. Article 10.6 of the Directive (the so called 'Bolar provision') enables pharmaceutical companies to commence the studies and clinical trials necessary for the marketing approval of a generic product before the patent underlying the referenced product has expired. The objective of the Bolar provision is that a generic product shall be available to market immediately after the expiration of the patent or SPC protection of the reference product concerned and the applicant will not have to wait for the expiry of such protection to commence the marketing authorisation approval procedure.

The Bolar provision effectively constitute part of the balance between (a) the provision for a uniform ten year period of data exclusivity for innovative products and (b) to allow the appropriate studies and trials to be carried out during the period in which the products are protected by a patent right.

Article 10.6 of Directive provides as follows:

> 'Conducting the necessary studies and trials with a view to the application of paragraphs 1, 2, 3, and 4 and the consequential practical requirements shall not be regarded as contrary to patent rights or to supplementary protection certificates for medicinal products').

17.6.2 'Bolar'

The term 'Bolar' derives from the 1984 US Court decision of *Roche Products Inc v Bolar Pharmaceutical Co* in which the Court of Appeals for the Federal Circuit held that research conducted by Bolar in support of a submission to the US Food and Drug Administration (FDA) was not exempt from patent infringement. The decision gave rise to concerns that pharmaceutical companies would have an effective extension of the term of a patent as generic companies could not commence the FDA process until after patent expiration. This decision gave rise to the Hatch-Waxman Act which created the FDA testing exemption by restoring the experimental use exception for research conducted for the purpose of seeking FDA approval. The same legislation also expanded patent terms for pharmaceutical companies under certain prescribed scenarios.

In the more recent US Supreme Court Decision of *Merck v Integra* (2005), the United States Supreme Court held that the exemption from an infringement extends to all uses of patented inventions that are reasonably related to the development and submission of any information under the US Federal Food, Drug, and Cosmetic Act.

17.6.3 Irish legislation

PA 1992, s 42 provided that the rights conferred by a patent shall 'not extend to.... acts done for experimental purposes relating to the subject-matter of the relevant patented invention.' The equivalent provision in the equivalent United Kingdom legislation (Patents Act 1975) has been the subject of a number of court cases, including the case of *Monsanto v Stauffer Chemical Co* [1985] RPC 515. The relatively narrow construction by the English Courts may be contrasted with the broader experimentation exemptions available under the laws of other European countries including Germany.

A transitional provision in the First Schedule of PA 1992, paragraph 4, applied to patents granted under the previous Patents Act 1964 which had their terms extended from 16 to 20 years as a result of the 1992 Act. During the final 2 years of the extended term, it was not an infringement of such a patent for a person to make preparations to put the invention into effect commercially after the term of the patent expired, provided that the preparations did not include the importation or placing on the market of a product protected by the patent. This provision would have allowed testing for regulatory purposes, but only if the active ingredient was manufactured in Ireland, not imported.[5] The paragraph has been repealed in the 2006 Act.

Until the Directive was implemented the nature and extent of what pre-patent-expiry development work could be conducted was not regulated at EU level. Article 10.6 (referenced at para **17.6.1** above) was designed to put the EU generics industry on a more equal footing with its competitors in other parts of the world such as the US, Canada and Asia. The nature and scope of what is meant by the Directive (as implemented in Ireland) gives rise to a number of issues. The recently published 'Gowers Review' of Intellectual Property (which was published in response to a request by the UK Government to conduct an independent review into the UK Intellectual Property framework) shares a concern of many commentators that what is meant by the equivalent UK provision is not entirely clear and needs clarification.

The 'Bolar' exemption was implemented into Irish law by the European Communities (Limitation of Effect of Patent) Regulations 2006 (SI 50/2006) on 30 January 2006. The Regulations amend PA 1992, s 42 of the by inserting an additional exemption as s 42(g) to the effect that acts done in conducting the necessary studies, tests and trials which are conducted with a view to satisfying the application requirements for marketing authorisation for a generic or similar biological medicinal product for human use or for veterinary use would not constitute an infringing act, or any other act which is required as a consequence of the acts referred to, as appropriate.

17.6.4 UK guidance

In the United Kingdom, guidance has been provided by the MHRA (Medicines and Healthcare Product Regulatory Agency) and the UK Patent Office (now renamed the UK Intellectual Property Office). The UK Patent Office has confirmed that the exemption would cover the scheduled activities conducted as and from 30 October 2005 as long as those activities are for the purposes of submitting an application under the Directive regardless of whether the referenced products are submitted for authorisation before or after the implementation of the new regulatory legislation, (that is whether protected by old or new periods of data and market exclusivity).

The Guidance of the UK Patent Office provides that the following acts are exempted from infringement:

- manufacture and importation of active substance(s) to conduct trials and validate manufacturing processes to the satisfaction of the competent authorities;
- the development of the final pharmaceutical form of the active substance;
- conduct of pre-clinical-tests, clinical and bioavailability trials and stability studies.
- manufacture and supply to the regulatory authorities of samples of the active substances, intermediates etc;
- compilation and submission of an application for a marketing authorisation.

[5.] It was doubtful whether this aspect was in conformity with EU law. There was also doubt as to how the final two years of the term of the patent was to be interpreted if an SPC had been granted.

It would therefore appear that the manufacture and supply of active substances or finished products which are not required for trials and tests required to obtain a marketing authorisation (as per the MHRA guidelines).

In other countries, a more expansive implementation of the applicable provision has taken place. For example, in Germany, the carve out from patent infringement applies to studies and trials and consequential practical requirements which are necessary to obtain an authorisation according to drug law for the marketing in the EU or an authorisation according to drug law for the marketing in the member states of the EU or in third countries. As such, in Germany, the research exemption is not limited to generic applications or indeed to applications for marketing authorisations in the EU.

The scope of the Bolar clause will need to be defined by the courts or clarified by further guidelines. The EU Council explicitly rejected a proposal by the European Parliament to include products for exports. In conclusion, the implementation of the Irish legislation leaves uncertain whether other clinical trials conducted for the purpose of obtaining marketing authorisation, but not of the abridged procedure, may be exempt. It is not specified, and so remains unclear whether other actions, such as, the conduct of feasibility studies or the supply or export of materials, is covered by the Bolar provision. What is meant by 'consequential practical requirements' is particularly vague and will inevitably lead to dispute. This may require clarification by the ECJ. As such, it seems the protection offered by the amendment is limited to acts done supporting an application made under the abridged procedure.

17.7 Patent Settlement Agreements

Para **17.1.6.2** (Bolar) has referenced the Hatch-Waxman legislation which, *inter alia*, provided for an accelerated process for approval of generic drugs in the United States of America. The generic applicant is required to make a 'Paragraph (iv)' certification in which the generic applicant confirms that either (a) the generic product does not infringe the patent or (b) the patent is invalid. The proprietary drug producer has a 45 day period in which to file suit for patent infringement. Under the Hatch-Waxman legislation, the first generic applicant will obtain a period of exclusivity for its generic product.

The US anti trust authority (FTC) has attacked a number of these arrangements. The US courts have assessed a number of patent settlement agreements entered into between innovator companies and generic companies under which the generic companies are paid consideration to suspend challenges to patents. The courts have concluded that it was legitimate for the parties to conclude the appropriate commercial arrangements until the pharmaceutical company's patents had been declared to be invalid or the competing product had been found not to infringe the applicable patent.

It is likely that the European Commission will closely examine equivalent arrangements in an EU context. As such this is likely to constitute a further area of overlap and tension between the exercise of intellectual property rights and EU competition law.

INDEX

All references are to heading numbers

A

Access Regulations
And see **Electronic communications regulation**
'access', 6.3.5.1
interconnection, 6.3.5.1
introduction, 6.3.5
local loop unbundling, 6.3.5.3
pricing, 6.2
SMP obligations, 6.3.5.2

Active date
electronic discovery, and, 8.3.1

Adaptation
computer programs, and, 16.6.3

Administrative law
electronic communications regulation, and, 6.5.2

Adware
computer crime, and, 7.2.2

Anti-copying devices
copyright, and, 12.1.2

Appeals
electronic communications regulation, and, 6.3.3.4
postal sector regulation, and, 6.6.2.6

Archival data
electronic discovery, and, 8.3.2

Articles of association
technology start-ups, and, 2.3.4

Artistic works
copyright, and, 12.2.2

Artists' resale rights
copyright, and, 12.1.2

Auctions
distance communications, and, 1.4.2.5

Authorisation Regulations
electronic communications regulation, and, 6.3.4
postal sector regulation, and
appeals against refusal, 6.6.2.6
generally, 6.6.2.2

Authorised officers
electronic communications regulation, and, 6.4.2

Authorship
copyright, and, 12.2.2

B

B2B services
distance communications, and, 1.1

Back-up copies
computer programs, and, 16.7.1

Bad faith
domain names, and, 3.7.2

Berne Convention
copyright, and, 12.1.3

Bespoke agreements
software licensing, and, 5.2.5.1

'Best' evidence
computer crime, and, 7.8

Best-of-breed outsourcing
generally, 9.5

Biological medicinal products
generally, 17.5.4

Biotechnological inventions
generally, 17.2.1.2
patents, and, 10.3.1.1

Bolar exemption
background, 17.6.1
case decision, 17.6.2
Irish legislation, 17.6.3
UK guidance, 17.6.4

Business plan
technology start-ups, and, 2.4.1

C

Cable retransmission
copyright, and, 12.1.2

Cancellation of contracts
distance communications, and, 1.4.2.7

Certificate of contested validity
patents, and, 10.9.4

Certification marks
And see **Trademarks**
generally, 11.20

Character merchandising
passing off, and, 13.6

Civil liability
electronic communications regulation, and
    introduction, 6.4.1
    procedural outline, 6.4.1.1
    urgent directions, 6.4.1.2
software licensing, and, 5.2.5.3
computer crime, and, 7.8

Civil remedies
computer crime, and, 7.4.4
copyright, and
    damages, 12.4.1
    delivery up, 12.4.2
    seizure of infringing material, 12.4.3

Collective marks
And see **Trademarks**
generally, 11.20

Commercial contracts
technology start-ups, and, 2.12

Communication to the public
copyright, and, 12.1.2

Communications Regulations Act 2002
establishment of ComReg, 6.3.1
regulatory impact assessment, 6.3.1.1

Communications sector regulation
broadcasting, 6.7.1
conclusion, 6.8
electronic communications
    And see **Electronic communications regulation**
    administrative law, 6.5.2
    background, 6.1
    competition law, 6.5.1
    concepts, 6.2–6.2.1
    enforcement, 6.4.1–6.4.3
    introduction, 6.1
    legal framework, 6.3–6.3.7
    terminology, 6.2
postal sector
    introduction, 6.6
    Postal Regulations, 6.6.2–6.6.2.6
    role of ComReg, 6.6.1
spectrum, 6.7.2

Community Patent Convention
patents, and, 10.2.4

Community trade mark (CTM)
acquiescence, 11.24.9
applications, 11.24.1
assignment, 11.24.6
duration, 11.24.2
infringement, 11.24.3
invalidity, 11.24.7
jurisdiction, 11.24.4
licensing, 11.24.6
remedies, 11.24.5
revocation, 11.24.7
seniority, 11.24.9

Company particulars and details
distance communications, and, 1.4.4

Competition law
electronic communications, and
    duties of ComReg, 6.3.3.6
    generally, 6.5.1

Compulsory licences
patents, and, 10.16.4

Computer crime
adware, 7.2.2
'best' evidence, 7.8
civil remedies, and, 7.4.4
common law, at, 7.4.3
computer hijacking, 7.2.7
computer-specific fraud
    denial of service, 7.2.4
    identity theft, 7.2.6
    introduction, 7.2
law, and, 7.4–7.4.4
maliciously developed software, 7.2.2–7.2.3
other forms, 7.2.8
response to discovery of, 7.3
unauthorised access, 7.2.5

Computer crime (contd)
    unsolicited bulk commercial emails, 7.2.1
  criminal liability
    Garda Bureau of Fraud Investigation, 7.4.2
    generally, 7.4.1
    introduction, 7.4
  denial of service, 7.2.4
  evidence
    'best' evidence, 7.8
    generally, 7.6
    proper practice, 7.7
  forensics, 7.5
  'hacking', 7.2.5
  harassment, 7.2.8
  identity theft, 7.2.6
  introduction, 7.1
  malware
    generally, 7.2.2
    legal issues, 7.2.3
  'pharming', 7.2.6
  'phishing', 7.2.6
  'spam', 7.2.1
  spyware, 7.2.2
  summary, 7.9
  Trojans, 7.2.7
  unauthorised access, 7.2.5
  unsolicited bulk commercial emails, 7.2.1
  viruses, 7.2.2
  'vishing', 7.2.6
  worms, 7.2.2

Computer hijacking

computer crime, and, 7.2.7

Computer programs

adaptation, 16.6.3
authorship, 16.5
background, 16.1.1
back-up copies, 16.7.1
conclusion, 16.9
copyright, and
  EC law, 12.1.2
  Irish law, 12.1.1
database right
  introduction, 16.8
  non-original databases, 16.8.2
  'original database', 16.8.1
  qualifying for protection, 16.8.3
  restricted acts, 16.8.4
  term of protection, 16.8.5
decompilation right, 16.7.2
definition, 16.3
distribution right, 16.6.2
incidental acts, 16.7.3
international treaty law
  EU developments, 16.2.1
  introduction, 16.2
  Software Directive, 16.2.2
making available right, 16.6.2
ownership, 16.5
protection, 16.4
reproduction right, 16.6.1
restricted acts
  adaptation, 16.6.
  back-up copies, and, 16.7.1
  decompilation right, 16.7.2
  distribution right, 16.6.2
  exceptions, 16.7–16.7.3
  generally, 16.6
  incidental acts, 16.7.3
  reproduction right, 16.6.1
Software Directive, 16.2.1–16.2.2

ComReg

electronic communications regulation, and
  appeals, 6.3.3.4
  consultation, 6.3.3.3
  dispute resolution, 6.3.3.7
  generally, 6.3.1
  independence, 6.3.3.2
  market analysis, 6.3.3.6
postal sector regulation, and, 6.6.1

Confidential information

background, 15.4
celebrities, 15.7
employment cases, 15.5
essential elements, 15.2
introduction, 15.1
meaning, 15.2
non-employment cases, 15.6
purpose of protection, 15.3
remedies, 15.8

Confusing similarity

domain names, and, 3.7.3

Constitutional rights

data protection, and, 4.2.4
privacy, and, 4.2.2

Construction of buildings

distance communications, and, 1.4.2.5

Consultation
electronic communications regulation, and, 6.3.3.3

Consumer law
Consumer Protection Act 2007, 1.4.5.1
introduction, 1.4.5
Unfair Terms in Consumer Contracts Regulations 1995, 1.4.5.2

Consumer Protection Act 2007
ebusiness, and, 1.4.5.1

'Consumers'
distance communications, and, 1.4.2.2

Contract law
outsourcing, and
   default and remedies, 9.8.2
   exclusion of liability, 9.8.4
   generally, 9.8
   limitation of liability, 9.8.4
   risk allocation, 9.8.1
   service credits, 9.8.3
   service levels, 9.8.3
software licensing agreements, and, 5.3.1

Convergence
electronic communications regulation, and, 6.2

Cooling off period
distance communications, and, 1.4.2.7

Copyright
anti-copying devices, 12.1.2
artistic works, 12.2.2
artists' resale rights, 12.1.2
authorship, 12.2.2
basic concepts, 12.2.1–12.2.3
Berne Convention, 12.1.3
cable retransmission, 12.1.2
civil remedies
   damages, 12.4.1
   delivery up, 12.4.2
   seizure of infringing material, 12.4.3
communication to the public, 12.1.2
computer programs
   EC law, 12.1.2
   Irish law, 12.1.1
   copyright works, 12.2.2
conclusions, 12.6
criminal remedies, 12.5.1–12.5.4
damages, 12.4.1
databases, 12.1.2
delivery up, 12.4.2
distribution rights
   background, 12.1.2
   generally, 12.2.4
dramatic works, 12.2.2
duration of protection
   EC law, 12.1.2
   generally, 12.2.2
   Irish law, 12.1.1
EC law, 12.1.2
enforcement
   EC law, 12.1.2
   generally, 12.3.1
   presumptions applying in court, 12.3.21
   presumptions applying in proveedings, 12.3.2
fair compensation for rightsholders, 12.1.2
incidental acts, 12.1.4
information society, and, 12.1.2
infringement, 12.3.3
international treaty law, and, 12.1.3
'Internet' treaties, 12.1.2
introduction, 12.1
legislative background, 12.1.1–12.1.5
lending rights
   background, 12.1.2
   generally, 12.2.4
literary works, 12.2.2
making available right
   background, 12.1.4
   generally, 12.2.4
moral rights, 12.4.45
musical works, 12.2.2
nature, 12.2.1
originality, 12.2.2
ownership, 12.2.2
primary infringements, 12.3.3
remedies
   civil, 12.4.1–12.4.5
   criminal, 12.5.1–12.5.4
   generally, 12.3.4
rental rights
   background, 12.1.2
   generally, 12.2.4
reproduction rights
   background, 12.1.2
   generally, 12.2.3
resale rights, 12.1.2
restricted works. 12.2.3
rights management systems, 12.1.2
satellite broadcasting, 12.1.2

Copyright (contd)
secondary infringements, 12.3.3
seizure of infringing material
    applications to court, 12.4.3
    rights of copyright owner, 12.4.4
software
    EC law, 12.1.2
    Irish law, 12.1.1
software licensing agreements, and, 5.3.2.1
spare parts drawings, 12.1.1
transient acts, 12.1.4
WIPO, and, 12.1.3

Council Regulation 44/2001
ebusiness, and, 1.4.7

Country of origin principle
ebusiness, and, 1.4.3.4

Co-ownership
patents, and, 10.6.1

Credit card fraud
distance communications, and, 1.4.2.7

Criminal liability
computer-related fraud, and
    Garda Bureau of Fraud Investigation, 7.4.2
    generally, 7.4.1
    introduction, 7.4
copyright, and, 12.5.1–12.5.4
designs, and, 14.7
electronic communications regulation, and, 6.4.3
trademarks, and, 11.22

Cyber-squatting
domain names, and, 3.2

D

Damage
passing off, and, 13.5

Damages
copyright, and, 12.4.1
patents, and, 10.9.1

Data exclusivity
8+2+1, 17.4.2.1
additional one year new indication, 17.4.2.2
introduction, 17.4.2
orphan medicines, 17.4.2.4

paediatric use, 17.4.2.5
well-established substances, 17.4.2.3

Data Privacy Regulations
electronic communications regulation, and, 6.3.7

Data protection
acceptable email and Internet usage policies, 4.6.2
access to data, 4.3.7.3
automatic processing of data, 4.3.7.6
blocking data, 4.3.7.4
breaches of data security, 4.3.3.1
constitutional right, as, 4.2.4
data controllers
    duties, 4.3.3.1–4.3.3.3
    generally, 4.3.2.1
    relevant controllers, 4.3.2.2
data processor contracts, 4.3.3.1
data retention, 4.5
data subject's rights
    access to data, 4.3.7.3
    automatic processing, 4.3.7.6
    blocking data, 4.3.7.4
    erasure of data, 4.3.7.4
    informed of data being kept, 4.3.7.1
    prevent use of date for direct marketing, 4.3.7.2
    prevent processing, 4.3.7.5
direct marketing, and, 4.3.7.2
duties of data controllers
    general principles, 4.3.3.2
    non-compliance, and, 4.3.3.3
    security of data, 4.3.3.1
Electronic Communications Regulations 2003, and, 4.4
erasure of data, 4.3.7.4
human right, as, 4.2.4
introduction, 4.3.1
legislative basis, 4.3.1
personal data
    generally, 4.3.2.1
    processing, 4.3.5
    transfer outside EU, 4.3.8.1–4.3.8.8
    use for marketing purposes, 4.3.4
practice, in, 4.2.4
processing of data
    personal data, 4.3.5
    sensitive personal data, 4.3.6
registration with Commissioner, 4.3.9
retention of data, 4.5
safe harbour principles, 4.3.8.4

Data protection (contd)
security of data, 4.3.3.1
sensitive personal data, 4.3.6
transfer of personal data outside EU
    adequacy of protection in recipient state, 4.3.8.3
    binding corporate rules, 4.3.8.6
    introduction, 4.3.8.1
    meaning, 4.3.8.2
    model contracts, 4.3.8.5
    other derogations and exceptions, 4.3.8.7
    safe harbour principles, 4.3.8.4
    SWIFT controversy, 4.3.8.8
unsolicited communications, 4.4
use of personal data, 4.3.4
workplace, in, 4.6.1–4.6.2

Data Retention Directive 2006
data protection, and, 4.5

Database right
introduction, 16.8
non-original databases, 16.8.2
'original database', 16.8.1
qualifying for protection, 16.8.3
restricted acts, 16.8.4
software licensing agreements, and, 5.3.4
term of protection, 16.8.5

Databases
copyright, and, 12.1.2

Debit card fraud
distance communications, and, 1.4.2.7

Declaration of invalidity
designs, and, 14.6.2

Declaration of non-infringement
patents, and, 10.14

Decompilation right
computer programs, and, 16.7.2

Deleted files
electronic discovery, and, 8.14.2–8.14.3

Delivery up
copyright, and, 12.4.2
patents, and, 10.9.2

Denial of service
computer-related fraud, and, 7.2.4

Designs
authorship, 14.8.1
conclusion, 14.12
criminal offences, 14.7
declaration of invalidity, 14.6.2
'design', 14.3.1
filing date, 14.9.2
groundless threats, 14.4.4
Hague Agreement, 14.2.3
infringement
    actions, 14.4.3
    defences, 14.5–14.5.3
    groundless threats, 14.4.4
    prior user, 14.5.3
    rights conferred 14.4.2
    scope of protection, 11.4.1
    spare parts for repair of complex products, 14.5.2
interconnection, 14.3.3
introduction, 14.1
invalidity
    counterclaim, and, 14.6.2
    grounds, 14.6.1
legislation
    generally, 14.2
    Hague Agreement, 14.2.3
    interpretation, 14.2.4
    Registered Community Design, 14.2.1
    Unregistered Community Design, 14.2.2
novelty, 14.3.5
OHIM, and, 14.2.1
ownership, 14.8.2
prior disclosure, 14.3.6
prior user, 14.5.3
priority right, 14.9.2
'product', 14.3.2
protectable designs
    'design', 14.3.1
    designs of interconnection, 14.3.3
    grace period for own disclosures, 14.3.7
    novelty, 14.3.5
    prior disclosure, 14.3.6
    'product', 14.3.2
    requirements for protection, 14.3.4
    technical function, 14.3.3
registered community design, 14.2.1
registration
    application, 14.9.1
    classification by products, 14.9.3
    deferment of publication, 14.9.5
    filing date, 14.9.2

Designs (contd)
    multiple designs in one application, 14.9.4
    priority right, 14.9.2
    term of protection, 14.9.6
  relationship to other forms of protection
    copyright, 14.9.8–14.10
    introduction, 14.9.7
    trademarks, 14.11
  right of designer to be cited, 14.8.3
  spare parts for repair of complex products, 14.5.2
  technical function, 14.3.3
  term of protection, 14.9.6
  trademarks, and, 14.11
  unregistered community design, 14.2.2

Declaration of non-infringement

patents, and, 10.14

Detention of goods

infringement of patents, and, 10.16.5

Direct mailing

ebusiness, and, 1.4.3.5

Direct marketing

data protection, and, 4.3.7.2

Directors' duties

technology start-ups, and, 2.3.3

Discovery

patent actions, and, 10.16.2

Discovery (electronic)

Australian position, 8.11
categorisation of data
  active data, 8.3.1
  archival data, 8.3.2
  forensic data, 8.3.4
  hidden data, 8.3.3
  introduction, 8.3
conclusion, 8.17
deleted files, of, 8.14.2–8.14.3
document management systems, 8.16
extent, 8.14.1
general conclusions, 8.14
identification of relevant data, 8.4
introduction, 8.1
Ireland, in, 8.9
legal issues, 8.8
litigator problems
  privilege, 8.15.2
  spoliation, 8.15.1
metadata, 8.7

New Zealand position, 8.12
presentation of evidence, 8.5
process, 8.2
quantity of data, 8.6
UK position, 8.10
US position, 8.13

Distance Communications Regulations 2001

application, 1.4.2.2
background, 1.4.2.1
businesses affected, 1.4.2.3
cancellation of contracts, 1.4.2.7
confirming contract terms, 1.4.2.7
'consumers', 1.4.2.2
cooling off period, 1.4.2.7
coverage, 1.4.2.6
'distance contracts', 1.4.2.6
effect on online contracts, 1.4.2.7
exclusions, 1.4.2.4–1.4.2.5
financial services, and, 1.4.2.4
fraudulent credit and debit cards, 1.4.2.7
inertia selling, 1.4.2.7
'means of distance communication', 1.4.2.6
non-compliance, and, 1.4.2.7
prior information, 1.4.2.7
software licensing agreements, and, 5.4.2
substitute goods or services, 1.4.2.7
time limits, 1.4.2.7
transactions covered, 1.4.2.6

'Distance contracts'

generally, 1.4.2.6

Distribution right

background, 12.1.2
computer programs, and, 16.6.2
generally, 12.2.4

Document management systems

electronic discovery, and, 8.16

Domain names

bad faith, 3.7.2
.com domains, 3.5
confusing similarity, 3.7.3
cyber-squatting, 3.2
dispute resolution
  bad faith, 3.7.2
  case law, 3.6
  confusing similarity, 3.7.3
  generally, 3.2
  ICANN UDRP, 3.4–3.4.2
  legitimate rights or interests, 3.7.4

Domain names (contd)
   principles, 3.7.1–3.7.4
   recent .ie domain disputes, 3.8
   standing, 3.7.1
   WIPO, and, 3.3
Domain Name System (DNS), 3.1
.eu domains, 3.1.1.2
ICANN, 3.1
.ie domains
   generally, 3.4.2
   recent disputes, 3.8
legitimate rights or interests, 3.7.4
meaning, 3.1
parody sites, 3.2
standing, 3.7.1
top level domains
   country code (ccTLDs), 3.1.1.2
   generic (gTLDs), 3.1.1.1
Uniform Domain Name Dispute Resolution Policy (UDRP)
   background, 3.4
   case law, 3.6
   effect of determination, 3.4.1
   .ie domains, 3.4.2
WIPO, and, 3.3

Dramatic works

copyright, and, 12.2.2

Due diligence

technology start-ups, and, 2.6

E

Ebusiness

auctions, and, 1.4.2.5
B2B services, and, 1.1
cancellation of contracts, 1.4.2.7
company particulars and details, 1.4.4
conclusion, 1.5
construction of buildings, and, 1.4.2.5
consumer law
   Consumer Protection Act 2007, 1.4.5.1
   introduction, 1.4.5
   Unfair Terms in Consumer Contracts Regulations 1995, 1.4.5.2
Consumer Protection Act 2007, 1.4.5.1
'consumers', 1.4.2.2
cooling off period, 1.4.2.7
Council Regulation 44/2001, 1.4.7
country of origin principle, 1.4.3.4
credit and debit card fraud, 1.4.2.7
direct mailing, and, 1.4.3.5

Distance Communications Regulations 2001
   application, 1.4.2.2
   background, 1.4.2.1
   businesses affected, 1.4.2.3
   cancellation of contracts, 1.4.2.7
   confirming contract terms, 1.4.2.7
   'consumers', 1.4.2.2
   cooling off period, 1.4.2.7
   coverage, 1.4.2.6
   'distance contracts', 1.4.2.6
   effect on online contracts, 1.4.2.7
   exclusions, 1.4.2.4–1.4.2.5
   financial services, and, 1.4.2.4
   fraudulent credit and debit cards, 1.4.2.7
   inertia selling, 1.4.2.7
   'means of distance communication', 1.4.2.6
   non-compliance, and, 1.4.2.7
   prior information, 1.4.2.7
   substitute goods or services, 1.4.2.7
   time limits, 1.4.2.7
   transactions covered, 1.4.2.6
'distance contracts', 1.4.2.6
EC Companies Regulations, 1.4.4
E-Commerce Regulations 2003
   application, 1.4.3.2
   background, 1.4.3.1
   country of origin principle, 1.4.3.4
   direct mailing, and, 1.4.3.5
   online contracts, and, 1.4.3.6
   'relevant service', 1.4.3.3
   transparency requirements, 1.4.3.3
Electronic Commerce Act 2000
   background, 1.4.1.1
   consent, and, 1.4.1.9
   electronic signatures, 1.4.1.4–1.4.1.6
   excluded areas, 1.4.1.3
   key requirement, 1.4.1.9
   objectives, 1.4.1.2
   place of dispatch and receipt of communications, 1.4.1.8
   "postal rule", and, 1.4.1.7
   purpose, 1.4.1.2
   time of dispatch and receipt of communications, 1.4.1.7
electronic signatures
   advanced, 1.4.1.6
   generally, 1.4.1.4
   special cases, 1.4.1.6
   validity, 1.4.1.5

Ebusiness (contd)
enforcement of judgments, 1.4.7
financial services, and, 1.4.2.4
fraudulent credit and debit cards, 1.4.2.7
inertia selling, 1.4.2.7
jurisdiction of contracts, 1.4.7
legislation
    Consumer Protection Act 2007, 1.4.5.1
    Council Regulation 44/2001, 1.4.7
    Distance Communications Regulations 2001, 1.4.2.1–1.4.2.7
    EC Companies Regulations, 1.4.4
    EC Directive Regulations 2003, 1.4.3.1–1.4.3.6
    Electronic Commerce Act 2000, 1.4.1–1.4.1.9
    Sale of Goods and Supply of Services Acts, 1.4.6
    sources, 1.2
    Unfair Terms in Consumer Contracts Regulations 1995, 1.4.5.2
National Consumer Agency, 1.4.5.1
nature of electronic contracts, 1.3
online contracts, and, 1.4.3.6
overview, 1.1
pay-phones, and, 1.4.2.5
primary legislation, 1.2
prior information
    online contracts, and, 1.4.3.6
    generally, 1.4.2.7
    'relevant service', 1.4.3.3
recognition and enforcement of judgments, 1.4.7
'relevant service', 1.4.3.3
Sale of Goods and Supply of Services Acts, 1.4.6
sale of property, 1.4.2.5
sources of law, 1.2
transparency requirements
    online contracts, and, 1.4.3.6
    generally, 1.4.2.7
    'relevant service', 1.4.3.3
unfair commercial practices, 1.4.5.1
Unfair Terms in Consumer Contracts Regulations 1995, 1.4.5.2
vending machines, and, 1.4.2.5

E-Commerce Regulations 2003

application, 1.4.3.2
background, 1.4.3.1
country of origin principle, 1.4.3.4
direct mailing, and, 1.4.3.5
online contracts, and, 1.4.3.6
'relevant service', 1.4.3.3
transparency requirements, 1.4.3.3

Electronic Commerce Act 2000

background, 1.4.1.1
consent, and, 1.4.1.9
electronic signatures
    advanced, 1.4.1.6
    generally, 1.4.1.4
    special cases, 1.4.1.6
    validity, 1.4.1.5
excluded areas, 1.4.1.3
key requirement, 1.4.1.9
objectives, 1.4.1.2
place of dispatch and receipt of communications, 1.4.1.8
"postal rule", and, 1.4.1.7
purpose, 1.4.1.2
time of dispatch and receipt of communications, 1.4.1.7

Electronic communications regulation

access pricing, 6.2
Access Regulations
    'access', 6.3.5.1
    interconnection, 6.3.5.1
    introduction, 6.3.5
    local loop unbundling, 6.3.5.3
    SMP obligations, 6.3.5.2
administrative law, 6.5.2
appeals, 6.3.3.4
Authorisation Regulations, 6.3.4
authorised officers, 6.4.2
background, 6.1
civil liability
    introduction, 6.4.1
    procedural outline, 6.4.1.1
    urgent directions, 6.4.1.2
Communications Regulations Act 2002
    establishment of ComReg, 6.3.1
    regulatory impact assessment, 6.3.1.1
ComReg
    appeals, 6.3.3.4
    consultation, 6.3.3.3
    dispute resolution, 6.3.3.7
    generally, 6.3.1
    independence, 6.3.3.2
    market analysis, 6.3.3.6
competition law
    duties of ComReg, 6.3.3.6
    generally, 6.5.1
concepts

Electronic communications regulation (contd)
    generally, 6.2
    policy making and collaboration, 6.2.1
  consultation, 6.3.3.3
  convergence, and, 6.2
  criminal liability, 6.4.3
  Data Privacy Regulations, 6.3.7
  enforcement
    authorised officers, 6.4.2
    civil liability, 6.4.1–6.4.1.2
    criminal liability, 6.4.3
    search and seizure powers, 6.4.2
  Framework Regulations
    appeals, 6.3.3.4
    consultation, 6.3.3.3
    definitions, 6.3.3.1
    dispute resolution, 6.3.3.7
    independence of NRAs, 6.3.3.2
    introduction, 6.3.3
    market analysis, 6.3.3.6
    scope, 6.3.3.1
    SMP Guidelines, 6.3.3.6
    SSNIP test, 6.3.3.6
    transparency, 6.3.3.3
  interconnection, 6.3.5.1
  introduction, 6.1
  legal framework
    Access Regulations, 6.3.5–6.3.5.3
    Authorisation Regulations, 6.3.4
    Communications Regulations Act 2002, 6.3.1
    Data Privacy Regulations, 6.3.7
    Framework Regulations, 6.3.3–6.3.3.7
    introduction, 6.3
    Universal Service Regulations, 6.3.6–6.3.6.5
  local loop unbundling, 6.3.5.3
  market analysis, 6.3.3.6
  national regulatory authority
    generally, 6.3.1
    independence, 6.3.3.2
  number portability, 6.3.6.5
  policy making and collaboration, 6.2.1
  purpose, 6.2
  regulatory impact assessment, 6.3.1.1
  search and seizure powers, 6.4.2
  significant market power (SMP)
    generally, 6.2
    Guidelines, 6.3.3.6
    obligations, 6.3.5.2
    universal service, and, 6.3.6.3
  SSNIP test, 6.3.3.6
  terminology, 6.2
  transparency, 6.3.3.3
  universal service obligations
    background, 6.2
    financing, 6.3.6.2
    generally, 6.3.6.1
  Universal Service Regulations
    consumer protection, 6.3.6.4
    introduction, 6.3.6
    number portability, 6.3.6.5
    SMP obligations, 6.3.6.3
    universal service obligations, 6.3.6.1–6.3.6.2
  VoIP, 6.3.3.6

Electronic Communications Regulations 2003
data protection, and, 4.4

Electronic discovery
active data, 8.3.1
archival data, 8.3.2
Australian position, 8.11
background, 8.1
categorisation of data
  active data, 8.3.1
  archival data, 8.3.2
  forensic data, 8.3.4
  hidden data, 8.3.3
  introduction, 8.3
conclusion, 8.17
deleted files, of, 8.14.2–8.14.3
document management systems, 8.16
evidence handling, 8.2
extent, 8.14.1
forensic data, 8.3.4
general conclusions, 8.14
hidden data, 8.3.3
identification of relevant data, 8.4
introduction, 8.1
Ireland, in, 8.9
legal issues, 8.8
litigator problems
  privilege, 8.15.2
  spoliation, 8.15.1
metadata, 8.7
New Zealand position, 8.12
presentation of evidence, 8.5
process, 8.2
quantity of data, 8.6

Electronic discovery (contd)
UK position, 8.10
US position, 8.13
Electronic signatures
advanced, 1.4.1.6
generally, 1.4.1.4
special cases, 1.4.1.6
validity, 1.4.1.5
Email usage policies
data protection and privacy, and, 4.6.2
Employee share option schemes
technology start-ups, and, 2.11
End-to-end outsourcing
generally, 9.5
Enforcement
copyright, and
    EC law, 12.1.2
    generally, 12.3.1
    presumptions applying in court, 12.3.21
    presumptions applying in proceedings, 12.3.2
electronic communications regulation, and
    authorised officers, 6.4.2
    civil liability, 6.4.1–6.4.1.2
    criminal liability, 6.4.3
    search and seizure powers, 6.4.2
Enforcement of judgments
ebusiness, and, 1.4.7
Escrow agreements
software licensing agreements, and, 5.2.5.5
European Convention on Human Rights
data protection, and, 4.2.4
privacy, and, 4.2.3
European Patent Convention
patents, and, 10.2.3
Evidence
computer-related fraud, and
    'best' evidence, 7.8
    generally, 7.6
    proper practice, 7.7
electronic discovery, and, 8.2
Exclusion of liability
outsourcing, and, 9.8.4

software licensing agreements, and, 5.5.7
Exclusive licences
trademarks, and, 11.17
Export control
software licensing agreements, and, 5.4.3

F
Fair compensation
copyright, and, 12.1.2
Famous marks
trademarks, and, 11.21
Financial services
distance communications, and, 1.4.2.4
Forensic data
electronic discovery, and, 8.3.4
Forensics
computer-related fraud, and, 7.5
Fraudulent credit and debit cards
distance communications, and, 1.4.2.7

G
Generic medicines
supplementary protection certificates, and, 17.2.1.4.5
Generic medicinal products
definition, 17.5.2
generally, 17.5.1
Generic products
biosimilars, 17.5.4
introduction, 17.5
line extensions, 17.5.3
medicinal products, 17.5.1–17.5.3
Goodwill
passing off, and, 13.4
Grant of licence
software licensing agreements, and, 5.5.3
Groundless threats
patents, and, 10.13

H
'Hacking'
computer-related fraud, and, 7.2.5
Hague Agreement
designs, and, 14.2.3
Harassment
computer crime, and, 7.2.8

Heads of agreement
technology start-ups, and, 2.5

Hidden data
electronic discovery, and, 8.3.3

Human rights
data protection, and, 4.2.4
privacy, and, 4.2.3

Human tissue
patents, and, 17.2.1.2

I

ICANN
domain names, and, 3.1

Ideas
patents, and, 10.4–10.4.1

Identity theft
computer-related fraud, and, 7.2.6

Incidental acts
computer programs, and, 16.7.3
copyright, and, 12.1.4

Incorporation of companies
articles of association, 2.3.4
duties of directors and secretaries, 2.3.3
founding shareholders and directors, 2.3.5
generally, 2.3
information requirements, 2.3.1
memorandum of association, 2.3.4
name of company, 2.3.2

Inertia selling
distance communications, and, 1.4.2.7

Information society
copyright, and, 12.1.2

Infringement
copyright, and, 12.3.3
designs, and
    actions, 14.4.3
    defences, 14.5–14.5.3
    groundless threats, 14.4.4
    prior user, 14.5.3
    rights conferred 14.4.2
    scope of protection, 11.4.1
    spare parts for repair of complex products, 14.5.2
patents, and
    And see **Infringement of patents**
    generally, 10.1–10.16

Infringement of patents
actions, 10.8
aircraft, 10.10.10.2
breach of restrictive conditions, 10.10.10.3
certificate of contested validity, 10.9.4
compulsory licences, 10.16.4
consent of proprietor, and, 10.10.1
continuation of use, and, 10.10.5–10.10.6
costs, 10.9.5
damages, 10.9.1
declaration of non-infringement, 10.14
defences
    aircraft, 10.10.10.2
    breach of restrictive conditions, 10.10.10.3
    consent of proprietor, 10.10.1
    continuation of use, and, 10.10.5–10.10.6
    Euro-defences, and, 10.10.2
    experimental use, and, 10.10.8
    extemporaneous preparation on prescription, 10.10.9
    generic medicine trials, 10.10.8.1
    hovercraft, 10.10.10.2
    invalid patent, 10.10.4
    private use, and, 10.10.7
    ships, and, 10.10.10.1
delivery up, 10.9.2
detention of goods, 10.16.5
direct infringing acts, 10.7.1
disclosure action, 10.16.3
discovery, 10.16.2
Euro-defences, and, 10.10.2
experimental use, and, 10.10.8
extemporaneous preparation on prescription, 10.10.9
generally, 10.7
generic medicine trials, 10.10.8.1
groundless threats, 10.13
hovercraft, 10.10.10.2
indirect infringement, 10.7.2
partially valid patent, 10.9.3
private use, and, 10.10.7
privileged communications, 10.16.1
publication of judgment, 10.9.6
remedies
    account of profits, 10.9.1
    certificate of contested validity, 10.9.4
    costs, 10.9.5
    damages, 10.9.1

Infringement of patents (contd)
    delivery up, 10.9.2
    introduction, 10.9
    relief for infringement of partially valid patent, 10.9.3
  role of patent agents, 10.15
  ships, and, 10.10.10.1

Infringement of trademarks

defences, 11.12
exceptions, 11.12
groundless threats, 11.14
infringing use, 11.11
introduction, 11.10
proceedings, 11.13

Intellectual property

And see under individual headings
computer programs
    authorship and ownership, 16.5
    background, 16.1
    exceptions to restricted acts, 16.7–16.7.3
    international treaty law, 16.2–16.2.2
    meaning, 16.3
    protection, 16.4
    restricted acts, 16.6–16.6.3
confidential information
    celebrities, and, 15.7
    employment cases, 15.5
    historical background, 15.4
    introduction, 15.1
    meaning, 15.2
    non-employment cases, 15.6
    purpose of protection, 15.3
    remedies, 15.8
copyright
    basic concepts, 12.2.1–12.2.3
    civil remedies, 12.4.1–12.4.5
    conclusions, 12.6
    criminal remedies, 12.5.1–12.5.4
    enforcement, 12.3.1–12.3.4
    introduction, 12.1
    legislative background, 12.1.1–12.1.5
database rights
    conclusion, 16.9
    introduction, 16.8
    non-original database, 16.8.2
    original database, 16.8.1
    protection, 16.8.3
    restricted acts, 16.8.4
    term of protection, 16.8.5
  designs
    authorship and ownership, 14.8.1–14.8.3
    conclusion, 14.12
    exploitation, 14.10
    infringement, 14.4.1–14.5.3
    introduction, 14.1
    invalidity, 14.6.1–14.6.2
    legislation, 14.2–14.2.4
    offences, 14.7
    protectable designs, 14.3.1–14.3.7
    registration, 14.9.1–14.9.9
    trade marks, and, 14.11
life sciences
    Bolar exemption, 17.6.1–17.6.4
    EU regulatory law, 17.4.1–17.4.2
    generic products, 17.5–17.5.4
    introduction, 17.1
    patent settlement agreements, 17.7
    patents, 17.2.1
    trade marks, 17.3.1–17.3.3
passing off
    business or goodwill, 13.4
    character merchandising, 13.6–13.6.2
    damage, 13.5
    introduction, 13.0
    misrepresentation, 13.1
    prospective customers, 13.3
    trader in the course of trade, 13.2
patents
    amendment, 10.12
    applications, 10.5–10.5.7
    declarations of non-infringement, 10.14
    groundless threats, 10.13
    ideas and know-how, 10.4–10.4.1
    infringement, 10.7–10.10.10
    international conventions and agreements, 10.2.1–10.2.5
    law, 10.1
    miscellaneous matters, 10.16.1–10.16.5
    ownership, 10.6–10.6.1
    patent agent's role in litigation, 10.15
    patentability, 10.3.1–10.3.4
    revocation, 10.11
software licensing, and
    copyright, 5.3.2.1
    database rights, 5.3.4
    generally, 5.5.6
    patents, 5.3.2.2
    trademarks, 5.3.3
technology start-ups, and, 2.7

Intellectual property (contd)
trade marks
    certification marks, 11.20
    collective marks, 11.20
    community trade marks, 11.24–11.24.9
    dealings, 11.15
    duration, 11.8
    effects of registration, 11.10
    famous marks, 11.21
    filing applications, 11.5
    infringement, 11.11–11.14
    introduction, 11.1
    jurisdiction, 11.23
    licensing, 11.16–11.18
    limitation on rights, 11.9
    meaning, 11.2
    offences, 11.22
    place of registration, 11.4–11.4.4
    procedure, 11.7
    registrability, 11.6–11.6.2
    registrable marks, 11.3
    surrender, revocation and invalidity, 11.19–11.19.3

Interconnection
designs, and, 14.3.3
electronic communications regulation, and, 6.3.5.1

International treaty law
copyright, and, 12.1.3

Inventions
biotechnological, 10.3.1.1
computer-implemented, 10.3.1.2
introduction, 10.3.1

Inventive step
patents, and, 10.3.2

IT contracts
See also **Software licensing agreements**
introduction, 5.1
software, 5.2.1

J

Judicial review
postal sector regulation, and, 6.6.2.6

Jurisdiction of contracts
ebusiness, and, 1.4.7

K

Key performance indicators
outsourcing, and, 9.6

Know-how
patents, and, 10.4–10.4.1

L

Legitimate rights or interests
domain names, and, 3.7.4

Lending rights
background, 12.1.2
generally, 12.2.4

Licensing
trademarks, and
    exclusive licences, 11.17
    generally, 11.16
    non-exclusive licences, 11.18

Life sciences
biological medicinal products, 17.5.4
biotechnological inventions, 17.2.1.2
Bolar exemption
    background, 17.6.1
    case decision, 17.6.2
    Irish legislation, 17.6.3
    UK guidance, 17.6.4
data exclusivity
    8+2+1, 17.4.2.1
    additional one year new indication, 17.4.2.2
    introduction, 17.4.2
    orphan medicines, 17.4.2.4
    paediatric use, 17.4.2.5
    well-established substances, 17.4.2.3
EU regulatory law, 17.4.1–17.4.2
generic medicines, 17.2.1.4.5
generic medicinal products
    definition, 17.5.2
    generally, 17.5.1
generic products
    biosimilars, 17.5.4
    introduction, 17.5
    line extensions, 17.5.3
    medicinal products, 17.5.1–17.5.3
human tissue, 17.2.1.2
importance of sector, 17.1.1
introduction, 17.1
medical treatment, 17.2.1.1
orphan medicines, 17.4.2.4
patents
    biotechnological inventions, 17.2.1.2

Life sciences (contd)
    compulsory licences, 17.2.1.3
    exceptions to patentability, 17.2.1.2
    human tissue, 17.2.1.2
    legislation, 17.2.1–17.2.1.4
    medical treatment, 17.2.1.1
    patentability, 17.2.1.1
    settlement agreements, 17.7
    stem cells, 17.2.1.2
    supplementary protection certificates, 17.2.1.4
stem cells, 17.2.1.2
supplementary protection certificates
    duration, 17.2.1.4.3
    EU competition law, 17.2.1.4.4
    generic medicines, 17.2.1.4.5
    introduction, 17.2.1.4
    medicinal product, 17.2.1.4.1
    requirements, 17.2.1.4.2
trade marks
    counterfeiting, 17.3.3
    data exclusivity, 17.4.2
    EU regulatory law, 17.4.1–17.4.2.5
    free movement, 17.3.2
    generic products, 17.5–17.5.4
    orphan medicines, 17.4.2.4
    paediatric use, 17.4.2.5
    parallel trade, 17.3.2—17.3.2.1
    selection, 17.3.1
well-established substances, 17.4.2.3

Limitation of liability
outsourcing, and, 9.8.4
software licensing agreements, and, 5.5.7

Literary works
copyright, and, 12.2.2

Local loop unbundling
electronic communications regulation, and, 6.3.5.3

M
Madrid Protocol
trademarks, and, 11.4.3

Making available right
background, 12.1.4
computer programs, and, 16.6.2
generally, 12.2.4

Malware
generally, 7.2.2
legal issues, 7.2.3

Market analysis
electronic communications regulation, and, 6.3.3.6

Medical treatment
patents, and, 17.2.1.1

Memorandum of association
technology start-ups, and, 2.3.4

Metadata
electronic discovery, and, 8.7

Misrepresentation
passing off, and, 13.1

Moral rights
copyright, and, 12.4.45

Musical works
copyright, and, 12.2.2

N
Name of company
technology start-ups, and, 2.3.2

National Consumer Agency
ebusiness, and, 1.4.5.1

National regulatory authority
generally, 6.3.1
independence, 6.3.3.2

Non-exclusive licences
trademarks, and, 11.18

Non-use
trademarks, and, 11.9

Novelty
designs, and, 14.3.5
patents, and
    generally, 10.3.2
    infringement action, and, 10.10.3
    searches, 10.5.1

Number portability
electronic communications regulation, and, 6.3.6.5

O
OHIM
designs, and, 14.2.1
trademarks, and, 11.4.2

Online contracts
prior information, and, 1.4.3.6

Open-source agreements
software licensing agreements, and, 5.2.5.4
Originality
copyright, and, 12.2.2
Orphan medicines
trade marks, and, 17.4.2.4
Outsourcing
background, 9.4
best-of-breed, 9.5
commercial drivers, 9.6
contracts
    default and remedies, 9.8.2
    exclusion of liability, 9.8.4
    generally, 9.8
    limitation of liability, 9.8.4
    risk allocation, 9.8.1
    service credits, 9.8.3
    service levels, 9.8.3
customer-supplier requirements, 9.2
end-to-end, 9.5
exclusion of liability, 9.8.4
introduction, 9.1
key performance indicators, 9.6
limitation of liability, 9.8.4
market, 9.7
meaning, 9.2
overview, 9.1
processes, 9.5
quality standards, 9.3
risk allocation, 9.8.1
service credits, 9.8.3
service levels, 9.8.3
transfer of undertakings
    affected employees, 9.9.4
    case law, 9.9.5
    effect, 9.9.2
    generally, 9.9
    objection, 9.9.3
    transfer of a business, 9.9.1
types, 9.3
Ownership
copyright, and, 12.2.2

P

Paris Convention
patents, and, 10.2.1
Passing off
business or goodwill, 13.4
character merchandising, 13.6
damage, 13.5
elements
    business or goodwill, 13.4
    damage, 13.5
    introduction, 13.0
    made by trader in course of trade, 13.2
    misrepresentation, 13.1
    prospective customers, 13.3
generally, 13.0
made by trader in course of trade, 13.2
misrepresentation, 13.1
personalty rights, 13.6.1
practical steps in dealings, 13.6.2
prospective customers, 13.3
Patents
advantages, 10.4.1
amendment, 10.12
applications
    amendment, 10.12
    claiming priority, 10.5.5
    co-ownership, 10.6.1
    Europe, in, 10.5.6
    filing, 10.5.3–10.5.4
    international jurisdictions, in, 10.5.7
    introduction, 10.5
    Ireland, in, 10.5.3
    novelty searches, 10.5.1
    preparation, 10.5.2
biotechnological inventions, 10.3.1.1
certificate of contested validity, 10.9.4
claiming priority, 10.5.5
Community Patent Convention, 10.2.4
compulsory licences, 10.16.4
computer-implemented inventions, 10.3.1.2
co-ownership, 10.6.1
damages, 10.9.1
declaration of non-infringement, 10.14
delivery up, 10.9.2
detention of goods, 10.16.5
disadvantages, 10.4.1
discovery, 10.16.2
EC legislation, 10.1
Europe, in, 10.5.6
European Patent Convention, 10.2.3
filing
    first application elsewhere, 10.5.4
    first Irish application, 10.5.3
general law, 10.1
groundless threats, 10.13

Patents (contd)
HMRC procedure, 10.16.5
ideas and know-how, 10.4–10.4.1
infringement
    actions, 10.8
    aircraft, 10.10.10.2
    breach of restrictive conditions, 10.10.10.3
    certificate of contested validity, 10.9.4
    compulsory licences, 10.16.4
    consent of proprietor, and, 10.10.1
    continuation of use, and, 10.10.5–10.10.6
    costs, 10.9.5
    damages, 10.9.1
    declaration of non-infringement, 10.14
    defences, 10.10.1–10.10.10
    delivery up, 10.9.2
    detention of goods, 10.16.5
    direct infringing acts, 10.7.1
    disclosure action, 10.16.3
    discovery, 10.16.2
    Euro-defences, and, 10.10.2
    experimental use, and, 10.10.8
    extemporaneous preparation on prescription, 10.10.9
    generally, 10.7
    generic medicine trials, 10.10.8.1
    groundless threats, 10.13
    hovercraft, 10.10.10.2
    indirect infringement, 10.7.2
    partially valid patent, 10.9.3
    private use, and, 10.10.7
    privileged communications, 10.16.1
    publication of judgment, 10.9.6
    remedies, 10.9–10.9.4
    role of patent agents, 10.15
    ships, and, 10.10.10.1
international conventions and agreements
    Community Patent Convention, 10.2.4
    European Patent Convention, 10.2.3
    Paris Convention, 10.2.1
    Patent Co-operation Treaty, 10.2.2
    TRIPS Agreement, 10.2.5
international jurisdictions, in, 10.5.7
invalidity, 10.10.4
inventions
    biotechnological, 10.3.1.1
    computer-implemented, 10.3.1.2
    introduction, 10.3.1
inventive step, 10.3.2
legislative basis, 10.1
life sciences, and
    biotechnological inventions, 17.2.1.2
    compulsory licences, 17.2.1.3
    exceptions to patentability, 17.2.1.2
    human tissue, 17.2.1.2
    legislation, 17.2.1–17.2.1.4
    medical treatment, 17.2.1.1
    patentability, 17.2.1.1
    settlement agreements, 17.7
    stem cells, 17.2.1.2
    supplementary protection certificates, 17.2.1.4
novelty
    generally, 10.3.2
    infringement action, and, 10.10.3
    searches, 10.5.1
ownership of right
    co-ownership, 10.6.1
    generally, 10.6
Paris Convention, 10.2.1
patent agents, 10.15
Patent Co-operation Treaty, 10.2.2
patentability
    inventive step, 10.3.2
    novelty, 10.3.2
    patentable inventions, 10.3.1
patentable inventions
    biotechnological, 10.3.1.1
    computer-implemented, 10.3.1.2
    introduction, 10.3.1
priority, 10.5.5
privileged communications, 10.16.1
revocation, 10.11
secondary legislation, 10.1
short-term patents, 10.3.3
software licensing agreements, and, 5.3.2.2
supplementary protection certificates, 10.3.4
TRIPS Agreement, 10.2.5

Pay-phones
distance communications, and, 1.4.2.5

Payments
software licensing agreements, and, 5.5.4

Personal data
generally, 4.3.2.1
processing, 4.3.5

Personal data (contd)
transfer outside EU, 4.3.8.1–4.3.8.8
use for marketing purposes, 4.3.4

Personalty rights
passing off, and, 13.6.1

'Pharming'
computer-related fraud, and, 7.2.6

'Phishing'
computer-related fraud, and, 7.2.6

Postal sector regulation
authorisation
    appeals against refusal, 6.6.2.6
    generally, 6.6.2.2
ComReg, and, 6.6.1
introduction, 6.6
judicial review, 6.6.2.6
legislative basis, 6.6
Postal Regulations, 6.6.2–6.6.2.6
reserved service, 6.6.2.3
service quality standards, 6.6.2.4
transparent cost accounting, 6.6.2.5
universal service obligation, 6.6.2.1

Primary infringements
copyright, and, 12.3.3

Prior disclosure
designs, and, 14.3.6

Prior information
online contracts, and, 1.4.3.6
generally, 1.4.2.7
'relevant service', 1.4.3.3

Prior user
designs, and, 14.5.3

Priority
designs, and, 14.9.2
patents, and, 10.5.5

Privacy
constitutional right, as
    generally, 4.2.2
    introduction, 4.2.1
data protection, and
    constitutional right, as, 4.2.4
    data controllers, 4.3.2.1–4.3.2.2
    data subject's rights, 4.3.7.1–4.3.7.6
    duties of data controllers, 4.3.3.1–4.3.3.3
    human right, as, 4.2.4
    introduction, 4.3.1
    practice, in, 4.2.4
    processing of personal data, 4.3.5
    processing of sensitive personal data, 4.3.6
    registration with Commissioner, 4.3.9
    transfer of personal data, 4.3.8.1–4.3.8.8
    use of personal data, 4.3.4
    workplace, in, 4.6.1–4.6.2
Data Retention Directive 2006, 4.5
Electronic Communications Regulations 2003, 4.4
European Convention on Human Rights, and, 4.2.3
human right, as
    generally, 4.2.3
    introduction, 4.2.1
introduction, 4.1

Privilege
electronic discovery, and, 8.15.2
infringement of patents, and, 10.16.1

Q

Quality standards
outsourcing, and, 9.3
postal sector regulation, and, 6.6.2.4

R

Recognition and enforcement of judgments
ebusiness, and, 1.4.7

Registered community design
And see **Designs**
generally, 14.2.1

Regulatory impact assessment
electronic communications regulation, and, 6.3.1.1

'Relevant service'
ebusiness, and, 1.4.3.3

Rental rights
background, 12.1.2
generally, 12.2.4

Reproduction right
background, 12.1.2
computer programs, and, 16.6.1
generally, 12.2.3

Resale rights
copyright, and, 12.1.2

Restricted works
copyright, and, 12.2.3

Rights management systems
copyright, and, 12.1.2

Risk allocation
outsourcing, and, 9.8.1

S

Safe harbour principles
data protection, and, 4.3.8.4

Sale of goods
ebusiness, and, 1.4.6
software licensing agreements, and, 5.3.1

Sale of property
distance communications, and, 1.4.2.5

Satellite broadcasting
copyright, and, 12.1.2

Search and seizure powers
electronic communications regulation, and, 6.4.2

Secondary infringements
copyright, and, 12.3.3

Secretaries' duties
technology start-ups, and, 2.3.3

Seizure of infringing material
copyright, and
    applications to court, 12.4.3
    rights of copyright owner, 12.4.4

Service agreements
technology start-ups, and, 2.10

Shareholders agreement
technology start-ups, and, 2.9

Shrink-wrap agreements
software licensing agreements, and, 5.2.5.2

Significant market power (SMP)
generally, 6.2
Guidelines, 6.3.3.6
obligations, 6.3.5.2
universal service, and, 6.3.6.3

Software
adaptation, 16.6.3
authorship, 16.5
background, 16.1.1
back-up copies, 16.7.1
conclusion, 16.9
copyright, and
    EC law, 12.1.2
    Irish law, 12.1.1
database right
    introduction, 16.8
    non-original databases, 16.8.2
    'original database', 16.8.1
    qualifying for protection, 16.8.3
    restricted acts, 16.8.4
    term of protection, 16.8.5
decompilation right, 16.7.2
definition, 16.3
distribution right, 16.6.2
incidental acts, 16.7.3
international treaty law
    EU developments, 16.2.1
    introduction, 16.2
    Software Directive, 16.2.2
making available right, 16.6.2
ownership, 16.5
protection, 16.4
reproduction right, 16.6.1
restricted acts
    adaptation, 16.6.
    back-up copies, and, 16.7.1
    decompilation right, 16.7.2
    distribution right, 16.6.2
    exceptions, 16.7–16.7.3
    generally, 16.6
    incidental acts, 16.7.3
    reproduction right, 16.6.1
Software Directive, 16.2.1–16.2.2

Software licensing agreements
bespoke agreements, 5.2.5.1
click-wrap agreements, 5.2.5.3
conceptual difficulties, 5.2.4
contract law, 5.3.1
copyright, 5.3.2.1
database rights, 5.3.4
definition of software, 5.5.2
distance communications, 5.4.2
escrow agreements, 5.2.5.5
exclusion of liability, 5.5.7
export control, 5.4.3
generally, 5.2.2
grant of licence, 5.5.3
intellectual property, 5.5.6
intellectual property law
    copyright, 5.3.2.1
    database rights, 5.3.4
    patents, 5.3.2.2

Software licensing agreements (contd)
   trademarks, 5.3.3
   legal principles
      contract law, 5.3.1
      intellectual property law, 5.3.2
   limitation of liability, 5.5.7
   nature, 5.2.2
   open-source agreements, 5.2.5.4
   other legal issues
      distance communications, 5.4.2
      export control, 5.4.3
      introduction, 5.4
      unfair terms, 5.4.1
   patents, 5.3.2.2
   payments, 5.5.4
   preliminary issues, 5.2.1–5.2.5
   purpose, 5.2.3
   sale of goods, and, 5.3.1
   shrink-wrap agreements, 5.2.5.2
   'software', 5.2.1
   terms and conditions
      definition of software, 5.5.2
      exclusion of liability, 5.5.7
      grant of licence, 5.5.3
      intellectual property, 5.5.6
      introduction, 5.5.1
      limitation of liability, 5.5.7
      payments, 5.5.4
      undertakings, 5.5.5
      warranties, 5.5.5–5.5.6
   trademarks, 5.3.3
   turnkey agreements, 5.2.5.6
   types, 5.2.5
   undertakings, 5.5.5
   unfair terms, 5.4.1
   warranties
      generally, 5.5.5
      intellectual property, 5.5.6
   Wassenaar Agreement, and, 5.4.3

'Spam'
computer-related fraud, and, 7.2.1

Spare parts
copyright in drawings, and, 12.1.1
designs, and, 14.5.2

Spoliation
electronic discovery, and, 8.15.1

Spyware
computer-related fraud, and, 7.2.2

SSNIP test
electronic communications regulation, and, 6.3.3.6

Start-up technology companies
articles of association, 2.3.4
commercial contracts, 2.12
directors' duties, 2.3.3
due diligence, 2.6
employee share option schemes, 2.11
finance
   business plan, 2.4.1
   potential sources, 2.4.2
heads of agreement, 2.5
incorporation
   articles of association, 2.3.4
   duties of directors and secretaries, 2.3.3
   founding shareholders and directors, 2.3.5
   generally, 2.3
   information requirements, 2.3.1
   memorandum of association, 2.3.4
   name of company, 2.3.2
intellectual property, 2.7
introduction, 2.1
memorandum of association, 2.3.4
name of company, 2.3.2
overview, 2.2
secretaries' duties, 2.3.3
service agreements, 2.10
shareholders agreement, 2.9
sources of information, 2.13
subscription agreement, 2.9
warranties, 2.8

Stem cells
patents, and, 17.2.1.2

Subscription agreement
technology start-ups, and, 2.9

Supplementary protection certificates
duration, 17.2.1.4.3
EU competition law, 17.2.1.4.4
generally, 10.3.4
generic medicines, 17.2.1.4.5
introduction, 17.2.1.4
medicinal product, 17.2.1.4.1
requirements, 17.2.1.4.2

Supply of services
ebusiness, and, 1.4.6

T

Technical function
designs, and, 14.3.3

Technology start-ups
articles of association, 2.3.4
commercial contracts, 2.12
directors' duties, 2.3.3
due diligence, 2.6
employee share option schemes, 2.11
finance
    business plan, 2.4.1
    potential sources, 2.4.2
heads of agreement, 2.5
incorporation
    articles of association, 2.3.4
    duties of directors and secretaries, 2.3.3
    founding shareholders and directors, 2.3.5
    generally, 2.3
    information requirements, 2.3.1
    memorandum of association, 2.3.4
    name of company, 2.3.2
intellectual property, 2.7
introduction, 2.1
memorandum of association, 2.3.4
name of company, 2.3.2
overview, 2.2
secretaries' duties, 2.3.3
service agreements, 2.10
shareholders agreement, 2.9
sources of information, 2.13
subscription agreement, 2.9
warranties, 2.8

Top level domains
country code (ccTLDs), 3.1.1.2
generic (gTLDs), 3.1.1.1

Trademarks
cancellation, 11.9
certification marks, 11.20
collective marks, 11.20
community trade mark (CTM)
    acquiescence, 11.24.9
    applications, 11.24.1
    assignment, 11.24.6
    duration, 11.24.2
    infringement, 11.24.3
    invalidity, 11.24.7
    jurisdiction, 11.24.4
    licensing, 11.24.6
    remedies, 11.24.5
    revocation, 11.24.7
    seniority, 11.24.9
dealings, 11.15
duration of registration, 11.8
effects of registration, 11.10
exclusive licences, 11.17
famous marks, 11.21
filing applications, 11.5
infringement
    defences, 11.12
    exceptions, 11.12
    groundless threats, 11.14
    infringing use, 11.11
    introduction, 11.10
    proceedings, 11.13
introduction, 11.1
invalidity, 11.19.3
jurisdiction, 11.23
licensing
    exclusive licences, 11.17
    generally, 11.16
    non-exclusive licences, 11.18
life sciences, and
    counterfeiting, 17.3.3
    data exclusivity, 17.4.2
    EU regulatory law, 17.4.1–17.4.2.5
    free movement, 17.3.2
    generic products, 17.5–17.5.4
    orphan medicines, 17.4.2.4
    paediatric use, 17.4.2.5
    parallel trade, 17.3.2—17.3.2.1
    selection, 17.3.1
limitation on rights, 11.9
Madrid Protocol, 11.4.3
meaning, 11.2
non-exclusive licences, 11.18
non-use, 11.9
offences, 11.22
place of registration
    generally, 11.4
    individual countries, in, 11.4.4
    Ireland, in, 11.4.1
    Madrid Protocol, under, 11.4.3
    OHIM, at, 11.4.2
procedure before Patents Office, 11.7
registrability
    absolute grounds, 11.6.1
    introduction, 11.6
    relative grounds, 11.6.2
registrable marks, 11.3

Trademarks (contd)
registration
    duration, 11.8
    effects, 11.10
    place, 11.4–11.4.4
revocation, 11.19.2
software licensing agreements, and, 5.3.3
surrender, 11.19.1

Transfer of undertakings
affected employees, 9.9.4
case law, 9.9.5
effect, 9.9.2
generally, 9.9
objection, 9.9.3
transfer of a business, 9.9.1

Transient acts
copyright, and, 12.1.4

TRIPS Agreement
patents, and, 10.2.5

Trojans
computer-related fraud, and, 7.2.7

Turnkey agreements
software licensing agreements, and, 5.2.5.6

U

Unauthorised access
computer-related fraud, and, 7.2.5

Undertakings
software licensing agreements, and, 5.5.5

Unfair commercial practices
ebusiness, and, 1.4.5.1

Unfair Terms in Consumer Contracts Regulations 1995
ebusiness, and, 1.4.5.2
software licensing agreements, and, 5.4.1

Uniform Domain Name Dispute Resolution Policy (UDRP)
background, 3.4
case law, 3.6
effect of determination, 3.4.1
.ie domains, 3.4.2

Universal service obligations
electronic communications regulation, and
    background, 6.2
    financing, 6.3.6.2
    generally, 6.3.6.1
postal sector regulation, and, 6.6.2.1

Universal Service Regulations
And see **Electronic communications regulation**
consumer protection, 6.3.6.4
introduction, 6.3.6
number portability, 6.3.6.5
SMP obligations, 6.3.6.3
universal service obligations, 6.3.6.1–6.3.6.2

Unregistered community design
And see **Designs**
generally, 14.2.2

Unsolicited communications
computer-related fraud, and, 7.2.1
data protection, and, 4.4

V

Vending machines
distance communications, and, 1.4.2.5

Viruses
computer-related fraud, and, 7.2.2

'Vishing'
computer-related fraud, and, 7.2.6

Voice over Internet Protocol (VoIP)
electronic communications regulation, and, 6.3.3.6

W

Warranties
software licensing agreements, and
    generally, 5.5.5
    intellectual property, 5.5.6
technology start-ups, and, 2.8

Wassenaar Agreement
software licensing agreements and, 5.4.3

Well-established substances
data exclusivity, and, 17.4.2.3

World Intellectual property Organisation (WIPO)
copyright, and, 12.1.3
domain names, and, 3.3

Worms
computer-related fraud, and, 7.2.2